FROM AFRICA TO ZEN

FROM AFRICA TO ZEN
An Invitation to World Philosophy

Edited by
Robert C. Solomon
Kathleen M. Higgins

Rowman & Littlefield Publishers, Inc.

ROWMAN & LITTLEFIELD PUBLISHERS, INC.

Published in the United States of America
by Rowman & Littlefield Publishers, Inc.
4720 Boston Way, Lanham, Maryland 20706

British Cataloging in Publication Information Available

Library of Congress Cataloging-in-Publication Data

From Africa to Zen : an invitation to world philosophy / edited by
Robert C. Solomon, Kathleen M. Higgins.
p. cm.
1. Philosophy—History. I. Solomon, Robert C. II. Higgins, Kathleen
Marie.
B73.F76 1993 109—dc20 92-28469 CIP

ISBN 0-8476-7774-5 (cloth : alk. paper)
ISBN 0-8476-7775-3 (pbk. : alk. paper)

Printed in the United States of America

 ™ The paper used in this publication meets the minimum requirements of
American National Standard for Information Sciences—Permanence of
Paper for Printed Library Materials, ANSI Z39.48–1984.

For our parents,
our ancestors,
and for the memory
of all ancestors
everywhere.

When we discuss modern philosophy, must it be defined by the latest books and ideas on the same old subjects out of Oxford or Berkeley, or are there other sources of contemplation and wisdom, lacking academic credentials perhaps but closer to the pulse of the human heart? What about, for example, so-called New Age philosophy? What about liberation theology? What about various folk philosophies, passed on from generation to generation by way of myths and stories, admonitions and advice? What about the philosophy of multiculturalism as such? What counts as philosophy today is very much at issue, but this should not be seen as a crisis but rather as a fruitful and exciting opening and an opportunity for other traditions to come spilling in with their own ideas and influences. As one twentieth-century leader put it, in a quite different situation, "let a thousand flowers bloom." That doesn't mean, as some would fear, that we have to jettison Socrates, Descartes, Kant, and Hegel and the wisdom of the West, nor does it mean that we should throw up our hands, refrain from criticism, and agree that every idea is as good as any other. What it does mean is that we are now ready to open our eyes and our ears to voices and ideas that have for too long been excluded or pushed to the margins of philosophy. They are demanding to be heard, and in their own terms. And where the voices are soft and distant, largely buried in the past, or the ideas seem the oddest and most foreign, that is where we should listen hardest. For that is often where we have refused to listen longest.

Contents

Introduction

As everyone who has recently set foot in a university or read the editorials of our more cosmopolitan newspapers knows, there is a vigorous attempt in academia to combat the ethnocentrism of the traditional ("male, white European") college curriculum and the implicit chauvinism (if not racism) it represents. In philosophy in particular, some administrations have all but mandated that as a field of study it should become increasingly conscious of and attentive to other philosophical traditions. Even a casual review of the standard course offerings and dissertation topics demonstrates an embarrassing one-dimensionality, stretching through time from Socrates to Sartre or Quine with nary a mention of Confucius or Nāgārjuna. There is no mention of African philosophy or any African philosopher (except Augustine, whose origins are conveniently ignored) and no Latin American philosophy. No matter what one's position on the politically hot, and even explosive, topic of "multiculturalism," it must be admitted that the demand for global sensitivity in philosophy is healthy for a subject that has indeed become overly narrow, insulated from other disciplines, and in many quarters oblivious even to its own culture as well as to others.

Coming to appreciate those other cultures and their philosophies is hampered, however, by the very narrow strictures on what deserves the honorific name of "philosophy." For example, the current emphasis on argumentation—often summarized as rationality—as the essence of philosophy excludes much of the more poetic and nondisputational wisdom of non-Western cultures, and even gives rise to the remarkable suggestion that these cultures are therefore nonrational or prerational. In the East and in the South, the ideas by which people guide their lives are often expressed in song, slogan, and poetry, not disputational prose—and poetry has been banned from philosophy since Plato. In many cultures, philosophy places an overwhelming emphasis on ethics and religion, often expressed in myth and allegory. Such traditions are therefore dismissed as "not philosophy" not only because ethics and religion themselves have been relegated to second place since the onset of the obsession with epistemology that began with Descartes and "the New Science" but because myth and allegory (except for a few canonized exceptions in Plato) have also been declared to have no role in philosophy. The obsession with logical argumentation and epistemology reached its zenith only recently, with the logical positivists in the era of World War II, when virtually every concern of substance was dismissed as "meaningless." That terrible war may have been global, but the philosophy it provoked in its aftermath became even more isolated and provincial. Indeed, as recently as 1989, one of our best and most broad-minded philosophers could write that "Philosophy has really arisen only twice in the history of civilization, once in Greece and once in India" (Arthur Danto, *Connections to the World,* p. 14).

What we call Western philosophy is studied, of course, by students from around the globe, but instead of adding new dimensions to the overly well-defined Western tradition many or most of those graduating philosophers and philosophy teachers who learned their trade in the pubs and tutorials of Oxbridge or the seminar rooms of the best American and Canadian universities returned to their native cultures and taught, in essence, the same one-dimensional Anglo-American philosophy and the supposedly "neutral" remnants of logical positivism. Local philosophies may have affected the course of instruction in quaint ways, but most culturally specific and significant ideas were dismissed as prerational, intellectually primitive, and unprofessional. Even Buddhism and Confucianism, with credentials as ancient as those of the pre-Socratics and on which we have far more substantial extant texts, have been excluded. And one still hears the claim, in not just a few philosophy departments, that the discipline of philosophy is defined, as a matter of power if not by way of tautology, as what its practitioners say it is, namely, as that emaciated subject matter which as a matter of anthropological and sociological curiosity has emerged as the standard curriculum in most of our universities and colleges.

One obvious complication with the idea of cross-cultural philosophical education is that in reading other philosophical traditions we are not only trying to understand other authors, other languages, other ideas. We are also trying to embed ourselves in another culture, engage in another life. If Hegel was right, that philosopohy is the spirit of its time (and place) rendered conceptually articulate, then understanding a philosophy is necessarily understanding the strains and structures of the culture it expresses and through which it is expressed. This raises deep questions about our ability to read such philosophy. It is not enough to know the language (one can readily enough learn Sanskrit, Swahili, or Chinese if one is sufficiently motivated), or even to have something more than a tourist's view of the land, its peoples, and customs. One must, it seems, put oneself "in another's skin," to see "from the inside" a life that is as routine and unexceptional to others as our lives are to us, so defined as well as convenienced by technology, the notions of privacy, individual possessiveness, and the separation of the secular from the sacred. It is, therefore, not enough to show that early Indian philosophers developed an epistemology displaying remarkable similarities to that of the British empiricists or that certain Buddhists had a concept of self resembling some arguments in David Hume or Jean-Paul Sartre. In this sense one can grossly misunderstand a philosophy precisely by "understanding" it, that is, by embracing and absorbing a few seemingly familiar ideas while ignoring the surrounding mysteries and the underlying structure, which, for those who promulgated them, allowed them to make sense.

What we call world philosophy isn't a single discipline or way of thinking. It is not variations on a single set of themes expressed and speculated upon now in an African way, now in a Latin way, now in an Arabic or Persian way, now in the Anglo-American way (whatever that may be). For the embarrassing fact long submerged in the tyrannical reign of the "history of philosophy"—that exclusionary artifice invented largely by Hegel to embrace all of European philosophy in a single narrative—is that what we call "Western" philosophy isn't really that at all. Even assuming that one wants to include Greece in what we now call "the West," it is evident that much of the definitive influence on the great Greeks came from Asia Minor and the Orient, from northern Africa and the migrations of many tribes north and south, east and west. Judaism and Christianity were not, despite their now official designation as such, "Western" religions, nor was Islam, which produced some of the greatest medieval philosophy. In addition to the radical differences in philosophy and culture we find across the globe, we also find, almost everywhere we turn except among a few, soon-to-be-destroyed long-isolated rain forest or African bush peoples, confluences and influences, ideas swapped and shared along with foodstuffs, satins and spices, amalgamated theories evolved from once-warring myths and ideologies, global philosophy as a long-cooking stew instead of a scattering of "centers" or a worldwide intellectual "human condition."

Of course, there is such a "condition"—all people everywhere are born into families and communities; they are vulnerable to cuts and burns, suffer pain and illness; they die. They have to eat and sleep; they fear for their lives, for their children, for a few favorite belongings. They have sex. They have parties. And more than occasionally, they think. But, of course, what they think and how they think, as well as what they do at parties, how they enjoy but also restrict their sex lives, what they fear, how they suffer, and how they die are all born of sometimes widely different strategies. How do we understand these strategies? How do we put ourselves "into another's skin"? How do we break out of what most of us now believe to be a readily understandable but nevertheless no-longer-justifiable ethnocentric trap to get into another philosophy and another culture? One can always suggest the standard glib solution: Seek out similarities. Appreciate differences. But how does one do this without manufacturing the similarities and glossing over (or, just as bad, exaggerating and celebrating) the differences?

In attempting comparative philosophy, it is important not to "look down" on the various masterpieces of Western and Eastern philosophy as if from a great height or an interplanetary perspective, taking them all in at a sweep. For the reader who is not yet familiar with many of the world's great philosophical traditions, who can grasp the idea of a Chinese skeptic only by drawing some dim parallel with Hume, the idea of a different tradition—not just an incidental parallel—gets lost. One has to get "into" the other tradition, its background, its problems, and its language. The attempt will be, for most people, merely a token of appreciation and understanding; yet the effort may be enough to gain that glimmer of comprehension that makes mutual understanding and cross-fertilization possible. We have therefore tried to avoid mere high-flying observations illustrated with various bits of text in favor of chapters in which the authors try to situate themselves within various philosophical traditions. The tone and structure of the various discussions are, accordingly, quite distinct. One would not expect the oral traditions of Africa and native America to pass through the same stages and transformations as the 3,000-year-old textual traditions of China and India. It would have been a sure sign of failure if, indeed, these chapters had all come out looking pretty much the same.

One recent and now influential approach comes through the discipline of hermeneutics, an academic cocktail-party word that has come to signify mainly a certain professional affiliation but that originally meant "understanding interpretation." It was and is a technique for understanding texts, neither from the inside nor from the outside but by a kind of immersion in which one uses already familiar concepts and categories to understand something strange and novel. Originally, it was a technique employed to understand the half-hidden messages of the Bible, the strange but wondrous word of God. In the nineteenth century, the technique was expanded to texts and nontexts—works of art, religious rituals, social activities—of all kinds. It is particularly appropriate, therefore, for understanding another culture's philosophy, and some of our authors have made use of it in the chapters that follow. The virtue of hermeneutics, at least as practiced by its modern archetype Hans Georg Gadamer, lies in its insistence on appreciating differences as differences, but hermeneutics, by its very nature, insists on finding some common framework, albeit a comparative framework, and therein lies its promise. Ideally, this common framework emerges through extensive dialogue, in which mutual misunderstandings are corrected and overly narrow interpretations are broadened and enriched.

This means that we should give up the "interplanetary perspective" that is the aspiration of most global philosophers. Those high-flying observations allow clear vision of only those markings and ideas that are already expected or so generic that they are all but uninformative, like touring Paris, Nairobi, and Delhi from a Boeing 747. Nor can we expect to get wholly within other philosophical traditions. We will always be tourists, at best, in cultures that we are merely visiting. What is wrong with much of the world philosophy and multicultural movement today is that it clings to the notion of *teaching* rather than *conversing:* Where the former consists of one person or culture lecturing to (or at) another, the latter consists of questions and answers, anecdotes and personal stories, honest disagreements and arguments. Respect for another culture is not the same as uncritical acceptance.

It is too often thought that world philosophy is simply sampling a taste of China, a taste of Africa and Latin America, perhaps taking a slightly fuller serving of India, because it is the most developed and thoroughly studied alternative culture, but not engaging with them. That is a mistake. There is nothing wrong with preferring one system of philosophy to another; indeed, one would be hard put not to, even if, as is natural, that preferred system is usually one's own. But there is much to admire in other cultures, and what we learn can sometimes serve as a basis on which to judge our own. The Native American philosophy of the environment is a popular case in point. There is much to criticize in other cultures too, and it is no sign of respect but rather a sign of intimidation or moral sloth when one wholly abstains from judgment. One must always be careful, of course. What looks like a fallacy in the context of an alien argument may in fact be a legitimate piece of reasoning within an alternative mode of practical reasoning, and what at first appears to be nonsense in another culture may well make sense in the context of a large problem or way of thinking. (What do first-time philosophy students think of such astounding yet standard claims in European philosophy as "perhaps I am dreaming right now" or "I don't see how matter can exist"?) It is only by way of engagement, not by a high-flying tour, that one will gain some sense of another philosophy.

The best way to learn a new kind of philosophy, accordingly, is through dialogue, asking questions, raising challenges, requesting more details, making comparisons and contrasts. There are limits, of course, to what a book can provide, but one of the most important skills taught in Western philosophy is of particular value here, namely, the ability to read other cultures critically as well as appreciatively. It is a mistake simply to dismiss other philosophies, to reduce them to familiar Western themes, or to glorify the differences and place them beyond criticism and evaluation. Whether a lecture or textbook is traditional "white male Western" philosophy routinely promulgating its ways in Oxbridge-type universities in Africa or Asia or the new demand for "equal time" so that Third World societies can lecture white American students on the virtues of alternative cultures and the horrors and guilt of oppression, the problem remains the same. It is through dialogue and differences that the philosophies of other cultures will emerge. Part of these conversations, of course, will involve readings from the great texts of each culture and its past. These are not scriptures but influential voices. They can be disputed not only by foreigners who do not share their framework but by natives who do. Indeed, that is what philosophy ultimately comes to in any culture, not great texts or even great teaching so much as the will to disagree, to question, to seek understanding in place of mere acceptance.

In the chapters that follow, we have tried to allow the voices of world philosophy to speak for themselves. There is no prearranged order or structure imposed, which would distort or in some cases eliminate a philosophical appreciation of how various cultures see and think about the world. There has been no attempt to map Confucian, Buddhist, and Arabic traditions of philosophy onto (or against) the Western tradition, and we have taken great pains not to take the Greek-medieval-European tradition of Socrates through Sartre as the prototype of what philosophy should be. Such biased comparisons too readily lead to the wholesale dismissal of oral traditions such as we find in Africa and in America before the arrival of the Europeans, for example, and more subtly condemn the very different approaches to reasoning and dialogue that are to be found even in the most sophisticated philosophical traditions. One of the recurrent and often destructive arguments we find within these traditions, in fact, concerns what is and what is not philosophy. The professional philosophers of Europe and the United States have long pummeled each other and interrupted conferences with this accusatory concept, and African philosophers, to point to a very different instance, have spent much of their time debating the question whether Africa has any philosophy at all. In some of the traditions discussed, religion encompasses virtually the whole of philosophy. In others, it plays a relatively modest role. In some of the traditions, ethics is the focus, while in others it will be logic or metaphysics or art or the environment.

There is and will be, of course, considerable room for debate about what is included and what is not in a book brazenly subtitled *Essays in World Philosophy*. There is, as always, a space problem, and the respect for the endurance, patience, and pocketbook of the reader. There are also questions of priority and discretion. We have not included a chapter on Jewish philosophy, for example, despite a rich history of nearly 5,000 years. Our view, with which we remain somewhat uncomfortable, is that Jewish philosophy and such philosophers as Spinoza and Maimonides have been so often studied and written about and are interwoven so tightly into the fabric of what is usually called Western philosophy that they did not require a separate chapter here. So, too, Russian philosophy borders on and borrows from Europe throughout its history but nevertheless has undergone a fascinating, if sometimes tragic, intellectual odyssey of its own. It is, accordingly, with some hesitation that we do not include it here. One might make innumerable distinctions within Africa and Latin America, of course, and so too with Native American philosophy, where there are, in a sense, as many philosophies as there are tribes and nations. But we have tried, in each case, to be as comprehensive as possible while acknowledging the differences and variations. In the Middle East, on the other hand, we have included both Arabic and Persian philosophies, despite the obvious overlap of boundaries and influences. Again, our only justification is that lines have had to be drawn somewhere, sometimes here and not there, but the overall scope of the book, we hope, will provide a rich global portrait of the ideas and traditions that are just beginning to be understood together as the philosophies of the world.

The reader might well be taken aback by the fact that there is no chapter on Western philosophy. Is it not part of world philosophy? Or are we bowing to the most ridiculous voices of the recent multiculturalism, who dismiss the West, its ideas, and masterpieces as nothing more than the imperialism of "Dead White European Males"? The answer, of course, is that so-called Western philosophy, that is, the allegedly linear tradition that starts with certain Greek ontologists and builds from Socrates, Plato, and Aristotle to the Hellenistic and early medieval philosophers and then shifts abruptly from the Mediterranean to France and then England and Germany and on to modern times, is no doubt the dominant philosophy of the world. (American philosophy, interestingly enough, is virtually omitted from most accounts of this tradition, except, perhaps, for a late, passing, and often perfunctory reference to William James or John Dewey.) The Western tradition is often the subject (even the sole subject) of philosophical study even in all those countries with philosophical traditions of their own and is so often summarized and analyzed that the last thing that this book needs is one more survey of "Socrates to Sartre." Its place in the philosophical world is well established, and if the reader wants to supplement the chapters in this book with a slim volume on Western philosophy, there are any number of such readily available. What we have tried to do here is to give pride of place and a proper voice to those traditions that are usually excluded from the study of philosophy, because they do not seem appropriate for philosophical study, because there are so few extant texts and so little evidence about them, or simply because, despite a rich written history, they seem too foreign or remote.

As an exercise, one might ask, however, what the schematized linear philosophical tradition of the West would look like from a foreign shore, encapsulated in thirty to fifty pages as are the traditions covered in this book. It would no doubt seem as strange and confusing as any other exotic tradition of ideas. Premises and logical inferences would appear not only less than self-evident but suspicious or downright dubious.

Indeed, the very emphasis on logic and proof that has characterized so much of the philosophical discipline of the West will itself seem like a curiosity at best, or perhaps—for instance, to a Taoist sage—like vulgar foolishness. Western ethical rules and social practices may seem arbitrary, if not foolish or politically manipulative, and, again, the relatively low status and high abstraction of ethics since the seventeenth century or so would also seem peculiar or even perverse. Our most fundamental, though often embattled, religious beliefs, needless to say, would seem to be superstitions if not hallucinations and much of what is considered most spiritual in other parts of the world would be deemed missing. Montesquieu once tried to take on the intellectual traditions and practices of his countrymen in his *Persian Letters,* and his later Enlightenment followers Voltaire and Diderot similarly tried to gain some perspective by envisioning some South Sea or Oriental philosopher contemplating the inscrutable curiosities of the West. In this book, several of our authors have tried to come to grips with the Western tradition in philosophy by way of contrasts not always flattering to the West. What that tradition has gained in clarity and power it has often lost in other dimensions, many of them systematically ignored. The power of reason has marginalized or vilified the passions. The success of science has eclipsed the importance of art and religion. The emphasis on control and domination has endangered and sometimes destroyed the environment. Sometimes, to see oneself from the outside is essential to one's own salvation.

But, of course, the term *Western* is already a problem, standing for a mixed salad of traditions too readily disguised by the simplicity of the traditional linear summaries, incorporating but not embracing Jews, Arabs, immigrants from all sorts of places, and displaced natives, whether Indians or Gypsies, or "guest workers" or foreign subversives plotting their own revolutions. And even with the supposedly linear development of philosophy, one can distinguish any number of threads and conflicts and discontinuities. Socrates, for example, was on the one hand the seeker after absolute truth, the crafter of definitions, and the precursor of the analytic and linguistic thrust of later philosophy. On the other hand, he was the great conversationalist, a dialectician who loved the exchange, the witty comeback, the subtle put-down. He was a jovial skeptic, a personality, a celebrity, and there is a history of Western philosophy that could be written focusing only on that very different influence. Plato and Aristotle in turn mark off two very different paths in philosophy, and the absorption of philosophy in theology during the Middle Ages could be interpreted either as the further development of the tradition or as a detour, depending on where (if anywhere) one thinks that philosophy was or is going. About forty years ago, Hans Reichenbach, one of the logical positivists, celebrated what he called "the rise of scientific philosophy," dismissing most of ancient and medieval (and much of modern) philosophy as an unfortunate detour. About the same time, the German philosopher Martin Heidegger was bemoaning the sacrifice of "Being" to science and scientific thinking, and according to whom the ancients and many medieval thinkers had it right and scientific philosophy was the detour. It is no longer wise to think of Western philosophy as a single tradition or even as a fabric of interwoven threads stretching from the ancient Greeks, and as one probes deeper into the origins and influences of the so-called Western tradition, many other voices begin to be heard.

1

Understanding Order: The Chinese Perspective

David L. Hall and Roger T. Ames

Late in the evening of June 4, 1989, government tanks rolled into Beijing's Tiananmen Square, the symbolic center of China, to clear the square of protesters. *Snapshot:* Scorching lights advancing across the square reduce everything to outline as a tent is caught and half-flattened beneath the treads of a tank steamrolling its straight line across the square. *Snapshot:* A terrified young soldier with rifle still hot and smoking is being dragged from a jeep by faceless arms into the maw of a frenzied crowd. *Snapshot:* Three students stand atop a tour bus that has been detained and searched, and as proof that its civilian occupants are People's Liberation Army soldiers, the students hold up an automatic weapon and two helmets for the crowd to see. *Snapshot:* The plaster Goddess of Democracy lies broken in several pieces. A heavy armored vehicle has pulled it from its wooden stand, and it has toppled through the many institutional flags that still fly around its base. *Snapshot:* A student turns back with contorted face as he sees the young woman in a pink dress running beside him reel and fall face forward onto the pavement. *Snapshot:* The stiff, charred body of a PLA soldier, naked except for his hat and shoes, is kept upright against the shell of a burned-out bus by taut wire wrapped around his neck; "He killed four people" is written with masking tape on the bus beside him.

Unfortunately, we have become increasingly familiar with scenes such as these over the past generation. The news media have provided vivid accounts of events apparently similar to the Tiananmen incident: protesters with placards and loudspeakers exhorting liberal reforms and proclaiming certain victory for their cause; soldiers, in helmets and khaki uniforms, firing upon their fellow citizens.

Were we to look at Tiananmen through Chinese eyes, however, would we really see an event explicable in the terms used to explain student protests in our own country or, for that matter, the broader acts of governmental violence in the Middle East, South Africa, or Eastern Europe?

Instinctively, we believe that pain and the brutality that causes it are the same around the globe. But much of what we are coming to understand about China and its people tells us that there is an otherness about the Chinese sensibility which defies immediate understanding in either the terms of our common sense or the terms of the abstract categories and principles associated with the sort of intellectual analysis philosophers are apt to attempt.

For example, how are we to interpret the incident at Tiananmen as a democratic revolt if in our democracy there is a prevailing conception of personhood that entails natural rights, free choice, independence, autonomy, and so on, while in China such values, far from being self-evident and normative, have traditionally been regarded by even the sagest Chinese as sociopathic?

Of course the rhetoric of a democratic society such as ours must insist that the dictum "all men are created equal" applies to *all* human beings and that, therefore, the Chinese are fundamentally the same as us, differing only in such incidentals as their use of chopsticks, the shape of their eyes, and so forth. Such rhetoric was responsible for the blithe, clichéd interpretation assumed by much of the American news coverage of Tiananmen: An unpopular and tyrannical government crushes young George Washingtons.

Yet this belief in a "common humanity" is belied by the xenophobic stereotypes that have become part of our understanding of things Chinese. The most familiar associations of the word *Chinese* in our popular discourse are "puzzling," "confusing," "absurd." There are many examples of this sort of understanding. A perplexing puzzle that is found to have no solution is called a "Chinese puzzle." When someone does mischief to himself to spite another, he has taken a "Chinese revenge." A "Chinese flush" in poker has only the same color to recommend it. "Chinese screwdriver" is Australian slang for a hammer. A "Chinese fire drill" is a college prank in which, while stopped at a traffic signal, students leap from an automobile, run around in circles, and reenter the car just as the light changes. Finally, to end this rather ignoble litany, there is a familiar expression: Someone or something has a "Chinaman's chance"—that is, practically no chance at all.

The sense of difference is, if anything, even more profound on the side of the Chinese. More often than not, Westerners have been characterized as barbarians who, though obviously possessed of superior military technology, are physically unfit for battle because of their straight legs, rigid waists, and extremely poor night vision. Visitors from the West have been depicted for the Chinese people, the vast majority of whom would never have the chance to see one for themselves, as demons—grotesquely hairy monsters, with beaks and claws. Even today, the phrase "foreign devil" is commonly used among Chinese to refer to Western individuals. And though the connotation of this term has lost most of the sense of physical monstrosity, the epithet still evokes an understanding of Westerners as clumsy, tactless, and vulgar. A popular saying in the nineteenth and early twentieth centuries captured this impression of the intruding foreigner as unmannered and graceless: "The sage fears nothing in this world, save for one thing only: the foreign devil attempting to speak Chinese."

Of course, not all recognitions of difference are grounded in bigotry and suspicion. Lin Yutang's claim that "the reason why the Chinese failed to develop botany and zoology is that the Chinese scholar cannot stare coldly and unemotionally at a fish without immediately thinking of how it tastes in the mouth and wanting to eat it"[1] expresses this sense of difference in a wry, humane, even humorous manner.

From the sixteenth to the close of the eighteenth century, European opinion of China as reflected in the literature of this period was usually quite high. The Jesuit Matteo Ricci (1551–1610) found the Chinese to be a humane and eminently civilized people. Seventeenth- and eighteenth-century Europeans idealized China as a remarkable and "curious land" requiring the utmost scrutiny.[2] Individuals such as Leibniz and Voltaire often proclaimed the knowledge and virtues of the Chinese to be superior to those of Europeans.

Things changed markedly in the nineteenth century. G.W.F. Hegel was typical of nineteenth-century Western thinkers in his unsympathetic interpretation of Chinese civilization:

> Its distinguishing feature is, that everything which belongs to spirit—unconstrained morality, in practice and theory, heart, inward religion, science and art properly so called—is alien to it. . . . While *we* obey, because what we are required to do is confirmed by an *internal* sanction, there the law is regarded as inherently and absolutely valid without a sense of the want of this subjective confirmation.[3]

The engine of the industrial revolution had added another dimension to this negative evaluation. Europe and America, marching under the banner of scientific and industrial progress, lost all esteem for China. The earlier visions of an exotic Shangri-La plummeted from "Cathay" idealizations to the depths of disaffection for the inertia of a culture cast as backward-looking and moribund.

How are we to approach the question of Chinese philosophy against the background of this general recognition on the parts of both China and the West of vast cultural differences? In the first place, we had better not overload the term *philosophy* with its Western connotations. What serves as "philosophic thinking" in China is significantly different from that with which most of us are familiar. Second, we must be prepared to understand the differences between Chinese and Western thinking as both cause and consequence of those broader cultural differences perhaps more easily observed.

The religious writer Gerald Heard once characterized the civilizations of Europe, India, and China in terms of a fundamental question presumably asked by the thinkers and seers of each tradition. For the European that question was "*Where* am I?" Curiosity about the nature of the external world led to the development of the natural and social sciences. Indians asked the question "*Who* am I?" and as a consequence discovered subtle techniques of spiritual self-examination and articulation. The Chinese, claimed Heard, asked the question "*What* am I?" This question was answered in terms of rituals and roles establishing the parameters of one's identity as a social being.

Granted the simplistic character of Heard's suggestions, there is something to be gained if we realize that we in the West have oriented our interests principally toward discovering the objective nature of things. This is reflected in the traditional interests of philosophers: Metaphysicians search out the *being* of things, epistemologists most often ask how we come to know the reality that lies behind appearances, and so forth. But the overriding concern of the Chinese has always been the establishment of harmonious relationships with their social ambience. Their "philosophic" thinking is always concrete, this-worldly, and, above all, practical. Keeping in mind this contrast between Chinese and Western interests will prevent us from too readily believing that the Chinese thinkers whom we might wish to call philosophers are somehow ignoring the most important philosophical issues.

William James said that philosophy is nothing other than the uncommonly stubborn attempt to think clearly. That's not a bad conception with which to begin, though we might wish to supplement it with the equally fruitful definition provided by the contemporary American thinker Wilfred Sellars: Philosophy is the attempt to discover how things, in the most general sense, hang together, in the most general sense.

On first approach, seeking to think clearly about the Chinese seems to give us the sense that things just don't "hang together" in any way that we recognize as stable, rational, or appropriate. We must presume that our puzzlement is caused by the difficulty of adjusting to a cultural sensibility so utterly distinct from our own. Of course, part of this difficulty is due to the fact that we cannot be prepared to appreciate the Chinese ways of thinking unless we have a reasonably articulate grasp of the beliefs and desires that shape our own sensibility.

There is a Chinese expression:

> I do not know the true face of Mount Lu
> Simply because I'm standing on top of it.

We must begin to see the face of our own Mount Lu before we shall be able to make out the contours of the Chinese mountain.

Meanings of Order

We have just said that Western thinkers observing the Chinese may experience a frustrating perplexity when trying to make sense of the order of things Chinese. Jorge Luis Borges advertises just such perplexity by his well-known citation of "a certain Chinese encyclopedia" in which the category "animals" is divided into: (i) belonging to the Emperor, (ii) embalmed, (iii) tame, (iv) sucking pigs, (v) sirens, (vi) fabulous, (vii) stray dogs, (viii) included in the present classification, (ix) frenzied, (x) innumerable, (xi) drawn with a very fine camel-hair brush, (xii) etcetera, (xiii) having just broken the water pitcher, and (xiv) that from a long way off look like flies.[4]

Borges's parody of the Chinese manner of organizing things will appear somewhat less extreme if we consider the following parable of the fourth-century B.C.E. Taoist thinker Chuang Tzu:

> The Ruler of the Southern Ocean was *Shu* (Heedless), the Ruler of the Northern Ocean was *Hu* (Sudden), and the Ruler of Center was Chaos. *Shu* and *Hu* were continually meeting in the land of Chaos, who treated them very well. They consulted together how they might repay his kindness, and said, "Men all have seven orifices for the purpose of seeing, hearing, eating, and breathing, while this (poor) Ruler alone has not one. Let us try and make them for him." Accordingly they dug one orifice in him every day; and at the end of seven days Chaos died.[5]

The means of organizing the world through the senses, the very basis of a reasonable sense of order, destroys kindly Lord Chaos. James Legge, the translator of this passage, advertises the Western bewilderment with the Chinese conception of order in his footnote to his translation of this text: "But surely it was better that Chaos should give way to another state. 'Heedless' and 'Sudden' did not do a bad work." Unquestionably, it is better that confusion and disorder give way to harmony, but Chaos *(Hun-tun)* is not for Chuang Tzu identified with pernicious disorder but rather with the innocent spontaneity and harmony of the "original condition" before things received artificial and deadening organization.

This story about Lord Hun-tun could be considered a cosmogonic myth—a story of how the world comes into being. But it certainly isn't like the myths of origins with which most of us are familiar. Our traditional sense of order is grounded in cosmogonic myths that celebrate the victory of Cosmos over Chaos. Chaos is a "yawning gap" and a "gaping void." It is an emptiness or absence, a nothingness; it is a confused mass of unorganized surds. And however conceived, Chaos is the enemy of order. Hesiod's *Theogony* tells how the yawning gap of Chaos separating Heaven and Earth was overcome by Eros—love thereby creating harmony. The Book of Genesis tells how, from a "dark formless void," order was created by Divine Command. In the *Timaeus*, Plato's Demiurge "persuades" the disorganized, intransigent matter into reasonable order—"a victory of persuasion over necessity."

In accordance with the profound influence of our cosmogonic tradition, Western understandings of the way things hang together rest on the presumption that order and harmony must be vigilantly maintained by appeal to a creative agent or objective rules, laws, and principles.

Classical Chinese culture was little influenced by any sort of cosmogonic myth that contrasted an irrational Chaos with an ordered Cosmos. The relative unimportance of cosmogonic myths in China accounts for the dramatically different intellectual contexts from which the Chinese and Western cultural sensibilities emerged.

In the Western tradition, thinking about the order of things began with questions such as "What kinds of things are there?" and "What is the nature *(physis)* of things." This inquiry, which later came to be called metaphysics, took two principal forms. One, which the scholastics later termed *ontologia generalis* ("general ontology"), is the investigation of the most essential features of things. General ontology seeks to uncover the *Being* of beings. A slightly less abstract mode of metaphysical thinking, *scientia universalis* ("universal science"), involves the attempt to construct a science of the sciences, a way of knowing that organizes and accounts for the various ways of knowing the world about us.

Both general ontology and universal science serve to interpret the order of the cosmos advertised by the cosmogonic myths. Both suppose that there are general characteristics—the Being of beings, or universal principles—that tell us how things hang together.

Neither of these forms of metaphysical thinking were ever influential in China. One important reason for their unimportance is reflected in the character of the Chinese language. The usual Chinese equivalents for "being" and "not-being" are *yu* and *wu*.[6] But the meanings of these terms are markedly different from their uses in Indo-European languages. The Chinese *yu* means not that something "is" in the sense that it *exists;* it means rather that "something is present." "To be" is "to be available," "to be around." Likewise, "not be" means "not to be around." Thus, the Chinese sense of "being" overlaps with "having." A famous line from the Taoist classic *The Tao Te Ching,* often translated as "Not-Being is superior to Being," may as easily be translated "Not-having is

superior to having" (or, as a Marxist-inspired translator has rendered it, "Not owning private property is superior to owning private property").
The Chinese language disposes those who employ the notions of *yu* and *wu* to concern themselves with the presence or absence of concrete particular things and the effect of having or not having them at hand. Moreover, the practical, concrete disposition of Chinese thinkers is not merely a consequence but, just as important, a cause of the Chinese meanings of *yu* and *wu*.

Were we asked to come up with a name for the most general "science" of order in the Chinese tradition, we might offer the term *ars contextualis*. The Chinese seek the understanding of order through the "art of contextualization," which does not presume that there are essential features, or antecedent determining principles, serving as transcendent sources of order. The art of contextualization seeks to understand the manner in which particular things present to hand are, or may be, most harmoniously correlated. The reason the classical Chinese were disinclined toward the creation of myths accounting for the origin and structure of the cosmos is that they found harmonious interrelations among the particular things around them to be the natural condition—a *given* that requires no external principle or agency to explain it.

Our contrast of Western and Chinese senses of order has provided us two distinctive understandings of the term. The dominant meaning of order in the West is associated with uniformity and pattern regularity. In its most general sense, this "logical" or "rational" ordering is expressed in terms of the structure, or *logos,* of the cosmos. The Chinese understanding of order is one in which the natural and social worlds are comprised of concrete particulars whose uniqueness is essential to any context to which they belong. Aesthetic order emerges from the way in which these details are juxtaposed and correlated. As such, the order is resolutely immanental. This is true not only of social order but of "natural" order as well: The striations in stone, the coloration that differentiates the various layers of the earth, the veins in the leaf of a plant, the wind piping through the orifices of the earth—all are understood in the same manner as are the rituals and roles that constitute a communal grammar.

Our two senses of order may be illustrated in the following way: Think of the contrast between mathematical objects such as a triangle or a circle and art objects such as J.M.W. Turner's painting *Slave Ship.* What are the relevant differences? An important difference is that almost anyone can construct a triangle, but only Turner could have painted that particular work of art he named *Slave Ship.* Further, a triangle may be constructed from ink, chalk, or string, or elements of our imaginations. As a mental scheme or concept, the triangle is indifferent to such construction. All our individual constructions are imitations of "triangularity" as conceptually defined. With respect to Turner's painting, only that particular canvas and those particular pigments can comprise it. There is no antecedent pattern that Turner wishes to imitate. The work of art comes into being as a function of its unique particular elements. Few would believe that an imitation, a copy, of *Slave Ship* could ever be valued as much as the original.

In the West, the objective, formal character of mathematical order has been deemed nearest to perfection. In China, a notion of order that abstracted from the concrete details of this-worldly existence would be seen as moving away from relevancy. The crucial difference between these two senses of order is that in the one case there is the presumption of an objective standard which one perforce must instantiate; in the other, there is no source of order other than the agency of the elements comprising the order. The claim that the Chinese create order aesthetically rather than by recourse to logical or rational operations of the sort familiar to Western metaphysical thinkers requires us to reevaluate our most common stereotypes. Through the persuasion of our most popular sources on China, we have become accustomed to thinking of China as a stagnant society paralyzed by inertia, almost wholly inflexible, defiantly resistant to entering the modern world—if no longer a slumbering, certainly a lumbering, giant.[7] Can it really be true that the country identified with cultural continuity, intractable tradition, and the most provincial intolerance toward other civilizations illustrates an *aesthetic* understanding of order?

This seeming paradox may be resolved if we pursue the analogy with art. In painting there are the "greats," the innovators who create and master a style or manner, influencing their successors to emulate and augment the style and technique of the master. In China, the "Sage-Kings" such as the Emperors Yao and Shun, and exemplary figures such as Confucius, Lao Tzu, and Chuang Tzu, are the creators, the innovators whose contributions help to shape the ritualistic practices that order the present. But it would be a mistake to label as imitators those who practice rituals that they themselves did not create. For the proper effect of ritual practices is to liberate rather than to stultify the feelings of the participants in them. Those who play a musical instrument know very well how liberating technique can be. Once we master the scales and chords and gain sufficient dexterity in the use of our fingers, we can play the piano in such a manner as to release our aesthetic feelings. This inner ecstasy of performance is open to those who practice ritual as well. Ritual, like artistic technique, is not a tyrant but a liberator.

Rational order depends on the belief in a single-ordered world, a cosmos. Aesthetic order speaks of the world in much less unitary terms. In China, the cosmos is simply "the ten thousand things." The claim that the things of nature may be ordered in any number of ways is the basis of philosophical thinking as *ars contextualis*. Rational order, on the other hand, is based on the notion that this world is one, rendered coherent by laws guaranteeing its rationality.

Each of these understandings of order existed at the beginnings of both Western and Chinese cultures, and both persist as interpretative options in the two cultures. It so happens that in the course of their respective histories the two cultures made distinctly different choices, which led to the dominance of alternative understandings of the grounding of cosmic, social, and personal order.[8]

Confucians are often distinguished from Taoists by the observation that though both seek aesthetic harmony, the Taoists seek harmony with nature whereas Confucians are concerned with harmony in the social sphere. "Nature" ("the ten thousand things") and "society," as contexts, are both aesthetic products whose order is a creation of the elements of the contexts. In the Taoist texts, the central notion of *tzu-jan* (self-so-ing) means that each of the ten thousand things comes into being out of its own inner reflection and that no one can tell how it comes to be so. The Confucian version of this claim is that "it is the person who extends order in the world *(tao)*, not order that extends the person."[9] Later on, with the penetration of Buddhism into China, a rich vocabulary permitting an articulation of the inner life of the individual will be added to the Chinese cultural resources. Thus, the introduction of Indian Buddhism brought with it a conception of human interiority that neither early Confucianism or Taoism provided.

The Chinese exercise of the naming of persons is a good illustration of how one ritually "extends order in the world." The process of naming is a correlative procedure that has its most familiar illustrations in totemic classifications. In an Amerindian tribe, the name *Running Deer* may suggest to the person so named how he or she is to behave toward others of the tribe, as well as indicate to others how they are to behave toward him or her. The ordering of attitudes, actions, and expectations through the act of naming does not create an objective, rational order; nonetheless, real social harmony can result from such ordering.

In something like this fashion, the giving of proper names in the Chinese tradition provides a disposition to act on the part of the individual named and a disposition to treat the named one as his or her name indicates. As dispositional, a name is a ritual form. Thus, the Chinese proper name *An Lo-che* ("Contented in philosophy")[10] advertises a wish to fulfill the promise of the name. If, in turn, family and associates respond in however small a manner to the name as more than a mere "tag," there is support for the philosophical life of An Lo-che. Thus, a family may be a society of names that, as dispositions-to-act, define the character of the beliefs and desires of the family.

As a harmony of names, the family is determinate and focused at the center, but becomes increasingly vague as it stretches out both historically in the direction of one's own lineage, one's clan, one's surname, and as a present community immediately transformed into "uncles" and "aunties" as soon as social contact is made. The family is radial, articulated in terms of a ritual "wheel" of social relations that "ripple out" in a field of "discourse" to define the person as a network of roles.[11]

To speak of the relationship of the Chinese to their various social contexts, we must avoid language suggesting the relation of "part" and "whole." It is better to speak of the relation of a "focus" to the "field" it focuses. Thus, the togetherness of heaven and man suggests that the particular human being is focus and that "heaven" or "the ten thousand things" are the field focused by that person. The culture is the field and its exemplary models—the Sage Kings, Confucius, Lao Tzu, and so forth—are foci. The political order of any given epoch is field and the present ruler is the principal focus.

Although the family, the society, the state, or the tradition itself as the most extended context is vague *as a grouping,* this vagueness is focused and made immediate through its embodiment by the particular father, the communal exemplar, the ruler, the historical model. This is but to say that the meaning of the group is made present in "supreme personalities": one's own father, one's teacher, one's Confucius, and one's Mao Tse-tung. Although the concreteness and immediacy of the center preclude any but the vaguest and indeterminate definitions of "Chineseness," this notion comes alive *to a particular historical person* in his or her image of a Tseng Kuo-fan or a Yang Yu-wei.[12]

Clearly the Chinese sense of social order cannot be understood in terms of Western individualism. None of the principal ideas undergirding individualism in the West had much influence in China. That is to say, neither the idealist conception of the human being as possessed of a unique soul that serves to individuate him or her from other ensouled beings, nor the materialistic, atomistic understanding that identifies the person with his or her body, only extrinsically related to other such bodies, nor, for that matter, the existential interpretation that identifies the individual with the creative exercise of will played much part in the formation of Chinese cultural resources.

Chinese society cannot be interpreted as a complex of distinct and autonomous individuals protected by natural rights, living in a society ordered by codes of law backed by power and sanctions. One confronts dramatic evidence of the inappropriateness of individualism in the Chinese context when attempting to translate the rhetoric of liberal democracy into the Chinese language. The English sentence "Liberalism rests on individualism under the supremacy of law" would read to the Chinese something like this: "The doctrine of spontaneous license *(tzu-yu chu-yi)* rests on the doctrine of self-centeredness *(ko-jen chu-yi)* under the supremacy of administrative regulation *(fa-lü)."*[13]

The defect of individualism from the Chinese perspective is its challenge to a ritually ordered society in which the boundaries of the self may be only vaguely delineated. The Chinese "self" is a complex of roles and functions associated with the obligations to the various groupings to which one belongs. One is son, father, brother, husband, citizen, teacher. Subtract each of these roles from him and nothing constituting a coherent personality remains: no soul, no mind, no ego, not even an "I know not what."

The sense of personal identity is determined in part by tension with others. Without at least a tacit conflict between self and others, the distinctive character of the self becomes vague and diffuse, difficult to distinguish from its various social contexts. Ritual actions significantly decrease the occasions on which one would experience tension with others.

The phenomenon of the individuated self was in fact a rather late development in our own tradition. At the beginning of Greek culture, the tribal character of social organization effectively precluded a strong sense of otherness.[14] This sense increased markedly with the growth of cosmopolitan cities. In fact, as the word suggests, "civilization" in the West was a process of "citification."

Attendant upon the rise of cities and of the commercial relations with foreign peoples that sustained these urban centers, the Greeks enforced a strong distinction between the private and the public spheres. This separation of the intimate relations of the family from the more impersonal relations of public life further enhanced the possibility of a sense of self-identity. The family became a training ground for public life.

Things went quite differently in China. Ancient China overcame the threat of the tensions and conflicts attendant upon ethnic and cultural pluralism by the device of employing the language itself, rather than the process of urbanization, as the medium for transmitting the culture. A class of literati developed; a canon of classical works was instituted along with a commentarial tradition that served to perpetuate the doctrines of these classical works; an examination system based on these texts was introduced in the early Han dynasty.[15]

Further, the Chinese never stressed a distinction between private and public realms. Because the family was the model of all types of relationship, including the nonfamilial relations among subjects and between ruler and subjects, there was no effective public sphere. One can hardly overestimate the importance of these contrasting developments in determining Chinese and Western attitudes toward individual autonomy.

Our contrast between the Chinese and Western understandings of order appears to challenge the conviction that the West surely prizes novelty and spontaneity more than do the traditionalist Chinese. But, on reflection, it becomes clear that the profound concern for creativity in the West is a response to the realization that any presumption of an objective reality providing the standards for the world of appearance leaves very little room for the production of novelty. In China, by contrast, where the standards themselves are created through the activity of the agents comprising society or the "ten thousand things," novelty is the norm. Tradition-based models available in the culture ensure that novel contributions will not lead to disharmony.

In China, the phrase "the togetherness of man and heaven" *(t'ien-jen ho-yi)* has been construed to mean that personal, societal, political, and cosmic order are coterminous and mutually entailing, and that, from the human perspective, this order is emergent in the process of one's own self-cultivation and articulation. If we think of the various contexts that are to be harmonized as so many concentric circles, we can see that there is an interdependence between one's self-realization at the center and cosmic order at the outer extreme.

Classically, this is expressed through the notion of the Sage as exemplar of both tradition in its broadest sense and "the Will of Heaven," that is, the specific environing conditions that set up the viable possibilities in a particular social situation or historical epoch. This is the sense of Mencius's (ca. 380–289 B.C.E.) assertions that "all of the myriad things are complete here in me" and "one who applies exhaustively his heart-and-mind realizes his character, and in thus realizing his character, realizes the whole of nature *(t'ien)*."[16]

The "myriad things" is an expression denoting the natural world as a complex of particular elements. It lacks the suggestion of unity or coherence carried by the term *cosmos,* which is thought to be organized in terms of natural laws characterizing causal relationships among things. Its order is a shifting set of aesthetic harmonies construed from the perspective of the human world.

The *Lao Tzu,* the classic of the Taoist tradition, expresses this notion of harmony: "The myriad things shoulder *yin* and embrace *yang* and blend their energies *(ch'i)* together to constitute a harmony *(ho).*" The intelligible patterns created by different perspectives upon the world are all pathways that can in varying degrees be traced out to make one's place and its context coherent. *Tao* is, at any given time, both *what* the world is and *how* it is. There is no final distinction between an independent source of order and that which it orders. The world and its order at any particular time is self-causing so-of-itself *(tzu-jan).* For this reason, explanation does not lie in the discovery of some antecedent agency or the isolation and disclosure of relevant causes. Rather, any particular event or phenomenon can be understood by mapping out the conditions that collaborate to sponsor it. Once understood, these conditions can be manipulated to anticipate the next moment.

In the Han dynasty, vast tables of correspondences were developed in order to define and organize the sorts of things in the natural and social world that were thought to provide a meaningful context for one's life. One such set of tables, called "tables of five," compared "the five phases" (wood, fire, earth, metal, water), "the five directions" (north, east, south, west, and center), "the five colors" (green, red, yellow, white, black), "the five notes", and so forth.

Other types of correlation employed the twelve months, the twelve pitches, the twenty-eight constellations, the heavenly roots and earthly branches. Such classifications include body parts, psychophysical and affective states, styles of government, weather, domestic animals, technological instruments, heavenly bodies, and much more.[17]

One of the important devices employed in Chinese correlative thinking is the contrast of *yin* and *yang*. Given the uniqueness of each thing and the continuity that exists among things, each phenomenon is thought to be bound to every other thing in a pattern of interchanging hierarchical relationships. The old teacher Lao Tzu is wiser than his young student, and hence overshadows him in this respect. Lao Tzu is *yang* and the student is *yin*. The student, however, is stronger physically than the old master; hence in strength, the student is *yang* to Lao Tzu's *yin*. It is when these various strengths and weaknesses that define the relationship can be balanced to maximum effect that the relationship is most productive and most fully harmonious.

The contents of many of these correlative schemes are apparently the same as the subject matters of the Western natural sciences. But there is a crucial difference in the manner in which they are treated. In China, correlations were not undertaken as a means of dispassionately investigating the nature of things. Rather, in accordance with the query "*What am I?*" correlative schemes oriented the individual in a very practical manner to the external surroundings. Thus, the Chinese were concerned less with astronomy than with astrology; they were far more enthusiastic over the development of geomancy than over the development of geology.

In China, social order was construed as a harmony achieved through personal participation in a ritually constituted community. Thus the ideal of social order could not be realized by appeal to law. Such appeal, far from being respected as a legitimate resource for adjudicating social conflicts, was seen as an admission of communal failure. This attitude was so much a part of the Chinese character that the profession of the lawyer, thought to be a potential source of dissension among citizens, was discouraged. Judges often acted as the sole arbiters of legal disputes.

It is the emphasis on social harmony achieved through personalized ritual relationships *(li)* that most dramatically distinguishes the Chinese *ritual community* from the Western *society of laws*. The term most often translated by the English "society" in modern Chinese is *she-hui*, which, taken literally, refers to the traditional practice of gathering around the sacred pole erected in the center of the community.[18]

The characteristic of ritually shaped order that distinguishes it from the more legalistic rule-based order is the personal cultivation of a sense of shame, and the self-rectification that ensues from it. Confucius compared these two alternative models of communal order in the following terms:

Lead the people with administrative policies and organize them with penal law, and they will avoid punishments but will be without a sense of shame. Lead them with an example of excellence and organize them with ritual practices, and they will have a sense of shame and, moreover, will order themselves harmoniously.[19]

This sense of the self-attuning harmony of society led Confucius to claim that "the various Chinese states without their rulers are better than the barbarian tribes with them."[20]

Ritual has broad compass in the Chinese social and political order. It is the performance of any formalized, meaning-invested conduct, role, or institution that serves to organize particular human beings in community. Thus, ritual spans everything from table manners to court ceremony, from living familial relations to observances for the dead.

The People of the Han

One of the well-known generalizations concerning the Western intellectual tradition is captured by Whitehead's apothegm: "All of Western philosophy is a series of footnotes to Plato." The Chinese version of this sort of claim has equal force: "All of Chinese thinking is a series of commentaries on Confucius." The validity of this assertion is dependent upon historical developments occurring within the period of the Han dynasty (206 B.C.E.–220 C.E.). It is these developments that have led the Chinese to call themselves "the People of the Han."

The first volume of the *Cambridge History of China* describes the career of the Han empire from its emergence under Liu Pang to its gradual disintegration three and a half centuries later.[21] In this volume, Yü Ying-shih uses the "five zones" *(wu-fu)* theory of submission as a device for describing the dynamics of the Han world order[22]:

According to this theory, China since the Hsia dynasty (2205–1766 B.C.E.?) had been divided into five concentric and hierarchical zones or areas. The central zone *(tien-fu)* was the royal domain, under the direct rule of the king. The royal domain was immediately surrounded by the Chinese states established by the king, known collectively as the Lords' zone *(hou-fu)*. Beyond the *hou-fu* were Chinese states conquered by the reigning dynasty, which constituted the so-called pacified zone *(sui-fu* or *pin-fu,* guest zone). The last two zones were reserved for the barbarians. The Man and I barbarians lived outside the *sui-fu* or *pin-fu* in the controlled zone *(yao-fu),* which was so called because the Man and I were supposedly subject to Chinese control, albeit of a rather loose kind. Finally, beyond the controlled zone lay the Jung and Ti barbarians, who were basically their own masters in the wild zone *(huang-fu)* where the sinocentric world order reached its natural end.

This hierarchical system, with patterns of deference sustaining a central authoritative focus, seems pervasive in Chinese society. These concrete, functioning patterns of deference contribute in varying degrees to, and are constitutive of, the authority at the center, shaping and bringing into focus the standards and values of the social and politically entity.

The full spectrum of Han peoples—some under traditional hereditary houses, others organized religiously, yet others under clan or tribal regulation—was suspended in the Han harmony, with each contributing in greater or lesser degree to the definition of Han culture. This transition from contending diversity in the latter years of the Chou dynasty to unity in the Han is best expressed in a language of incorporation and accommodation.

Three and a half centuries later, well after the establishment of social and political unity, the center of the Han court weakened and the political order gradually dissolved into a period of disunity. Contending forces precipitated out of the harmony to reassert themselves. What had been their contribution to the center became the energy of contest among them. What was a tightening spire in the early Han became a gyre, disgorging itself of its disassociating contents.

Broadly, then, the disintegration of social order in the Chinese context is occasioned by a weakening of the center that is both cause and consequence of corruption among those responsible for the order. Because the political ruler is also a moral exemplar, any hint of corruption can lead to demoralization on the part of the people. If the ruler cannot institute proper reforms, he will suffer a loss of filial respect on the part of the people, who will claim that he has lost "the Mandate of Heaven" *(t'ien-ming)*. With increasing demoralization, what was a participatory authoritative order becomes impositional and authoritarian.

The order discernible in the constitution of Han dynasty China is precisely that captured in the Confucian concept of ritually ordered community, where ritual, defined at the center by the authority of the tradition, not only demands personalization and participation but reflects the quality of its specific participants. There is an immediate analogy between an official's participation in an order defined by the court and a person's performance of those roles and rituals that define the tradition.

To this point we have been speaking about the notion of order and harmony in such a manner as to suppress suggestions of intellectual differences and conflicts. This is in keeping with the Chinese disposition to tell a story of the harmony rather than of the conflict of ideas.

It is generally recognized that Confucian orthodoxy, which came to dominance in the Han dynasty, is a river that over time was fed by three powerful streams: Confucianism, Taoism, and Buddhism. A typical Chinese, even into the modern period, might be heard to say, "With respect to family and society, I am Confucian; with respect to Nature I am Taoist, and with respect to things beyond the world of nature and society, I am Buddhist."[23] The stress here is on the harmony of the three traditions. There is no suggestion that one separates family from nature or from "things apart from nature." Though Confucianism remains dominant, the three sensibilities provide distinct foci in accordance with which one can construe one's life.

The distinguished interpreter of the Chinese tradition Wing-tsit Chan refers to the story of Chinese philosophy as "an intellectual symphony in three movements."[24] In the first movement the diverse themes introduced by the various schools were harmonized by Confucianism. In the second movement, from the Han synthesis until approximately the tenth century C.E., strong Buddhist chords provided counterpoint to the Confucian themes. The third movement, from the eleventh century to the modern period, again resolved all thematic tensions in what has come to be called Neoconfucianism. Throughout these three movements it was the Confucian themes that provided the harmonic unity.

Granted the disposition on the part of the Chinese to promote a harmonious narrative of China's cultural development, a closer look at the actual events yields a slightly greater sense of conflict. In the approximately one hundred years between the death of Confucius and the birth of Mencius, a complex variety of philosophical schools developed. In the Taoist work, the *Chuang Tzu,* this growth in diversity is referred to as the period of the "Hundred Schools." Far from seeing in this a healthy pluralism of opinion, Mencius, a representative of the Confucian tradition, described this phenomenon in the most negative of terms: "Sage-kings have failed to arise. The feudal lords do whatever they want and scholars who are not employed in government are quite ready to pronounce on affairs."[25] This sort of contentiousness is thought to be destructive of the Confucian order.

The period of the conflicting schools of thinking began when Mo Tzu, the founder of Mohism, called Confucian ideas into question. Mohist thinking, generally associated with a kind of utilitarianism, constituted a significant challenge to the ritually grounded traditionalism of Confucius. Legalism, associated with Han Fei Tzu (ca. 280–233 B.C.E.), differed from both Confucianism and Mohism by beginning its social thinking not with the people but with the laws and sanctions presumed to be devices necessary to bring order to the people. With the Legalists came at least the adumbration of a theory of rational political order. During the succeeding centuries, until about 200 B.C.E., a plethora of alternative schools emerged, and court-sponsored academies were established in different parts of the empire.

In the beginning, the competing schools engaged primarily in debates about doctrine. Conservative Confucians who sought the meaning of life by appeal to family and social obligations were opposed by those Taoists who sought a hermit's retreat from the social world.[26] There were fierce debates among the Confucians, Taoists, and Legalists (among many others) concerning the original goodness or evil of human nature. Soon, however, issues became procedural and logical rather than substantive.

Thinkers began to argue about the meaning of argument itself. Mohism and the School of Names developed complex paradigms of logical thinking and puzzled over the linguistic paradoxes that advertise the limits of language. Thus, as was the case in the history of early Greek thinking, rationalism developed in China primarily as a means of adjudicating doctrinal conflict.

But interest in logic and rationality, along with the analytical and dialectical modes of discourse attendant upon these, very soon faded into the background of Chinese intellectual culture. China emerged as a culture grounded in the immanent aesthetic order of a ritually grounded society that precludes rational conflict. Attendant upon this emergence was the rapid decline in the importance of the Mohists, the Legalists, the School of Names, and so forth, and the rise of Confucian orthodoxy.

That this orthodoxy did not lead to the eradication of other important strains, principally those associated with the Buddhists and Taoists, is testimony to the flexibility of a ritually based society.

The Buddhist influence is most obvious in the magnificent landscape paintings of the Sung dynasty (960–1279 C.E.), and the spare, imagistic poetry produced during that same period. With respect to the landscapes, the only avenue of understanding is to envision oneself moving through the scape to enjoy the world as construed from perspectives within the painting. And the economy of the poetry requires a proportionate interpretive response. Likewise, Taoist contributions such as herbal medicines and acupuncture have helped to form the character of what we know as "Chineseness." Nonetheless, by the beginning of the first century B.C.E. Confucianism had become the permanent victor over all contending forces—in large measure because of its ability to accommodate within a ritually grounded society the most profound elements of Taoism and Buddhism, as well as many other lesser movements and sensibilities.

With the dominance of Confucian orthodoxy came a new method of adjudicating doctrinal conflict. Beginning in the early Han, commentaries on Confucian texts would be produced and would vie for proximity to the center defined by the canon. The authors of these commentaries were almost never interested in overthrowing the traditional authority in favor of their own ideas, but they sought to enrich the authority of the classic by claiming to better understand its original meaning.

Further, since tradition was the sole ready resource for principles and doctrines, critics of a particular doctrine depended as much as did proponents on a shared cultural repository. This is evidenced in the frequent canonical allusions employed to focus one's criticisms. The appeal to canonical authority is again a way of reinforcing a sense of shared community, and stands in sharp contrast to dialectical arguments that depend on appeal to "canons" of reason or logic.

In our tradition we find it possible to disagree with particular opinions while remaining respectful of the person holding those opinions. But in the Chinese tradition, there is not a discernible distance between the belief or opinion and the person. Good people write good books; good rulers promulgate good policies. One would not expect to hear from a Chinese scholar anything like Aristotle's statement "I love my teacher, Plato, but I love truth more." Such a declaration would have been seen as indulgence in the sort of contentiousness and self-assertiveness that threatens social harmony.

Characteristic of scholarly dispute after the emergence of Han ortho-doxy is a fundamental commitment to mutual accommodation.[27] There is a general distaste for contentiousness and an active cultivation of the art of accommodation. In the exercise of criticism, the ritual basis of order comes into play because rituals serve as patterns of deference that accommodate and harmonize differences in desires, beliefs, and actions.

Criticism assumes a context of common concern and becomes thereby a cooperative exercise among responsible participants that proceeds to search for alternatives on which all can agree. One important constraint on self-assertiveness, as well as an encouragement to consensual resolu-tion, is that the critic himself is always implicated in the existing context, and hence any criticism of it is ultimately self-referential. Contentious-ness, by contrast, betrays a concern for personal advantage. Such self-assertion threatens to disrupt rather than reinforce or improve the har-mony of the existing context. The proper goal of criticism in China, whether it be scholarly or social and political, is the strengthening of communal harmony.

Dismantling the Stereotypes

The attempt to discern how, in China, things hang together in the most general sense has led us to a number of insights which, properly em-ployed, can help us avoid some of the more serious stereotypes that threaten to besot our thinking about China. Paradoxically, the stereotypes we must avoid are not those based on a confused sense of Chinese inscrutability. Rather, the most damaging stereotypes are those which make us believe that, when all is said and done, being human has to mean being pretty much as we are.

We in the scientific, liberal democratic West must recognize that our tendencies toward universalism and the acceptance of objective ideas and values merely advertise the content of our own cultural sensibility. The West has masked its ethnocentrism by the claim that its self-understand-ing has universal applicability. One paradoxical element of our peculiar form of ethnocentricity is the rejection of ethnocentrism. But we do not escape provincialism simply because we make naive claims to objectivity and universality.

The comparison of Chinese and Western cultures is, therefore, the comparison of two sets of ethnocentric beliefs. Most of us who occupy a privileged place in a Western democracy consider ourselves autonomous individuals, possessing natural rights, with a faith in our ability to search out the truth of things for ourselves, generally confident that reason and goodwill can solve most of our problems. We are respectful of governmental authority when it serves to nurture freedom and autonomy for its citizens, but are perfectly capable of becoming an adversary of the government if it threatens those same values. We identify ourselves with ideas, values, and principles that we believe are reasonable and employ our religious, scientific, or political institutions as instruments for the implementation of those ideas and values. We deplore censorship and believe that free and open enquiry will result in consensus upon what is true about the needs and desires of the majority of human beings.

Above all, we believe in the ideals that emerged from the French Revolution and have found their specific instantiation in documents such as the American Declaration of Independence, the U.S. Constitution, and the Bill of Rights. These ideals we hold to be the guarantees of our individual autonomy, our liberal democracy, and our science and technology—all of which we believe to be the necessary vehicles of progress for all countries and peoples around the world.

Among our intellectual elites there is doubtless a great deal less naive assent to these beliefs, but the trust in objectivity lingers. The visions of natural and social scientists, and of philosophers too, still reflect the belief that there is an objective order to things and that the discovery of this order requires the responsible application of the methods of logic and science.[28] This faith extends for many of us into the idea that human beings have objective natures, identifiable characteristics that make us essentially the same from one society or culture to another.

Many might believe that while it is important to reckon with the sort of differences discussed in this essay if our aim is to understand the ideas and institutions of classical China, we need not take these differences too seriously when approaching the modern period. Surely, such individuals believe, the events of the twentieth century have radically changed the character of China. The pressures of the West have been felt from without and internal revolution experienced from within. Must not China begin to adopt the principles of Western democracy and science?

These beliefs are admixtures of wishful thinking and of serious misunderstandings of contemporary China. Such is the power of China's tradition that the long-standing meaning of "Chineseness" remains intact. If asked whether we ought still to refer to the Chinese as people of the Han, we must answer "yes."

The relatively slight impact of Marxism on contemporary China reveals the persistence of the Chinese tradition. When the leadership of China decided to import Marxism, it solicited advice from Russia, which had just gone through its Communist revolution. Russian advisers, appalled by the absence of a proletarian class in China, in effect told the Chinese to call on them again when they had developed a proletariat! Undaunted by the absence of the "essential conditions" for the success of Marxism, Mao Tse-tung adopted that ideology as "a Western heresy with which to combat the West." By idealizing those elements of Marxism which condemned the disharmonious effects of competition and private property, he actually increased the weight of basic Confucian values. And, however much the nuclear family was affected by Marxist ideas, the family as a model of the larger society, and the paternalistic character of rule that follows from this model, remained intact. There are all too many illustrations of this sort that demonstrate the almost incidental character of Marxism as a force for change in contemporary China.

There is little evidence to suggest that contemporary China has abandoned any significant elements of its Confucian orthodoxy. The leadership of contemporary China maintains the same characteristics that have dominated since the Han dynasty—the understanding of the nation as a "family," the filial respect for the ruler as "father," and the consequent sense of rule as a *personal* exercise.[29]

With respect to the personal character of rule, it continues to be the case in China that to object to the policies that articulate the existing order is in fact to condemn the ruler's person.

> In Mao's China political deviance had been a treasonous crime far more serious than theft or homicide. It was not possible to separate policy from patriotism and tolerate a loyal opposition. Today the old Confucian tenets seem imbedded in the CCP system: that one rules by virtue of wisdom and rectitude; that theory and practice are a unity, policies a form of conduct manifesting one's character, and attacks on policy therefore attacks on the ruling power.[30]

The Chinese have remained people of the Han. Contemporary China is still a ritually constituted society without grounding in the objective principles associated with reason or natural law, its order defined by the exemplars of its tradition. The members of the society are themselves possessed of their "humanity" not as a gift from God or as a common genetic inheritance, but as created by ritual enactment. The Chinese have no inalienable rights. Citizens have been deemed to possess only those rights that are granted by China's various constitutions.

Contrary to the ethnocentricity of the West, which insists on the universality of certain values and principles, Chinese ethnocentrism is based on the centrality of a culture defined by racial and linguistic identity. Thus, ethnic pluralism is still a threat to social harmony. Foreigners *as foreigners* can be absorbed into the society only with extreme difficulty. China remains a culture grounded in filiality and the model of the family that cultivates filial dependency. Individualism is still a signal of selfishness and license. The Chinese have no means of cultivating what we would consider to be a healthy suspicion of governmental power without at the same time challenging the personal character of the ruler. Technology, the idol of the Western world, is a serious threat to China. As a rational means of organizing social and economic interactions, technology undermines the ritual grounding of interpersonal relationships. Further, the existence of "specialists," "experts," and "professionals" subverts the belief in the omnicompetence and sagely wisdom of those who guide society. It is still the case in China that not only saying but *thinking* as well is a kind of "doing." The inhibition of free speech is not a modern invention of the Chinese Communists but a persistent feature of a Confucian society in which ideas are always dispositions to act.

We began this essay with a reference to the relatively recent incident at Tiananmen Square, suggesting that this event might be easily misunderstood if we did not take into account the real differences that exist between our own and the Chinese perspectives. Were we to yield for a moment our ethnocentric beliefs and look at contemporary China through Chinese eyes, we would see Tiananmen as symbolic of a struggle the causes of which have little to do with a desire for individual autonomy or liberal democracy. Indeed, when a young student at Tiananmen—asked for his understanding of democracy—said, "I don't know what democracy is, but we need more of it," he advertised the general level of understanding of democratic institutions in China.

The Chinese expression *(min-chu chu-yi)* that translates our word *democracy* refers, for most Chinese, to the classical Confucian tenet "taking the people as the root of government" *(min-pen)*, where "people" must mean an interdependent family rather than a society of free, self-determining individuals. "Government of, by, and for the people" can never mean the same thing for the Chinese as for the citizens of a Western democracy.[31]

Asking the Chinese to recognize that they have inalienable rights is to ask them to become, *per impossibile,* beings with essences or natures. Wishing for increased autonomy and freedom for the Chinese people, along with access to the technologies and economic institutions that make for the Western standard of living, is to condemn the Chinese order to dissolution. And, after the deluge, there is little hope that any alternative order could be put in its place.

There is good reason to believe that the Chinese intellectual, social, and political orders are in crisis. Perhaps the rulers no longer occupy the center; perhaps they have lost the "Mandate of Heaven." Whether China will continue to hang together in the traditional manner is a very real question. But it does seem clear that only if China chooses (or is forced by circumstances beyond its control to choose) to emulate the order of Western societies as a means of entering the "modern world" will the Chinese lose their claim to call themselves "the people of the Han."

Notes

1. *The Importance of Living* (New York: John Day, 1937), p. 46.

2. See the Introduction to D. E. Mungello's *Curious Land: Jesuit Accommodation and the Origins of Sinology* (Honolulu: University of Hawaii Press, 1985) for a discussion of the interest in China on the part of the Jesuit missionaries and other intellectuals.

3. F. Hegel, *Philosophy of History,* trans. J. Sibree (New York: Dover, 1956 repr.), pp. 111–12.

4. This passage from Borges was the inspiration for Michel Foucault's *The Order of Things: An Archaeology of the Human Sciences* (a translation of *Les Mots et les choses*) (New York: Vintage Books, 1973), Preface.

5. *The Texts of Taoism,* trans. James Legge (New York: Dover, 1962), Vol. 1, pp. 266–67.

6. See A. C. Graham's "Being in Western Philosophy Compared with *Shih/Fei* and *Yu/Wu* in Chinese Philosophy" in *Studies in Chinese Philosophy and Philosophical Literature* (Singapore: Institute of East Asian Philosophies, 1986), pp. 322–59, and "The Relation of Chinese Thought to Chinese Language," Appendix 2, *Disputers of the Tao* (La Salle, Ill.: Open Court Press, 1989), pp. 408–12.

7. Paul Cohen in his *Discovering History in China: American Historical Writings on the Recent Chinese Past* (New York: Columbia University Press, 1984) concerns himself with the currency of just such an image of China in the most influential historical sources that define the intellectual understanding of China and its culture in the West.

8. We have pursued the reasons for these differing choices in our *Anticipating China: The Circle and the Square,* forthcoming from SUNY Press. One of the things we discuss in that work is how leading developments in contemporary Anglo-European philosophy—those associated with such thinkers as Foucault, Derrida, and the American pragmatist Richard Rorty—express a critique of the Western notion of rational order and a movement in the direction of the aesthetic understanding resident in our tradition.

9. *Analects* 15/29.

10. An Lo-che is in fact the Chinese name of one of the authors of this essay.

11. The Chinese language is organic, and a cluster of cognate terms expresses this sense of community: wheel *(lun),* relationship *(lun*),* discourse *(lun**),* and ripple *(lun***).*

12. Yang Yu-wei is our Taiwan teacher and surrogate "father," and has taught our best students from his grotto in Taipei.

13. This illustration is from John Fairbank's review of John Lubot's "Liberalism in an Illiberal Age" in *China Quarterly* 96 (December 1983): 739.

14. See Alvin Gouldner's *The Hellenic World: A Sociological Analysis* (New York: Harper and Row, 1969), p. 104ff, for a discussion of the development of the Greek notion of the self.

15. This examination system persisted in China with relatively little change for 2,000 years. It was abolished only in 1905.

16. *Mencius* 7A/4 and 7A/1.

17. A rather complete table of one variation of these correspondences is

contained in Joseph Needham, *Science and Civilisation in China*, Vol. 2 (Cambridge: Cambridge University Press, 1954): 262–63.

18. For a discussion of the concentric structure of Chinese society from which Han social organization emerged, see Nishijima Sadao, "The economic and social history of Former Han" in *The Cambridge History of China*, Volume I: *The Ch'in and Han Empires 221* B.C.–A.D. *220* (Cambridge: Cambridge University Press, 1986).

19. *Analects* 2/3.

20. *Analects* 3/5.

21. Denis Twitchett and Michael Loewe, eds., *The Cambridge History of China*, Volume I: *The Ch'in and Han Empires 221* B.C.–A.D. *220* (Cambridge: Cambridge University Press, 1986).

22. Ibid., pp. 379–80.

23. On visiting a temple in Taipei some years ago, we received in reply to the question "What kind of temple is this?" the answer "It is the temple of this place." Persisting, we asked, "Is it Taoist, Buddhist, or Confucian?" The reply was "It is our neighborhood temple." And actually, the practices in the temple suggested the influences of all three sensibilities.

24. See Chan's "The Story of Chinese Philosophy" in *The Chinese Mind*, ed. Charles Moore (Honolulu: East-West Center Press, 1967), pp. 31–76.

25. *Mencius* 3B/9.

26. Taoism is a complex movement in early China. There were certainly Taoists—some would argue that these were in the majority—who enjoined participation in the political order.

27. In his *Ethical Argumentation: A Study in Hsün Tzu's Moral Epistemology* (Honolulu: University of Hawaii Press, 1985), A. S. Cua provides a general analysis of the "style" of argumentative engagement in Han China. See especially pp. 6–12. In the following we shall be borrowing heavily from Cua.

28. As we mentioned in note 8, however, there are rapid changes in these beliefs—especially at the level of philosophic thinking. These changes could eventually lead to a somewhat greater sympathy with the Chinese sensibility. But we are still far from abandoning our sense of rational order. This is particularly so with respect to the belief in universal rights and a common human nature—the very ideas that the Chinese aesthetic understanding of order most directly challenges.

29. See John Fairbank, *China Watch* (Cambridge, Mass.: Harvard University Press, 1987), pp. 83–94.

30. Ibid., p. 209.

31. See David L. Hall and Roger T. Ames, *Thinking Through Confucius* (Albany: State University of New York Press, 1987), pp. 138–56, for a discussion of early Confucian attitudes toward "the people" *(min)*. See also Roger T. Ames, *The Art of Rulership* (Honolulu: University of Hawaii Press, 1983), pp. 157–64, for the history of the Confucian tenet "benefitting the people" *(li-min)*.

2

Ways of Japanese Thinking

Graham Parkes

In February of 1936, twenty-one junior officers in the Imperial Army of Japan led an uprising calculated to overthrow the government and restore supreme command of the armed forces to the emperor. They managed to assassinate three government ministers and occupy a small area of Tokyo near the imperial palace. Emperor Hirohito, however, demanded that the uprising be quashed. Overwhelmed by the imperial forces, two of the officers committed *seppuku* (ritual suicide by disembowelment), and the rest were executed.

In 1960, Mishima Yukio, who was becoming one of the best-known writers in Japan, wrote a short story entitled "Patriotism," which was based on the abortive rebellion of 1936.[1] The hero of the story is a young officer in the Imperial Guard from whom his comrades have kept the dangerous conspiracy a secret because he is newly married, and they want to obviate the risk of his young bride's being prematurely widowed. After the rebellion is launched, the officer is ordered to participate in the attack on the rebel forces, but rather than take up arms against his comrades, he resolves to commit *seppuku*. His wife expresses her desire to join him in death, and the officer agrees.

The husband and wife bathe and then make love, the eroticism of the scene heightened by the prospect of imminent death. Mishima is one of the great prose stylists in modern Japanese, and the story builds to a climax that is overwhelmingly powerful even in English translation. The officer's self-disembowelment is described in loving and excruciating detail, as he plunges the sharp sword into the left side of his abdomen and pulls it across to the right. It is almost a relief when the wife follows her husband in death by stabbing herself in the neck with a dagger.

Five years after writing "Patriotism," Mishima made a film of the story, entitled *The Rite of Love and Death,* in which he himself played the role of the young officer who commits *seppuku.* Five years later, in 1970, at the head of a small band of comrades in a paramilitary organization he had founded, Mishima gained entry to the headquarters of the Army Self-Defense Force in Tokyo and captured its commander. From a balcony on the second floor he proceeded to harangue the troops whom he had ordered assembled outside, encouraging them to abolish the democratic form of government that had been established after World War II and to restore to Japan its true identity by reestablishing the emperor system.

Greeted by howls of derision, Mishima went back into the room where his comrades were holding the commander hostage, knelt down facing the balcony, and committed *seppuku.* His right-hand man, a university student by the name of Morita, followed his previous orders to behead him so as not to prolong the agony. (The beheading by a "second" was a part of the ancient ritual.) Morita then disemboweled himself and was beheaded in turn by a third member of the group. Mishima had been the most admired writer of his generation, and the Japanese public was profoundly shocked by his death—in part because this was the first incident of *seppuku* in Japan since just after World War II.[2] A number of critics have remarked that with Mishima's death a special epoch of Japanese literature came to an end.

Although there have been some forms of ritual suicide in the Western tradition, there is something profoundly alien to the Western sensibility about the particular form of *seppuku.* We can, many of us, imagine killing ourselves, but the idea of plunging a sword into one's abdomen and having the strength of will to keep the blade in (the musculature of the lower body naturally tries to eject it) as one pulls it across to the other side, slicing through a variety of vital organs and entrails, is surely incomprehensible to the large majority of Westerners. Mishima was a gifted writer of extraordinary intelligence, and his voracious intellectual appetite encompassed a wide range of European literature and philosophy as well as classical East Asian learning. Being a great admirer of the German philosopher Friedrich Nietzsche, he was surely familiar with the chapter in *Thus Spake Zarathustra* called "On Free Death," and his suicide can certainly be seen as a consummate response to Zarathustra's dictum "Die at the right time!" On the other hand, the method of his self-annihilation is quite alien to Western sensibilities, and he chose *seppuku* precisely because it is so quintessentially Japanese.

Insofar as philosophy is "the uncommonly stubborn attempt to think clearly," it is hard for us to be "philosophical" about Mishima's suicide. But if we try to think clearly about this man who saw his life and death as embodying traditional Japanese ideas, we stand to learn some things about the way the Japanese have traditionally thought about life—and death. As in the case of China, however, we cannot expect philosophical thinking to look the same as it does in the Western tradition. Insofar as philosophy seeks "to discover how things, in the most general sense, hang together, in the most general sense," Japanese philosophy tends to concentrate on concrete things and relations *within* the world rather than on abstractions beyond it. In this it is again like Chinese philosophy, in part because the development of Japanese thought was greatly influenced by Confucianism, Taoism, Chinese Buddhism, and Neo-Confucianism.

Indeed, the Japanese tradition is, above all, *multiple,* being composed of many heterogeneous elements, and Japan is one of the most fascinating of modern cultures because of the ways its enduring indigenous tradition has continually incorporated a wide range of foreign influences. A feature of this tradition that makes it quite different from its Western counterparts is that philosophy did not develop as a separate discipline in isolation from life, but was rather embodied in particular forms of practice. (It is significant that the Japanese word for philosophy, *tetsugaku,* was coined only a little over a hundred years ago to refer to the European systems of thought that began to be studied when Japan was opened up to the West.)

This is not to say that there are no texts in the Japanese tradition that contain thinking of the kind we call philosophical in the West. There are many such works, but relatively few of them have been translated into English, and many of these make very difficult reading. For one thing, the content is often inherently complex, being an amalgam of native ideas with ideas from India, China, or—in the modern period—Europe. For another, the Japanese language possesses far more inherent ambiguity and indeterminacy than do Indo-European languages, which makes a faithful translation quite taxing for the reader accustomed to Western philosophy.

Because Japanese philosophy is so closely allied to a variety of practices, one of the best ways to approach it is to read Japanese literature in translation, to look at Japanese art and architecture, see Japanese films, study Japanese martial arts, go to Japanese theater, visit Japanese restaurants, and so on. The last part of this suggestion is not as frivolous as it may sound. In fact, it is worth developing a little so that we may appreciate how reflecting upon a practice can bring to light the philosophy behind it—and also how an approach informed by inappropriate presuppositions can blind us to what is really going on.

The first thing to notice about a Japanese meal is that how it *looks* is as important as how it tastes: The best Japanese cuisine is almost as much a feast for the eyes as it is a treat for the palate. Even in the most modest eating establishment, far from the metropolis, care is taken as a matter of course concerning the aesthetic appearance of the meal. And insofar as it provides satisfaction for the senses of sight and touch as well as taste, one usually eats less than usual before feeling satisfied. (The particular sense of satisfaction experienced after a good Japanese dinner is rarely accompanied by a feeling of overfulness—perhaps in part because savoring of the visual and tactile pleasures inclines one to eat more slowly.) Another thing to notice is that most of the meal is served at one time, rather than course by course as in the West. The advantage of this "nonlinear" way of eating is a remarkably wide range of tastes, as one gradually works one's way through the various combinations of flavors afforded by a large number of small dishes laid out at the same time.

One of these dishes is usually miso soup served in a lacquer bowl.[3] Now if the diners, following the injunction so beloved of Western mothers to "Drink your soup before it gets cold," finish the soup first, before going on to the other dishes, they will have lost the opportunity to appreciate what Japanese cuisine is really about. But if they consume the soup Japanese-style, slowly and intermittently, they are able not only to savor the progression of different tastes as it cools but also to orchestrate the combinations of these changing tastes with the flavors of the other dishes. The meal can then be appreciated as a multilayered process rather than as a single linear event—an appreciation that is impossible if the meal is approached from the perspective of Western preconceptions of ingestion.

But let us return from the sustenance of life to its curtailment in suicide. The death Mishima chose to end his life with and that life itself are emblematically Japanese. (On being criticized for affecting a Western life-style—a home furnished in European rococo and a wardrobe of Italian suits, Levi's, and T-shirts—Mishima responded that his possessions were just the outer trappings. His real life, as a writer working late at night in his study, was Japanese through and through.) It is possible to extract from that life some salient features that serve to articulate a kind of intellectual framework with which to approach some of the ways of thinking that are the topic of this chapter. In short, Mishima chose his *death,* through destroying the *body,* in a *ritual* action that consummated his life as an *aesthetic* whole.

To choose one's death as Mishima did is to consummate one's life in a way that is impossible if one just lets things take their course and dies from natural causes. This kind of suicide affirms an understanding of death as inseparable from life rather than as an event that simply comes after it. When Socrates describes the true philosopher as "practicing dying," or the Christian advocates "dying to the world" in order to be reborn, it is on the basis of an understanding of death as a separation of the soul from the body that grants access to a world beyond. But when the Japanese Zen thinkers speak of the "great death," they refer to death experienced *within* life that leads to a rebirth in *this* world; and thus insofar as they distinguish something like a soul from the body, the major focus tends to be on the latter. Modern Japanese thinkers like to remark that whereas in the West philosophies of life have predominated, Eastern thought has tended to produce philosophies of life-*and*-death such as

Buddhism and Taoism. In broad terms this is true, with some of the more recent "existential" philosophies in the West providing the exception that strengthens the general rule.[4]

The tendency of the Platonic-Christian tradition to privilege the soul over the body is manifest in the fact that it was not until Schopenhauer and Nietzsche in the nineteenth century—and then, later, Merleau-Ponty—that European thinkers began to develop extensive philosophies of the body. In East Asian thought, by contrast, the body has consistently been a focus of philosophical reflection, whether by virtue of the emphasis on ritual performance in the teachings of Confucius, the development of breathing and concentration techniques or physical skills in Taoism, or the practice of meditation in sitting, walking, and other physical activity in Zen Buddhism.[5]

Even though the ancient Greeks attached great importance to the training of the body, Plato's association of the head with intellect and rational thought distracted the attention of the subsequent philosophical tradition from the body as a whole. Thinking came to be understood as an "internal" process, the outward somatic manifestations of which are relatively unimportant. Descartes's denial of the body as in any way essential to our true nature as "thinking beings" exaggerated this trend. The idea of mental interiority was, however, quite foreign to the thinkers of the classical Chinese tradition. For Confucius, the major task was to cultivate oneself as a human being in society by engaging in the ritual practices handed down from the ancestors: Tradition was in this way literally *embodied*. By disciplining the movements and postures of the body through ritual practice, one could refine the faculties and capacities of the whole human being. This attitude was maintained in the Taoist tradition that developed after Confucius—and was thus incorporated in Chinese Buddhism as well as in the Japanese forms of Buddhism that were descended from it. This is why the ideas of Zen have traditionally embodied themselves in such activities as archery, swordplay, tea ceremony, Noh drama, painting, and calligraphy.

We saw in an earlier chapter how Chinese thought is predicated upon an aesthetic rather than a rational notion of order, and the same is true in general of the Japanese tradition. Aesthetics did not develop as a separate field of Western philosophy until the eighteenth century, and philosophies of art have traditionally been regarded as peripheral by comparison with metaphysics, epistemology, and ethics. In East Asian thought there has been no such marginalization of the aesthetic viewpoint: The texts of classical Taoist philosophy are some of the finest poetry ever written; the eighth-century Japanese thinker Kūkai was a Buddhist priest and an accomplished painter and calligrapher; the Zen thinker Dōgen (born 1200 C.E.) wrote exquisite poetry as well as poetic works of philosophy; the eighteenth-century Zen master Hakuin was a renowned poet, painter, and calligrapher as well as a thinker of the first rank.

But let us begin our approach by stepping back for some historical perspective. Because in Japan—more so than in most cultures—the past persists alongside (beneath or behind) the present, our understanding of Japanese ways of thinking will be enhanced if we can get a sense of some of the factors that have historically conditioned them.[6]

The Major Sources: Shinto, Confucianism, Buddhism

The drama of Mishima's "Patriotism" is played out against the backdrop of a devotion to Shinto. Holding pride of place in the young lieutenant's home is a tablet from the Great Shrine at Ise, the religion's most sacred site, and a photograph of the emperor, the high priest of Shinto—before which the lieutenant and his wife solemnly bow every morning. The code of honor and ethics followed by the hero of "Patriotism"—and the philosophy that Mishima himself came to espouse—was that of *bushidō,* "the way of the samurai." This philosophy is precisely a synthesis of elements of Shinto with ideas from the Confucian tradition and Buddhism.

Up until the last part of the nineteenth century, when Japan was opened to the West after several hundred years of self-imposed isolation, Japanese thinking had been fed by the three streams of Shinto, Buddhism, and Confucianism. Let us begin with Shinto, which was the indigenous religion of Japan prior to the influx of any influence from outside, and which still informs many aspects of life in Japan today. (There are thousands of well-attended Shinto shrines in Japan, and most marriage ceremonies are still performed by Shinto priests.)

Shinto—the Japanese word means literally "way of the divine spirits"—is an animistic nature religion, according to which the entire cosmos is "ensouled" and animated by spirits, and which is in many respects similar to the religion of ancient Greece. Its two major components are a *cult of nature,* in which the sun, mountains, trees, waterfalls, rocks, and certain kinds of animals are worshiped as divine, and an *ancestor cult,* in which reverence is paid to the spirits of the ancestors, again often as divinities. Another important idea in Shinto is that the Japanese nation is one large, extended family, with the emperor—as high priest and "father"—at the head. This notion began to be literalized in the so-called nativist philosophies of the eighteenth and nineteenth centuries, which held that the Japanese imperial family was directly descended from the gods of the primeval period. The idea of the Japanese nation as a family whose forefathers were of divine origin tends to give rise to a belief in the inherent superiority of the Japanese to all other races—a belief that formed the basis of the ultranationalist movements of the 1930s.

A salient feature of Shinto illustrates a contrast between the Japanese and the Western understandings of age and the reality of the past. The

Great Shrine at Ise is dedicated to the ancestor of the imperial family, the sun goddess Amaterasu. This most ancient shrine in the country is also the newest: In order to avoid the impurity that comes with the decay of aging, the Ise shrine is destroyed and built anew every twenty years. Whereas in the West the age of a building depends on how old the materials of which it is made are, in Japan it is the *form* that counts. Not form in the Platonic sense of some antecedent pattern beyond the world of change, but form as concretely embodied in a finite, impermanent building. The ephemeral nature of existence, of which the Japanese appear to possess an especially keen awareness, is enacted in the perpetual destruction and reconstruction of the most sacred structure of the national religion.

The Japanese propensity for the intelligent and thorough appropriation of foreign influences is nowhere more apparent than in the massive borrowings from Chinese culture that took place in the sixth century and continued, on and off, over the next thousand years. The Japanese had developed no writing system of their own, and so the first and most basic thing to be "imported" was the ideographic system of written Chinese. Along with it came the philosophies embodied in that writing, namely, Confucianism, Buddhism, and Taoism.

The first two of these had originated around a thousand years prior to their arrival in Japan. Buddhism, which arose in India in the sixth century B.C.E., was transmitted in the first century of the Christian era to China, where its development was influenced by the indigenous philosophy of Taoism during the five hundred years before it spread to Japan. A primary feature of Buddhist thinking is expressed in what it calls the "three characteristics of existence"—which turned out to harmonize especially well with the Japanese worldview. Most forms of Buddhism view existence as being characterized by *duhkha*, frustration or unsatisfactoriness, *anitya*, impermanence, and *anatman*, which refers to the idea that nothing possesses an intrinsic "selfness." In the Buddhist view, it is the failure or refusal to acknowledge that existence is transitory through and through that gives rise to frustration. If existence is a continual process of "arising and passing away," then the idea that there are enduring, self-identical things—including human egos or selves—may be shown to be an illusion, a fabrication designed to mask the radically ephemeral nature of existence.

Buddhist thought is particularly opposed to the substantialist view that there are *independently* existing things, claiming instead that everything is "itself" only in relation to a set of conditions that make it what it is. And again, the same is true for the "non-thing" that is the human self: It, too, is what it is only in relation to other things. The idea that things do not possess any inherent "self-nature" was already current in some schools of Chinese thought, as was the idea of the world as constant process or flux. Thus when Buddhism spread from India to China, certain forms of it resonated especially with the indigenous philosophies of Confucianism and Taoism.[7]

Some major features of the philosophies of Confucius and Taoism have been discussed in an earlier chapter. With respect to the influence of Confucian thought on Japanese thinking, the important ideas concern the ethical teachings: the "virtues" of sincerity, humaneness, rightness, and filial piety. Equally important are the ideas underlying these virtues: an understanding of the self as a matrix of familial and social relationships rather than as something substantial, and an emphasis on ritual activity as a means toward a harmonious "ritual community."

Out of the interactions among Buddhism and Confucianism and Taoism there arose in the Tang dynasty in China (seventh and eighth centuries) an eminently practical form of Buddhism known as *Chan*—the Chinese rendering of the Sanskrit *dhyana,* meaning "enlightenment." Chan Buddhism renounced the reciting of holy scriptures (sutras) and the discussion of metaphysical theories in favor of the practice of meditation. However, the goal of this practice, enlightenment, was understood not as the attainment of some transcendent realm beyond the world of everyday affairs, but rather as the realization of a more authentic way of being *within* the realm of day-to-day life.

The basic premise of Chan Buddhism (as of its transformation into Zen in Japan) is that our normal, pre-enlightenment experience is conditioned by layers of conceptualization that prevent us from experiencing the world *the ways* it is. (The plural marks a difference from the common Western conception of *the way* the world is.) This conceptualization is something we all grow up into quite naturally as we are acculturated into a particular social context through the acquisition of language. To use a visual metaphor for experience generally, it is as if the linguistic categories we acquire as we grow up place various kinds of filters over our eyes that color and distort our experience of the world.

The practice of Zen effects a return to the preconceptual level of the individual's being and to the most basic context of the person, which is understood as *mu,* or nothingness. The radical nature of this return is brought into relief when we recall that in China and Japan the person is normally understood as a function of social relationships. In stark contrast to the modern Western notion of the individual (especially as developed in the liberal democratic tradition), in East Asian thought it is the group—whether the nation or the family—that is ontologically primary, and the individual a derivative aberration. Thus when one enters a Zen monastery—giving up one's former possessions, clothing, social standing, head of hair, and even one's name—all ties to one's former existence are severed and the context of one's personal identity is completely abandoned. In spite of the new and highly disciplined order prevailing within the monastery, the point of the Zen regime is to show the novice that the ultimate context for his being is precisely *nothing.*[8]

Dōgen, the founder of the Soto school of Zen, refers to this process of self-transformation in which one's ordinary identity falls away as "the molting of body-mind." This molting allows one to experience and act from the "field of emptiness"—another Zen expression for the context of nothingness—without preconceptions, which in turn allows one's experience and actions to be totally spontaneous and appropriate to the current situation. (People sometimes fail to realize that, according to Zen, if the situation happens to call for conceptualization, the appropriate response is to conceptualize.)

The founder of the other major school of Zen, the ninth-century Chinese master Rinzai, expresses a similar conception of the person by talking about "the true human of no rank." We have seen that the Japanese understanding of the self is above all relational, and especially in terms of social standing; the Rinzai Zen idea of "no rank" suggests that all human relations (to things as well as persons) are possible only in the deeper context of nothingness. Hakuin, a Japanese Zen master who flourished in the early eighteenth century and is responsible for a revitalization of the Rinzai school, was fond of talking about the "great death" rather than the return to nothingness. In order to see into the depths of one's true nature it is necessary, according to Hakuin's quite existential understanding of Zen, to undergo the "great death": One must "be prepared to let go one's hold when hanging from a sheer precipice" if one is to be able to "die and return again to life."[9] This talk of the "great death" brings us now to a consideration of the philosophy and practice of *bushidō*, the major tenet of which is summed up in the dictum "The way of the samurai is death."

The Way of the Sword

The pretext on which Mishima paid his apparently cordial visit, on the day of his suicide, to the commander of the Army Self-Defense Force was that of showing him a beautiful ceremonial sword. From ancient times in Japan the sword has been regarded with an almost religious awe, and famous swordsmiths, who regard their art as being primarily spiritual rather than material, pass down the secrets of their special craft from master to pupil over the generations. Zen ideas and practice began to influence swordsmanship (the use as well as the making of the sword) around the beginning of the fourteenth century, and they played an increasingly important role in the development of the way of the sword over the succeeding centuries of civil strife in the country.[10]

Because Buddhism, with its emphasis on cultivating compassion for all sentient beings, has a reputation for being one of the world's more peaceable religions, it may be thought strange that Zen should have such a close connection with swordsmanship. But from the Zen perspective everything depends on the character and integrity of the one wielding the sword: If one's will is directed toward annihilating evil and against agents that stand in the way of justice and harmony, then the sword—even though it kills—becomes what Zen calls a "sword of life" rather than of death.

The *bushi,* or samurai warrior, carried two swords: a long one for combat, and a short one to kill himself with, if that should be necessary. The most important thing for a samurai was his honor as a loyal servant of his master, and if he were humiliated by defeat or about to be taken prisoner, he would have no hesitation in turning the short sword upon himself. This attitude is a manifestation of a more general readiness to die—and especially to die for one's lord—that is the distinguishing mark of the Japanese samurai. Let us consider the role of this idea that "the way of the samurai is death" in the teaching and discipline of swordsmanship.[11]

The most important principle of samurai swordsmanship is the injunction to enter combat, when combat is unavoidable, *absolutely prepared to die*—with no concern whatsoever for saving one's skin. This somewhat paradoxical idea is more comprehensible if one considers the combination of Confucian and Zen Buddhist elements in bushido. In speaking of the difficulty of attaining the ideal of true "humaneness," Confucius emphasized that the requisite ritual activity must not only be technically precise but must also be informed by the performer's heart or spirit. Similarly, bushido stresses the discipline of the whole person, the training of the psychological and spiritual aspects of the warrior as well as the physical. The idea is that once one has undergone the requisite self-discipline and trained the body to its utmost limits, the appropriate activity will flow effortlessly.

To understand this idea (which is also quite Taoist) it may help to consider an example from the field of competitive sports in the West. Even given an innate talent for tennis, for instance, the training necessary to acquire the psychological coordination that it takes to win a championship game is long and demanding. But once one has undergone such training, which may involve considerable analytical reflection upon various swings and strokes (not to mention a good deal of boredom and frustration), the appropriate frame of mind in which to play a championship match would appear to be one of relative "emptiness." As in Zen, the idea is to free oneself of preconceptions and expectations. If one starts to think about how to respond to a particular serve, one is certain to fluff the return. And even amateur players learn early on that emotional upset or nervousness about losing a crucial point virtually guarantees that one will lose it.[12]

What is called for—and the corresponding point can surely be made about most competitive sports—is an attitude that is open, yet free from all extraneous influences, a relaxed but intense concentration on the event of the opponent's striking the ball. Then the return happens as if "by itself," without one's having to think "Now the opponent is in that part of the court moving in this direction, so I need to place the ball over there" and then issue commands to the musculature to move in such and such a way so as to put one's body in the right position to execute a forehand volley at the appropriate angle.

In the Zen Buddhist tradition one enters into the spirit of a physical discipline by cultivating the condition of *mushin,* or "no-mind," which again connotes an openness untrammeled by ego-centered prejudices or preconceptions. (The Sino-Japanese word *shin* means "heart," and thus carries broader and less strictly intellectual connotations than the English "mind.") The term also suggests the respect accorded to what one might call the deep "wisdom of the body." As mentioned earlier, the Japanese tradition in general, and Zen in particular, tends not to employ as strict a dichotomy between mind and body as Western thought does—as evidenced by the common use in Zen texts of Dōgen's compound term "body-mind."

On the question of where to direct the mind or focus one's body-awareness, the master of the sword is likely to tell the student at first to keep the mind in the lower part of the abdomen, just below the navel. (This area is regarded by the Chinese and the Japanese as the center of the body's vital activity. The Japanese call it the *hara,* which is why the alternative reading of *seppuku* is *hara-kiri,* "cutting the abdomen.") The more advanced student is instructed to expand that focus throughout the entire body. In the words of Takuan addressed to the sword master Yagyū Munenori: "If you don't put the mind anywhere, it will go to all parts of the body and extend throughout its entirety."[13] In this way one's awareness will extend through to the sword as well, which thus virtually becomes part of the body—just as the racket becomes an extension of the arm in the case of the championship tennis player.

The parallel with tennis goes only so far, however, because the stakes in swordsmanship are infinitely higher. An instant of emotional upset or a moment's reflective thought on the court at Wimbledon can mean the loss of a valuable prize, it is true. But the Japanese sword is such a fiendishly sharp instrument that a corresponding lapse in a sword fight means the loss of a hand, a limb, or one's head. And losing one's head in that context is a literal and irrevocable loss.

If we recall now that the samurai is encouraged to enter combat absolutely prepared to die and with no thought of preserving himself, we can see that the openness or emptiness of "no-mind" coincides in an interesting way with the nothingness of death. We can also appreciate the further paradox that the Zen emphasis on *natural* action, when it re-emerges as a consequence of intense physical and mental discipline in something like the spontaneous activity of the consummate swordsman, coincides now with a way of being that is quite *unnatural.* This is not meant to suggest that it is artificial, but rather that the way to realize one's full humanity lies in going against what is naturally given so that one may sublimate, as it were, one's human nature.

In animals the instinct for self-preservation is fundamental and pervasive, and it is naturally strong in humans, too. However, the almost superhuman achievement of the Zen swordsman, which manifests itself in activity that appears equal to the most finely honed instinctual responses in the animal world, goes hand in hand with a remarkable suspension of the instinct for self-preservation. Many of the stories told about the best-known Zen masters of the sword suggest that they have acquired extraordinary powers (some of the better samurai films convey a sense of this). At this level of achievement, it is as if the life force is negated in such a way that one becomes totally—and almost supernaturally—alive.

Let us now go on to consider some other, less violent arts of the hand that have been inspired by the ideas of Zen.

Arts of the Hand

Although Mishima was a writer, he lived in an era during which writing was less an art of the hand than it was before the advent of printing (a Chinese invention). Formerly in Japan, as in China, writing well meant not only authoring fine poems and essays, but also producing manuscripts that were themselves works of art. Because of the special nature of the Chinese ideographic writing system, the fine poem will look as beautiful as it sounds—and indeed the way it looks is an important part of the poetry. For someone writing after the invention of printing, the act of writing is bound to seem a less immediate type of action than it was in the days when readers would have before them the actual traces of the author's moving hand.

We shall see later how this perceived lack of connection with the world drove Mishima to take up arts of the hand and body more dynamic than writing, like *kendō* (a kind of fencing with swords of bamboo, but more in the style of sabers than foils). In so doing he was following an East Asian tradition—grounded in the teachings of Confucius, among others—with respect to which the Western dichotomy between theory and practice, or reflection and action, fails to hold. Japanese history is full of figures whose achievements undercut such dichotomies: emperors who were exquisitely cultured individuals, Zen masters who were consummate swordsmen, and warriors who were exemplary men of letters. Over the centuries in which Japan was torn by civil wars, there grew up a tradition of samurai who were at the same time literati, men of refined culture who wielded the pen (or, rather, the brush) with as much skill as the sword.

Closely related to the art of calligraphy (*shōdō:* literally, "the way of writing'') is *sumi-e,* monochrome painting with brush and ink. The most striking thing about both Chinese and Japanese brush painting at first sight is the large amount of "empty space." Until fairly recently it was traditional in most Western painting to have the canvas completely covered with paint, for the space outlined by the picture frame to be filled. By contrast, in many masterpieces of Japanese brush painting as little as 15 to 25 percent of the surface of the scroll has ink on it. In view of the influence of Taoism and Zen on this art form, the relative emptiness of the canvas can be understood as an evocation of the nothingness that forms the context of all particular things.

The technique of monochrome painting has much in common with that of swordsmanship: The training under a master is long and rigorous, and the goal is to let the brush move itself. The appropriate condition for painting is one of "no-mind," and one's awareness is dispersed throughout the whole body—and even beyond the brush to the blank paper. In the case of painting a persimmon, a branch, or a bird, the idea is to have contemplated the subject long enough so that one has actually become one with it; then the subject literally paints itself. (Something like this can happen in the case of still life or landscape painting in the West, too, insofar as the artist contemplates the subject with sufficient concentration to achieve a kind of union with it.)

While it is a delight to watch the exquisite movements of a master calligrapher or *sumi-e* artist letting the ink flow on to the paper, it is the product rather than the process that is regarded as the work. But in several other art forms inspired by Zen the moving body of the artist is itself part of the work of art.

One of the most quintessential expressions of Japanese culture is the tea ceremony (*chadō,* "the way of tea," or *chanoyu,* literally, "hot water for tea").[14] Tea was originally brought to Japan from China some time during the sixth or seventh century, and the practice of drinking tea appears to have established itself first of all in the Buddhist seminaries and schools. The green tea that is still the staple in Japan is a vitalizing beverage that helps keep one alert during meditation—and in life in general. After relations with China were broken off at the end of the ninth century, the custom went into decline, and was not revived again until the twelfth century, thanks to the Zen master Eisai.

At first, tea gatherings were rather grand social affairs that took place in elaborate Chinese-style tea pavilions and often involved tea-tasting competitions. In the course of the Middle Ages the ceremonies gradually became simpler and at the same time more strictly governed by rules of ritual. This happened in part through the adoption of the tea ceremony by the samurai class, whose rules of conduct were being formulated at the time, and also under the influence of the simple rules of life-style of the Soto school of Zen, whose founder was Dōgen. There is also a strong Confucian element in the tea ceremony, as we shall see.

While the primary requisite for the tea ceremony consists of simplicity and an avoidance of ostentation, the specifications for the utensils, the room, and the surroundings are remarkably strict, on the principle, not entirely foreign to Western thinking, that it is only within a context of the most rigid discipline that the utmost freedom for creativity can be exercised. On the surface, the ceremony is simple; a small number of guests gather in an anteroom. They proceed through a modest but carefully laid-out and well-tended garden to a simple thatched hut built of wood and plaster. Before entering the hut, which usually consists of one rather small room, each guest washes his or her hands in a stone water basin—a symbolic cleansing from the dust of the everyday world. They enter across a stone threshold and through a low entranceway with a simple sliding door covered with white rice paper.

The room is small, some ten feet square, and suffused by a subdued light coming through the translucent sliding screens that make up much of the walls. The only form of ornament is in an alcove built into one of the walls: a vase with a simple arrangement of flowers in it, or else a hanging scroll inscribed with Chinese characters or a monochrome painting. In the middle of the floor of tatami (rectangular mats made of tightly woven rice straw) is a hearth in which charcoal is burned to heat the iron kettle for the water.

The host enters through a sliding door in one of the other walls, greets the guests, and passes around a dish of small cakes while preparing the tea. In a precisely determined sequence of ritual movements, the host uses a special ladle to rinse the tea bowl with hot water, puts two spoonfuls of powdered tea into the bowl, pours a ladleful of hot water into the tea bowl, and stirs the tea with a whisk made of split bamboo. Originally the guests would share one bowl, wiping the rim with a piece of rice paper before passing it on; a variation of the ceremony uses one bowl for each guest. As the guests slowly sip the tea, they may compliment the host on its taste and color, admire the tea bowls and utensils, and converse for a while before taking their leave. That is all; and yet when it goes well, those present have the impression of contacting the deepest levels of human being, and of experiencing from the narrow confines of that simple hut a far wider world.

All features of the room, of the ornaments, and the utensils for brewing and serving the tea are precisely specified as to the optimal size, shape, color, and so on. The specifications change, however, according to the time of day the ceremony is performed as well as the season of the year. Certain kinds and colors of flowers, for example, are recommended for certain times of day but not for others. The ritual gestures of the hands with which the host makes and serves the tea are too complex to be described: They have to be seen to be appreciated. As in the practice of the Zen sword, the techniques are learned over a long period of instruction under a master of the discipline, until they can be performed quite naturally. To watch an accomplished tea person simply lay the ladle on top of the kettle, for instance, is to witness an action quite awe inspiring in its elegance and economy.

The Zen ideas that inform the ceremony ensure that all the participants are *there* with full attention to the present activity. At the same time, aware of the age of the ceremony itself and of many of the utensils being used to perform it (the form of the activities being centuries old, and the utensils fashioned long before the participants were born), they feel the flow of the past rise up through the present moment. A beautiful account of this phenomenon is to be found in the well-known short novel by Kawabata Yasunari, *A Thousand Cranes*.[15] The tea ceremony serves as a background to the entire narrative, and two or three bowls play a role in the story that is—strangely—almost human, insofar as they are three to four hundred years old and so have passed through the hands of generations of tea connoisseurs.

More recently the bowls in question have been owned by the young protagonists' parents and their respective lovers, and after the deaths of the parents the bowls evoke the presence of the deceased with an almost supernatural power, at the same time prompting premonitions of the deaths of the survivors in turn. The young man and woman, Kikuji and Fumiko, are looking at a bowl that was a favorite of Kikuji's deceased father, when Fumiko remarks how like the father the bowl is. And so reminiscent of its previous owner is a bowl inherited from her late mother that the bowls together look like "two beautiful ghosts." And yet since the bowls are completely "sound and healthy," "life seemed to stretch taut over them in a way that was almost sensual."

In the tea ceremony the bowl is handled with such care and reverence that—while of course it will not last forever—it is likely to survive beyond the death of any particular owner or user. (Should the bowl be broken, it is often repaired using gold.) The awareness that this bowl will continue to exist long after I have passed on, even though a part of my being may somehow survive with it—to the extent that it has been closely associated with me during my lifetime—helps me to focus on the series of unique moments in which I drink from it. The realizations that there are a finite number of such moments yet to come and that every sip is potentially the last, serve to intensify the experience of the present moment.

An important dimension of the ceremony is illuminated if we recall the Confucian conception of the place of ritual activity in human life, where such practice is understood to be integral to captivating and refining one's essential humanity. For a ceremony to be genuine in the Confucian sense, not only must the technique be faultless and effortless, but the performer must perform the actions with "heart and soul." (Lack of heart is as obvious to a connoisseur as a perfunctory handshake is to a sensitive individual, or a coldly mechanical rendition of a piano sonata to a true music lover.) In the case of tea, consummate technique must be accompanied by a sense that the participants are fully engaged in the human interaction. As the host serves the tea, or the guest bows to the host, the activity expresses an awareness that here are two human beings who have come together under the heavens and on a particular piece of the earth, and in the context of a particular configuration of the elements of fire and water, wood and metal, in order to partake of a unique and vivifying beverage.

Just as in Zen the awareness that accompanies sitting meditation *(zazen)* is to be extended throughout one's waking life, so the atmosphere of the tea ceremony optimally comes to pervade the practitioner's entire being, so that every meal and all other waking activities may become occasions for experiencing the ultimate context of nothingness that is the womb of all human possibilities. The greatest contrast would be the kind of "eating on the run" encouraged by the institution of the drive-through fast food outlet. The consumption while driving of a bland styrofoam-enclosed mass is something that—even if it helps sustain life—barely enters the consumer's consciousness (perhaps just as well) let alone vivifies the experience of life itself.

Even as present-day Japan succumbs to the institution of fast food, there remains a custom that faintly recalls the Zen attitude underlying the way of tea. In the otherwise prosaic situation of drinking beer, for example, whether in a public place or a private home, one may find one's companion proffering bottle, neck first. The appropriate response is to lift one's glass a little off the table so that the other person can fill it. The roles are usually reversed on the second round. Rather than dismiss this custom as a minor bit of useless ritual, one might see it as analogous to the tea ceremony in its function of bringing to awareness the uniqueness of the human situation in which the participants find themselves.

Noh Drama: Poetry, Music, Dance

Several critics maintain that the plays Mishima wrote based on the traditional Noh drama are among his finest accomplishments. Noh (the word means literally "accomplishment," was used early on to refer to the special abilities of actors, singers, and dancers) is another Zen-influenced art form in which the human body is part of the work.[16] It was developed during the fourteenth century from a mixture of art forms such as the sacred dances of Shinto, court dances concerning warriors, and other forms of recitation and proto-opera. The traditional founder, Kan'ami, had a son, Zeami, who became a protégé of the shogun of Japan at the time, an enlightened ruler who was a great patron of the arts and a devotee of Zen. This high regard for Zen was shared by Zeami, and

Buddhist ideas influenced both the many classic plays he authored and his treatises laying out the basic principles of the art.

Noh is a highly refined art form that combines poetry, drama, music, song, and dance in a way that is somewhat reminiscent of ancient Greek tragedy. The plays are generally based on simple, ancient, and archetypal themes deriving from some of the most familiar poems, stories, and legends in the Japanese canon. (This is just as well, since the highly poetic dialogue is delivered in such an idiosyncratic combination of song and chant that it is more or less incomprehensible even to native Japanese speakers, many of whom attend the plays equipped with the written texts.) There is generally very little in the way of plot in these plays; they aim rather at the development of a particular mood or emotion or attitude basic to human psychology.

A primary aim of the drama, according to Zeami, is the production of the mood of *yūgen,* a Zen term that connotes "what lies beneath the surface," the subtle as opposed to the obvious. The original meaning of the word is "obscure and dark," but it came to refer to a special kind of beauty that is only partly revealed, that is elusive yet full of meaning and tinged with a wistful sadness. It also has connotations of the graceful elegance of the refined aristocrat. The talk of something "beneath the surface" is not meant to suggest the dichotomy between appearance and reality familiar in Western metaphysics, but comes rather from the Zen ideas that layers of conceptualization obscure our experience, and that certain art forms may enable us to "see through" those layers.

There is no attempt in Noh at realism. The back of the stage consists of simple wood paneling on which is painted a stylized pine tree, and a chorus and several musicians sit on the stage in full view of the audience. The "orchestra" comprises a flute and two hand drums, with sometimes a third stick drum in addition. The rhythms of the percussion are based on an extremely long and often irregular beat, which has the effect after a while of profoundly altering the audience's sense of time. (Zen adepts might claim that the rhythms help one to break through the conceptual overlay; psychologists, that they modify the brainwaves in such a way as to activate the deep unconscious.) On occasion, in some of the dances, the music can become remarkably Dionysian in its frenzied crescendos, evoking no doubt the music of the Shinto festivals of which Mishima was so enamored. The singing of the chorus sometimes comments on the action and sometimes substitutes for the singing of the principal actor when he is too involved in the dance to be able to sing. But the most striking feature of the Noh is the way the acting techniques combine with the specially designed costumes and masks.

With the movements and gestures of Noh drama we are again on familiar ground—a ground prepared by our discussion of the role of ritual activity in refining the human being. The gestures are highly stylized and for the most part extremely subtle and restrained—only occasionally building up into climaxes of wild dance—and they are perfected only after years of the most intense physical training on the part of the actor. The costumes, which generally cover the entire body, are themselves works of art, and when worn by an accomplished actor they become kinetic sculptures of breathtaking beauty. Some of the costumes have an uncanny way of making the wearer appear to be defying the laws of gravity. It sometimes looks, for instance, as if it is physically impossible for a human being to stand that way without falling over; this phenomenon conduces to the often desired effect of a more-than-human presence.

The Noh mask is carved from wood, usually cypress, and then covered with layer upon layer of paint. The making of these masks is another Japanese art that has been handed down from master to apprentice over the centuries, and some of the older ones are today regarded as "national treasures." There are many different types of mask, and one of their primary functions is to enable the principal actor (all Noh actors and musicians are men) to play a wide range of parts: young girl, old man, angry demon, and so on. Sometimes a different mask is used for the second part of the play, since the text often requires a warrior or a woman to turn into a ghost, a demon, an animal, or even a god.

Unlike the masks that were used in Greek tragedy, the Noh mask is slightly smaller than the face, and this has the effect of delocalizing the sound of the actor's voice in such a way that it seems to come, strangely, from "around" the figure rather than from it. The masks are designed to have a neutral, intermediate expression, so that very slight movements of the actor's head, in combination with the appropriate bodily gestures, are able to produce the illusion of a remarkable variety of facial expressions. The synergism of all these features gives the masked figure of the actor a strangely nonhuman or even superhuman appearance—again in a way similar to the overall effect of the masked actors of Greek tragedy.

During the half hour before he goes on stage, the Noh actor sits alone and in silence in what is called the "mirror room" and contemplates the mask he is about to put on. During the last five minutes, he looks into the eyes of the mask, at the center of which is nothing, in order to "see" the character about to be acted. This period of meditation allows him to empty himself so that he will be able to act out of the context of no-mind, or nothingness, thus letting the archetypal figure he is to portray "play through" him. Correspondingly, the more the audience is able to let its preconceptions concerning what it is seeing fall away, the more profound the experience that will ensue. The effects of the music and the somewhat hypnotic chanting of the poetry of the text can thus combine to short-circuit everyday consciousness and elicit a profound response from the deeper layers of the self.[17]

Because Zen is not a set of dogmas but rather a practice that transforms one's relationships to the world, it is not surprising that the ideas behind it should continue to inform Japanese thought and culture even after the radical break effected by modernization, which began a little more than a century ago. In the last part of this chapter we shall consider some later transformations of Japanese thinking through the correspondingly modern medium of cinema.

Projections in a Western Medium: The Art of Film

In 1853 several warships of the U.S. Navy commanded by Commodore Matthew Perry sailed into Edo Bay, carrying a request (amounting to a demand) that Japan open her ports to foreign trading ships. The island had been closed to foreign influence for almost three hundred years. A number of people in the government were quick to gauge the situation. They realized that the only way for Japan to avoid the fate of colonization that had befallen all her neighbors in Asia was to modernize quickly enough to develop technology to defend the country against foreign aggression. In 1868 the feudal system that had held sway for several centuries was abolished, and some measure of political power was restored to the imperial house of Meiji (hence the name *Meiji Restoration*). Western technology and culture were imported with amazing rapidity and thoroughness: Promising Japanese political leaders and scholars in all areas of the arts and sciences were sent by the hundreds to the major countries of Europe, as well as to the United States. Their assignment was to learn the ways of the West so that they could return home and supervise the appropriation of Western ideas in fields ranging from philosophy to physics.

Toward the end of the nineteenth century, not only were French positivism and British utilitarianism being received with special enthusiasm, but also—in the interests of a thorough historical understanding of Western thought—ancient Greek and Roman thought. But it was German philosophy that found the most fertile ground for transplantation—from Leibniz and Kant, through German Idealism, to the more recent philosophies of Schopenhauer and Nietzsche.[18] To this day, philosophers in Japan are more likely to be fluent in German than in English or French; and if one wants to study Buddhist philosophy there, for example, one has to go to a department of religious studies, since most philosophy departments are concerned only with continental European thought and Anglo-American (analytic) philosophy.

The fact that relatively few contemporary philosophers in Japan are interested in Japanese philosophy is a symptom of just how massive and comprehensive the importation of Western ideas after the Meiji Restoration was. While the appropriation of Western philosophical ideas has greatly enriched Japanese culture, it was undertaken with such zeal as to almost preclude a continuing engagement with the indigenous tradition of Japanese thought. It is true that Shinto still functions on the everyday level as a vessel for whatever thoughts and feelings the average Japanese may have concerning "the meaning of life," the nature of death and the beyond, and so on. However, it seems that the majority of the contemporary population has been cut off from the traditional ideas and practices of Buddhism and Confucianism—and the arts and disciplines that sprang from them—which sustained the development of so many centuries of Japanese culture. The "Kyoto School" philosopher Nishitani Keiji argues in a book on nihilism written in 1949 that this severance from the tradition on the intellectual and existential levels has introduced into modern Japanese life a deep-seated nihilism that is all the more powerful for remaining mostly unconscious.[19]

There is really no equivalent in the West to the shock caused by modernization in Japan. A country with a two-thousand-year-old tradition cuts itself off from the rest of the world for a period of a dozen generations, and then is suddenly forced into the wholesale adoption of a totally alien set of values—a process that necessitates in large part a radical break with indigenous traditions. The situation was exacerbated because the importation of Western ideas was carried out uncritically, so it passed unnoticed that many of the systems of thought that were brought in were themselves beginning to collapse. The import of Nietzsche's proclamation of "the death of God" was lost on the avid Japanese appropriators of turn-of-the-century European culture. Nobody realized that the ideals that had sustained the enormous expansion of the Western powers were themselves crumbling from within, that the virus of nihilism was present in the ideational stock that was so indiscriminately transplanted to Japanese soil.

This is not to deny that much of the past persists alongside the manifestations of modernity in Japan. But while the integration of modern Western ideas with the quite different ways of thinking that formerly sustained the development of the indigenous culture has been enormously fruitful—as evidenced by Japan's current economic domination of the world—it has also engendered a certain tension between an outer fullness and an inner void. Nietzsche remarked on the efficacy of hard and prolonged work as a way of covering over the abyss of nihilism, and it is hard to resist the impression that the frenetic industriousness of contemporary Japanese life serves to conceal a yawning emptiness at the core of it. The question of what "Japaneseness" consists in has been something of a national obsession since even before the Meiji period, and one suspects that the periodic outbreaks of aggressive nationalism that have occurred during this century may also stem from an inadequate response to the issue of nihilism. If all other sources of meaning for one's life appear to have dried up, then at the very least the meaning of it all is that one is Japanese.[20]

This line of thinking is going to take us back full circle to Mishima, but on the way let us consider another engagement with the problem of nihilism that dates from shortly after the publication of Nishitani's book on the topic. The art of film, which provides another example of the way Japan has appropriated from the West in order to produce work of the first rank, will afford us a final approach to Japanese thought by way of a peculiarly modern medium.

Although Kurosawa's *Rashomon* (1950) is probably the Japanese film that is best known in the West, his *Ikiru* (1952) is in many ways more profound.[21] The title is the plain form of the verb "to live" and may best be translated as "living." In any case, the topic of the film is living, or how to live, in the face of death—and with this we return to a major theme in our discussion of bushido.

The film begins with a close-up of an X ray of the protagonist's stomach, which (the narrator's voice-over tells us) shows symptoms of cancer. The protagonist's exterior is presented in the next shot, where we see him—his name is Watanabe and he is the chief of the Citizens' Section in City Hall—sitting at his desk. Shortly thereafter the narrator informs us that the main character "is not very interesting yet. He's just passing the time. . . . It would be difficult to say that he is really alive." As Watanabe looks through a pile of papers, stamping them as he goes— the epitome of the automatonlike bureaucrat—the narrator remarks, "This is pretty bad. He is like a corpse, and in fact he has been dead for the past twenty-five years."

In the context of the strict work ethic of postwar Japan, the film's opening scenes are a stinging indictment of the stultifying nature of office work in the public sector—but also, by extension, of all the kinds of work with which modern Japanese narcotize their existence. And because a much larger part of one's identity in Japan comes from one's occupation than is the case in most other countries, Kurosawa's criticism cuts deeply into the question of what it means to be a human being in modern Japanese society. On the other hand, one could argue that at least one feature of bushido persists in contemporary Japanese life: the sense of honor and duty to one's superiors. It is common, for example, for politicians or heads of companies in Japan to resign at the first public sign of impropriety on their part, in order to save face and leave the image of the party or company untainted. (This response seems incomprehensible to chief executive officers in this country, where the immediate reaction is always to announce one's intentions to fight to the bitter end while one searches for someone else to lay the blame on.)

Watanabe goes to the hospital to get the results of some tests that have been done because of a stomach problem. The doctor has diagnosed the cancer and reckons that the patient has only six months to live, but when Watanabe comes in, the doctor lies to him (as is still the custom in Japan in such cases), saying "it's just a light case of ulcers." But, as a result of a strange encounter just before going into the doctor's consulting room, Watanabe knows the truth. The realization of his imminent death serves to pull him out of his absorption in his job, with the result that he abruptly stops going to the office—after not missing a day's work for twenty-five years!

He hopes for some solace from his son and daughter-in-law, with whom he lives, but they callously reject him before he can tell them about his devastating realization. Thus an even more fundamental context for Watanabe's identity than his job—his relationship to his family—is shattered. We learn later that after Watanabe's wife died he declined to remarry out of consideration for his son, and Watanabe himself at one point explains his total dedication to his deadening work as being "all for my son's sake." Such parental self-sacrifice (though usually on the part of the mother) is the norm in Japan, and is the counterpart of the Confucian filial piety that parents expect from their offspring. So, to a degree that may be extreme even in Japan, Watanabe has devoted himself to the raising of his son in addition to this work; and now, with his son's rejection of him, as well as his alienation from his job, everything that gave his life meaning has collapsed. The abyss of nothingness yawns as it seldom does in a normal Japanese life; the nothingness of death stares him in the face in true existentialist fashion.[22]

The protagonist's response to his confrontation with death is quite consonant with Western existentialist thinking as well as with Zen. Rather than reject or attempt to transcend the everyday routines of his life, Watanabe reengages them, transfigured, with an unprecedentedly vital enthusiasm. He throws himself back into his job, but in a completely new way, devoting his energies to having an insalubrious swampy area drained and a neighborhood park built in its place. He thereby succeeds, in his last months, in getting something genuinely meaningful done in the context of his formerly deadening occupation. But this account of some of the major themes of the film gives no indication of the cinematic techniques with which Kurosawa elaborates these themes and lends them such power. The movie is one of the great masterpieces of mid-twentieth-century cinema—as are the works of another Japanese director during the same period, whose primary concern is with stresses within the family that are occasioned by the modernization of the country. (With this focus we move away from the major concerns of Mishima, but the Japanese sense of self is so intimately bound up with the family that the detour is justified.)

Ozu Yasujiro, who between 1927 and 1962 made around sixty-five feature films, is often referred to as the most "Japanese" of Japanese film directors.[23] If a feature of being "Japanese" is being eclectic in one's ability to appropriate foreign influences—Ozu was a keen admirer of early Hollywood movies—then this judgment is apt. At any rate, there are few better ways to get a feel for the modernizing Japanese culture of the 1950s than to see some of Ozu's films of the period.[24]

Ozu's films almost invariably take as their subject the family, with whatever drama there is being provided by the process of the family's dissolution. Since the sense of self in Japan is always closely bound up in relationships, and especially family relationships, the breaking up of the family provides rich material for human drama. Ozu's treatment is sufficiently penetrating psychologically that in his films the family becomes a microcosm for the whole society and even—insofar as his characters transcend cultural boundaries—for the human world in general.

The portrayal of the family takes place mostly in the home, and no other director has been as successful as Ozu in presenting the internal architecture of the Japanese house as an embodiment of the soul and spirit of its inhabitants. Ozu is also famous for his low positioning of the camera: It is usually only three feet from the floor, which might seem odd until one realizes that this is eye level for someone sitting in the traditional Japanese way (on one's heels or cross-legged) on a tatami-matted floor. Ozu uses silence, stillness, and the stark contrasts of black and white film in ways that evoke a mood strongly reminiscent of Zen. Over the decades he refined his filmic technique relentlessly, returning repeatedly to the same stories and themes, and using the same actors and cowriter over long periods of time, in order to strip down the essentials of his art to the bare minimum. In his mature work, pretty much the only form of transition is the cut; the camera hardly ever moves, and the length of the shots stays remarkably constant. On the one hand, this pacing gives Ozu's films a somewhat meditative tone with an occasionally hypnotic effect, and on the other it conveys a strong sense of the inevitability of fate in human affairs.

Some of Ozu's films directly invoke the spirit of Zen. *Late Spring,* for instance, contains scenes of a tea ceremony (though very much a "society" affair), a Noh play, and the famous sand and rock garden at Ryoanji temple in Kyoto. (There are also several scenes in this film where characters pour drinks for each other.) The extent to which Ozu has distilled the essence of Japanese culture of that period is remarkable. And in the course of elaborating his customary theme of the breakup of the family, he conveys a powerful sense of the dichotomy that is probably more radical in Japan than in any other modern society: that between outer appearances and one's true inner feelings.

The story of *Late Spring* is simple: A widowed university professor lives with his daughter Noriko, who in her fondness for her father is happy to take care of him. Being in her late twenties, however, she is under tremendous social pressure—both from other members of her family and from her friends—to get married, since that is simply what "one does." (Arranged marriages were still the norm in 1949 and are common to this day in Japan.[25]) Noriko is able to resist this pressure until she is tricked into believing that her father is going to remarry and will thus have someone else to take care of him. Her aunt arranges a meeting with an excellent prospective husband (who is said to resemble Gary Cooper!), and after the meeting Noriko eventually—for the sake of some peace, one imagines—consents to marry the man. She leaves on her honeymoon, and the father is left alone in the house.

The film conveys an extreme sense of the overwhelming power of social pressures on individual freedom in Japanese society, and is at the same time—thanks to the superb acting—a very moving film emotionally. Just as restraint is a quality highly prized in human relationships in Japan because of the harmony it imparts to social interactions (and restraint is the keynote of Ozu's technique as a director), so does it also characterize the emotional lives of the protagonists in this film. Thanks to the consummate artistry with which the actors play the father and daughter, the emotional power generated (but never directly expressed) is excruciating in its intensity. On several occasions the daughter says "yes" when every fiber of her being is screaming "no" (or vice versa), and yet that scream comes silently, through facial expression alone. The film's ending is extremely poignantly because both the main characters are unhappy. The viewer is left with the impression that the daughter has condemned herself to a life of utter misery and that the father will miss her terribly—and yet they have done what "one does." But such is life in the world of Japan.

Ozu worked with the same actors over and over again from film to film, and he was able to elicit performances from them that are on occasion overwhelming in their hieratic beauty. Whether Ozu was aware of it or not, his technique in directing his actors had a great deal in common with the Zen approach to physical discipline, as well as with the technique of the Noh. He apparently had his actors and actresses repeat certain movements and gestures over and over again, ad nauseam, until every drop of spontaneous feeling had been eliminated. After that point was surpassed, he would film, and the results are often uncanny in the impression they give of controlled spontaneity. The combination of this technique and the reappearance in film after film of the same actors— often in very similar roles and even bearing the same names—further enhances the archetypal quality of the characters.[26]

Having left the world of Mishima, it will be in the spirit of Ozu to effect an abrupt cut back, in order to gather together the threads of Japanese thought we have been considering.

Mishima's Ends

At the age of thirty, having devoted the major part of his life up to then to literature, which—though itself a form of action—is hardly a very physical activity, Mishima resolved to take up bodybuilding, a discipline he engaged in for the rest of his life. This was partly an attempt (apparently successful) to overcome a tendency toward ill health, but it was also Mishima's way of counteracting the tendency of writing to "corrode reality away" before he had a chance to experience life directly. Over the ensuing fifteen years he became proficient at boxing, karate, and kendo. Having been born into an aristocratic family, Mishima may, in a certain sense, have been returning to his roots in these endeavors. He also saw himself as participating in a revival of the old samurai ideal of combining the ways of the martial and the literary arts. He gives a fascinating and, at times, enigmatic account of this aspect of his life in the long essay *Sun and Steel,* written in 1968.[27]

While there was surely a strong element of narcissism in Mishima's concern for the body during the last part of his life (a concern intensified, it seems, by his homosexuality), his devotion to various forms of physical regimen nevertheless situated him authentically in the Japanese tradition of arts and letters. He was obsessed from early on by the desire to die "a beautiful death," and believed this would be impossible unless the body had been developed to perfection. It is an impressive fact about Mishima's suicide that on the morning of the day he ended his life he sent to the publisher the final installment of the fourth volume of his last work, *The Sea of Fertility.*[28] There is a sense that Mishima had reached the height of his powers, that he knew it, and that he had no wish to go on to live a life of both physical and artistic decline. His suicide would thus be his ultimate aesthetic act.

Toward the end of his life, Mishima developed an interest in Japanese Neo-Confucianist philosophy, and especially in its idea of the importance of the unity of thought and action.[29] Since he had come to think that Japanese culture had degenerated lamentably since World War II, and his recent attempts to call attention to this decline through polemical essays had fallen on deaf ears, it was a logical consequence of his philosophy that he should take more drastic action. To this extent Mishima's suicide was in keeping with the tradition of *kanshi,* a type of *seppuku* whose purpose was remonstration with one's feudal lord or a more general reproach of the ruling powers.[30]

One can assemble a multiplicity of plausible perspectives, negative as well as positive, on Mishima's suicide—which appropriately reflects the inherent multiplicity of Japanese thought. One can see him as the consummate exemplification of the way of the samurai, in knowing the right time to die and having the courage to act accordingly. He can be reproached for vain egocentrism in his irresponsible disregard for his wife and the sacred institution of the family. One can argue that since he was beyond the peak of his powers, nothing of value was lost in his ending his life when he did, and that a great deal was gained, because all was not right in the state of Japan at the time, and his *seppuku* shocked at least some people into a realization of the crisis. We can say that he acted out of pure vanity, unable to bear the prospect of the disintegration of the body he had worked so hard to perfect. A Nietzschean could argue that he died at just the right time—or else that his obsession with the body was too literal and blinded him to the fact that old age would be incapable of destroying the magnificent body of work he had produced. Or one could say from the perspective of someone like Nishitani Keiji that his response to the problem of nihilism was too shallow: that the way in which he wanted to reassert the ancient Japanese spirit suggests that he failed to plumb the depths of the self sufficiently to reach a layer deeper than that of national identity.

Mishima came in for a great deal of criticism, both in Japan and abroad, for the right-wing views and support of the emperor system expressed in his later polemical essays and speeches. However, it is hard to take those views too seriously, in view of Mishima's quite apolitical stance during most of his career. And indeed they are peripheral to his main work—a body of literature, some of which is the finest in any modern language, and which embodies an important philosophy of existence that partakes genuinely of the best of the Japanese tradition.

Notes

1. An English translation of the story by Geoffrey W. Sargent can be found in Yukio Mishima, *Death in Midsummer and Other Stories* (New York: New Directions, 1966). When not used in citations, Japanese names will be given in Japanese style, with the family name first.

2. Two biographies of Mishima are available in English: John Nathan, *Mishima: A Biography* (Boston: Little, Brown, 1974), and Henry Scott Stokes, *The Life and Death of Yukio Mishima* (New York: Farrar, Straus & Giroux, 1974). An outstanding poetic celebration of Mishima's work is by Marguerite Yourcenar, *Mishima: A Vision of the Void* (New York: Farrar, Straus & Giroux, 1986). Available on videotape, and well worth seeing, is Paul Schrader's film *Mishima: A Life in Four Parts*. A comprehensive list of films and videos on Japan, entitled *Audio Visual Resources,* is available on request from the New York Office of the Japan Foundation.

3. The novelist Tanizaki Junichiro offers a lyrical description of the aesthetic delights of eating soup from a lacquer bowl in his essay *In Praise of Shadows,* trans. Thomas J. Harper and Edward G. Seidensticker (New Haven: Leete's Island Books, 1977). Although amusingly cranky in parts, this essay is an excellent introduction to certain aspects of Japanese aesthetic culture by one of the country's greatest novelists.

4. The most striking example would appear to be the existential conception of death elaborated by Martin Heidegger in his masterpiece *Being and Time,* which bears a remarkable similarity to the understanding of death that informs the philosophy of the Japanese samurai tradition. For some evidence that Heidegger may have been influenced by Japanese ideas concerning death, see Graham Parkes, "Heidegger and Japanese Thought: How Much Did He Know, and When Did He Know It?" in Christopher Macann, ed., *Heidegger: Critical Assessments* (London: Routledge, 1992).

5. For a good account of East Asian philosophies of the body, see Yuasa Yasuo, *The Body: Toward an Eastern Mind-Body Theory,* trans. Thomas P. Kasulis and Nagatomo Shigenori (Albany: SUNY Press, 1987).

6. An excellent cultural history of Japan is by H. Paul Varley, *Japanese Culture* (Honolulu: University of Hawaii Press, 1973).

7. A helpful overview of the transmigration of Buddhist ideas from India to China and then Japan is provided by Alan Watts, *The Way of Zen* (New York: Pantheon Books, 1957). For a more detailed analysis, see the monumental two-volume study by Heinrich Dumoulin entitled *Zen Buddhism: A History,* trans. James W. Heisig and Paul Knitter (New York: Macmillan, 1989).

8. An excellent treatment of the philosophy of Zen Buddhism, with a special focus on Dōgen and Hakuin, is T. P. Kasulis, *Zen Action, Zen Person* (Honolulu: University Press of Hawaii, 1971). See, on the present topic, the section entitled "*Mu* as the Context of the Zen Person" (pp. 40–42).

9. A selection of Hakuin's writings is available in English: *The Zen Master Hakuin: Selected Writings,* trans. Philip Yampolsky (New York: Columbia University Press, 1971). The experience of the "great death" as described by Hakuin bears a striking resemblance to the revelation of "the abyss" in Nietzsche and the encounter with the nothingness disclosed by *Angst* described by Heidegger. For a comparative treatment of some of the ideas of Rinzai Zen, see Graham Parkes, "The Transformation of Emotion in Rinzai Zen and Nietzsche," *The Eastern Buddhist* 23/1 (1990): 10–25.

10. An account of the relation of Zen to swordsmanship can be found in Daisetz T. Suzuki, *Zen and Japanese Culture* (Princeton: Princeton University Press, 1959), chapters 5 and 6. A real gem of a Zen treatise relating the way of the sword to experience in general is Takuan Sōhō, *The Unfettered Mind,* trans. William Scott Wilson (Tokyo and New York: Kodansha International, 1986); see especially the first section, "The Mysterious Record of Immovable Wisdom."

11. Excerpts from the classic text of bushido have been translated into English: Yamamoto Tsunetomo, *Hagakure: The Book of the Samurai,* trans. William Scott Wilson (Tokyo and New York: Kodansha International, 1979). Also of interest are Mishima's reflections on the contemporary relevance of the text in *Yukio Mishima on Hagakure: The Samurai Ethic and Modern Japan,* trans. Kathryn Sparling (Tokyo and Rutland, Vt.: Tuttle, 1978).

12. Not surprising is the appearance of a number of books about sports with titles like "Zen and the Art of . . ." and "The Tao of . . ." The first of these is still, I think, the best: Eugen Herrigel, *Zen in the Art of Archery* (London: Routledge & Kegan Paul, 1953).

13. Takuan, *The Unfettered Mind,* pp. 30–31.

14. A concise introduction to the tea ceremony is Horst Hammitzsch, *Zen in the Art of the Tea Ceremony* (New York: St. Martin's Press, 1980). For a more detailed account, see A. L. Sadler, *Cha-no-yu: The Japanese Tea Ceremony* (London, 1933).

15. Kawabata Yasunari, *A Thousand Cranes,* trans. Edward G. Seidensticker (New York: Knopf, 1958).

16. A good introduction is Donald Keene, *Nō: The Classical Theater of Japan* (Tokyo and Palo Alto: Kodansha International, 1966). Classic translations of some of the classic plays can be found in Arthur Waley, *The Nō Plays of Japan* (London, 1921), and Ezra Pound and Ernest Fenollosa, *The Classic Noh Theater*

of Japan (New York: New Directions, 1959). The latter was first published in the United States in 1917, but the 1959 edition includes an interesting essay on the Noh by William Butler Yeats.

17. A modern version, as it were, of Noh drama is *Butoh,* a quintessentially Japanese form of theater involving music and dance, but which generally uses whiteface, makeup, and body paint instead of masks. The only comprehensive treatment in English is Jean Viala, *Butoh: Shades of Darkness* (Tokyo: Shufuno-tomo, 1988). A fine collection of photographs can be found in Mark Holborn et al., *Butoh: Dance of the Dark Soul* (New York: Aperture, 1987). See also the videotape *Butoh: Body on the Edge of Crisis.*

18. The only overview of modern Japanese philosophy in English has unfortunately long been out of print: Gino K. Piovesana, S.J., *Contemporary Japanese Philosophical Thought* (New York, 1969). Some aspects of the early appropriation of Western philosophy in Japan are touched on in my essay, "The Early Reception of Nietzsche's Philosophy in Japan," in Graham Parkes, ed. *Nietzsche and Asian Thought* (Chicago: University of Chicago Press, 1991), pp. 177–99. Discussions of correspondences between Japanese philosophy and the thinking of Martin Heidegger can be found in Graham Parkes, ed., *Heidegger and Asian Thought* (Honolulu: University of Hawaii Press, 1987).

19. An excellent account of this process, in the context of an insightful discussion of the phenomenon of nihilism in general, is to be found in Keiji Nishitani, *The Self-Overcoming of Nihilism,* trans. Graham Parkes with Setsuko Aihara (Albany: SUNY Press, 1990).

20. This suggestion is based on Nishitani's discussion of the import of nihilism in the Japanese context in *The Self-Overcoming of Nihilism.*

21. *Ikiru* is available under that title both on videotape and on laser disc.

22. There is no evidence that Kurosawa was familiar with the writings of the European existential thinkers, but the film is uncannily reminiscent of the treatments of such themes as anxiety, nothingness, and death in Kierkegaard, Nietzsche, and Heidegger.

23. If this output seems considerable, one should bear in mind that the Japanese film industry has always been one of the most prolific in the world. It is just that most of it has been, until fairly recently, for domestic consumption only.

24. An excellent trio of films by Ozu (available on videotape) dealing with the stresses on the Japanese family structure caused by modernization is: *Late Spring* (1949), *Early Summer* (1951), and *Tokyo Story* (1953). An exquisite later film dealing with a slightly earlier period (available on laser disc as well as videotape) is *Floating Weeds* (1959; one of Ozu's few films in color). Two good sources in English on Ozu are Donald Richie, *Ozu* (Berkeley & Los Angeles: University of California Press, 1974), and David Bordwell, *Ozu and the Poetics of Cinema* (Princeton: Princeton University Press, 1988).

25. A survey a few years ago estimated that as recently as 1966 fully 50 percent of marriages in urban areas in Japan were arranged *(o-miai)*—in rural areas the figure was 63 percent—while nowadays the figure has dropped to around 25 percent.

26. After seeing *Late Spring, Early Summer,* and *Tokyo Story,* the viewer is bound to see Hara Setsuko as *the* (good) daughter, Ryu Chishu as *the* (benevolent) father, and so on. Ozu's apparently obsessive return to the same characters and themes in film after film has, of course, its counterparts in Western art—in Cézanne's persistent return to the Montagne St. Victoire, for example.

27. Yukio Mishima, *Sun and Steel,* trans. John Bester (Tokyo and New York: Kodansha International, 1970).

28. The novels of the tetralogy, which—though they are perhaps not his best works—contain many interesting philosophical ideas, are: *Spring Snow, Runaway Horses, The Temple of Dawn,* and *The Decay of the Angel.* His greatest novels, and the most interesting philosophically, are (in my opinion) *The Temple of the Golden Pavilion* (1956) and *The Sailor Who Fell from Grace with the Sea* (1963).

29. Japanese Neo-Confucianism arose in the sixteenth and seventeenth centuries, the major interest being in the work of the medieval Chinese philosophers Chu Hsi and Wang Yang-ming.

30. A discussion of the various types of *seppuku* can be found in Jack Seward, *Hara-Kiri: Japanese Ritual Suicide* (Tokyo and Rutland: Tuttle, 1968).

3

Traditional American Indian Attitudes Toward Nature

J. Baird Callicott and Thomas W. Overholt

There's a big debate going on about hunting for sport. On one side are the "antis," as they are often labeled—advocates of animal rights, who think that shooting and killing a deer or a duck is almost as bad as murdering a human being. The fact that it is done for sport only makes matters worse, because hunters evidently get a sadistic pleasure from spilling the blood of other living, sensitive creatures.

On the other side are the "pros"—sportsmen (and sportswomen) and their supporters. The pros believe, to the contrary, that people are totally superior to animals and have a God-given right to do whatever they like to "lower" forms of life, provided no injury is done another human being. An important element in the justification of modern sport hunting is the "objectification" of the "game," the minimization of animal conscious-ness. Animals have no thoughts or feelings beyond their immediate sensations and get around largely by "instinct," or so many of the pros allege. Thus to hunt and kill these moving targets is a far cry from doing similar things to another genuine "subject," another fully conscious, thinking, feeling person.

Among traditional American Indian peoples, whose livelihood con-sisted primarily of hunting and gathering wild foods, we might expect to find attitudes similar to the pro side of the sport hunting controversy—if such folk had any thoughtful opinions at all on the matter. Once upon a time, even anthropologists believed that the aboriginal peoples of the Western Hemisphere lived in a rude and primitive estate, only a notch above the beasts they preyed upon. If so, one could hardly imagine that these "savages" (then a perfectly acceptable term in anthropology) entertained any other notion about animals than which ones were good for eating and what was the easiest way to catch them.

But when anthropologists began to study the cognitive as well as material cultures of American Indian peoples, a startlingly different set of native attitudes and values was revealed. Thus, by the 1930s, the distinguished American anthropologist Frank Speck could claim that

> Among Indians in the hunting level, . . . various families and clans . . . held themselves in special relationships to groups of animals, associations which have earned the name of "totemism." . . . The animal world, in their view, enjoyed the right to exist in close association with human beings. . . . Numerous regulations govern the taking and killing of plant and animal life. With these people no act of this sort is profane, hunting is not war upon the animals, not a slaughter for food or profit, but a *holy occupation*.[1]

Though Speck doesn't mention it, above all for the Indians, neither is hunting a sport. And not because it is their work instead of their play. Hunting an animal for sport would violate its dignity, sanctity, and right to be respected by human beings.

Hunters who believe in animal rights?! That sounds like a contradiction.

Gifted contemporary writers such as Richard Nelson, Gary Snyder, and Calvin Martin have tried to work us imaginatively into the seemingly paradoxical mind-set of pre-Columbian American Indian hunter-gatherers, and, for that matter, into the mind-set of the animals and plants they pursued. Nelson subverts the assumption that for traditional hunters the animal is a mere object, not a subject, and suggests that, according to their beliefs, when we look out upon the natural world, there are many sets of eyes—most concealed—looking back at us.[2] Martin suggests that as incredible as it may seem to those of us in the grip of the modern Western worldview, the traditional American Indian hunter did not attempt to attack his prey so much as to seduce it.[3] The sacred game must want to give itself to the tender, loving human carnivore and to go willingly, even cheerfully, to its fate.[4] Gary Snyder tries to explain why it would: The animal is seized with a desire to come into the lodge, teepee, or hogan of the hunter, to smoke his tobacco, and to hear him and his friends tell their stories and sing their songs.[5]

Assuming that these authors are reporting their facts straight, is this some kind of collective madness . . . or what? But it just might be that American Indian peoples had a coherent philosophy to support such seemingly ludicrous beliefs. We think that they did, and what we're going to try to do here is to bring it out and make it seem both clear and reasonable.

Problems of Unity and Method

Here we sketch, in broadest outline, the picture of nature endemic to pre-Columbian North America. And, more specifically, we argue that the view of nature typical of traditional American Indian peoples has included and supported an environmental ethic that helped to prevent them from overexploiting the ecosystems in which they lived.

We do not enter into this discussion unaware of the difficulties and limitations lying in ambush at the very outset. In the first place, there is no *one* thing that can be called *the* American Indian belief system. The aboriginal peoples of the North American continent lived in environments quite different from one another and culturally adapted to these environments in quite different ways. For each tribe there were a cycle of myths and a set of ceremonies, and from these materials one might abstract *for each* a particular view of nature.

However, recognition of the diversity and variety of American Indian cultures should not obscure a complementary unity to be found among them. Despite great differences there were common characteristics that culturally united American Indian peoples. Joseph Epes Brown claims that

> this common binding thread is found in beliefs and attitudes held by the people in the quality of their relationships to the natural environment. All American Indian peoples possessed what has been called a metaphysic of nature; and manifest a reverence for the myriad forms and forces of the natural world specific to their immediate environment; and for all, their rich complexes of rites and ceremonies are expressed in terms which have reference to or utilize the forms of the natural world.[6]

Calvin Martin has more recently confirmed Brown's conjecture:

> What we are dealing with are two issues: the ideology of Indian land-use and the practical results of that ideology. Actually, there was a great diversity of ideologies, reflecting distinct cultural and ecological contexts. It is thus more than a little artificial to identify a single, monolithic ideology, as though all Native Americans were traditionally inspired by a universal ethos. Still, there were certain elements which many if not all these ideologies seemed to share, the most outstanding being a genuine respect for the welfare of other life-forms.[7]

A second obvious difficulty bedeviling any discussion of American Indian views of nature is our limited ability to accurately reconstruct the cognitive—as opposed to the material—culture of New World peoples prior to their contact with (and influence by) Europeans. Arrowheads, bone awls, and other cultural artifacts that were made before 1492 still exist and can be carefully examined. But documentary records of precontact Indian thought do not.

American Indian metaphysics was embedded in oral traditions. Left alone, an oral culture may be very tenacious and persistent. If radically stressed, it may prove to be very fragile and liable to total extinction. Hence, *contemporary* accounts by contemporary American Indians of *traditional* American Indian philosophy are vulnerable to the charge of inauthenticity, in that for several generations American Indian cultures, cultures preserved in the living memory of their members, have been both ubiquitously and violently disturbed by transplanted European civilization.

Perhaps we ought, therefore, to rely where possible upon the earliest written observations of Europeans concerning American Indian belief. The accounts of the North American "savages" by sixteenth-, seventeenth-, and eighteenth-century Europeans are, however, invariably distorted by ethnocentrism, which today appears so hopelessly benighted as to be more entertaining than illuminating. The written observations of Europeans who first encountered American Indian cultures provide, rather, an instructive record of the implicit European metaphysic. Because Indians were not loyal to the Christian religion, it was assumed that they had to be conscious servants of Satan, and that the spirits about which they talked and the powers their shamans attempted to direct had to be so many demons from hell. Concerning the Feast of the Dead among the Huron, Jean de Brébeuf wrote in the *Jesuit Relations* of 1636 that "nothing has ever better pictured for me the confusion among the damned."[8] His account, incidentally, is very informative and detailed concerning the physical requirements and artifacts of this ceremony, but the rigidity of his own system of belief makes it impossible for him to enter sympathetically into that of the Huron.

Reconstructing the traditional Indian attitude toward nature is, therefore, to some extent a speculative matter. On the other hand, we must not abandon the inquiry as utterly hopeless. Postcontact American Indians do tell of their traditions and conceptual heritage, and the critical ear can filter out the European noise in such accounts. Among the best of these nostalgic memoirs is John G. Neihardt's classic, *Black Elk Speaks,* one of the most important and authentic sources available for the reconstruction of an American Indian attitude toward nature.[9] The explorers', missionaries', and fur traders' accounts of woodland Indian attitudes are also useful, despite their ethnocentrism, since we may also critically correct for the distortion of their biases and prejudices.

Further, disciplined and methodical modern ethnographers have recorded an American Indian oral narrative heritage, a diverse body of myths and stories that convey the cognitive structure and values of the people who told and retold them, generation after generation. Folktales have a life of their own and may survive the demise of the material culture in which they originated. Consider the fairy tales we Euro-Americans tell our children. They are set an ocean away in a material culture of castles and knights-in-shining-armor that no longer exists. Yet they remain relatively unchanged when we retell them in our present world of skyscrapers, fast-food joints, and TV. From them we might learn something about the enchanted-thought world of our medieval ancestors. Similarly, American Indian folktales may represent a relatively transparent window on the pre-Columbian mind-set of Stone Age North America.

Using these three sorts of sources—first-contact European records, transcribed personal recollections of tribal beliefs by spiritually favored Indians, and Native American folktales—we may achieve a fairly reliable reconstruction of traditional Indian attitudes toward nature.[10]

The Western Worldview as an Intellectual Foil

The distinct flavor of the typical American Indian conception of nature may be brought out most vividly by contrasting it with the typical Western European concept of nature, which now also prevails in North America and has, until recently, eclipsed native thought.

The European style of thought was set by the Greeks of classical antiquity. Whatever else it may have come to be, modern science is a continuation and extrapolation of certain concepts originating with the Greeks of the sixth, fifth, and fourth centuries B.C.

Salient among the originally Greek notions of nature to find its way into modern science is the atomic theory of matter. The ancient atomists imagined all material things to be composed of indestructible and internally changeless particles, of which they supposed there were infinitely many. Each of these atoms was believed to be solid and to have a shape and a relative size. All other qualities of things normally disclosed by perception exist, according to the atomic theory, only by "convention," not by "nature." In the terms of later philosophical jargon, characteristics of things such as flavor, odor, color, and sound were regarded as *secondary* qualities, the privately experienced effects of the primary qualities on the sensory subject. The atoms move about haphazardly in the "void" or space. Macroscopic objects are assemblages of atoms; they are wholes exactly equal to the sum of their parts. Such objects come into being and pass away, but process and change were conceived as the association and dissociation of the eternally existing and unchanging atomic parts. The atomists claimed to reduce all the phenomena of nature to a simple dichotomy, variously expressed: the "full" and the "empty," "thing" and "no-thing," the atom and space.

The eventual Newtonian worldview of modern science included as one of its cornerstones the atomists' concept of free space, thinly occupied by moving particles or "corpuscles," as the early moderns called them. It was one of Newton's greatest achievements to supply a quantitative model of the regular motion of the putative material particles. These famous "laws of motion" made it possible to represent phenomena not only materially but also mechanically: All change could be reduced to bits of matter moving through space impacting on other bits.

That the *order* of nature can be successfully disclosed only by means of a quantitative description is an idea that also originated in sixth-century B.C. Greece and is attributed to Pythagoras. The prevailing modern concept of nature might be oversimply, but nonetheless not incorrectly, portrayed as a merger of the Pythagorean idea that the order of nature is mathematical with the atomists' ontology of void space (so very amenable to geometrical analysis) and material particles.

As Paul Santmire characterizes the modern European concept of nature that took root in North America,

> Nature is analogous to a machine; or in the more popular version nature *is* a machine. Nature is composed of hard, irreducible particles which have neither color nor smell nor taste. . . . Beauty and value in nature are in the eye of the beholder. Nature is the dead *res extensa,* perceived by the mind, which observes nature from a position of objective detachment. Nature in itself is basically a self-sufficient, self-enclosed complex of merely physical forces acting on colorless, tasteless, and odorless particles of hard, dead matter. That is the mechanical view of nature as it was popularly accepted in the circles of the educated [Euro-Americans] in the nineteenth century.[11]

Santmire is careful to mention the nineteenth century because developments in twentieth-century science—the general theory of relativity, quantum theory, and ecology—have begun to replace the modern mechanical model of nature with another paradigm. A cultural worldview, however, lags behind the leading edge of intellectual development and so most Westerners still apprehend nature through a mechanistic-materialistic lens, blissfully unaware that the Newtonian worldview is obsolete. In any case, Santmire's comments bring to our attention a complementary feature of the prevailing (albeit theoretically defunct) modern classical European and Euro-American worldview of particular interest to our overall discussion. If no qualms were felt about picturing rivers and mountains, trees, and even animals as inert, material, mechanical "objects," only a few hard-nosed materialists (Democritus among the ancients and Hobbes among the moderns) were willing to try to provide a wholly mechanical account of mental activity.

The conception of the soul as not only separate and distinct from the body but as essentially alien to it (that is, of an entirely different, antagonistic nature) also was first introduced into Western thought by Pythagoras. Pythagoras conceived the soul to be a fallen divinity, incarcerated in the physical world as retribution for some unspecified sin. The goal in life for the Pythagoreans was to earn the release of the soul from the physical world upon death and to reunite the soul with its proper (divine) companions. The Pythagoreans accomplished this by several methods: asceticism, ritual purification, and intellectual exercise, particularly in mathematics.

Plato adopted Pythagoras's concept of the soul as immortal, otherworldly, and essentially alien to the physical environment. Influenced by Plato, Saint Paul introduced it into Christianity. Although Plato and Pythagoras had not restricted the soul to human beings, but believed that all sorts of animals are inhabited by one too, Christian orthodoxy limited the earthly residence of souls to human bodies. The "father of modern philosophy," René Descartes, reiterated in especially strong terms both the ancient Pythagorean/Platonic dualism and the Judeo-Christian insistence that only human beings are ensouled. Thus the essential self, in the eventual modern Western worldview, the part of a person by means of which he or she perceives and thinks, and in which resides virtue or vice, is less a citizen of Earth than of Heaven; and while living here on Earth we are lonely strangers in a strange land. Worse, the natural world is the place of trial and temptation for the quasi-divine human soul, its moral antipode.

So what attitude to nature does modern classical European natural philosophy convey? In sum, nature is an inert, material and mechanical plenum completely describable by means of the arid formulae of pure mathematics. In relation to nature, human beings are lonely exiles sojourning in a strange and hostile world, alien not only to their physical environment but to their own bodies, both of which they are encouraged to fear and to attempt to conquer. These Christian-Cartesian ideas were added to the core concepts, thoroughly criticized by Lynn White, Jr., Ian McHarg, and others, forthrightly set out in Genesis: God created man in his own image to have dominion over nature and to subdue it. The result, the Judeo-Christian/Cartesian-Newtonian worldview, was a very volatile mixture of ingredients that exploded during the nineteenth and twentieth centuries in an all-out European and Euro-American war on nature, a war that, as we rush headlong into the third millennium, has very nearly been won. (To the victors, of course, belong the spoils!)

The prevailing Western worldview, rooted in ancient Greek natural philosophy, is in fact doubly atomistic. Plato accounted for the existence of distinct species by means of his theory of ideal and abstract forms. Each individual or specimen "participated," according to Plato, in a certain essence or form, and it derived its specific characteristics from the form in which it participated. The impression of the natural world conveyed by Plato's theory of forms is that the various species are determined by the static logical-mathematical order of the formal domain, and then the individual organisms (each with its preordained essence) are loosed into the physical arena to interact adventitiously, catch-as-catch-can.

Nature is thus represented as like a room full of furniture, a collection, a mere aggregate of individuals of various types, relating to one another in an accidental and altogether external fashion. This picture of the world is an atomism of a most subtle and insidious sort. It breaks the highly integrated functional ecosystem into separate, discrete, and functionally unrelated sets of particulars. Pragmatically, approaching the world through this model—which we might call "conceptual" in contradistinction to "material" atomism—it is possible to radically rearrange parts of the landscape without the least concern for upsetting its functional integrity and organic unity. Certain species may be replaced by others (for example, wildflowers by grain in prairie biomes) or removed altogether (for example, predators) without consequence, theoretically, for the function of the whole.

Plato's student Aristotle rejected the otherworldliness of Plato's philosophy, both his theory of the soul and his theory of forms. Aristotle, moreover, was a sensitive empirical biologist and did as much to advance biology as a science as Pythagoras did for mathematics. Aristotle's system of classification of organisms according to species, genus, family, order, class, phylum, and kingdom (as modified and refined by Linnaeus) remains a cornerstone of the modern life sciences. This hierarchy of universals was not real or actual, according to Aristotle; only individual organisms fully existed. However, Aristotle's taxonomical hierarchy, as it was formulated long before the development of evolutionary and ecological theory, resulted in a view of living nature that was no less compartmentalized than was Plato's. Relations among things again are, in Aristotle's biological theory, accidental and inessential. A thing's essence is determined by its logical relations within the taxonomical schema rather than, as in ecological theory, by its working relations with other things in its environment—its trophic niche, its thermal and chemical requirements, and so on.

Evolutionary and ecological theory suggest, rather, that the essences of things, the specific characteristics of species, are a function of their relations with other things. Aristotle's taxonomical view of the biotic world, untransformed by evolutionary and ecological theory, thus has the same ecologically misrepresentative feature as Plato's theory of forms: Nature is seen as an aggregate of individuals, divided into various types, that have no functional connection with one another. And the *practical* consequences are the same. The Earth's biotic mantle may be dealt with in a heavy-handed fashion, rearranged to suit one's fancy without danger of dysfunctions. If anything, Aristotle's taxonomical representation of nature has had a more insidious influence on the Western mind than Plato's "real" universals, because the latter could be dismissed, as often they were, as abstracted Olympians in a charming and noble philosophical romance, whereas metaphysical taxonomy went unchallenged as "empirical" and "scientific."

Also, we should not forget another Aristotelian legacy, the natural *hierarchy,* or great chain of being, according to which the world is arranged into "lower" and "higher" forms. Aristotle's belief that everything exists for a purpose resulted in the commonplace Western assumption that the lower forms exist for the sake of the higher forms. Since we human beings are placed at the top of the pyramid, everything else exists for our sakes. The practical tendencies of this idea are too obvious to require further elaboration.

American Indian Animism

The late John Fire Lame Deer, a reflective Sioux Indian, comments, straight to the point, in his biographical and philosophical narrative, *Lame Deer: Seeker of Visions,* that although the "whites" (that is, members of the European cultural tradition) imagine earth, rocks, water, and wind to be dead, they nevertheless "are very much alive."[12] In the previous section we tried to explain in what sense nature is conceived as "dead" in the mainstream of European and Euro-American thought. To say that rocks and rivers are dead is perhaps a little misleading, since to say that something is dead might imply that it was once alive. Rather in the usual Western view of things, such objects are considered inert. But what does Lame Deer mean when he says that they are "very much alive"?

He doesn't explain this provocative assertion as discursively as one might wish, but he provides examples, dozens of examples, of what he calls the "power" in various natural entities. According to Lame Deer, "Every man needs a stone. . . . You ask stones for aid to find things which are lost or missing. Stones can give warning of an enemy, of approaching misfortune."[13] Butterflies, coyotes, grasshoppers, eagles, owls, deer, and especially elk and bear all talk and possess and convey power. "You have to listen to all these creatures, listen with your mind. They have secrets to tell."[14]

It would seem that for Lame Deer the "aliveness" of natural entities (including stones, which to most Europeans are merely "material objects" and epitomize lifelessness) means that they have a share in the same consciousness that we human beings enjoy. Granted, animals and plants (if not stones and rivers) are recognized to be "alive" by conventional European conceptualization, but they lack awareness in a mode and degree comparable to human awareness. According to Descartes, the most extreme and militant dualist in the Western tradition, even animal behavior is altogether automatic, resembling in every way the behavior of a machine. A somewhat more liberal and enlightened view allows that animals have a dim sort of consciousness, but operate largely by "instinct," a concept altogether lacking a clear definition and one very nearly as obscure as the notorious occult qualities (the "sporific virtues," and so on) of the medieval Scholastic philosophers. Of course, plants, although alive, are regarded as totally lacking in sentience. In any case, we hear that only human beings possess *self*-consciousness, that is, that only we are aware that we are aware and can thus distinguish between ourselves and everything else!

Every sophomore student of philosophy has learned, or should have, that solipsism is an impregnable philosophical position, and corollary to that, that every characterization of other minds—human as well as nonhuman—is a matter of conjecture. The Indian attitude, as represented by Lame Deer, apparently was based on the reasonable consideration that since human beings have a physical body *and* an associated consciousness (conceptually hypostatized or reified as "spirit"), all other bodily things—animals, plants, and, yes, even stones—were similar in this respect. Indeed, this strikes us as an eminently plausible assumption. One can no more directly perceive another human being's consciousness than one can that of an animal or a plant. One *assumes* that another human being is conscious because he or she is very similar to oneself in physical appearance. Anyone not hopelessly prejudiced by the metaphysical apartheid policy of Pauline Christianity, Descartes, and the Western worldview that is their legacy would naturally extend the same consideration to other natural beings. Human beings closely resemble other forms of life in anatomy, physiology, and behavior. The myriad organic forms themselves are obviously closely related, and the organic world, in turn, is continuous with the whole of nature. Thus virtually all things might be supposed, without the least strain upon credence, like ourselves, to be "alive," that is, conscious, aware, or possessed of spirit.

Lame Deer offers a brief, but most revealing and suggestive, metaphysical explanation:

> Nothing is so small and unimportant but it has a spirit given it by *Wakan Tanka*. *Tunkan* is what you might call a stone god, but he is also a part of the Great Spirit. The gods are separate beings, but they are all united in *Wakan Tanka*. It is hard to understand—something like the Holy Trinity. You can't explain it except by going back to the "circles within circles" idea, the spirit splitting itself up into stones, trees, tiny insects even, making them all *wakan* by his ever-presence. And in turn all these myriads of things which make up the universe flowing back to their source, united in one Grandfather Spirit.[15]

This Lakota panentheism (the belief that there exists a single unified holy spirit that is, nevertheless, also manifest in each thing) presents a conception of the world that is, to be sure, dualistic: It posits the existence of a personal spirit in otherwise material bodies. But it is important to emphasize that, unlike the Platonic-Pauline-Cartesian tradition, it is not an *antagonistic* dualism in which body and spirit are conceived in contrary terms and pitted against one another in a moral struggle. Further, and most important for our subsequent remarks, the pervasiveness of spirit in nature, a spirit *in* each thing which is a splinter of the Great Spirit, facilitates a perception of the human and natural realms as akin and alike.

Consider, complementary to this Native American panentheism, the basics of Siouan cosmogony. Black Elk (a Lakota shaman of the generation previous to Lame Deer's) rhetorically asks, "Is not the sky a father and the earth a mother, and are not all living things with feet or wings or roots their children?"[16] Accordingly, he prays, "Give me the strength to walk the soft earth, a relative to all that is!"[17] Black Elk speaks of the great natural kingdom as, simply, "green things," "the wings of the air," "the four-leggeds," and "the two-legged."[18] Not only does everything have a spirit; in the last analysis, all things are related as members of one universal family, born of one father, the sky, the Great Spirit, and one mother, the Earth herself.

More is popularly known about the Sioux metaphysical vision than about those of most other American Indian peoples. The concept of the Great Spirit and of the Earth Mother and the family-like relatedness of all creatures seems, however, to have been a very common, not to say universal, American Indian idea and, likewise, the concept of a spiritual dimension or aspect to all natural things. Pulitzer Prize-winning American Indian poet and essayist N. Scott Momaday remarked, " 'The earth is our mother. The sky is our father.' This concept of nature, which is at the center of the Native American world view, is familiar to us all. But it may well be that we do not understand entirely what the concept is in its ethical and philosophical implications."[19] And North American ethnomusicologist Ruth Underhill has written that "for the old time Indian, the world did not consist of inanimate materials. . . . It was alive, and everything in it could help or harm him."[20]

Concerning the Ojibwa Indians, who speak an Algonkian language and at the time of first contact maintained only hostile relations with the Lakota, Diamond Jenness reports:

Thus, then, the Parry Island Ojibwa interprets his own being; and exactly the same interpretation he applies to everything around him. Not only men, but animals, trees, even rocks and water are tripartite, possessing bodies, souls, and shadows. [These Indians, Jenness earlier explains, divided spirit into two aspects—soul and shadow—though, as Jenness admits, the distinction between the soul and shadow was far from clear and frequently confused by the people themselves.] They all have a life like the life in human beings, even if they have all been gifted with different powers and attributes. Consider the animals which most closely resemble human beings; they see and hear as we do, and clearly they reason about what they observe. The tree must have a life somewhat like our own, although it lacks the power of locomotion. . . . Water runs; it too must possess life, it too must have a soul and a shadow. Then observe how certain minerals cause the neighboring rocks to decompose and become loose and friable; evidently rocks too have power, and power means life, and life involves a soul and shadow. All things then have souls and shadows. And all things die. But their souls are reincarnated again, and what were dead return to life.[21]

A. Irving Hallowell has noted an especially significant consequence of the pan-spiritualism among the Ojibwa: "Not only animate properties," he writes, "but even 'person' attributes may be projected upon objects which to us clearly belong to a physical inanimate category."[22] Central to the concept of *person* is the possibility of entering into social relations. Nonhuman persons may be spoken with, may be honored or insulted, may become allies or adversaries, no less than human persons.

The philosophical basis for attributing personhood to nonhuman natural entities also helps to explain the American Indian understanding of dreams. Like eating, getting sick, falling in love, having children, and other such things, dreaming is an experience common to all peoples. But the meaning, the interpretation of the dream state of consciousness differs from culture to culture. A culture's understanding of dreams, no less than its explanation of disease, reflects its more general worldview. Thus, a culture's representation of dreams can also be very revealing of its more general worldview.

For example, the ancient Greeks, before philosophy had thoroughly undermined their mythic worldview, believed both illness and dreams to be visitations from the gods. In Plato's *Symposium,* to take a case in point, Socrates remarks that the woman who taught him the mysteries of love was believed to have postponed a god-sent plague in Athens by performing certain religious rites; and in the *Phaedo,* Socrates remarks that over the course of his life the same dream had come to him, sometimes wearing one countenance, sometimes another, but always commanding him to work and make music. Most of us modern Europeans and Euro-Americans follow Descartes in believing that to be sick is to experience a mechanical breakdown in our bodies and that dreams are confused phenomena of the mind (though some of us add to this generic idea Freud's more specific hypothesis that dreams are confused manifestations of the unconscious dimension of a person's psyche).

The French fur traders and missionaries of the seventeenth century in the Great Lakes region were singularly impressed by the devotion to dreams of the "savages" with whom they lived. According to Vernon Kinietz, Paul Ragueneau, in 1648, first suggested that among the Algonkians, dreams were "the language of the souls."[23] This expression lacks precision, but we think it goes very much to the core of the American Indian understanding of dreams. Through dreams, and most dramatically through visions, one came into direct contact with the spirits of both human and nonhuman persons, as it were, naked of bodily vestments. In words somewhat reminiscent of Ragueneau's, Hallowell comments, "It is in dreams that the individual comes into direct communication with the *atiso'kanak,* the powerful 'persons' of the other-than-human class."[24] Given the animistic or panspiritualistic worldview of the Indians, acute sensitivity and pragmatic response to dreaming make perfectly good sense.

Dreams and waking experiences are sharply discriminated, but the theater of action disclosed in dreams and visions is continuous with and often the same as the ordinary world. In contrast to the psychologized contemporary Western view in which dreams are images of sorts (like afterimages) existing only "in the mind," the American Indian while dreaming experiences reality, often the same reality as in waking experience, in another form of consciousness—as it were, by means of another sensory modality.

As one lies asleep and experiences people and other animals, places, and so on, it is natural to suppose that one's spirit becomes temporarily dissociated from one's body and moves about encountering other spirits. Or, as Hallowell says, "when a human being is asleep and dreaming his *otcatcakwin* (vital part, soul), which is the core of the self, may become detached from the body *(miyo).* Viewed by another human being, a person's body may be easily located and observed in space. But his vital part may be somewhere else."[25] Dreaming indeed may be one element in the art of American Indian sorcery (called "bear walking" among the Ojibwa in which the sorcerer skulks around at night in the form of a bear, and appears indeed to be a bear to persons unskilled in detecting the subtle differences between a mischievous bear walker up to no good and an ordinary well-meaning bear minding its own business).[26] If the state of consciousness in dreams is seized and controlled, and the phenomenal content of dreams volitionally directed, then sorcerers may go where they wish in order to spy on enemies or perhaps affect them in some malevolent way.

It follows that dreams should have a higher degree of "truth" than ordinary waking experiences, because in the dream experience the person and everyone he or she meets is present in spirit, in essential self. This, notice, is precisely contrary to the European assumption that dreams are "false" or illusory and altogether private or subjective. For instance, in the second of his *Meditations on First Philosophy,* Descartes, casting around for an example of the highest absurdity, says that it is "as though I were to say 'I am awake now, and discern some truth; but I do not see it clearly enough; so I will set about going to sleep, so that my dreams may give me a truer and clearer picture of the fact.'" Yet this, in all seriousness, is precisely what many Indians have done. An episode from Hallowell's discussion may serve as illustration. A boy claimed that during a thunderstorm he saw a thunderbird. His elders were skeptical, since to see a thunderbird in such fashion, that is, with the waking eye, was almost unheard of. He was believed, however, when a man who had dreamed of the thunderbird was consulted and the boy's description was "*verified*"![27]

The Ojibwa, the Sioux, and, if we may safely generalize, most American Indians lived in a world that was peopled not only by human persons but by persons and personalities associated with all natural phenomena. In one's practical dealings in such a world it is necessary to one's well-being and that of one's family and tribe to maintain good social relations not only with proximate human persons, one's immediate tribal neighbors, but also with the nonhuman persons abounding in the immediate environment. For example, Hallowell reports that among the Ojibwa "when bears were sought out in their dens in the spring they were addressed, asked to come out so that they could be killed, and an apology was offered to them."[28]

In characterizing the American Indian attitude toward nature, we have tried to limit our discussion to concepts so fundamental and pervasive as to be capable of generalization. In sum, we have claimed that the typical traditional American Indian attitude was to regard all features of the environment as enspirited. These entities were believed to possess a consciousness, reason, and volition no less intense and complete than a human being's. The earth, the sky, the winds, rocks, streams, trees, insects, birds, and all other animals therefore had personalities and were thus as fully persons as human beings were. In dreams and visions the spirits of things were directly encountered and could become powerful allies to the dreamer or visionary. We may therefore say that the Indians' social circle, their community, included all the nonhuman natural entities in their locales as well as their fellow clan and tribe members.

Now a most significant conceptual connection obtains in all cultures between the concept of a person, on the one hand, and certain behavioral restraints, on the other. Toward persons it is necessary, whether for genuinely ethical or purely prudential reasons, to act in a careful and circumspect manner. Among the Ojibwa, for example, according to Hallowell, "a moral distinction is drawn between the kind of conduct demanded by the primary necessities of securing a livelihood, or defending oneself against aggression, and unnecessary acts of cruelty. The moral values implied document the consistency of the principle of *mutual obligations* which is inherent in all interactions with 'persons' throughout the Ojibwa world."[29]

The implicit overall metaphysic of American Indian cultures locates human beings in a larger *social,* as well as physical, environment. People belong not only to a human community but to a community of all nature as well. Existence in this larger society, just as existence in a family and tribal context, places people in an environment in which reciprocal responsibilities and mutual obligations are taken for granted and assumed without question or reflection. Moreover, a person's basic cosmological representations in moments of meditation or cosmic reflection place him or her in a world all parts of which are united through ties of kinship. All creatures, be they elemental, green, finned, winged, or legged, are children of one father and one mother. One blood flows through all; one spirit has divided itself and enlivened all things with a consciousness that is essentially the same. The world around, though immense and overwhelmingly diversified and complex, is bound together through bonds of kinship, mutuality, and reciprocity. It is a world in which a person might feel at home, a relative to all that is, comfortable and secure, as one feels as a child in the midst of a large family. As Brown reports:

> But very early in life the child began to realize that wisdom was all about and everywhere and that there were many things to know. There was no such thing as emptiness in the world. Even in the sky there were no vacant places. Everywhere there was life, visible and invisible, and every object gave us great interest to life. Even without human companionship one was never alone. The world teemed with life and wisdom, there was no complete solitude for the Lakota (Luther Standing Bear).[30]

The Ethics of the Multispecies Society

In this section we develop a little more formally the hypothesis that the American Indian concept of nature supported an environmental ethic. And we illustrate and document the existence of an American Indian environmental ethic with reference to specific cultural materials.

Aldo Leopold's land ethic has been the contemporary ecology movement's environmental ethic of choice. It may serve thus as a familiar model of environmental ethics with which we may compare the American Indian worldview and its associated environmental attitudes and values.

According to Leopold, "All ethics so far evolved rest upon a single premise: that the individual is a member of a community of interdependent parts. . . . The land ethic simply enlarges the boundaries of the community to include soils, waters, plants and animals, or collectively: the land."[31] Ethics depend ultimately, Leopold suggests, upon a sense of community. One will acknowledge moral obligations only to those persons whom one recognizes as fellow members of one's own society or group. And if one's sense of community includes nonhuman natural entities and is coextensive with the whole of nature, one has the cognitive foundations of a land ethic.

What we have already discovered about the American Indian concept of nature amply shows that nonhuman natural entities are personalized. Whereas in the Western worldview only human beings are fully persons, nature in the Indian worldview abounds with other-than-human-persons, among them "plants and animals" and even "soils and waters," as Leopold's specifications for an environmental ethic would require. For Leopold, the personhood of the nonhuman world is a sadly neglected implication of evolutionary biology. We are, from an evolutionary point of view, animals ourselves. Since we experience sensations, feelings, and thoughts, then only pre-Darwinian prejudices about the uniqueness of people would blind us to similar capacities in other animals. The reasoning indeed is not unlike that of the Indians as outlined by Jenness, quoted in the previous section. Leopold summed up the moral implications of the theory of evolution this way:

It is a century now since Darwin gave us the first glimpse of the origin of species. We know now what was unknown to all the preceding caravan of generations: that men [and women] are only fellow voyagers in the odyssey of evolution. This new knowledge should have given us by this time, a sense of kinship with fellow-creatures; a wish to live and let live; a sense of wonder over the magnitude and duration of the biotic enterprise.[32]

Although it would be presumptuous to think that American Indians had anticipated Darwin in discovering the evolutionary origin of species, the American Indian worldview certainly supported a similar upshot: a continuity among all beings. That nonhuman persons form with us a community or society Leopold inferred from the science of ecology, which represents plants and animals, soils and waters as "all interlocked in one humming community of cooperations and competitions, one biota."[33] Pre-Columbian American Indians were no more informed by scientific ecology than they were by the theory of evolution, but they did regard themselves as members of multispecies socioeconomic communities of interlocked cooperations and competitions. Traditional Ojibwa narratives amply document this aspect of the pre-Columbian American Indian worldview. The stories tell again and again of the transformation of a human being into an animal (or vice versa) and of a marriage between the transformed human (or animal) person with a person of another species.

One especially representative example is "The Woman Who Married a Beaver." In this story, a young woman on her vision quest meets a person "who was," as the narrator puts it, "in the form of a human being."[34] He asks her to come to his attractive and well-appointed home by a lake and to be his wife. The man was a very good provider; the woman was in want of nothing; and their home was very beautiful. For her part, she collected firewood, made mats and bags out of reeds, and kept the house in very neat order. She has two clues that the person she married was not really of her own species: "When they beheld their first young, four was the number of them"; and "sometimes by a human being were they visited, but only round about out of doors would the man pass, not within would the man come." "Now," the story goes, "the woman knew that she had married a beaver."

The meaning of this oft-repeated theme may not be obvious to Westerners, but a little basic anthropological information should help to make it entirely clear. In tribal societies, alliances between different clans (or extended families) are established through marriage. Further, in many tribal societies, clans are distinguished from one another through totem representation. Within a tribal group, in other words, there may be the bear clan, the snake clan, the crane clan, and so on. (Entertaining the notion of interspecies marriages, therefore, would probably seem less weird to people who think of themselves in terms of totem identities—the bear people, the snake people, the crane people, and so on.) Further, each clan may assume both ceremonial and economic specialties metaphorically associated with their totems. For example, only the bear clan may be permitted to kill bears for the annual bear ceremony, and thus the bear clan may be the principal provider of bear meat and grease for the whole tribe. Or, to take another hypothetical example, the crane clan may specialize in organizing seasonal migrations and gathering wild rice. Intermarriages between clans—what anthropologists call the rule of exogamy or out-marriage—binds them all together in a functioning tribal whole. More especially, it facilitates the exchange of specialized goods and services among all the subgroups. Such exchange of goods and services was typically less a matter of barter than of gift-giving, as would befit clans united by matrimonial ties.[35]

So the basic meaning of "The Woman Who Married a Beaver" and of similar tales seems to be this: The marriage between the two groups, the people and the beavers, establishes an alliance with economic implications. Gifts are exchanged that are mutually beneficial. Our suggestion is confirmed as the plot develops.

The odd couple of this story is very prolific and the beaver-man (though not the woman herself) and their offspring would go home with the human beings who visited them from time to time. "The people would then slay the beavers, yet they really did not kill them; but back home would they come again." When they came home, "All sorts of things would they fetch—kettles and bowls, knives, tobacco, and all the things that are used when a beaver is eaten. Continually were they adding to their great wealth." Here is the clearest possible representation of a mutually beneficial economic relationship between two matrimonially united "clans"—the beaver "people" and the people proper—executed through gift exchange. The beavers give the people all that they have to give, their flesh and fur, and the people give the beavers what the aquatic rodents could not otherwise obtain: hand-crafted articles (like kettles and knives) and cultivars (like tobacco), which they highly prize.

But of course the animals could not benefit from the gifts they are given in return if they were dead. So the Indians conveniently supposed that they were not really dead. How did that work? We have already seen that in pre-Columbian North America there prevailed a ubiquitous belief in nature spirits. The spirits of the slain animals would, it was assumed, survive the killing of their bodies and, if their bones were not broken or burned and if they were returned to their appropriate element (water in the case of beavers), the bones might be reincarnated and reclothed in fur.

The existence of many taboos respecting the bones of game animals and the preoccupation of many stories with the proper treatment of animal bones may be understood in one or the other of two possible ways: The spirit may reside in or take refuge in the bones. Or at a stage of American Indian thought before the formation of the concept of an immaterial spirit, the immortal thing may have been supposed to be the skeleton—which, after all, is more lasting than the softer parts.

People, obviously, are economically dependent not only on one another but on many other species as well. To people who live largely by hunting and gathering, this dependence is more palpably apparent on a daily basis than it is to us who are insulated from the natural economy by a series of middlepersons. The Ojibwa represented their dependence upon other species through a social metaphor, not altogether unlike that of contemporary ecology. Ecologists draw an analogy between the economic structure of human societies and the "economy" of the "biotic community." The Ojibwa similarly pictured their interspecies economic relationships with beavers, moose, bears, and other creatures in terms of their intraspecies economic relationships with one another. Again, "The Woman Who Married a Beaver" is almost didactically explicit about this:

> That was the time when very numerous were the beavers, and the beavers were very fond of the people; in the same way as people are when visiting one another, so were the beavers in their mental attitude toward the people. Even though they were slain by the people, yet they were not really dead. They were very fond of the tobacco that was given them by the people; at times they were also given clothing by the people.

Now, as we earlier observed, social interaction among persons is facilitated by ethical protocols. The conclusion of the story of the woman who married a beaver is explicitly moral. Having grown old together, the beaver-man instructs his wife to return to her people, and he departs for another land.

> Thereupon she plainly told the story of what had happened to her while she lived with the beavers. . . . And she was wont to say: "Never speak you ill of a beaver! Should you speak ill of a beaver, you will not be able to kill one."
>   Therefore such was what the people always did; they never spoke ill of the beavers, especially when they intended hunting them. . . . Just the same as the feelings of one who is disliked, so is the feeling of the beaver. And he who never speaks ill of a beaver is very much loved by it; . . . particularly lucky then is one at killing beavers.

In addition to forging the alliance between the human clan and the beaver clan necessary for the gift exchange of goods and services typical of a tribal economy, the human changeling often serves in such stories as the emissary from the animals about their special requirements and demands. As we have just seen in this story, when the woman who married a beaver returns to her own kind she informs them of the feelings of the beavers and the appropriate attitude of respect that the beavers demand if people wish successfully to engage in this particular form of fur trading. In another story, "Clothed-in-Fur," in addition to reciprocal gift-giving and respect, the moral of the story focuses on the proper treatment of the beavers' bones.

The Practical Implications of the American Indian Worldview

Let us now explore a little more deeply the suggestion made at the beginning of this chapter, namely, that in its *practical* consequences the traditional American Indian view of nature was on the whole more productive of a cooperative symbiosis of people with their environment than is the view of nature predominant in the prevailing Western European and Euro-American tradition.

Respecting the latter, Ian McHarg writes that "it requires little effort to mobilize a sweeping indictment of the physical environment which is [Western] man's creation [and] it takes little more to identify the source of the value system which is the culprit."[36] According to McHarg, the culprit is "the Judeo-Christian-Humanist view which is so unknowing of nature and of man, which has bred and sustained his simple-minded anthropocentricism."[37]

Since the early 1960s popular ecologists and environmentalists (perhaps most notably Rachel Carson and Barry Commoner, along with McHarg and Lynn White, Jr., and, more recently, Norman Myers, Paul Ehrlich, and Bill McKibben) have, with a grim fascination, recited a litany of environmental ills. They have spoken of "polychlorinated biphenyls," "chlorofluorocarbons," "nuclear tinkering," "acid rain," and "the gratified bulldozer" in language once reserved for detailing the precincts of Hell and abominating its seductive Prince. Given the frequency with which we are reminded of the symptoms of strain in the global biosphere and the apocalyptic rhetoric in which they are usually cast we may be excused if we omit this particular step from the present argument. Let us stipulate that modern technological civilization (European in its origins) has been neither restrained nor especially delicate in manipulating the natural world.

With somewhat more humor than other advocates of environmental reform, Aldo Leopold characterized the modern Western approach to nature thus: "By and large our present problem is one of attitudes and implements. We are remodeling the Alhambra with a steam shovel, and we are proud of our yardage. We shall hardly relinquish the shovel, which after all has many good points, but we are in need of gentler and more objective criteria for its successful use.''[38] So far as the historical roots of the environmental crisis are concerned, we have here suggested that the much maligned attitudes arising out of the Judaic aspect of the Judeo-Christian tradition (man's God-given right to subdue nature, and so forth) have not been so potent a force in the work of remodeling as the tradition of Western natural philosophy that originated among the ancient Greeks, insidiously affected Christianity, and fully flowered in modern classical scientific thought. At least Western natural philosophy has been as formative of the cultural milieu (one artifact of which is the steam shovel itself) as have Genesis and the overall Old Testament worldview. In any case, mixed and blended together, they create a mentality in which unrestrained environmental exploitation and degradation could almost have been predicted in advance.

It seems obvious (especially to philosophers and historians of ideas) that attitudes and values *do* directly "determine" behavior by setting goals (for example, to subdue the Earth, to have dominion) and, through a conceptual representation of the world, by providing means (for example, mechanics, optics, and thermodynamics) expressed in technologies (for example, steam shovels and bulldozers). Skepticism regarding this assumption, however, has been forthcoming. Yi-Fu Tuan says in "Discrepancies Between Environmental Attitude and Behavior: Examples from Europe and China":

> We may *believe* that a world-view which puts nature in subservience to man will lead to the exploitation of nature by man; and one that regards man as simply a component in nature will entail a modest view of his rights and capabilities, and so lead to the establishment of a harmonious relationship between man and his natural environment. But is this correct?[39]

Yi-Fu Tuan thinks not. The evidence from Chinese experience that he cites, however, is ambiguous, while the evidence from European experience that he cites misses an important point that we earlier made about the origins of Western environmental attitudes and values.

According to Tuan, traditional Chinese attitudes toward nature shaped by Taoism and Buddhism are supposed to have been "quiescent" and "adaptive." But, he points out, China's ancient forests were seriously overcut, suggesting that the traditional Chinese were no more concerned about living in harmony with the natural Tao (or Way of nature) or about respecting the Buddhahood of plants and animals than were their European counterparts. On the other hand, Tuan reports that China's first railway was decommissioned because it was believed to have been laid out contrary to the principles of *feng shui*—the art of siting human works in accordance with the flow of rivers, the direction of prevailing winds, and the contours of land forms—thus suggesting that the Chinese *were* in fact more concerned about living in harmony with nature than were their European counterparts. One can hardly imagine a European or American railway being pulled up solely because it was incompatible with principles of environmental aesthetics. Generally speaking, among the Chinese before Westernization, the facts that Yi-Fu Tuan presents indicate as many congruences as discrepancies between the traditional Taoist and Buddhist attitudes toward nature and Chinese environmental behavior.

Concerning European experience, we would expect that the ancient Greeks and Romans—who deified nature—would not have trashed the environment, if they really believed what they said they did *and* if human actions are determined by human belief. But Tuan marshals examples and cases in point of large-scale transformations, imposed, with serious ecological consequences, on the Mediterranean environment by the Greeks and Romans of classical antiquity. He concludes this part of his discussion with the remark that "against this background of the vast transformations of nature in the pagan world, the inroads made in the early centuries of the Christian era were relatively modest."[40]

Our discussion in the second section of this chapter, however, should explain the environmental impact of "pagan" Greek and Roman civilization consistently with the general thesis that worldview substantially affects behavior. The Greeks and Romans of classical antiquity lived in an age of increasing religious skepticism. By the mid-fifth century B.C., materio-mechanistic, dualistic, and humanistic philosophy had undercut and replaced the earlier sincere paganism of the ancient Greeks. The same religious skepticism eventually spread to the ancient Romans, who habitually followed Greek intellectual fashions. In the absence of religious restraint, the ancients exploited, despoiled, and defiled the natural (but no longer sacred) world.

Nevertheless, a simple deterministic model will not suffice with respect to this question: Do cultural attitudes and values really affect the collective behavior of a culture? At the one extreme, it seems incredible to think that *all* our conceptualizations, our representations of the nature of nature, are, as it were, mere entertainment, a sort of Muzak for the mind, while our actions proceed in some blind way from instinctive or genetically programmed sources. After all, our picture of nature defines our theater of action. It defines both the possibilities and the limitations that circumscribe human endeavor. We attempt to do only what we think is possible, while we leave alone what we think is not. Moreover, what we believe human nature to be, and what we take to be our proper place and role in the natural world, represents an ideal that, consciously or not, we strive to realize. At the other extreme, the facts of history and everyday experience do not support any simple cause-and-effect relationship between a given conceptual and valuational set and how people actually behave. Notoriously, we often act in ways that conflict with our sincere beliefs, especially our moral beliefs, and with our values.

Here is our suggestion for understanding the relationship between human environmental attitudes and values, on the one hand, and actual human behavior in respect to nature, on the other. Inevitably, human beings must consume other living things and modify the natural environment. Representations of the order of nature and the proper relationship of people to that order may have either a tempering, restraining effect on our manipulative and exploitative tendencies or an accelerating, exacerbating effect. They also give form and direction to these inherently human drives and thus provide different cultures with their distinctive styles of doing things. It appears, further, that in the case of the predominant European mentality, shaped both by Judeo-Christian and by Greco-Roman images of nature and man, the effect was to accelerate the inherent human disposition to consume "resources" and modify surroundings. A kind of "takeoff" or (to mix metaphors) "quantum leap" occurred, and Western European civilization was propelled—for better or worse—into its industrial, technological stage, with a proportional increase in ecological and environmental distress. The decisive ingredient, the sine qua non, may have been the particulars of the European worldview.[41]

If the predominant traditional Chinese view of nature and man has been characterized by Yi-Fu Tuan and others as quiescent and adaptive, the American Indian view of the world has been characterized as in essence "ecological"—for example, by Stewart Udall in *The Quiet Crisis*. The general American Indian worldview (at least the one central part of it to which we have called attention) deflected the inertia of day-to-day, year-to-year subsistence in a way that resulted, on the average, in conservation. Pre-Columbian American Indian conservation of resources may have been a *consciously* posited goal. But probably it was not. Probably conservation was neither a personal ideal nor a tribal policy because the "wise use" of "natural resources" would, ironically, appear to be inconsistent with the spiritual and personal attributes that the Indians regarded as belonging to nature and natural things. So-called natural resources are represented by most conservationists, whose philosophy was shaped by Gifford Pinchot, the nation's first chief forester, as only commodities, subject to scarcity, and therefore in need of prudent "development" and "management." The American Indian posture toward nature was, we suggest, more moral or ethical. Animals, plants, and minerals were treated as persons, and conceived to be coequal members of a natural social order.

Our cautious claim that the American Indian worldview supported and included a distinctly ethical attitude toward nature and the myriad variety of natural entities is based on the following basic points. The American Indians, on the whole, viewed the natural world as enspirited. Natural beings therefore felt, perceived, deliberated, and responded voluntarily as persons. Persons are members of a social order (that is, part of the operational concept of *person* is the capacity for social interaction). Social interaction is limited by (culturally variable) behavioral restraints—rules of conduct—which we call, in sum, good manners, morals, and ethics. Thus, as N. Scott Momaday maintains: "Very old in the Native American world view is the conviction that the earth is vital, that there is a spiritual dimension to it, a dimension in which man rightly exists. It follows logically that there are ethical imperatives in this matter."[42] The American Indians, more particularly, lived in accordance with an "ecological conscience" that was structurally similar to Aldo Leopold's "land ethic."

Examples of wastage—buffalo rotting on the plains under high cliffs or beaver all but trapped out during the fur trade—are supposed to deliver the coup de grace to all romantic illusions of the American Indian's reverence for nature. But examples of murder and war also abound in European history. Must we conclude therefrom that Europeans were altogether without a humanistic ethic of any sort?[43] Hardly. What confounds such facile arguments is a useful understanding of the function of ethics in human affairs.

As philosophers point out, ethics bear a normative relation to behavior. They do not describe how people actually behave. Rather, they set out how people *ought* to behave. People remain free to act either in accordance with a given ethic or not. The fact that on some occasions some do not scarcely proves that, in a given culture, ethical norms do not exist, or that ethics are not on the whole influential and effective behavioral restraints.

The familiar Christian ethic, with its emphasis on the dignity and intrinsic value of human beings, has long been a very significant element of Western culture, and has exerted a decisive influence within European and Euro-American civilization. Certainly, it has inspired noble and even heroic deeds both by individuals and by whole societies. The documented existence and influence of the Christian ethic are not in the least diminished by monstrous crimes on the part of individual Europeans. Nor do shameful episodes of national depravity, like the Spanish Inquisition, and genocide, as in Nazi Germany, refute the assertion that a human-centered ethic has palpably affected average behavior among members of the European culture and substantially shaped the character of Western civilization.

By parity of reasoning, examples of occasional destruction of nature on the pre-Columbian American continent and even the extirpation of species, especially during periods of enormous cultural stress, as in the fur trade era, do not, by themselves, refute the assertion that American Indians lived not only by a tribal ethic but by a land ethic as well. The overall and usual effect of such an ethic was to establish a greater harmony between the aboriginal American peoples and their environment than that enjoyed by their Euro-American successors.

We are living today in a very troubling time, but also a time of great opportunity. The modern mechanistic worldview and its technological expression are collapsing. A new, more organic ecological worldview and a corresponding technological esprit are beginning to take shape. But how can we translate this essentially scientific realization and its techno-social analogue into terms easily grasped by ordinary people so that we may all begin to see ourselves as a part of nature and as dependent on it for our sustenance? Only then can we hope to evolve a sustainable society.

The Indians were hardly evolutionary ecologists, but their outlook on nature was, albeit expressed in the imagery of myth, remarkably similar to the concept of nature emerging from contemporary biology. They saw themselves as plain members and citizens of their respective biotic communities, humbly and dependently participating in the local economy of nature. Hence one way to help popularize the emerging new ecological worldview and its associated life-style would be to turn for help to the indigenous wisdom of the North American continent. American Indian mythology could put imaginative flesh and blood on the dry skeleton of the abstract environmental sciences.

American Indian thought remains an untapped intellectual resource for all contemporary Americans. Euro-Americans cannot undo the past injustices that our forebears inflicted on American Indians. What we can do, however, is to recognize and fully incorporate the cognitive cultural achievements evolved in this hemisphere. So doing would engender respect and honor for the peoples who created them and for their contemporary custodians.

Some may say that "mining" the so-far "untapped" intellectual "resource" represented by traditional American Indian cognitive cultures would only perpetuate the history of exploitation of Native Americans by Euro-Americans.[44] After appropriating Indian lands, now we propose to add insult to injury by appropriating Indian ideas. We disagree. Things of the mind are not diminished when they are shared. Teachers do not diminish their knowledge by sharing it with students. Quite the contrary. Similarly, American Indian thought could only be enlarged and enriched should it become a principal tributary to the mainstream of contemporary North American culture and civilization. And, vice versa, North American culture and civilization could at last become something more than an extension of its European matrix should it mix and merge with the rich legacy of its native peoples.

Notes

1. Frank G. Speck, "Aboriginal Conservators," *Bird Lore* [now *Audubon*] 40 (1938): 259–60 (Speck's emphasis).

2. Richard Nelson, *Make Prayers to the Raven* (Chicago: University of Chicago Press, 1983).

3. Calvin Martin, *Keepers of the Game: Indian-American Relationships and the Fur Trade* (Berkeley and Los Angeles: University of California Press, 1978).

4. The allusion is to Paul Shepard, *The Tender Carnivore and the Sacred Game* (New York: Scribner's, 1973).

5. Gary Snyder, *The Practice of the Wild* (San Francisco: North Point Press, 1990).

6. Joseph E. Brown, "Modes of Contemplation Through Action: North American Indians," *Main Currents in Modern Thought* 30 (1973–74): 60.

7. Calvin Martin, *Keepers of the Game*, p. 186.

8. Quoted in W. Vernon Kinietz, *Indians of the Western Great Lakes, 1615– 1760* (Ann Arbor: University of Michigan Press, 1965), p. 115.

9. John G. Neihardt, *Black Elk Speaks: Being the Life Story of a Holy Man of the Oglala Sioux* (New York: William Morrow, 1932). For its authenticity, see Raymond J. DeMallie, *The Sixth Grandfather: Black Elk's Teachings Given to John G. Neihardt* (Lincoln: University of Nebraska Press, 1984).

10. For a more complete discussion of the methodological problem of reconstructing American Indian worldviews, see J. Baird Callicott, "American Indian Land Wisdom?: Sorting Out the Issues," *Journal of Forest History* 33 (1989): 35– 42.

11. H. Paul Santmire, "Historical Dimensions of the American Crisis," reprinted from *Dialog* (Summer 1970) in *Western Man and Environmental Ethics*, ed. Ian G. Barbour (Menlo Park, Calif.: Addison-Wesley, 1973), pp. 70–71.

12. Richard Erdoes, *Lame Deer: Seeker of Visions* (New York: Simon and Schuster, 1976), pp. 108–9.

13. Ibid., p. 101.

14. Ibid., p. 124.

15. Ibid., pp. 102–3.

16. Neihardt, *Black Elk Speaks*, p. 3.

17. Ibid., p. 6.

18. Ibid., p. 7.

19. N. Scott Momaday, "A First American Views His Land," *National Geographic* 149 (1976): 14.

20. Ruth M. Underhill, *Red Man's Religion: Beliefs and Practices of the Indians North of Mexico* (Chicago: University of Chicago Press, 1965), p. 40.

21. Diamond Jenness, *The Ojibwa Indians of Parry Island, Their Social and Religious Life*, Canadian Department of Mines Bulletin no. 78, Museum of Canada Anthropological Series no. 17 (Ottawa, 1935), pp. 20–21.

22. A. Irving Hallowell, "Ojibwa Ontology, Behavior, and World View," *Culture in History: Essays in Honor of Paul Radin*, ed. S. Diamond (New York: Columbia University Press, 1960), p. 26.

23. Kinietz, *Indians of the Western Great Lakes*, p. 126.

24. Hallowell, "Ojibwa Ontology," p. 19.

25. Ibid., p. 41.

26. See Richard M. Dorson, *Bloodstoppers and Bearwalkers: Folk Traditions of the Upper Peninsula* (Cambridge, Mass.: Harvard University Press, 1952).

27. Hallowell, "Ojibwa Ontology," p. 32.

28. Ibid., p. 35.

29. Ibid., p. 47 (emphasis added).

30. Brown, "Modes of Contemplation," p. 64.

31. Aldo Leopold, *A Sand County Almanac: With Essays on Conservation from Round River* (New York: Ballantine Books, 1966), p. 239.

32. Ibid., pp. 116–17.

33. Ibid., p. 193.

34. This and all subsequent quotations from this story are taken from Thomas W. Overholt and J. Baird Callicott, *Clothed-in-Fur and Other Tales: An Introduction to an Ojibwa World View* (Washington, D.C.: University Press of America, 1982), pp. 74–75.

35. For a full discussion, see Marshall Sahlins, *Stone Age Economics* (Chicago: Aldine Atherton, 1972).

36. Ian McHarg, "Values, Process, Form," from *The Fitness of Man's Environment* (Washington, D.C.: Smithsonian Institution Press, 1968), reprinted in Robert Disch, ed., *The Ecological Conscience* (Englewood Cliffs, N.J.: Prentice-Hall, 1970), p. 25.

37. Ibid., p. 98.

38. Leopold, *Sand County*, pp. 263–64.

39. Yi-Fu Tuan, "Discrepancies Between Environmental Attitude and Behavior," in *Ecology and Religion in History*, eds. D. Spring and I. Spring (New York: Harper and Row, 1947), p. 92.

40. Ibid., p. 98.

41. For a full discussion, see J. Baird Callicott and Roger T. Ames, "Epilogue: On the Relation of Idea and Action" in J. B. Callicott and R. T. Ames, eds., *Nature in Asian Traditions of Thought* (Albany: State University of New York Press, 1989), pp. 279–89.

42. Momaday, "First American Views," p. 18.

43. The most scurrilous example of this sort of argument with which we are acquainted is Daniel A. Guthrie's "Primitive Man's Relationship to Nature," *BioScience* 21 (July 1971): 721–23. In addition to rotting buffalo, Guthrie cites alleged extirpation of Pleistocene megafauna by Paleo-Indians, ca. 10,000 B.P. (as if that were relevant), and his cheapest shot of all, "the litter of bottles and junked cars to be found on Indian reservations today."

44. A similar complaint about Western intellectual colonialism of Asian traditions of thought has been registered by Gerald James Larson, " 'Conceptual Resources' in South Asia for 'Environmental Ethics' " in Callicott and Ames, *Nature in Asian Traditions of Thought*, pp. 267–77.

4

Pre-Columbian and Modern Philosophical Perspectives in Latin America

Jorge Valadez

Nothing in the experience of the much-traveled soldiers of Hernán Cortés's invading army could have prepared them for what they saw when they marched into Tenochtitlán, the ancient site of present-day Mexico City, in 1519. They encountered great buildings and ceremonial centers, vast and beautiful floating gardens, splendid murals, impressive sculptures and other works of art, and large and well-organized markets. The Spaniards were witnessing the splendors of one of the greatest civilizations in history. Their amazement was magnified by the fact that this civilization was so utterly foreign and unexpected. The Spaniards were denizens of the Old World, where diverse cultures had interacted and influenced one another for thousands of years. But here was a civilization that had evolved in isolation from the rest of the world and yet was highly advanced in astronomy and agriculture, had created architectural wonders, practiced sophisticated types of surgery, and developed complex and unique systems of religious belief and social organization.

This unprecedented and extraordinary encounter of two diverse cultures was destined to have catastrophic consequences for the people of the Americas. In less than two centuries diseases like smallpox and diphtheria, which the inhabitants of the New World had no defenses against because of their genetic isolation, decimated approximately two-thirds of the population of the Americas. In Mesoamerica (a region covering the southern two-thirds of Mexico and Guatemala, El Salvador,

Belize, and certain areas of Nicaragua, Honduras, and Costa Rica), tens of millions of native people died either in battles with the technologically superior invading army or, more commonly, as the result of infection with these new diseases. The Spaniards eventually conquered the Aztec capital, Tenochtitlán, plundered it for its gold and silver (melting many pieces of jewelry and religious figurines into gold bullion), and enslaved many of its inhabitants.

But there was another kind of destruction that the Spaniards were to wreak on the Aztecs and other people of Mesoamerica—the almost wholesale destruction of their culture. The social, religious, and political organization of early Mesoamerican society—including the structure of its large urban centers, forms of religious ritual, cultural customs, artistic styles, philosophy of education, and architectural forms—were all based on a religious and cosmological perspective that was completely foreign and incomprehensible to the Europeans.

The worldview of the Spaniards was determined by their Christian beliefs, and hence they were at once amazed and repulsed by what they saw: human sacrifices, rituals involving bloodletting, adoration of pagan gods, cannibalism, sculptures of what they considered monstrous creatures, and so on. According to their Christian metaphysical perspective there was a clear and straightforward way to categorize these practices; they were to be considered evil and the work of the Devil. One of the most famous chroniclers of the native culture, the Spanish Franciscan priest Bernardino de Sahagun, firmly believed that the existence of Aztec religious beliefs and customs was an ingenious and elaborate manifestation of the power of Satan's influence. Thus, the religious practices of the Aztecs not only had no claim to cultural legitimacy, they had to be stopped at whatever cost. Bolstered by such ethical and cultural chauvinism, the Spaniards undertook what is perhaps the most extensive and systematic (and certainly the most large-scale) destruction of a civilization in the world's history. In that the civilizations of Mesoamerica were essentially grounded in a radically different religious and cosmological vision, this conquest was nothing less than an attempt at metaphysical annihilation, that is, an attempt to destroy the worldviews of the native people. Nevertheless, despite the efforts of the Spaniards to eradicate the cosmological roots of these cultures, we shall see that some important features of the ancient worldviews can still be found in some contemporary Mesoamerican cultures.

Given their imperialistic orientations and the closed nature of their religious perspective, it was perhaps inevitable that the Spaniards would fail so completely to understand the Aztec culture and the other cultures of ancient Mesoamerica. In fact, it is only in the latter half of the twentieth century that it has been possible, through a variety of archaeological sources and different kinds of interpretive techniques, to understand the religious and metaphysical worldview of early Mesoamerican cultures.[1]

This essay will present a systematic exposition of some of the central concepts and principles of the early Mesoamerican cosmological perspectives, concentrating on the Aztec and Mayan cultures.[2] An analysis of these two cultures will provide us with a fairly good understanding of the general structure of the cosmological vision that predominated in ancient Mesoamerica. I will then briefly discuss the philosophical worldview of the ancient South American culture of the Incas, and compare it to the Aztec and Mayan worldviews. In addition, I will draw contrasts and comparisons between the Mesoamerican metaphysical perspectives and some perspectives that have been of predominant importance in the Western philosophical tradition. These comparisons will help us to appreciate more fully the uniqueness and depth of the ancient Mesoamerican worldviews and will further our understanding of some of the Western European philosophical perspectives by placing them within a wider global cultural context.

Precolonial Latin American Cosmologies

Cultures throughout history have developed a variety of answers to certain fundamental and perennial questions: What place do human beings have in the universe? What is the structure of the cosmos? How can we explain or account for the origin of the world? The cultures of Mesoamerica developed complex and fascinating answers to such questions. In order to provide a general understanding of how they approached these questions, we will look first at some central metaphysical principles common to the Mayan and Aztec cosmologies, and then examine the structure of each of these worldviews in more detail.

One of the most striking features of the Mesoamerican metaphysical perspective was the remarkable degree to which it interconnected or integrated different aspects or components of reality. Four different kinds of integration characterized its cosmology: (1) the internal structural interconnection of the different components of the universe, (2) the integration of fundamental dualities that were perceived as complementary instead of oppositional, (3) the holistic integration of astronomical science and religious beliefs, and, most important, (4) the integration of everyday life with the cycles and rhythms of the cosmos through the practice of rituals that were perceived as necessary for sustaining the very existence of the universe. To arrive at a unified view of the Mesoamerican metaphysical perspective, we must to understand each of these four aspects of Mesoamerican cosmology. This will also help us to situate such practices as human sacrifice and ritual bloodletting in their proper cultural context.

The Interactive Universe

The people of Mesoamerica believed that the universe consisted of three different planes or levels: a celestial plane, a terrestrial plane, and an underworld plane. There were further divisions within the celestial and underworld levels. (The Aztecs, for example, believed that there were thirteen celestial levels and nine underworld levels.) There was also a constant interaction of supernatural forces or powers among these levels, which was made possible by the existence of spiral-shaped channels called *mallinalis*. These supernatural forces were thought to enter the terrestrial level through caves, sunlight, fire, and animals.[3] Some of the rituals of the Mesoamerican cultures were designed to tap and redirect or harness these supernatural cosmic forces. Thus their universe was not a static universe, but rather an interactive one, with three dynamic levels of reality.

Time itself also existed at different planes or levels: human or terrestrial time; the time of myth; and the transcendent time in which the gods dwelled. Terrestrial time originated in the interaction of cosmic forces from the celestial and underworld levels converging at the terrestrial level. In other words, human time originated in the interaction of forces from two distinct spatial planes.

Myth time existed prior to terrestrial time, and in it the actions of the gods, as they were depicted in their myths, took place. For example, in one of the Mayan myths about death, two heroic twin brothers descend to the underworld to challenge the Lords of Death. After a long series of trials and ordeals, the brothers defeat the Lords of the Underworld and emerge victorious. This myth is an expression of the Mayan belief that death represents a challenge which, through courage and fortitude, can be overcome. It was also during this myth time, which still progresses and has not ceased to be, that many supernatural beings who exert cyclical influences on humans at the terrestrial level were born or created.

In transcendent time lived the most powerful gods at the apex of the divine hierarchy who created and grounded the universe. (Apparently these powerful creator gods existed in two temporal dimensions, namely, mythic and transcendent time.) The gods and supernatural beings that inhabited transcendent time, like those that lived in mythic time, had periodic or cyclical influences on the events and beings that existed in terrestrial time.[4] The early Mesoamerican calendars marked the occasions during the year when these periodic influences occurred.

Thus, in the Mesoamerican worldview, space and time were not understood as existing independently of one another; instead, they formed a complex, unified whole. (When we analyze the cosmology of the Aztecs we will see more clearly the centrality of the notion that space/time is a unified whole.) For the ancient Mesoamericans, the world was replete with cosmic forces resulting from the intersection of the various spatial and temporal levels that comprised the universe.

In addition, their universe did not consist of isolated, discrete entities; rather, it consisted of entities, events, and forces that were in constant interaction with one another and that existed in different spaciotemporal planes. Absolute space, conceived as an empty vacuum in which entities exist and events take place, and absolute time, understood as an infinite linear progression of moments, had no reality in the Mesoamerican cosmological perspective. For the people of early Mesoamerica, space and time constituted the very fabric of existence; that is, they affected, shaped, and determined everything that exists. This is why Mesoamerican cultures were so preoccupied with developing accurate calendars and astronomical techniques for measuring time, determining the spatial location of celestial bodies, and anticipating the occurrence of astronomical events. The capacity to measure and predict the solar, lunar, planetary, and astral cycles enabled them to understand the various complex cosmic forces that they believed affected human events at the terrestrial level. By knowing the particular times at which certain cosmic forces affected events at the human level, they tried to mediate and channel these forces through rituals. From such observations we can appreciate the great extent to which the different components of the Mesoamerican universe were interrelated and interconnected with one another.

Complementary Dualities

The second kind of integration in Mesoamerican cosmology concerns the complementary nature of fundamental dualities. Dualities such as life/death, celestial world/underworld, male/female, night/day, and so forth were of central importance in the Mesoamerican worldview. These dualities were not conceived as being oppositional in nature; instead, they were understood as being different and necessary aspects of reality. One of the clearest examples of this type of nonoppositional duality was the supreme dual god of the Aztecs, Ometeotl. This supreme deity, who was the ultimate originator of all that exists, had a dual male and female nature. Ometeotl was sometimes called Tonacatecuhtli-Tonacacihuatl, which means "lord and lady of our maintenance," and often he/she was referred to as "our mother, our father."[5] The dual nature of Ometeotl enabled him/her to beget other beings and the universe from his/her own essence. It is clear that the Aztecs wanted to incorporate both the male and the female principle within a single supreme entity and that they saw no contradiction in a deity who was simultaneously male and female.

It is interesting and instructive to compare the conception of a male/female dual god with the monotheistic God of the Judeo-Christian tradition. Traditionally, the Christian god has been characterized primarily as having male qualities and has been referred to in explicitly male terms. For example, the first two substantive terms in the expression "the father, the son, and the holy ghost" refer to God in terms that are unequivocally male, while the third substantive term, "the holy ghost," has traditionally never been spoken of in female terms. And historically, rarely if ever have we heard the Christian God referred to by the female pronoun "she" or by the phrase "holy mother." He is usually characterized by predominantly male qualities that emphasized his power and authority instead of, say, his nurturance and unconditional acceptance. Some contemporary theologians have argued that these gender-specific characterizations of the Christian God deny women full spiritual participation in the Christian religious tradition. In any case, we can see that the Aztec conceptualization of the supreme deity Ometeotl incorporates the two aspects of the male/female duality into a single divine entity.

We find another case of the Mesoamerican tendency to think in terms of nonoppositional dualities in the Mayan understanding of the life/death duality. From the Mayan perspective, death, whether of humans or of plants, was an integral part of a never-ending life cycle of birth, death, and regeneration. Death was not seen as the discontinuity of life, but rather as a necessary phase in the regeneration of life. Upon death, humans went to the underworld of Xibalba, where they experienced various ordeals and struggles with the supernatural entities of the underworld. Then they would be reborn and ascend to the celestial or terrestrial level, where they might become a part of a heavenly body, an ancestral spiritual entity, or a maize plant.[8] Through this transformation and process of rebirth, individuals would be integrated into one of the eternal life cycles of the universe. In similar fashion, the death of plant life in the seasonal and agricultural cycles was merely one phase in the recurring pattern of sowing, sprouting, dying, and regenerating. One of the central ideas in the Mayan cosmology was that the earth was a living entity that was continually in the process of regeneration, and that the death of plant life was an integral part of this process.

In short, death was not seen as the negation, or as the polar opposite, of life. Rather, death was a process that either (1) made possible the continuation of the life process or (2) allowed for the integration of the life of the individual into the eternal cosmic cycles. In the plant world, the death of plants enabled new vegetation to sprout and develop; that is, death was an integral part of the process of regeneration. In the human realm, death was, as we have seen, a process in which the individual would eventually become a part of the astral or earthly cycles of the universe. In contrast to some Western views on death, in which the soul of the individual continues to exist in an otherworldly spiritual realm, in the early Mesoamerican cosmology the spirits of the dead return to become a part of the world we can see, touch, and feel. That is, they became part of the world of everyday experience.

A Scientific-Religious Worldview

The third kind of structural integration that characterizes the Meso-american cosmology concerns the intimate linkage between Mesoamerican scientific and religious perspectives. Astronomy was by far the most fully developed science of the cultures of Mesoamerica. The accuracy of their calendars equaled or surpassed those of other cultures in the world at that time, and their astronomical observations were as extensive and accurate as those of any other civilization. Insofar as they possessed a scientific, empirically validated form of knowledge, it was their astronomy. This was the knowledge that allowed them to correctly predict celestial events, carry out extensive and accurate calendrical computations (some of which involved dates many millions of years into the future), and measure agricultural cycles. But their astronomical science was also closely interconnected with their religious ideas and beliefs, especially the fundamentally important concept of the renewal or regeneration of agricultural and human life cycles. They believed that the influences of the supernatural forces and beings that permeated the earth and supported these life cycles could be tracked and predicted by their calendars. In addition, they maintained that through religious rituals they could harness and successfully mediate these cosmic forces.

Thus, the intense interest of the people of ancient Mesoamerica in astronomical observation and the measurement of time was not motivated merely by the desire to acquire knowledge for its own sake; the continuation of the life cycles of the universe depended on the performance of the appropriate religious rituals at specific points in time. Their scientifically validated observations were united with their fundamental religious ideas and with the rituals they believed were crucial for the continued existence of the cosmos. This unification of their two most basic kinds of knowledge gave rise to a holistic conceptual unity in their thinking that is difficult for us to understand and appreciate. The reason this conceptual integration is so foreign to us is that there is a fundamental fragmentation in modern thought between scientific knowledge and religious belief.

Science tells us that reality consists of physical entities and forces that exist independently of human consciousness and that are utterly indifferent to the human search for meaning and cosmic significance. According to the contemporary scientific worldview, everything that occurs in the universe is explainable in terms of universal physical laws, not in terms of the acts of a divine will. Because according to this worldview it is physics, and not the will of God, that explains why events occur, modern scientific knowledge conflicts with the age-old reliance on a supernatural, spiritual being to explain what happens in the universe. And if, as the modern scientific perspective tells us, reality consists exclusively of impersonal physical forces and entities governed by universal laws, where in such a universe can we find a basis for human spiritual meaning and significance? This scientific perspective has also deeply influenced non-religious, philosophical attempts to find a basis for the meaning of human existence. For the past several centuries (a period coinciding with the emergence of modern science and the decline of the religious worldview), Western philosophers have wrestled with questions concerning the meaning of life. Here again the problem has been to find a basis for grounding existential significance and human values in an indifferent, impersonal universe consisting solely of objective physical forces and entities. In short, a basic dilemma has arisen in modern Western thought as a result of the scientific view of the universe as an objectively existing physical realm in which there is no room for the principles of human subjective experience as expressed in religious and philosophic thought. By contrast, in the Mesoamerican cosmological view there was no conflict between science and religion; on the contrary, Mesoamerican scientific and religious worldviews complemented and reinforced one another.

Cosmic Responsibility

We have already alluded to the fourth kind of integration characteristic of the Mesoamerican metaphysical perspective. It concerns the belief that religious rituals were of central importance for maintaining the existence of the cosmos. Perhaps the clearest expression of this belief can be found in the Aztec Legend of the Four Suns. According to this legend, there have been four ages that have been dominated by four different suns. Each of these ages—which correspond to each of the four directions, east, south, west, and north—had ended in a catastrophic manner with the destruction of the human race and the world. The Aztecs believed that they lived in the age of the Fifth Sun, which was created at Tenochtitlán, the ancient site of Mexico City, as the result of the self-sacrifice of the gods Nanahuatzin and Tecuciztecatl. After the destruction of the Fourth Sun, all was darkness except for the divine hearth (the *teotexcalli*), where the gods gathered to create the new sun that would usher in the new age. The gods ordered Tecuciztecatl to leap into the great fire, but he was unable to do so out of fear. After Tecuciztecatl attempted and failed four times to leap into the fire, the gods ordered Nanahuatzin to sacrifice himself in the giant blaze. Nanahuatzin braced himself, closed his eyes, and threw himself in. Upon seeing this, Tecuciztecatl finally gained enough courage to jump into the fire. As the result of his courage and sacrifice, Nanahuatzin reemerges from the east as the new, blazing red sun.[7]

The Legend of the Suns expresses some central ideas of the Aztec cosmology. One of these is the centrality of cataclysmic change in the evolution of the universe. Each of the previous four ages had been destroyed by sudden, catastrophic disasters and the present age was also susceptible to an abrupt, massive destruction. The Aztec universe was thus highly unstable and vulnerable to extinction. Another prominent theme in this myth is that of sacrifice. The Aztecs believed that the present age began with a sacrifice by the gods, and that in order to prevent this age from ending they had continually to provide the sun with life-sustaining blood and with the energy concentrated in certain parts of the body of sacrificial victims. This is the primary explanation for the religious rituals involving human sacrifice.

The need for sacrificial victims demanded the continued capture of enemy warriors and the creation of a warrior class to satisfy this need. This sense of cosmic responsibility reinforced certain authoritarian orientations in Aztec culture. Theirs was a society that did not tolerate a great deal of individual freedom or challenges to the established social order.

Human actions had great significance in the cosmology of the Aztecs, because the very existence of the universe depended on the proper performance of religious rituals, including human sacrifice. Without a doubt, most of us would find the practice of human sacrifice, and the extent to which it was practiced by the Aztecs, to be morally objectionable and repugnant in the extreme. Nevertheless, this practice was based on a religious doctrine that was of central importance in the Aztec cosmological perspective. Within their worldview, human sacrifice was not only justified, it was absolutely essential. Indeed, the profound sense of cosmic responsibility that was so central to the Aztec worldview was a double-edged sword. It provided them with an unquestioned faith in their relevance and importance as a people, but it also burdened them with the heavy obligation of maintaining the existence of the cosmos. It can truly be said that the Aztecs elaborated a highly imaginative, though severe, answer to the question concerning the role and relevance of human existence in the universe.

The Mayan World

One way to begin a description of the world of the Maya is by discussing the sacred nature of Mayan kings. They were more than just high personages at the top of the social and political hierarchy of Mayan society. Kings were considered the *axis mundi* of the Mayan world; that is, they were regarded as living centers of divine powers and as links between the gods and humans. Their function as mediators between the worlds of the sacred and the mundane was most clearly expressed in a religious ritual that in Mayan society was closely associated with kingship: bloodletting. This practice involved the piercing and bleeding of various parts of the body during rituals. This ritualistic form was practiced on important occasions such as marriage ceremonies, political events, crucial points of transition in the calendar, and so on. As we shall see, through this religious ritual Mayan kings would use their bodies as conduits for mediating between the world of the gods and the world of mortals. The purpose of this practice was to invoke the spiritual presence of gods and ancestors, to direct and reinforce their influence on worldly events, and to renew the existence of, and even create, deities.

Many cultures throughout the world have employed a variety of means for inducing altered states of consciousness in which contact is made with supernatural beings, divine forces, or alternative realities. The Huichol people of northwestern Mexico use the peyote cactus to induce religious visions, while the Zapotecs in Oaxaca use hallucinogenic mushrooms for similar purposes. Buddhists and Hindus in India use fasting and meditation to attain higher states of awareness. The Mayan kings used a combination of fasting and bloodletting in order to attain such states of consciousness and to call forth the gods into the dimension of human space and time. It is a medical fact that the loss of blood can induce altered states of awareness, including hallucinations. The practice of fasting, which in itself can also lead to such states, probably reinforced the hallucinatory effect of the bloodletting.

The Mayan kings, sometimes accompanied by their wives, would usually perform the bloodletting ritual in an elaborate public ceremony. Typically, the king might use a stingray spine or a lancet made of obsidian (a hard volcanic rock) to lacerate his penis while the wife punctured her tongue with a thorned rope. They would let the blood soak onto a special piece of sacrificial paper made from bark and would then burn the blood-saturated paper. Then they gazed into the dark smoke produced by the burning paper in order to see the form of a deity or of one of their ancestors take shape. We can easily see that the preparatory fast combined with the effects of the loss of blood would have a powerful effect on what they experienced at that moment. During this important religious ceremony the Mayan kings would fulfill their function as spiritual intermediaries between the sacred and the human realms.[8]

As mentioned earlier, the purpose of the bloodletting ritual was to bring the gods and ancestors into being in the dimension of human space and time. By doing this the Mayan kings believed that they would reinforce or strengthen the existence of the gods and would show that they stood in the sacred relationship of reciprocity with their gods. The concept of reciprocity is important for understanding the relationship between people and gods in the Mayan world. The Mayan gods did not exist independently of humans; they relied on the spiritual sustenance that they received from the religious rituals of the people. Because the gods had struggled and sacrificed to create the world, it was incumbent upon humans to nourish and sustain the gods through the sacrificial ritual of bloodletting. By shedding their blood the Mayan kinds would show their willingness to reciprocate the sacrifice that the gods had endured to bring the world into existence.

The bloodletting rituals that the gods themselves engaged in are further illustrations of the relation of reciprocity holding between the gods and mortal beings. The following scene of divine bloodletting is depicted on an intricately carved Mayan pot.

The Sun God, the deity having the vision, sits in the center of the scene holding in each arm a Vision Serpent; they fold out from him as mirrored opposites, meeting head to head on the other side of the pot. The serpent in the God's right arm spits out the sun; its tail is night. . . . The serpent on the left belches forth his realized vision—the watery deep of the Underworld . . . The world of the day is contrasted with the watery Underworld; they are the two opposite halves that make up the universe. The actor is a god; his sacrifice of blood creates a mirrored vision, and from that vision are created day and night, birds of the sky, the waters of the primordial sea in which the world floats, the plants of the earth, death, and sacrifice. The god's bloodletting vision is thus the whole cosmos.[9]

This scene suggests that the creation of the universe came about through a ritual sacrifice by the gods. Thus we can see that the bloodletting ritual was an expression of the mutual existential dependence that united gods and kings (and, by extension, all humans) in a fundamental cosmic bond. This cosmic bond was cemented by means of the kings' very life essence—their own human blood. Bloodletting was the ultimate expression of the Mayan loyalty to and faith in their gods.

Once again, it is instructive to compare the Mayan conception of the relationship between human beings and the gods with the conception of God in the Judeo-Christian tradition. The Christian God is typically characterized as all-powerful and existentially independent, that is, not dependent on any other entity (including human beings) for its existence. Even though both the Christian God and the Mayan gods are described as having a caring and loving relationship with humans, the existential dependence of the Mayan gods on people expresses a conception of the divine that is profoundly different from that of the Christian tradition. This mutual existential dependence and reciprocity constitute an indication of the great extent to which the Mayan people participated in the divine and offer another example of the high degree of holistic integration that characterized the metaphysical perspectives of the people of Mesoamerica. For the Maya the gods were beings whose existence could be reinforced and made tangible through the religious ritual of bloodletting.

The Ecological Culture of the Maya

The need to renew the existence of the gods through ritual bloodletting brings us to another central theme in Mayan thought, namely, the necessity of religious rituals for regenerating or renewing the earth. The Mayans had what we might call an ecological culture, that is, a culture whose basic metaphysical perspective reflected the idea of the cyclical regeneration of the earth. Their agricultural orientation was manifested in several ways. First, they were an agriculturally advanced culture: They built canal systems for crop irrigation, practiced slope-field and raised-field farming, and cultivated corn, squash, beans, cotton, cacao, chili peppers, and other crops. Second, they recognized that the cultivation of maize and other crops had made possible the development of the permanent communities where the temples and pyramids that were important to the evolution of their culture and religion were built. Third, their rituals and their dominant metaphors indicated that they were intimately in tune with the seasonal and agricultural cycles of their rich vegetative environment.

The predominance of the ecological orientation in the Mayan world can be seen in the rich symbolism of the "cosmic tree." The cosmic tree is a symbol, used by many cultures throughout the world, of the earth as a fertile, living totality. In the Mayan culture this tree represents the earth as a living entity capable of periodic regeneration. Thus, according to the traditions of the present-day Tzutujil Mayas, the earth (and all that it contains) is seen as a tree or a maize plant that periodically sprouts, blossoms, dies, and is regenerated.[10] The significance of this metaphor in which the world is seen as a biological unit is twofold: First, there is recognition of the fact that just as there is an interconnection between the different parts of a plant, so there is an interconnection between the different biological units of the earth; second, there is the conviction that just as plants need nurturance from the sun, the soil, and water in order to live, so there is corresponding need for the world to be nurtured and renewed in order for it to continue to exist. This renewal was achieved by religious rituals performed at specific times as determined by the temporal cycles that were measured by Mayan calendars.[11] It is interesting to note here that the Mayan view of the earth as a regenerating biological unit is remarkably similar to the modern-day "Gaia hypothesis," which states that the earth consists of many complex, interacting ecological systems. Some biologists and ecologists have argued that by adopting this view of the earth we will be more aware of the need to maintain and protect the earth's own ecological balance.

One of the implications of the Mayan view of the earth is that because nature does not belong to human beings, they do not have the right to do with it as they please. Nature is not something to be "mastered" and controlled for human purposes. In the Mayan perspective people do not stand against nature, but are rather an integral part of it. Humans should take care of nature and nurture it, because they depend on the earth for their nourishment and survival, and because, as biological entities that are born, reproduce, and die, humans are also part of the natural life cycles that permeate the earth. Even among the contemporary Maya of Guatemala there is still a deep sense of respect for the earth because of the belief that ultimately it belongs to the gods and not to mortal man. People are the caretakers, not the owners, of the earth. This accounts for the traditional belief among members of such communities that it is not correct to partition tracts of land and sell them. The earth should be nurtured and cultivated for the good of the whole community; it is not something to be bought and sold for profit. The ancient Maya believed that it was not possible to buy and sell the earth in that it did not belong to them in the first place. This belief is maintained, though perhaps to a lesser degree, by some contemporary Mayan communities.

By contrast, Western culture has elevated the individual's right to own private property into a fundamental human right. We see this "right" as so basic that we consider it more important than the right of an individual to have enough to eat or to have adequate shelter. Nevertheless, despite the importance in the Western tradition of the individual right to own private property, it seems plausible to say that, as far as basic individual human rights are concerned, the individual right to have adequate nourishment or shelter is more basic or primary than the individual right to own private property. But perhaps even more important, an analysis of the ecological orientation of the Maya reminds us that it is only recently that Western societies have realized that a fundamental change in our attitude toward nature is necessary to ensure our ecological survival. We have used and abused nature to such an extent—through air pollutants, the use of toxic chemicals, the production of nonbiodegradable materials, and so forth—that we have placed our own survival, and the survival of other people in the world, in jeopardy. Our view of our relationship to the earth is starting to change so that we are beginning to see the world as an integrated ecological system that may be deeply affected by our actions.

Preparing for Victory over Death

One of the central legends of the Maya relates the adventures of two Hero Twins, Hunahpu and Xbalanque, who outwitted the Lords of Death of the Underworld of Xibalba. According to the legend, the twins were highly skilled players of a Mayan ball game in which a rubber ball was passed through a ring in order to score points. Their constant play disturbed the Lords of the Underworld, who ordered them to come to Xibalba to play against them. The twins underwent many trials and ordeals in their confrontations with the Lords of Death, but by using their wits they eventually succeeded in overcoming all of the trials imposed by the Lords. For instance, in one of the trials the twins were given a flaming torch and two lit cigars and were told that they had to keep them lit throughout the night and return them unconsumed in the morning. Hunahpu and Xbalanque fooled the Lords of Death by attaching the brightly colored tail feathers of a macaw to the torch and some fireflies to the end of the cigars to give the appearance that they were still lit. In another test the twins were placed in the House of Jaguars, where many hungry jaguars lived. They managed to survive by throwing bones to the jaguars, who then fought for the bones among themselves and forgot about the twins.

At the end of the story the twins perform several tricks before the Lords, like setting a house on fire without destroying it and sacrificing a dog and then reviving it. One of the twins even sacrifices the other and is then able to bring him back to life. The Lords are so impressed with this that they plead with the twins to let them participate in this magical sacrifice. The twins allow the Lords to play the role of the victims in the apparently nonlethal, magical sacrifice. However, the twins really sacrifice the Lords and do not bring them back to life. The twins then warn the Xibalbans that unless they stop trying to harm humans on their journey through the underworld, they too will meet the same fate as their rulers. The victorious Hunahpu and Xbalanque finally leave the underworld of Xibalba and ascend into the sky, where one of them acquires the ownership of the sun and the other the ownership of the moon.[12]

The legend of the Hero Twins embodies the Mayan conception of death as a journey through the underworld, involving challenges that could be overcome through courage, intelligence, and fortitude. It is a myth that recognizes the natural human fear of facing the unknown, but nevertheless it encouraged the Mayan people to face death with bravery, even boldness. It portrayed death as a transitional phase between life at the terrestrial plane and an eternal life that began upon one's victorious emergence from the underworld. Just as the sacred sun descended into the underworld every night only to reemerge in blazing glory every morning, so could the human spirit triumph over death and become integrated into the eternal cycles of the cosmos.

The Aztec World

As we have observed, one of the central themes of Aztec cosmology was the belief in the inherent metaphysical instability of the universe. Their universe, which was subject to the divine whim of the gods, was susceptible to sudden and cataclysmic extinction. It is within the context of this belief in the instability of the cosmos that we should understand the centrality of human sacrifice in the Aztec world. Aztecs thought they could prevent the annihilation of their world by offering the gods human blood and the vital energies concentrated in certain parts of the body. By means of these ritual sacrifices they would (1) repay the gods some of the life energy the gods had expended in creating the world and (2) strengthen the gods, who were the metaphysical ground of the universe.

But there was another tradition in Aztec culture that provided an alternative to the dominant doctrine based on human sacrifice. In this tradition there was a systematic analysis of issues dealing with the nature of reality and ultimate truth. The Aztecs created centers of higher learning that were the most advanced and egalitarian in Mesoamerica. They developed theories of knowledge in which artistic creativity was regarded as the only true way of attaining insight into the nature of reality. In what follows, we will first discuss the theological-militaristic doctrines of the Aztec culture, and then we will examine the legacy of the Aztec philosophers.

For the Aztecs the human body was the locus of cosmic life forces. *Tonalli, teyolia,* and *ihiyotl* were some of the life forces that were concentrated in various parts of the body.

The head (especially in the hair and the fontanel area, the soft spot on an infant's skull) was filled with *tonalli,* an animating force or soul that provided vigor and the energy for growth and development. The heart received deposits of *teyolia* (what gives life to people), which provided emotion, memory, and knowledge to the human. This was the soul that could live and have influence after the body was dead. The liver received *ihiyotl,* which provided humans with bravery, desire, hatred, love, and happiness.[13]

These life forces could be acquired or transferred by different means. Thus people could acquire *tonalli* from the sun, which was one of the primary providers of this kind of life energy, by exposing themselves to its rays. And the *tonalli* of a community could be increased by collecting the decapitated heads of enemy warriors.

It is not difficult to see that the ritualistic importance of human sacrifice demanded a constant supply of sacrificial victims. Ritual sacrifices occurred at least once a month and more frequently on certain occasions. For example, for the dedication of the Great Temple in the Aztec capital of Tenochtitlán, Aztec priests working in shifts sacrificed between 10,000 and 80,000 people (the estimate varies according to different sources) during a four-day period. A mythology of war and sacrifice that had evolved in Aztec culture supported the practice of human sacrifice. Native documents historically credit the Aztec political figure Tlacaelel with originating the metaphysical-militaristic philosophy that sustained this practice.

In 1424 the young Aztec nation, led by King Itzcoatl, found itself besieged by the tyrannical Maxtla, leader of Azcapotzalco. Itzcoatl and his advisers had decided to humbly surrender to Maxtla, when Tlacaelel appealed to them to resist and fight instead. Tlacaelel led the Aztec warriors to victory over the forces of Maxtla and as a result gained great influence with King Itzcoatl. Under Tlacaelel's influence the Aztecs burned their own codices (books of pictures that they used to record important events) and rewrote their history. In this process of mythological revision, the patron god of the Aztecs, the war god Huitzilopochtli, was identified with the sun and thus elevated to the status of a major god. Since Huitzilopochtli was also the god of war, the idea eventually took hold that by his periodical nourishment with the blood of captured enemy warriors, he would maintain the existence of the sun and stave off the end of the present age.[14]

Tlacaelel's conception of the new divine militaristic mission of the Aztecs is clearly expressed in his remarks to Motecuhzoma I concerning the dedication of the Great Temple:

> Our god need not depend on the occasion of an affront to go to war. Rather, let a convenient market be sought where our god may go with his army to buy victims and people to eat as if he were to go to a nearby place to buy tortillas . . . whenever he wishes or feels like it. And may our people go to this place with their armies to buy their blood, their heads, and with their hearts and lives, those precious stones, jade, and brilliant and splendid wide plumes . . . for the services of the admirable Huitzilopochtli.[15]

Thus the Aztecs came to accept a religious cosmological vision that had far-ranging social and political consequences. Almost every aspect of Aztec culture, including their economic and social structures, their education, their religions and festivals, was influenced by their metaphysical-militaristic philosophy. A powerful warrior class developed to implement this cosmological vision and it expanded the Aztec empire over large parts of Mesoamerica. Perhaps part of the appeal of this vision to the Aztec rulers was that it facilitated imperialist expansion while simultaneously providing a unified religious view of the divine mission of the Aztec people.

The Aztec Tradition of Philosophical Reflection

As pointed out earlier, another very different approach to the problem of finding a place in the great scheme of things was also developed by the Aztecs. It is important to understand this approach in order to avoid the facile conclusion that Aztec society was merely concerned with satisfying a collective bloodthirst through military conquest. This orientation challenged the validity of traditional religious doctrines and beliefs and sought to answer certain fundamental questions concerning the nature of truth and reality. The systematic questioning was carried out by Aztec wise men known as *tlamatinime*. In Nahuatl this word means "knowers of things." The *tlamatinime* were not satisfied with the answers given by religious myths to questions concerning the origin of the world, the nature of death and the afterlife, the nature of reality, and so on. They reflected in a systematic way on the difference between myth and reality, truth and illusion, knowledge and opinion.

These systematic reflections occurred in schools of higher learning called *calmecacs*. The purpose of these schools, which were open to all social classes and not just to the nobility, was to teach the moral codes, history, and arts of Aztec culture and to endow their students with the practical wisdom necessary for correct living. Other functions of these institutions of higher education included the assimilation of the students into the life of the community, the teaching of self-control and moderation in everyday activities, and the dissemination of the highest principles and ideals of Aztec society. Before a male child reached the age of fifteen, his father would decide whether to send him to the *calmecac* or to the *telpochcalli* (where he would be taught to be a warrior). It was in the *calmecacs,* which were educational institutions of central importance to Aztec society, that the *tlamatinime* proposed and analyzed alternative answers to fundamental questions about human existence. Insofar as the Aztec wise men engaged collectively in critical and rational discourse concerning such basic questions, they exemplified true philosophical reflection and can therefore be categorized as philosophers.

The traditions initiated by the *tlamatinime* are of particular philosophical interest because they provide an example of the emergence of philosophical discourse in a setting that was intellectually isolated from the rest of the world. Even though philosophical reflection arose in different cultures of the Old World (e.g., the Greek, Indian, and Chinese cultures), at the time at which such philosophical reflections arose none of these cultures had been intellectually isolated for thousands of years. Thus, the reflections of the *tlamatinime* indicate a genuine second birth of philosophy. It is also important to analyze their conception of the proper way to answer metaphysical questions, that is, questions concerning the ultimate nature of reality. After proposing various ways of achieving well-grounded philosophical knowledge, the *tlamatinime,* or Aztec philosophers, concluded that it was only through aesthetic and poetic inspiration, and not rational discourse, that one could get a glimpse of ultimate truth. That is, these Aztec philosophers elaborated an aesthetic approach to the acquisition of metaphysical knowledge.

Aesthetic Activity and Insight into the Transcendent

The doctrine that insight into the nature of reality could be achieved through artistic creativity was based on two considerations. First, the *tlamatinime* were skeptical about the possibility that human beings could attain discursive knowledge regarding the nature of reality. In particular, this skepticism applied to the belief that traditional religious legends and myths could provide genuine knowledge and to the belief that metaphysical insights could be articulated or expressed in rational discourse. Second, the *tlamatinime* maintained that true insight into the nature of reality could be achieved only by imitating the creative activity of the gods. That is, they believed that through artistic creation, humans could mimic the divine creative actions by which the gods gave rise to the world. Let us examine each of these basic considerations in turn.

In the following poem, one of the Aztec philosophers expresses personal misgivings concerning the capacity of human beings to know ultimate truth and the intentions of the gods.

> Perchance, oh Giver of Life, do we really speak?
> Even though we may offer the Giver of Life
> emeralds and fine ointments,
> if with the offering of necklaces you are invoked,
> with the strength of the eagle, of the tiger,
> it may be that on earth no one speaks the truth.[16]

This poem conveys the idea that religious traditions and religious offerings may not provide the *tlamatinime* with true insights into the divine. It expresses their reluctance to rely on the established doctrines for knowing the nature of the sacred. Also of importance is the idea that "on earth no one speaks the truth." This expressed the doubts of the *tlamatinime* regarding people's capacity to articulate the truth through discursive, rational discourse.

In order to understand the view that aesthetic creation provides insight into the nature of reality, let us first consider the following poem.

> With flowers you write,
> Giver of Life
> With songs you give color,
> With songs you shade
> those who live here on earth.
>
> Later you will erase eagles and tigers.
> We exist only in your book
> while we are here on the earth.[17]

One of the central ideas in this poem is that objects in the natural world exist only as painted images or representations on a divine canvas. The reality of these objects is as fleeting as the reality of painted images in a book. God creates the world through a process of divine creative activity, and the reality of the objects in the natural world lies in the models of these objects in the divine mind. But humans can also engage in an activity which is analogous to that of the divine creator, namely, the activity of artistic creation. The human artist can strive to create works that exemplify or capture the original aesthetic divine form of the objects of the world around us. It is futile for human beings to try to penetrate to a reality underlying the world of appearances, because the world in itself consists only of images and appearances. The best we can do is to imitate the divine creative process through the creation of works of art. Only then can we hope to get a glimpse of the divine models and the divine sacred vision that gave rise to the objects in the world.[18]

Poetry is one of the creative activities through which we can gain some insight into the nature of the real. In Nahuatl the phrase "in xochitl in cuicatl" means "flower and song" and it is a metaphor for poetry or for a poem. This semantical clarification will help us to understand the significance of the following poem, which speaks about the origins of poetic inspiration.

> Our priests, I ask of you:
> From whence come the flowers that enrapture man?
> The songs that intoxicate, the lovely songs?
> Only from His home do they come, from the innermost part of
> heaven,
> only from there comes the myriad of flowers . . .
> Where the nectar of the flowers is found
> the fragrant beauty of the flower is refined . . .
> They interlace, they interweave;
> among them sings, among them warbles the quetzal bird.[19]

As stated in this poem, poetic inspiration and insight come from heaven, from the world of the divine. The Aztec philosophers believed that true knowledge, that is, knowledge based on a solid foundation, cannot originate here on earth, but must be based on the insight given by the gods. The knowledge people can acquire through the senses and reason is transitory and unreliable. Poetic intuition is one of the ways in which it is possible to attain true insight into the nature of reality and the sacred. The *tlamatinime* thought that it was only occasionally, in the experience of aesthetic rapture, that one might come to have a glimpse of ultimate truth.

The view that true knowledge of the divine could be attained through artistic creation such as poetic inspiration challenged, and provided an alternative to, the idea that human sacrifice and warfare were necessary. If the insights provided by religious doctrines were, like all human knowledge, uncertain and unreliable, then how could we know that offering human sacrifices to the gods would ward off the destruction of the present age? Once the general basis of established religious doctrines was undermined, any particular religious belief could be questioned, including the one concerning the necessity of human sacrifice and warfare. The alternative view elaborated by the *tlamatinime* was that communion with the gods did not occur through the ritual of human sacrifice, but rather through the creation of aesthetic works. Through divine inspiration and artistic creation, the artist could convey the only real truth accessible to human beings.

At the time of the conquest, this aesthetic vision of the acquisition of knowledge existed side by side with the dominant theological-militaristic perspective. We can only speculate as to whether the alternative viewpoint of the *tlamatinime,* which had been in place for less than a century when the Spaniards arrived, would eventually have undermined, or even replaced, the dominant cosmological vision. The Spaniards burned countless "picture books" on which the Aztecs had recorded their history and their legends and myths. Because the Aztecs did not develop a written language, and because of the destruction of the vast majority of their codices, much of the information that we have concerning the aesthetic perspective on metaphysical knowledge developed by the *tlamatinime* comes from native writers who were taught by the Spaniards to write shortly after the conquest.

We can now appreciate the complexity and paradoxical character of Aztec culture. It was a culture whose major institutions were deeply influenced by a cosmological perspective of instability, conflict, and warfare. But it was also a culture that gave rise to highly organized and sophisticated forms of education, some of which involved the systematic analysis of philosophical questions concerning the nature of the divine and the nature of ultimate truth. The Aztecs' intellectual evolution reached the point where they had developed a metaphysical perspective that was an alternative to the dominant viewpoint based on conflict and domination. Aztec society was one in which the periodic ritualistic sacrifice of human beings was accepted as a matter of course; but it was also a society that took great care in the education of its citizens and the rearing of its children. The Aztecs believed in compulsory education for all their children; all boys and girls, whether they were children of the rich or poor, were taught the Aztec legends and traditions, the divine songs, and the proper methods of worshiping their gods. They were also taught to practice the central values of their society, which included self-control, self-knowledge, moderation, and respect for government institutions. These were the aspects of Aztec culture that the Spanish friar Bernardino de Sahagun had in mind when he remarked that in certain respects the Aztecs exhibited more signs of virtue and civility than many people in his own country.

The World of the Inca

The vastness of the Inca empire rivaled that of any other in the history of the world. The empire extended for 2,500 miles and included approximately 12 million people who spoke at least twenty different languages. For an early culture, the Incas achieved extremely high levels of skill in architecture, engineering, ceramics, textiles, and metallurgy. They devised methods for freeze-drying food and developed chemically sophisticated techniques for gilding ornaments and jewelry with very thin layers of precious metals. They built a highway network that covered 10,000 miles and that far surpassed that of the Roman empire or any other nation. Their well-built roads, which extended across raging rivers, enormous mountains, and deep valleys, were equipped with rest stops and lodgings located at regular intervals. Among their engineering marvels were suspension bridges that extended across enormous gorges and fortresses and buildings that consisted of boulders weighing more than a hundred tons. One of their religious buildings measured 307 feet in length and 40 feet in height. But perhaps the most remarkable feature of the Inca empire was the bureaucratic infrastructure that held together in cooperative unity the different ethnic and cultural groups comprising it.

The Incas had a profound understanding of the psychology of conquest and this understanding enabled them to unify a large number of widely dispersed communities. When they conquered a new group and integrated it into their empire, they respected the local leaders and chieftains and allowed the people to retain their religious rituals and customs. The religious tolerance of the Incas was shown by the fact that the conquered groups could continue to worship their gods; the Incas demanded only that they venerate the Sun as a principal deity. However, the Incas did force these groups to pay tribute to them in the form of labor, food, and raw materials, though the tribute exacted was in proportion to the resources at each group's disposal. In exchange, the Incas would teach them to cultivate various crops and help them to build roads, permanent shelters, and bridges. In some cases the Incas would even build schools and provide teachers for the newly conquered communities. The Incas would institute a form of agrarian collectivism that rigidly regulated everyday activities but that provided everyone with the basic necessities of life, such as food and shelter. The forms of economic and social organization of the Incas enabled them to amass great amounts of goods, which they stored in enormous warehouses. Their collectivism system, which involved exacting tribute from conquered communities that had undergone economic and social development, benefited both the communities and the central Inca empire. The effect of this enlightened, though ultimately self-interested, philosophy of conquest was that the conquered groups would eventually adopt Inca customs and forms of social organization. The way of life of the Incas, which these communities at first adopted out of fear and through coercion, before long became the accepted way of doing things.

Inca Cosmology

Inca society was basically agrarian, and the religion reflected a concern with the earth and its regenerative cycles and the propitious conditions for attaining successful crops. As in other cultures, Inca concerns and fears influenced their conceptions of the divine, and their gods were made the agents and protectors of their needs and preoccupations.[20] The principal god was Pachacamac, who was considered the creator of the earth and the animating force of all living creatures. Pachacamac was an invisible being whose form or shape was not capable of representation; in fact, it was prohibited to represent his form. Another major deity was Viracocha, who created humans and the astral bodies.

The Incas' most prominent and elaborate temples and their major festivals were devoted to the sun, who was denoted by the name Inti. The sun was looked upon as the deity who determined the destiny of individuals and the community and as the force that provided sustenance for crops and the plant world. The great importance attributed to the sun is understandable in a society that lived in the high altitudes of the Andes, where the earth freezes as the temperature plunges at night after the sun disappears. The moon was denoted by the name Quilla, and she was regarded as the wife and companion of the sun. In addition to these divine entities, the Incas practiced totemism (the belief in animals or natural objects that are related by blood to certain families or clans). Among the most common totems were the condor, the jaguar, the mountain lion, and the serpent. The Incas also venerated a number of objects and places, like rivers, great trees, mountains, the wind, and the earth.[21] The orderly functioning of the state religion was maintained by the priests; they kept track of the numerous festivals, rituals, and other observances of the Inca religion. This was an important task, given the complexity and variety of their religious observances. Like the Maya, the Incas had a tradition of divine kingship, in which the Inca rulers claimed descent from divine personages.

The word *huacas* was applied to a large number of entities, some of which were considered holy or sacred. The term was used to refer to various deities, places of worship like temples or shrines, and sacred places like mountaintops, but it was also used to denote any natural object that was extraordinary in size, shape, or form, like a very large rock or a deep gorge. Even people who were born with unusual traits or under unusual circumstances (like twins or triplets) were considered *huacas*. It seems unlikely that all of the objects that fell under this rubric were considered sacred or holy, but it is difficult to determine this with certainty. What is clear, however, is that the Incas believed that the gods created each of these unusual or extraordinary objects for a reason and that these objects were thus deserving of special care or veneration. The reasons why the gods created such objects were regarded as mysteries.[22] The Incas also held a quasi-Platonic[23] doctrine according to which every object had its archetype in heaven, which protected it and looked after its preservation. This archetype was regarded as a patron or "mother" of the objects it protected at the terrestrial level. The Incas did not have a general term for referring exclusively to their gods. They denoted their gods by their proper names, and used the word *huacas* as an inclusive term for all the kinds of entities just mentioned. Their conception of the divine or sacred included deities, the earth, and natural objects and places under a single category.

The Inca cosmos also had three levels: a heavenly level, a terrestrial level, and an underworld level. As in the Aztec and Mayan cosmologies, the beings in each of these levels interacted and influenced one another. Cosmic forces would flow between the terrestrial and the upper and lower levels through caves, gorges, and rivers. Propitiation of the gods was crucial for the well-being of the community and its members, and rituals were used to favorably direct the forces that affected the crops and the health of individuals and the community. Many aspects of the lives of the Incas were guided by religious belief. Of particular importance was divination, a practice to which they resorted before undertaking any decision of significance. They followed the peculiar practice of examining the entrails of sacrificed llamas for signs determining when and what decisions should be made.

The Inca religious cosmological perspective was similar in certain important respects to that of the Mayas and the Aztecs. The world of the Incas, like that of the latter, was replete with natural forces and powerful beings. The religious rites and rituals of the Inca cosmovision reflected an intimate knowledge of the cycles and forces of nature. That the forces of nature were venerated and granted divine status and that the major religious celebrations centered on the solar cycles attest to the importance the Incas assigned to nature in their agrarian society. Like the Mayas and, to a lesser extent, the Aztecs, the Incas promulgated the notion of divine kingship, that is, the idea that their rulers were direct descendants of sacred beings and were thus mediators between the terrestrial world and the realm of the divine. This notion was no doubt used by the Incas, as it was by the Aztecs, as an ideological justification for the tribute they extracted from the groups they conquered. Nevertheless, the Incas demonstrated a significant degree of religious tolerance, since they allowed these communities to continue to worship their own gods so long as they also venerated the sun god, Inti. But during the Spanish conquest, the Incas and the native cultures of Mesoamerica were to encounter a Christian culture that did not demonstrate such a tolerance for religious pluralism.

The Colonial Period

It is difficult to imagine the devastating effects of conquest on the people of the New World. During the span of years between 1500 and 1550, it is estimated that 70 million indigenous people died. In Mexico, in terms of the sheer number of members of a particular cultural group who died, the devastation was many times greater than that wrought by the Holocaust. In the year 1500 approximately 25 million people lived in Mesoamerica, but by 1600 only 1 million were alive. They died as the result of warfare, massacres, fatigue from overwork, and, most important, the new diseases the Spaniards brought with them. The impact of these diseases was magnified by slavery and by the stress and malnutrition caused by the destruction of the social infrastructure (including medical practices) of the native people.[24] To give an idea of the economic plundering of Latin America by the Europeans, it will suffice to point out that between 1503 and 1660, 407,000 pounds of gold and 35,200,000 pounds of silver were extracted from the New World. The shipments of silver alone amounted to three times the value of the total European reserves at that time.[25]

As stated earlier, the conquest of the New World was not only a military and political conquest; it was also a metaphysical conquest. The Spaniards made sure that the religious and cultural doctrines of the indigenous people were systematically vanquished. The Spanish priests knew perfectly well that the cosmological perspective of the native people formed the core of their culture, and that it was necessary to destroy this perspective in order for the conquest to be complete. The monuments, temples, and religious sculptures of the native people were torn down, and in many cases the people were forced to build Christian churches using the stones from their own sacred structures. Their educational, religious, political, and cultural institutions were dismantled, and the native people were enslaved or coerced into performing labor for their conquerors. It was a project of cultural annihilation of unparalleled proportions in world history.

A critical part of the dismantling of the native cultures involved the process of conversion to Christianity. This was not a completely straightforward matter, however, because there were some debates as to whether the native people were truly human, that is, whether they had souls. If they were merely animals closely resembling humans, then there was no point in trying to save their souls by converting them into Christians. Prominent among the Christian friars who maintained that the indigenous people did have souls was Bartolomé de las Casas. He argued that they were not only truly human, but that in terms of their educational and social institutions and their knowledge of astronomy, agriculture, and architecture, they were the equal of any nation in Europe. Those who advocated conversion prevailed, and thus began the process of transforming the cosmological perspectives of the native people into a Christian perspective.

Syncretism

In the area of religion, syncretism refers to the developmental process in which different or originally contradictory beliefs and practices are combined into new religious doctrines or belief systems. The conversion of the indigenous people of the New World to Christianity was not a simple affair in which the ancient religious beliefs completely disappeared while the Christian doctrines were accepted wholeheartedly. Instead, a syncretism between native and Christian beliefs occurred, which gave rise to a new religious perspective that included doctrinal and ritualistic elements of both traditions. The impetus for this syncretistic process often came from the efforts of mestizo (people of mixed Indian and Spanish blood) or Indian communities. The reason for this may lie in the fact that members of these communities had a stronger need to find a basis for identifying with the new religion; or perhaps it was an attempt to retain some measure of dignity and cultural solidarity in a situation in which they were politically, economically, and culturally disfranchised.

One of the most prominent cases of syncretism involves the appearance of the Virgen de Guadalupe to a poor Indian named Juan Diego at the hill of Tepeyac near Mexico City. The dark-skinned Virgin spoke to him in Nahuatl, the language of the Aztecs, and told him that a shrine should be built on the site of her appearance. When Juan Diego notified the archbishop of his experiences, his story was met with skepticism. But the Virgin appeared to him a second time and instructed him to pick some roses in a nearby area (even though it was not the season when roses could bloom) and take them to the archbishop as proof of her appearance. Juan Diego followed her instructions and placed the roses in his cloak. When he extended his cloak to show the archbishop the roses, both men were amazed to see that the image of the Virgin was miraculously imprinted on it. This incident convinced the archbishop of the truth of Juan Diego's story, and what is now the most famous basilica in Mexico was built at the bottom of the hill of Tepeyac. Juan Diego's cloak now hangs on the high altar of the basilica of the Virgen de Guadalupe.

The Virgin's dark-skinned, Indian features and her use of the Nahuatl language facilitated the Indians' acceptance of Catholicism by providing them with a means for racial and cultural identification with the new religion. Furthermore, the hill of Tepeyac, where she appeared, was a sacred site at which the Aztec fertility goddess Tonantzin had been worshiped for many years. Another connection between the goddess Tonantzin, who was associated with the moon, and the Virgen de Guadalupe is that the latter appeared standing on a half-crescent, which symbolizes the moon. It is clear that there were some important elements of syncretism between the Aztec's veneration of the goddess Tonantzin and the new Catholic virgin. Now the Indians had a Christian mother goddess of their own, one to whom they could speak and who was close to their hearts. She had appeared to one of them, and had spoken in their own tongue; she was thus an intermediary between the heavenly Christian God and the native people. The appearance of the Virgen de Guadalupe was a threshold event that signaled the emergence of a new cultural identity based on both Indian and Spanish features but uniquely different from each of these.

Honoring the Dead

In addition to the practice of venerating the Virgen de Guadalupe, there is another important case of religious syncretism that has survived to the present. The *Día de los Muertos* (Day of the Dead) rituals, which occur in Mexico and other countries of Mesoamerica at the end of October and beginning of November, also incorporate pre-Columbian and Christian beliefs. In the Day of the Dead ceremonies, people in Mesoamerica perform a number of religious rituals to remember and honor their dead friends and relatives. In some areas, saints and supernatural beings such as the spirits of rivers and mountains are also honored. Some of the rituals center on the home, while other rituals are public affairs that take place at the cemetery and involve the whole community. The careful construction of altars honoring the souls of dead friends and family members is of central importance in the home-centered rituals. These family altars typically consist of (1) religious symbols such as crosses and images of Christ, the Virgin Mary, and saints; (2) various kinds of breads, fruits, candies, liquors, and cooked dishes; (3) particular plants and flowers used especially for the occasion; and (4) objects that were of special significance to the deceased or that he or she enjoyed. Among the unique objects found in these altars are home-baked loaves of bread with crossbone-shaped crusts called *pan de muertos* (bread of the dead) and small sugar skulls that represent the dead friends and relatives being honored. According to tradition, during the afternoon of October 31 the souls of the dead begin to arrive at their former homes. Because the people believe that the souls of the deceased will best enjoy the offerings of the household altars in the absence of the living, for several hours no one enters the room that contains the altar.

On the evening of November 1, the community gathers at the local cemetery for an important public ceremony in which, according to the people's beliefs, the souls of the deceased, after enjoying the offerings of the family altars, join the living in a ritual that renews and reinforces the link between the living and the dead. Upon arriving at the cemetery, the people place candles at the previously decorated graves of dead family members and friends and then gather at a designated location. Between 1 A.M. and 2 A.M., the people pray together and entreat the souls of the dead to shelter them from tragedies and misfortunes and ensure that they enjoy health, happiness, plentiful crops, and success in their worldly endeavors. It is here that we can most clearly see the central ideological principle that underlies the rituals of the *Día de los Muertos,* namely, the belief in a covenant between the living and the dead in which the dead are propitiated, remembered, and honored in return for their intervention on behalf of the living. The deceased are seen as beings who act as intermediaries between individuals and the community and the Christian God and pagan supernatural beings. The centrality of this covenant is also corroborated by the importance given to those who died before the age of four. Such infants are seen as *angelitos* (little angels), whose purity of heart makes them especially effective in mediating between the world of the living and the realm of the supernatural, and special efforts are made to worship them and curry their favor.

The general tenor of the ceremonies of the Day of the Dead is not one of sorrow and lament, but rather one of communal unification, cohesion, and sometimes even celebration. The rituals honoring and remembering the dead not only bring the members of the community together; they also reinforce the belief that death is a transitional phase in which individuals continue to exist in a different plane while maintaining an important relationship with the living. The underlying philosophy of the Day of the Dead rituals goes beyond the notion (which is also a part of Christian ideology) that the souls of the dead continue to exist in a spiritual realm and should be remembered; rather, it contains important elements of a pre-Hispanic cosmology in which the universe is seen as an integrated whole consisting of numerous supernatural and terrestrial beings, existing in different planes, whose actions affect one another in important ways. In this syncretistic Christian and pre-Columbian cosmology, the dead care deeply about the actions and attitudes of the living toward them, while the living depend for their well-being on the willingness of the dead to intercede on their belief with God, the Virgin Mary, Christ, and the pagan beings associated with the natural elements such as the goddess La Malintzi and the supernatural personage El Cuatlapanga.[26] Thus, the observance of the *Día de los Muertos,* far from representing a morbid obsession with death, is a modern-day expression of an ancient vision of life and death as a seamless web in a metaphysically integrated universe.

In addition to syncretism, there were other ways in which pre-Columbian religious traditions and beliefs were preserved. Even though the Spanish colonizers could easily control public religious practices and institutions, it was much harder for them to monitor and control private religious rituals that occurred in the home and in the fields. Some traditions and rituals were kept secret from the Christian authorities and have survived even to the present. In some cases, there was a correspondence between the Christian symbols and beliefs and some elements of the native religions. For example, the Maya readily accepted the Christian tradition of venerating the cross because in the Mayan cosmology the cross symbolized the cosmic tree. They could thus retain some of their ancient traditions while outwardly appearing to follow the dictates of the Christian authorities.[27] The colonizers could force them to adopt their religious practices, but they could not control the subjective significance of their spiritual experiences.

With the arrival of the conquistadores, European philosophical influences also arrived in the New World. Scholasticism, a philosophical and theological tradition based on the works of Aristotle and his commentators, was the dominant philosophical perspective during most of the colonial period. The primary objective of this "official" Christian philosophy was to provide a philosophical, rational defense of Christian doctrines. Scholasticism, like other intellectual movements that influenced Latin America, was thus not an indigenous philosophical perspective. It was the first in a series of movements that were imported from Europe. Scholasticism was an intellectual tradition of the colonizers; it was not influential among the native people of the New World. The only institutionalized, indigenous philosophical tradition of the New World came to an end when the Aztec centers of higher education, the *calmecacs,* were dismantled and when the codices and traditions of the *tlamatinime* were destroyed. The social, political, and cultural effects of colonization were so devastating that it would take centuries before the people of Latin America developed philosophical doctrines that reflected their own concerns, needs, and aspirations.

The Modern Period

If there is a single great strand that connects the ancient and modern philosophers in Latin America, it is the conviction that philosophy is not a purely conceptual or cerebral activity that can be divorced from other dimensions of human experience. It is not possible to understand the philosophical perspectives that have been influential in Latin America in the twentieth century without understanding the role that colonialism, oppression, and poverty have played in the history of Latin American countries. Philosophical movements in Latin America have been influenced by political developments to a far greater degree than they have been in Europe or the United States. Generally speaking, Latin Americans have not seen philosophy as an intellectual activity detached from the sociopolitical milieu within which it takes place. Whereas in Europe and the United States philosophy has been understood as a theoretical enterprise concerned with proposing and answering questions of universal relevance and validity, in Latin America the relevant philosophical questions have been, for the most part, those which address the concrete sociopolitical and economic problems facing Latin Americans. Given its universalistic orientations, philosophy in the Western tradition has not considered cultural and sociopolitical factors as being of central significance for the philosophical enterprise.[28] But the legacy of colonialism and the poverty and political oppression that have been so much a part of the

Latin American experience have given the philosophers of these countries a keener awareness of the relevance and importance of such factors. There are several ways in which colonialism, poverty, and oppression have affected Latin American philosophical thought. First, the experience of colonialism raised the questions of cultural identity and self-determination. The destruction of the indigenous cultures and the imposition of alien religious and philosophical worldviews created dilemmas concerning cultural identity. The mestizos and the indigenous people knew that they were not Spaniards, and that, regardless of their social or economic status, they would never be accepted as such. Historically, the vision of reality of the colonizers had been forcibly imposed on the Indians and the mestizos, and thus they needed to define their own identity and their own vision of the world. For the colonized, the definition of who they were was imposed from without by the colonial powers. In the present century, these dilemmas have reemerged as the result of the imperialist policies of the United States toward Latin America.[29] The invasions of Nicaragua and Mexico in this century by U.S. troops, the CIA-inspired overthrow of the democratically elected government of Chile under Allende, and the Bay of Pigs invasion of Cuba are clear examples of these imperialist policies.[30] The economic underdevelopment and dependent status of Latin American countries and the numerous political and military interventions of the United States have made it more difficult for Latin Americans to develop and implement their own sociopolitical and philosophical conceptions of reality. In short, the collective experience of colonialism and oppression has underscored for Latin American philosophers and intellectuals the importance of addressing issues concerning cultural identity and self-determination.

The legacy of sociopolitical and cultural oppression in Latin America has also given rise to a distinctive conception of the nature and function of philosophical reflection. Philosophy is not seen as a discipline that is conceptually autonomous and isolated but rather as a field of intellectual discourse that incorporates sociology, economics, literature, politics, history, art, anthropology, culture, religion, and everyday life. This conception of philosophy is best exemplified by the Latin American *pensador,* who is a thinker who does not separate philosophy from other disciplines and who considers concrete action as an essential part of upholding particular philosophical positions. The spheres of action and reflection are thus not dichotomized from one another, but are understood as being intrinsically linked. The *pensador* is an intellectual who arrives at his or her philosophical viewpoint by drawing from all relevant areas of human investigation and by making connections between disciplines that are generally compartmentalized within the Western philosophical tradition.

Another important feature of this integrative conception of philosophy is that it takes the concrete sociopolitical setting in which one finds oneself as the point of departure for philosophical reflection. The idea here is that one's philosophical vision is necessarily conditioned by one's circumstances and life experiences. It is only from this concrete reality that one can address the supposedly "universal" philosophical issues of freedom, justice, value, existential significance, and so forth. Human beings are not cognitive machines who can engage in abstract philosophical reflection by disassociating themselves from their particular life circumstances; they are flesh-and-blood beings whose thoughts and feelings are grounded in the particularities of their cultural and historical backgrounds. By adopting this conception of philosophy, Latin American philosophers have sought to articulate their preoccupations and concerns by embracing the uniqueness and particularities of their collective cultural experiences.

The reason for focusing on the sociopolitical and economic effects of colonialism and imperialism on Latin America is that we need to be aware of these effects in order to frame properly the following discussion of some of the major philosophical movements in Latin America. Three of the four philosophical perspectives that we will discuss, namely, Marxism, the philosophy of liberation, and the theology of liberation, address in different ways the problems created by the legacy of colonialism and imperialism. These philosophical traditions have proposed different ideological paths by means of which the people of Latin America can become truly free and self-determined. And it is worthwhile to point out that the other philosophical movement we will analyze, positivism, despite its being categorized as politically conservative, also had as its stated pragmatic end the social, political, and economic progress of Latin America.

Positivism

Auguste Comte and his followers in the middle of the nineteenth century developed a philosophical perspective known as positivism. This perspective was inspired by the great advances in physics, mathematics, and the natural sciences that had occurred in the seventeenth and eighteenth centuries. Scientific knowledge was developing at an impressive rate, and there was a great eagerness on the part of philosophers and other intellectuals to use the emerging scientific worldview to analyze social and political problems. Reason and the scientific observation of physical phenomena were the twin pillars on which the new scientific perspective rested. Comte and the other adherents of positivism felt that by using the methodology of the natural sciences, social scientists could bring about the same advances in their fields as had been achieved in fields like physics, astronomy, biology, and mathematics. Comte maintained that the social and political order was governed by universal laws of human behavior that could be discovered through the use of reason and the methods of scientific investigation. By discovering the laws governing human behavior, one could create a utopian society in which all the social and political problems facing humanity would be resolved.

One of the central attractions of positivism, particularly in Latin America, was that it provided a blueprint for attaining progress and order. By following positivist principles, a society could move from the backward stages of underdevelopment in which ignorance and dogmatic beliefs predominated to a scientifically enlightened stage in which reason governed human behavior. These ideas were received favorably by some Latin American countries, which, after the struggles they had endured in attaining their independence, welcomed a philosophy that promised social progress and political stability.

Among those who were especially willing to embrace positivist doctrines were the members of the ruling classes of Latin American countries. This was partly because according to positivism, those individuals who were the best educated and most knowledgeable were the ones best fit to rule. Comtean positivism was essentially an elitist philosophy that placed great faith in the inherent rationality and goodness of the members of the ruling classes. Comte made the rather naive assumption that political leaders and powerful businessmen would base their decisions not on self-interest but on what was good for society as a whole. Positivism also provided political leaders with a justification for choosing policies that achieved social progress in a gradual, orderly manner instead of policies that would institute radical reform. Political leaders and members of the elite classes preferred a philosophy that advocated stability and order to doctrines that might threaten their power and control by demanding revolutionary change.[31]

Positivism influenced different Latin American countries in different ways. In Mexico, it helped the government free the educational system from the pervasive influence of the Catholic church. During the term of president Benito Juárez, an educational reform law was passed in 1867 that banned church schools and created primary and secondary lay schools throughout Mexico. This law also established a national center for higher education in Mexico City, which trained professionals for a variety of careers. However, positivism also had significant negative influences. Comte's belief that the people of Western Europe were intellectually superior to nonwhite races reinforced racist attitudes that were still deeply entrenched, especially among the elite. The educational reforms benefited mostly the children of the upper classes. Also, during the thirty-year rule of the dictator Porfirio Díaz, positivism was adopted as Mexico's official state doctrine and it was used to justify a policy of law and order. It thus provided a philosophical rationale for an authoritarian, often ruthless, government.

In Brazil, however, positivists were an influential force in challenging the legality of slavery in the 1880s. During this time, positivist thinkers were also at the forefront of those demanding institutional changes in the government of the emperor Dom Pedro II. The Brazilian positivists advocated more representative forms of government, even though they did not go so far as to argue for a truly egalitarian society. Even though positivism did not have a long-lasting influence on governmental policies, it was the first important philosophical school to emerge in Brazil and it furthered the development of the country's intelligentsia.[32]

In general, the promise of positivism was greater than the actual results it produced. This occurred primarily for two reasons: (1) Positivist proposals for social change were often couched in excessively abstract, general terms, and (2) positivists did not pay sufficient attention to the practical problems that stood in the way of implementing their proposals. To an important extent, positivism was a utopian philosophy that did not take seriously enough human greed for wealth and power. The positivist vision of a society founded on rational principles depended on the eradication, at every level of society, of ignorance, illiteracy, superstition, and poverty. But illiteracy, poverty, and powerlessness continued to exist among the lower classes even in those Latin American countries purportedly committed to positivist ideals. The elite's tenacious hold on political power and wealth made it practically impossible to implement the positivist vision of a new social and political order. Ultimately, the inability of positivism to provide an adequate analysis of the underlying factors that hindered the development of the countries of Latin America undermined its usefulness and viability as a philosophical doctrine capable of bringing about significant and lasting change.

The Appeal of Marxism

As a philosophical and political perspective, Marxism over the past thirty years has had a powerful appeal to intellectuals, writers, and artists in Latin America. This is because it provides the methodological techniques and conceptual categories with which to develop penetrating and extensive analyses of the economic, political, and social problems facing Latin America. Even more important, Marxism brings to the forefront the question of what concrete, revolutionary actions should be undertaken to resolve these problems. We need only recall Marx's famous dictum that the point of philosophy is "not only to understand reality, but to change it." Because, for most Latin American thinkers, contact with poverty and oppression is practically unavoidable, a philosophical perspective that can both analyze oppression and demand and articulate a practical response to it is deeply appealing.

Basically, Marxism is an economic, political, and philosophical doctrine which maintains that capitalism is an exploitative economic system because it allows the capitalists—those who own a society's means of production, such as factories, mills, machine shops, and so on—to accumulate great wealth at the expense of the workers. According to Marx, the workers are not paid for the full value of their work because the capitalists, in order to profit from workers' labor, keep part of the value of their work for themselves. The difference between the value of the workers' labor and what they get paid is called surplus value. By keeping the surplus value for themselves, capitalists are able to accumulate wealth by exploiting the labor of the workers.

Thus, capitalism is a system in which the workers produce objects of value (commodities), but in which they are prevented from enjoying the fruits of their labor because they are producing profit for someone else. The problem, for Marx, is that in a capitalist system the workers do not own the means of production and hence they do not have control over what they produce or the conditions under which they produce it. He argued that if the workers were to own the means of production, as they would in a communist society, they could work for their mutual benefit and not to enrich the capitalist owner. According to Marx, capitalism is essentially an oppressive economic system because it concentrates wealth in the hands of the few at the expense of the many. But Marx thought that this concentration of wealth would lead to the destruction of the capitalist system; the proletariat (the working class) would ultimately revolt and overthrow the bourgeoisie (the ruling class of capitalists), thus attaining power in a communist revolution. The workers would then establish a society free of economic exploitation, with common ownership of the means of production.

Marx believed that the political, legal, and social institutions of a capitalist society, as well as that society's values and cultural beliefs, reflected the interests of the rich. He thought that economic power was the basis for attaining political power and that the wealthy, using the political influence they gained by means of their wealth, shaped society for their own purposes. These Marxist views made sense to many Latin American thinkers who were historically aware of the great power and influence the Spaniards had enjoyed during the postcolonial period and who were also conscious of the vast inequalities in wealth and power between the different social classes in Latin American countries.

Also corroborated by the experiences of Latin American thinkers was Marx's analysis of economic exploitation at the international level. According to Marx, in order for capitalism to develop and survive, it must constantly expand production, seek new markets to exploit, and develop economic networks that transcend national boundaries. The existence of multinational corporations that placed profit over human needs, the unequal terms of international trade that Latin American countries were forced to accept, and the exploitation of their natural resources by the advanced industrialized countries substantiated Marx's claim that capitalism led to exploitation at both the national and international levels.[33] In short, Marxism provided a philosophical framework that enabled Latin American thinkers to make sense of many important sociopolitical and economic factors affecting Latin American countries.

Despite its potential usefulness as an analytical tool for Latin American philosophers, Marxist thought, as concretely applied, has often been determined by events and conditions outside of Latin America. The communist parties in Latin America have tried to remain loyal to international communist movements. During the first two decades of the twentieth century, Marxist thought in Latin America was deeply influenced by the ideological position of an international communist organization called the Second International.

The dominant view of the Second International, in which the communist parties of different countries were represented, was that communist revolutions would come about as a result of the expansion and evolution of capitalist forces and be initiated by the proletariat of advanced industrialized capitalist countries. Thus, the Second International did not appreciate the particular problems faced by the nonindustrialized, "backward" countries of Latin America (where capitalism was not highly developed), which were struggling to attain their autonomy from the imperialist countries on which they were economically dependent. The position of the Second International reflected a European bias that placed the locus of revolutionary change in the industrialized countries and that relegated the underdeveloped countries, with their masses of rural workers, to a secondary role in the evolution of communism.

In 1919, after the Russian Revolution, the Communist Third International was founded, and one of its primary purposes was to direct a worldwide communist revolutionary movement based on the organizational principles and strategies that had been successfully employed by the Bolsheviks in Russia. There were several important ways in which the position of the Third International differed from that of the Second International. There was a greater awareness of the sociopolitical and economic factors that affected the struggles for liberation of particular countries and there was an admission of the possibility, which had been denied in some previous interpretations of classical Marxism, that a country could undergo a communist revolution without first reaching the stage of advanced capitalism. Third World countries such as those of Latin America were now seen as facing special problems—such as liberating themselves from imperialism and attaining true national self-determination—not faced by the industrialized Western countries and as being autonomous agents of revolutionary change. Nevertheless, a Eurocentric bias remained in the Third Communist International insofar as the industrial proletariat of Western countries was still considered to be the force that would bring about the communist revolution. Furthermore, the Communist International never truly understood the role or importance of the indigenous populations in Latin American countries like Peru, Guatemala, Ecuador, and Bolivia.

Marxism from a Latin American Perspective

Thus, in the early part of this century Marxist analysis was rarely applied with an awareness of the specific circumstances facing Latin American countries. A notable exception was the work of the Peruvian writer José Carlos Mariategui. In what is widely considered to be one of the greatest works of Latin American Marxism, *Siete Ensayos de Interpretación de la Realidad Peruana,* Mariategui analyzed the economic and sociopolitical problems of Peru from a Marxist perspective.[34] He pointed out that Peru was basically an agricultural country with a feudalistic organizational structure and that the Indians, who constituted the great majority of the rural population, existed in a state of virtual servitude. Mariategui maintained that the highly efficient system of agricultural organization developed by the Incas had been destroyed by the Spaniards during the conquest, and that redistribution of the land to the Indians and restoration of the traditional, four-hundred-year-old agricultural structures were necessary for resolving the economic problems of Peru. In contrast to the orthodox Marxist position, which held that the industrial proletariat would be the agent of revolutionary change, Mariategui argued that in Peru it was the rural Indian who held the greatest potential for bringing about a Marxist revolution. Mariategui's application of Marxist ideology to the situation in Peru was solidly grounded in a thorough knowledge and understanding of the historical, cultural, and economic aspects of Peruvian reality. Mariategui clearly recognized the importance of taking into account specific national circumstances before applying Marxist analyses, and he managed to break away from the Eurocentrism that plagued Marxism in Latin America in the early part of the twentieth century.

An event having a great impact on the way Marxism was understood in Latin America was the Cuban revolution. In 1958, guerrilla forces led by Fidel Castro overthrew the government of Fulgencio Batista and took control of Cuba. The Cuban revolution violated the central tenets of the dominant interpretations of Marxism, which maintained that communist revolutions could take place only through the leadership of a core of enlightened Marxist revolutionaries who were actively supported by the proletariat. The Cuban Communist Party played practically no role in directing the overthrow of the Batista government, and it was not the urban proletariat that defeated the government forces, but rather a relatively small band of guerrillas based in the mountainous areas of Cuba. The Cuban revolution showed Latin American Marxists the necessity of remaining flexible regarding strategic alternatives for bringing about revolutionary change and underscored the diversity of conditions under which such change could take place.

From the 1960s to the present, Marxist ideology in Latin America has been used primarily in two ways: (1) as an analytical tool for examining a number of sociological, political, and economic issues such as the impact of foreign capitalism in Latin America, the nature of imperialism and dependent capitalism, and the basic features of the colonial past; and (2) as a theoretical perspective for devising political strategies for movements of national liberation. Concerning the first way in which Marxist ideology has been employed, Marxist researchers in Latin America have in recent years made social scientific contributions whose significance extends even beyond Latin America.[35] Regarding the second, Marxism has furthered the ideological development of national liberation movements in countries like Nicaragua and Guatemala. In these countries the rigidity of ideologically correct, externally imposed, party-line doctrines has given way to flexible pragmatism in dealing with concrete sociopolitical and economic issues. Latin American thinkers have recognized that even though Marxism can be a valuable analytical tool, it is not an inviolable doctrine that offers a privileged and infallible description of reality. A story is told in Nicaragua of a Sandinista worker who when asked by a reporter from the United States why he was a Marxist replied, "I am not a Marxist, I am a Sandinista. Marxism has important lessons to teach us, but it is not God's word come down from heaven."

Finally, it is important to point out that a critical factor affecting and impeding the implementation of Marxist alternatives in Latin America has been the economic, political, and military interventionism of the United States. We find prominent examples of this interventionism in the efforts of the CIA to undermine the democratically elected socialist government of Allende in Chile, the economic boycott and undermining of Cuba under Castro, and the economic and military support of the guerrilla forces trying to overthrow the Sandinista government in Nicaragua. It is difficult to determine with a high degree of certainty how these governments would have fared in the absence of U.S. efforts to subvert them. What is clear, however, is that the economic, political, and military interventionism of the United States has had a powerful negative impact on the attempts of Marxist-inspired governments in Latin America to implement their political and economic policies and reforms. What we have here is another illustration of how foreign influences and interests have hindered the efforts of the people of Latin America to determine their own destiny.

The Philosophy of Liberation

The philosophy of liberation refers to a set of philosophical doctrines that originated in Argentina in the 1970s. The various doctrines that fall under this rubric share certain philosophical orientations and objectives. First, there is a commitment to philosophize from the perspective of the poor and the oppressed. The philosophy of liberation focuses on the social needs and demands of the disfranchised. It articulates a vision of reality as seen through the perspective of those who have been excluded from the centers of power and influence. Second, philosophy is not seen as an abstract, purely conceptual enterprise disassociated from the political problems of the society in which it is situated; rather, it is seen as an instrument for bringing about concrete social and political change. Third, there is a reliance on interdisciplinary studies. The proponents of the philosophy of liberation believe that philosophy should incorporate, and be enriched by, the insights of sociology, history, economics, ethnology, and other studies. The disciplinary compartmentalization characteristic of academic institutions in the Western industrialized countries is rejected in favor of an integrated, comprehensive approach to philosophical reflection.

Perhaps the most prominent figure in the philosophy of liberation is the Argentinian philosopher Enrique Dussel. In the classic text *The Philosophy of Liberation,* he makes a fundamental distinction between the *center* and the *periphery*.[36] Within the context of the international balance of power between countries, the center refers to the countries in Western Europe, the United States, Japan, and the Soviet Union, while the periphery refers to the underdeveloped countries of the Third World (countries in Latin America would fall into this category). In the context of particular societies, however, the center refers to the socially and economically privileged classes, while the periphery denotes the classes of the poor and the oppressed. One of the central tenets of Dussel's work is that the philosophy of the center is a tool that furthers the interests of the countries and social classes of the center in maintaining their privileged positions of influence and power. Traditional philosophy has purportedly been concerned with issues of universal relevance and significance, that is, with issues of concern to all people, regardless of social class, gender, or cultural background. But in actuality, the philosophy of the center has been developed mostly by males belonging to the dominant cultural traditions or social classes. Thus, traditional philosophy, although pretending to speak for all people, in fact reflects the interests and concerns of the dominant groups.

Philosophizing from the perspective of the poor and the oppressed has wide-ranging and interesting consequences for philosophy. Philosophy becomes an intellectual enterprise grounded in the concrete sociopolitical and cultural experiences of people who have been excluded from an active role in history. Issues like the nature of justice, liberty, equality, and truth are analyzed from a unique and different perspective.

However, there are certain difficult questions that can be raised regarding Dussel's philosophy of liberation. First, it is not clear how, if at all, many important philosophical problems are affected by philosophizing from the viewpoint of the poor and the oppressed. For example, how is the analysis of the question of the existence of God, the nature of space and time, or the problem of induction affected by adopting the philosophy of liberation? It is easy to see how the analysis of some issues in social and political philosophy would be affected, but it is not obvious what it could mean to analyze many of the other classic philosophical issues from this stance.

Second, is there any guarantee that adopting the perspective of the poor and the oppressed necessarily leads to truly liberated and just points of view? Even though the experience of oppression is likely to give people some understanding of its nature, it is not necessarily the case that those who have experienced it are not capable of oppressing others. On the contrary, it is well established that groups that have experienced oppression, like working-class minority men, are quite capable of oppressing others, for example their wives or their children.

Finally, how is it possible to really take the stance of the poor and the oppressed if one is not a member of that class? What qualifies an individual as a representative of or speaker for the oppressed? Even though some philosophers who work within the tradition of the philosophy of liberation have experienced political persecution, one must nevertheless be very careful about privileging oneself by appropriating the voice of the poor and the oppressed. Most philosophers, by virtue of their education, knowledge, and skills, are not typical members of those groups for whom the philosophy of liberation aspires to speak. Any kind of appropriation of the voice of the poor and the oppressed must be carefully and critically examined.

Despite these dilemmas, however, the philosophy of liberation represents a genuine and productive attempt by Latin American philosophers to break away from dependence on European and American philosophy and to produce theoretical innovations within the philosophical arena.

The Theology of Liberation

The theology of liberation provides a radically new way of thinking about the meaning of Christian faith and commitment. Its founder, Gustavo Gutierrez, argues that a true understanding of the Bible and Christ's life leads to a commitment to fight against the poverty and oppression suffered by the people of Latin America (or the country where one happens to live).[37] Gutierrez maintains that one expresses one's faith in the teachings of Christ through one's actions in alleviating the suffering of the most marginalized and oppressed groups in society, and that one cannot claim to be a true Christian if one ignores the plight of those most in need of help. Being a Christian means following the example of Christ, who advocated loving one's neighbor and who spent his life helping the needy and outcasts of society. Thus, according to Gutierrez, it is not enough for Christians to be "saved" by accepting Christ in a personal act of faith; they must also be willing to express that faith in their daily lives by working for social justice for those in greatest need.

Gutierrez also argues that having the commitment to contribute to the human struggle for liberation from poverty and injustice involves more than merely performing acts of charity and goodwill for the poor; it also involves working to change the underlying social, political, and economic structures that give rise to poverty and oppression. As long as the basic structures that cause poverty and injustice remain intact, the suffering of the poor will continue. He maintains that poverty and social injustice exist in Latin America primarily because of the exploitation of the workers by foreign and domestic capitalists. He argues that multinational corporations make large profits by exploiting the cheap labor available in Latin American countries and that making profit (and not improving the lives of the workers) is the primary motivation for foreign investment in Latin America. He believes that it is only by restructuring their econo- mies and by eliminating their dependence on the major industrial powers that the countries of Latin America can deal with the problems of poverty and injustice.

The call for fundamental social change is one of the reasons the theology of liberation has had such a great impact in Latin America and in other parts of the world. But it is also the reason some critics of the theology of liberation have labeled it a Marxist ideology masquerading as Christian theology. In particular, conservative critics within the hierarchy of the Catholic church have alleged that the theology of liberation should be rejected because it espouses communist ideals. Saying that the theol- ogy of liberation is simply Marxism in disguise, however, is not really a fair criticism, because the central principles of the theology of liberation have an ethical and theological basis that is independent of Marxist principles. The theology of liberation employs Marxist analysis in arriving at an answer to the question of how, most effectively, to eliminate the poverty and economic injustices suffered by the poor of Third World countries. But there is no necessary or intrinsic connection between Marxism and the theology of liberation. One could retain the substance of the latter perspective while rejecting the contention that collective ownership of the means of production is the only way to achieve a just society in which the poor can live with dignity and respect.

The theology of liberation also proposes radical changes in the social and political role of the Catholic church. According to this theological perspective, the Catholic church should have a "preferential option for the poor."[38] In order to work toward a society in which people's basic needs for food, shelter, medical care, employment, and education can be met, the church needs to transform its ties to those in power in society.

The church must speak out against social injustices and abuses of power and must challenge the political and military authorities when they suppress the legitimate demands of the poor for political freedoms and the basic necessities of life. The theology of liberation maintains that the Catholic church has for too long been content to administer to people's spiritual needs while failing to involve itself in their everyday struggles against poverty and political injustices.

A concrete example of the way in which people in some Latin American countries have combined religious worship with political involvement is through the *comunidades de base* (grass roots communities). These community groups, besides studying the Bible and promoting living by Christian ideals, provide grass roots organizational structures that poor people can use to address such widespread problems as the torture or disappearance of relatives and friends while in the hands of the authorities, the consequences of extreme poverty and the lack of basic social services, and the often ruthless actions taken by the political and military authorities in response to their demands.

In assessing the adequacy of the theology of liberation from a philosophical or theoretical point of view, we must first of all note that it suffers from a rather obvious limitation, namely, its reliance on the truth or validity of Christian doctrines. From a theoretical perspective, this is a limitation because philosophers are likely to question the truth of such fundamental Christian views as that God exists, that Jesus was the son of God, and that there is an eternal life after death. But if the theology of liberation is viewed as a doctrine whose primary purpose is to provide spiritual guidance and to alleviate the suffering and oppression of poor and marginalized people, then we must assess its adequacy by its sociopolitical impact and influence. Seen from this perspective, the theology of liberation has been partly successful, since it has been able to call attention to the problems of the poor and the oppressed of Latin America and has been at the forefront of their struggles for political freedoms and adequate living conditions. Indeed, the theology of liberation has had greater sociopolitical impact than the philosophy of liberation, which is also concerned with the problems of the marginalized people of Latin America. Several factors may account for its greater influence.

First, the theology of liberation provides a spiritual dimension that is missing in other liberation ideologies like Marxism or the philosophy of liberation. It employs to good advantage the powerful and pervasive need that exists in many cultures (especially Latin American cultures) to make a spiritual connection with the transcendent. The theology of liberation is a perspective that unifies religious and political concerns by addressing both spiritual and physical needs. It recognizes that any theological or religious worldview that does not take into account people's basic economic needs is detached from concrete, everyday reality and that any revolutionary doctrine that does not address the spiritual dimension of life is limited and incomplete. Second, the theology of liberation success-fully uses both formal and informal religious and social structures to organize and mobilize the poor. At the formal level, church-centered activities and programs provide a forum for raising issues of concern to the poor and the oppressed and for developing strategies to deal with them. At the informal level, the grass roots *comunidades de base* provide the poor with the flexible organizational structures they need for devel-oping and implementing a wide variety of tactics and strategies for resolving their problems. Third, the basic principles and ideas of the theology of liberation are expressed in terminology that is understandable to the people it seeks to address. One of the great ironies of the philosophy of liberation and other doctrines of liberation is that they usually couch their ideas in a dense jargon that is practically unintelligible to anyone but the academic specialist. This makes it difficult, if not impossible, for the advocates of these ideologies to reach precisely those people they are trying to politicize. The proponents of the theology of liberation, by contrast, use symbolic and metaphorical language to make their ideas understandable to audiences who lack a formal education and even basic literacy skills. In summary, the theology of liberation has important lessons to teach philosophers who have an avowed interest in transforming the social and political consciousness of the poor and the oppressed.

Notes

1. This is especially true of our understanding of the Mayan civilization. In the past several decades the deciphering of Mayan writing and iconography and new archaeological discoveries have changed our conception of some basic aspects of Mayan culture. See, for example, David Carrasco, *Religions of Mesoamerica* (San Francisco: Harper and Row, 1990), pp. 13–14. In my accounts of the Aztec and Mayan cosmologies, I rely primarily on this excellent, philosoph-ically oriented text and on that classic work of philosophical anthropology by Miguel Leon-Portilla, *Aztec Thought and Culture* (Norman: University of Okla-homa Press, 1963).
2. Limitations of space and time preclude the analysis of some of the other pre-Columbian worldviews besides those of the Mayan, Aztec, and Inca cultures. These same limitations narrow the scope of my analysis of philosophical perspec-tives in both the colonial period and contemporary Latin America. My objective here is to provide an overview of some of the historically significant themes in the philosophical thought of the ancient and modern peoples of Latin America.
3. Carrasco, p. 51.
4. Carrasco, pp. 54–55.
5. Leon-Portilla, p. 84.
6. Carrasco, p. 118.
7. Leon-Portilla, pp. 44–45, citing Bernardino de Sahagun, *Historia General de las Cosas de Nueva España*, Vol. I, ed. Acosta Saignes, pp. 14–15.

122 Chapter Four

8. Linda Schele and Mary Ann Miller, *The Blood of Kings: Dynasty and Ritual in Maya Art* (Fort Worth, Tex.: Kimball Art Museum, 1986), pp. 177–78.

9. Ibid., p. 181.

10. Carrasco, p. 100.

11. I do not have the space here to go into a detailed explanation of the complex Mayan system of interlocking calendars. Suffice it to say that they developed their calendar system, which consisted of at least six different calendars, in order to pinpoint and keep track of the important events in their history. For an excellent explanation of their calendar system, see Schele and Miller, pp. 317–21.

12. Dennis Tedlock, trans., *Popul Vuh: The Definitive Edition of the Mayan Book of the Dawn of Life and the Glories of Gods and Kings* (New York: Simon and Schuster, 1985), p. 160.

13. Carrasco, p. 53.

14. Leon-Portilla, pp. 158–62.

15. Ibid., p. 163.

16. Ibid., p. 74.

17. Inga Clendinnen, *Aztecs: An Interpretation* (Cambridge: Cambridge University Press, 1991), pp. 213–14, citing Miguel Leon-Portilla, "Translating Amerindian Texts," *Latin American Indian Literatures* 7 (1983): 101–22, p. 119. In her book Clendinnen analyzes the implications of this poem for the Aztecs' vision of reality.

18. Clendinnen, pp. 214–16.

19. Leon-Portilla, p. 77.

20. *Ideología del Antiguo Perú*, diss., University of Lima, Peru, 1982.

21. Father Bernabe Cobo, *Inca Religion and Customs*, trans. and ed. Roland Hamilton (Austin: University of Texas Press, 1990), pp. 44–45.

22. Ibid., p. 56.

23. Plato (427–347 B.C.) maintained that there was an otherworldly, ideal abstract entity, or spiritual essence, for every type or category of concrete object in this world.

24. Carrasco, p. 129.

25. Eduardo Galeano, *Open Veins of Latin America: Five Centuries of the Pillage of a Continent*, trans. Cedric Belfrage (New York: Monthly Review Press, 1973), p. 33.

26. La Malintzi and El Cuatlapanga are beings associated with rain and other natural elements. They figure prominently in the beliefs of the people of traditional communities of the Tlaxcala region near Mexico City.

27. Sylvanus G. Morley and George W. Brainerd, rev. Robert J. Sharer, *The Ancient Maya* (Stanford, Calif.: Stanford University Press, 1983), p. 462.

28. There are, of course, exceptions to these tendencies in Western thought. Karl Marx, for example, maintained that economic and sociopolitical factors were of central importance for understanding the intellectual and philosophical perspectives of a society. Nevertheless, we can still speak in a general way of a Western philosophical tradition in which certain orientations have predominated.

29. Imperialism refers to the policy and practice that a more powerful country follows when it tries to control, either directly or indirectly, the territory, economic resources, and/or political events of another less powerful country (or countries).

30. The negative impact of U.S. economic policies and military interventionism in Latin America is well documented. See, for example, Jonathan L. Fried, Marvin E. Gettleman, Deborah T. Levenson, and Nancy Peckenham, eds., *Guatemala in Rebellion: Unfinished History* (New York: Grove Press, 1983). It is not my purpose here to discuss or assess the consequences of U.S. foreign policies in Latin America. It is important, however, to realize that the political and economic oppression of Latin America did not end with colonialism but continues into the present. This realization will help us to understand why certain issues have preoccupied Latin American philosophers.

31. Miguel Jorrin and John D. Martz, *Latin-American Political Thought and Ideology* (Chapel Hill: University of North Carolina Press, 1970), p. 126.

32. Ibid., pp. 140–43.

33. For an account of the economic exploitation of Latin American countries by the colonial powers and later by industrialized countries like the United States, see Eduardo Galeano, *Open Veins of Latin America,* op. cit.

34. José Carlos Mariategui, *Siete Ensayos de Interpretación de la Realidad Peruana: Escritos de Mundial y Amauta* (Lima: Ediciones Amauta, 1928).

35. Ibid., pp. 126–27.

36. Enrique Dussel, *The Philosophy of Liberation* (New York: Orbis Books, 1985). For a concise exposition of its central themes, see Douglas Kellner, "The Periphery, the Oppressed, and the Philosophy of Liberation," in *Theory, Culture, and Society* (London: Sage), Vol. 4 (1987), pp. 735–44.

37. Gustavo Gutierrez, *A Theology of Liberation,* trans. and ed. Sister Caridad Inda and John Eagleson (Maryknoll, N.Y.: Orbis Books, 1973), and *The Power of the Poor in History,* trans. Robert R. Barr (Maryknoll, N.Y.: Orbis Books, 1983).

38. This is the celebrated phrase used in the influential document prepared by the Catholic bishops at their conference in Medellín, Colombia, in 1968. This document signaled a significant change in the church's view of the poor in Latin America.

Glossary

axis mundi—A place or object regarded as the center of power of the cosmos or universe.

calmecacs—Aztec centers of higher education where the legends, traditions, and history of the culture were preserved and recorded. It was here that the Aztec wise men and poets raised questions about the nature of the world and their capacity to know reality.

cosmic tree—A symbol of the earth as a fertile, living entity capable of periodic regeneration.

Gaia Hypothesis—A view defended by some biologists and ecologists that the earth is a complex living organism consisting of many interacting ecological systems.

huacas—A general term used by the Incas to refer to deities, places of worship, and sacred places. It was also used to refer to natural objects that were extraordinary in size or shape.

Huitzilopochtli—The patron god of the Aztecs. He was also their war god, who was identified with the sun.

ihiyotl—A life force concentrated in the liver. The Aztecs believed it provided humans with bravery, desire, hatred, love, and happiness.

mallinalis—Spiral-shaped channels through which supernatural forces interacted between the celestial, terrestrial, and underworld levels in the Aztec universe.

metaphysical—Having to do with the area of philosophy that deals with the nature of reality beyond what is apparent to the senses.

Nahuatl—The language spoken by the Aztecs and most of the people of ancient central Mexico.

Ometeotl—The dual male/female god of the Aztecs who created the universe and sustains all life.

Pachacamac—One of the principal gods of the Incas, who created the earth and was the animating force of all living creatures.

5

Arabic Philosophy

Eric Ormsby

Reason is central to Islam. In the West, Islam is often depicted as a faith of unreasoning fanaticism, but in fact an intense preoccupation with reason is one of the most enduring and characteristic aspects of Islam and of Islamic culture, and this is especially evident in its philosophy. The bloodthirsty mobs of the evening news appear far removed from any shadow of reasonableness, and yet such images convey only a meager fraction of the truth. There is within Islam, as in many other theocentric cultures, a conflict between the dictates of reason and the prescriptions of revelation. Islamic philosophers, as well as jurists and theologians, experienced this conflict and confronted it, often in novel ways. But reason and the use of the human intellect, though seen by some as challenges to the all-encompassing mind of God, have occupied a position of unusual importance in the tradition of thought with which this chapter is concerned. Of course, faith is not the only source of fanaticism; a fanaticism of reason is also possible. But for Islamic thinkers, those philosophers who wrote in Arabic and whose works I will discuss here, the perennial problem was to strike a precarious and sometimes dangerous balance between reason and belief.

The great philosopher Abū Zakariyā' al-Rāzī has left an especially eloquent testimony to this central role of human reason. In his book entitled *Spiritual Medicine,* al-Rāzī wrote:

> Through reason we humans are made superior to inarticulate beasts so that we can own them and train them, tame them and manage them in ways by which advantages accrue to us as well as to them. Through reason we apprehend all that by which our life is elevated and made beautiful and good; through reason we attain our desires and the fulfillment of our wishes. . . .

Through reason we perceive distant and hidden matters that are veiled from us; through reason we know the shape of the earth and of the firmament and the magnitude of the sun and moon as well as the other stars, together with their distances and their motions. Through reason we arrive at knowledge of the Creator—He is exalted!—which is the most immense knowledge we can hope to attain, and the most beneficial object of our aspiration. In sum, reason is something without which our state would be the state of beasts, infants, and the insane.[1]

Al-Rāzī died in 925 A.D., and though he may be seen as atypical—by many critics he was considered to have been an outright atheist—his remarks are consistent with a point of view that recurs faithfully throughout the Islamic tradition. To appreciate this tradition and the philosophy it created, we must view it within a historical context.

The Historical Context of Islam

In the first half of the seventh century of the current era, Arab armies of conquest poured northward out of the obscurity of the Arabian peninsula—present-day Saudi Arabia—to establish the boundaries of a new empire stretching from the Straits of Gibraltar and Spain in the west to India and beyond in the east. These armies were made up of mostly illiterate tribesmen from the Hejaz, the western region of the Arabian peninsula, where a few moderately important caravan cities lay. These tribesmen were driven not only by the lure of conquest and plunder but by a newfound religious zeal. And wherever these Arab Muslims penetrated, the new faith of Islam took root. Islam did not prevail by the force of the sword alone but by example and persuasion as well. Islam, which literally means "submission" in Arabic, is supremely simple in its elements. It is also egalitarian. Equally important, those who converted were more likely to prosper under the new order. Jews and Christians especially, as members of "religions of the book," enjoyed respect and protection under Muslim rule in certain periods, but it was still distinctly advantageous to convert to Islam. In the sweep of conquest the Muslim conquerors left largely intact the bureaucratic structures established by earlier empires, such as the Byzantine and the Sassanian empires, though the language of official discourse did change from Greek or Persian to Arabic.

It is easy to forget how deeply into Europe the Arab conquests pressed, not solely into Spain, but far into southern France. The possible consequences of this remarkable incursion were drawn out by Edward Gibbon in a famous passage:

A victorious line of march had been prolonged above a thousand miles from the rock of Gibraltar to the banks of the Loire; the repetition of an equal space would have carried the Saracens to the confines of Poland and the Highlands of Scotland; the Rhine is not more impassable than the Nile or Euphrates, and the Arabian fleet might have sailed without a naval combat into the mouth of the Thames. Perhaps the interpretation of the Koran would now be taught in the schools of Oxford, and her pulpits might demonstrate to a circumcised people the sanctity and truth of the revelation of Mohammed.[2]

The ascendancy of the Arabic language is of the utmost importance in the rise of Arabic philosophy, by which we mean that body of thought formulated and preserved in classical Arabic. For the spread of the Islamic religion also carried with it the spread of Arabic as a language not merely of illiterate desert dwellers, but capable of the highest and most sophisticated levels of expression. Thomas Aquinas in the thirteenth century spoke disparagingly of the Arabs as "bestial people living in deserts," yet by his time Aquinas and his contemporaries were already immensely indebted to a long Arabic language tradition of translation of and textual commentary on the fundamental works of ancient Greek thought. For Arab thinkers did not merely transmit the works of Aristotle and other Greek philosophers to the West, as is so commonly noted; far more important, these Arab thinkers mediated the understanding of Greek thought to the West. And Aristotle, among others, was read and comprehended by Latin scholastics through the unfamiliar but compelling gaze of the Arab thinkers who had come before. The medieval understanding of Greek philosophy in Europe is inextricably entwined with, and dependent on, its interpretation and reformulation by Arab thinkers.

The Arabic philosophical tradition cannot be appreciated without recognition of two factors of great importance: the Islamic revelation itself as contained principally in such sacred texts as the Qur'ān (Koran) and the Sunnah, the exemplary conduct of the prophet Muhammad as preserved by his companions and others; and, of almost equal significance, the specific nature of the classical Arabic language.

The Religion of Islam

The beginnings of Islam can be documented with some precision. Muslims themselves commence their calendar with the *hijrah,* or emigration, of the prophet Muhammad from Mecca, his native city, to Madinah (Medina), a city some 200 miles away, in the year 622 A.D., which marks the Islamic year 1. Muslim traditional dating, which follows a lunar calendar, begins therefore in year 1 of the *hijrah,* or A.H. (for *anno hegirae*). Muhammad himself was a relatively unprosperous and illiterate merchant from the powerful and influential clan of the Quraysh. Eventually he made a fortunate marriage with an affluent older woman by the name of Khadījah. When he was in his forties, Muhammad withdrew for

a period of retreat, a common religious practice among the more devout
pagan Arabs of the time, and while he was in the mountains near the city
of Mecca, he experienced a profound revelation. The angel Gabriel—
Jibrīl, in Arabic—appeared before him and commanded him to recite
(iqra'). This revelation was the first of a continuous sequence of supernatural inspirations that Muhammad committed to memory and gradually
conveyed to a growing number of disciples and followers. The Qur'ān, or
"recitation" in the word's original sense, is the written expression of
these revelations to Muhammad over the remaining twenty or so years of
his life, and is considered sacrosanct by Muslims in both its contents and
verbal form. Indeed, traditional Muslims hold that the very letters of the
Qur'ān are sacred and represent direct utterances by God.

It is virtually impossible to overemphasize the centrality of both the
Qur'ān itself and the language in which it is expressed in discussing
philosophy in the Arabic tradition. Daily recitation of the scriptures, as
well as memorization of parts, or even the entire book, have been
incumbent upon pious Muslims for centuries. The Arabic of the Qur'ān,
originally the particular dialect of Arabic spoken in the Hejaz by certain
tribes, has become normative. This fact is of great importance for our
purposes here, for the creation of a lingua franca, a common language
available to all Muslims as well as to their non-Muslim subjects, made
possible an increasingly sophisticated medium of discourse. Of course,
the Qur'ān itself does not use a philosophical vocabulary; in fact,
Qur'ānic Arabic is extremely vivid and concrete as well as poetic. Thus,
the words of the angel Gabriel to Muhammad, given in sūrah 96, are (in
the translation of A. J. Arberry):

Recite: in the name of thy Lord who created, created man of a blood-clot.
Recite: and thy Lord is the most-bountiful,
who taught by the pen,
taught man what he knew not.
No, indeed: surely man waxes insolent,
for he thinks himself self-sufficient.
Surely unto thy Lord is the returning.

The direct and forceful language of the Qur'ān, by Muslims deemed
inimitable, gave to Arabic an incalculable prestige within Islamic culture
for centuries and made possible the creation of a distinctive Islamic
thought. In Muslim religious schools from Morocco to Iran, even today,
an indigenous tradition of study with its own canonical curriculum continues in force. Arabic philosophy, or what Arabic philosophy has become
after more than a millennium of development and refinement, remains
important in many of these schools today. Such a figure as the Ayatollah
Khomeini in Iran, whatever his political pronouncements, was himself
steeped in the traditional curriculum of the schools of Najaf and Qum, a

tradition upon which he himself and other clerics in Iran commented and drew. And a particular and characteristic type of philosophy formed an integral part of this curriculum, and continues to be important. This is not the "academic" philosophy of the West, nor is it strictly comparable to the philosophical or theological training given in Western seminaries. Rather, such Islamic, or Arabic, thought possesses its own original and distinctive characteristics, and is the product of a long and complicated development. What began as an eager assimilation and absorption of an alien tradition, the body of Greek thought that was translated into Arabic a century or so after the conquests, developed into a refined, original, and influential tradition of philosophical thought.

The Arabic Language and Its Diffusion

The classical Arabic in which this tradition is expressed is an immensely flexible and subtle language that possesses in its very structure a seemingly infinite capacity for expansion and invention. In this respect, certain intrinsic features of classical Arabic should be noted. First, as a Semitic language, Arabic depends upon a system of fixed verbal elements, or consonantal roots, with which it is possible to convey an enormous range of meanings and nuances. For example, the root *k-t-b*, which expresses the notion of "writing," accepts certain patterns of vowels by which various denotations are expressed, for example, *kataba* "he wrote," *kātib* "writer" or "scribe," *kitāb* "book," *maktab* "office," *maktabah* "library," *kuttāb* "Qur'ān school," *maktūb* "letter," and so on. The availability of certain fixed combinations of vowels and consonants with a variety of prefixes, suffixes, and infixes gives Arabic an immense potential for word building. (Indeed, the standard medieval dictionary of the classical language runs to twenty massive volumes.) In addition, existing words could be enlarged with new significations. The creation of a new and precise philosophical vocabulary was the first, and continuing, contribution of Arabic philosophy.

In the aftermath of the conquests, the Arab invaders came into contact with members of other, and older, civilizations. At the same time, as representatives of a vigorous and proselytizing faith, they encountered spokesmen for older faiths—Judaism, Christianity, and Zoroastrianism— who had the advantage of a well-developed language of discourse and sophisticated modes of argumentation. In the Arabian peninsula, to be sure, heathen Arabs had lived among Jews and Christians, but now, for the first time, they found themselves espousing an alternative worldview, and yet they lacked the intellectual weapons with which to pursue a conquest of minds and hearts, as well as of bodies. Christians and Jews, by contrast, possessed extremely supple and well-honed modes of discourse and persuasion. Even a cursory glance at the work of such a figure as John of Damascus with his intricate "negative" theology will reveal the vast gulf which in the seventh century still separated Muslims from their more sophisticated intellectual adversaries.

It is important to remember, too, that in their conquests the Arabs came to occupy territories formerly the possession of both the Sassanian and Byzantine empires. The Persians with their long and imposing cultural tradition might dismiss Arabs as mere "lizard eaters," but after the last Sassanian king, Yazdegerd III, was hunted down and killed, Persians came under Arab, and Islamic, dominance. It was thus significant not merely that Arabs themselves came up against more sophisticated civilizations, but that the inhabitants of these civilizations found themselves increasingly obliged to adopt Islam as their religion and Arabic as their medium of expression. One consequence of this intricate process of Islamization was that "Arabic philosophy," as we call it here, was in reality created by several different ethnic groups who adopted classical Arabic as their language of civilized discourse. Indeed, not only Persians, Greeks, Turks, and other nationalities elected Arabic; it became the preferred language of Christians, Jews, and Zoroastrians. How did this remarkable transformation occur? How did Arabic become such a powerful and nuanced vehicle of communication, such that centuries later the great Jewish philosopher Maimonides would compose his masterpiece, *The Guide of the Perplexed,* in Judeo-Arabic, Arabic written in Hebrew letters?

Translations into Arabic

Under the early Abbasid caliphs, and especially under the rule of the caliph Ma'mūn (reigned 813–833 A.D.), official patronage made possible the creation of a kind of early Islamic think tank, the "House of Wisdom" *(bayt al-ḥikmah),* perhaps on the model of such prestigious pre-Islamic academies as Gundishapur in Sassanian Persia, or others in late Hellenistic Alexandria. One of the principal achievements of this House of Wisdom was the translation of works of Greek medicine, science, and philosophy into Arabic. These translations were the accomplishment of Christian (Nestorian) scholars, such as Hunayn ibn Ishaq (d. 876 A.D.) and his son, among others, who worked from the original Greek texts; these texts, including not only the Hippocratic corpus of medical writings but such obscure and yet influential Aristotelian commentators as Alexander of Aphrodisias and John Philoponus, the Nestorian translators first converted into their native Syriac (the Christian dialect of Aramaic). From Syriac they then cast their translations into Arabic, coining and minting new technical terms where none had existed in Arabic before. Some terms were simply transposed into Arabic. Thus, Greek *philosophia* came directly into Arabic as *falsafah,* and a philosopher was henceforth to be known in Arabic as a *faylasūf;* a new quadriliteral verbal root was likewise coined: *tafalsafa,* "to philosophize." Again, the Greek word *genos* (genus) came into Arabic via Syriac as *jins.* For other foreign terms, Arabic words could be used with a new twist. Terms drawn from grammar or jurisprudence, disciplines developed with great ingenuity by Islam in its formative period, could be applied with a philosophical significance. Words such as *fā'il,* which basically denotes an agent, or the subject of an action, could come to denote the Supreme Agent, or God.

But the majority of new terms required translation; terms for which no term had hitherto existed, such as "substance" or "accident" or "contingency," as well as the complex technical vocabulary of such disciplines as logic, had to be discovered. Thus, for "substance" the Arabic word *jawhar* (taken from Persian *gawhar*) was employed; the term would also be used to designate "atom." Classical Arabic, the Arabic of the Qur'ān and of early Bedouin poetry, is an intensely vivid and concrete language with scores of terms for the physical world. The vast vocabulary pertaining to camels, sand, and climatic conditions is justly famous in this regard. Typical are the opening lines of the famous "Suspended Ode" of the pre-Islamic poet Labīd:

> The houses and the waystations have been wiped away at Mina;
> Ghawl and Rijam have reverted to wilderness,
> And the gorges of the torrents of Rayyām are blurred
> And worn like stones where old inscriptions cling.
> Where travelers bedded down, only black ash remains
> And the years with their daily rounds and festivals
> Have poured over them, fed by the rains of the spring stars,
> Thunderheads' downpour and the fine, vaporous, continual rain
> From every night-flowing cloud and darkening cloud of dawn,
> And from the evening clouds whose reverberations roar . . .[3]

One of the problems confronting translators was to find ways of rendering into this language abstract terms—universals such as "divinity," or "humanity," or "reality." Nevertheless, the adaptability of classical Arabic is such that abstractions begot abstractions to an almost dizzying extent, particularly in later texts, where a kind of formulaic jargon is common. Sometimes this seems to degenerate into excessively subtle hairsplitting, but more often, philosophical Arabic displays a marvelous capacity for nuance and distinction. For example, the eighteenth-century scholar al-Kalanbawī can distinguish almost twenty distinct senses of such a term as "possibility."

With the impact of Western thought on Arabic culture, beginning in the late eighteenth century, the language has continued to grow and accommodate new terms and new ideologies, from such alien notions as capitalism and socialism to Hegelian metaphysics.

Arabic Philosophy

The central importance of the Arabic language in the history of Arabic philosophy brings us squarely before two salient features of this tradition that deserve notice.

First, Arabic philosophy is a bookish philosophy. By and large, Arab philosophers took their agenda of philosophical topics and questions wholesale from Greek thought. And in an important sense, much of Arabic philosophy constitutes an extensive and continuing commentary on Greek philosophy. At the same time, however, Arab philosophers created a highly original and profound body of thought that deserves study in its own right. It is tempting to look for some rudiments of philosophical thought prior to the introduction of the Greek legacy into Islam, and occasionally, in some of the early poetry, for example, we do find vague musings of a quasi-philosophical nature, usually on the nature of destiny. In the Qur'ān, too, there are passages suggestive of, or conducive to, philosophical reflection and indeed, in the later tradition, Qur'ānic passages will often be given in confirmation of a disputed point. But philosophy, in any strict sense, can be said to begin within the Islamic world only with the study of translations from the Greek.

The extent of this translation was impressive. Works of immediate practical value were early translated, for example, the works of the Greek physicians, and especially Hippocrates and Galen, known to the Arabs as Buqrāṭ and Jālīnūs, respectively. Moreover, Galen was as influential for his philosophical writings as for his medical texts. Works of science were also important, including treatises on astronomy, alchemy, and mathematics. By far the most significant for our purposes, however, were the quite extensive and careful translations of such philosophers as Plato, Aristotle, Proclus, and Plotinus. For example, Arab philosophers such as al-Fārābī and Ibn Sīnā (Avicenna) had at their disposal translations of Plato's *Republic, Timaeus,* and *Laws,* as well as of Aristotle's *Metaphysics, Nicomachean Ethics,* and the *Organon* of logical treatises, among others.

Often the works of these thinkers were available only in fragments, or were subject to misattribution. For example, the *Elements* of Proclus, the Neoplatonic philosopher, was known to Arab thinkers as the *Book of Causes* and attributed to Aristotle. Certain portions of Plotinus's *Enneads* were translated as the *Theology of Aristotle,* and Plotinus himself was known only as "the Greek master." Obviously, in many instances, chance governed which works survived; thus, while Aristotle's *Metaphysics* was known and studied, his *Politics* remained unknown to Arab thinkers.

In general, the names of the great Greek philosophers were Arabicized: Aristotle became Arisṭūṭālīs, Plato Aflaṭūn, and Socrates Suqrāṭ, to mention but the most prominent.

Arab thinkers had a relatively wide knowledge of Greek thought. They were aware, for example, of certain of the pre-Socratic philosophers, such as Heraclitus and Empedocles, evidently through the account of them in Aristotle's *Metaphysics*. At the same time, however, works by Aristotle and Plato were occasionally confounded and, as in the case of al-Fārābī, an effort made to reconcile their apparently contradictory views. In general, the ancients and their works were held in high esteem; they themselves were known as "the wise" (*ḥakīm*, plural *ḥukamā'*), which is another rendering of "philosopher," the lover of "wisdom" (*ḥikmah*). The fact that these wise and ancient thinkers had not been Muslims did not seriously detract from their prestige; this finds a parallel in Dante's treatment of the "virtuous heathen," who are placed in the antechamber of the Inferno in a state of natural happiness.

In this chapter I will treat only the most characteristic aspect of Arab philosophy, that is, the "peripatetic" tradition, which begins with al-Kindī and comes to a conclusion in the monumental work of Ibn Rushd, or Averroes. This should not obscure the fact that other traditions of philosophy, though not called *falsafah,* have existed and continue to exist in Islamic and Arabic-speaking milieus. There is, for example, a highly sophisticated mystical tradition known as Sufism, which dates from the earliest period and thrives even today in a wide variety of permutations; in some very significant traditions, mystical and philosophical thought have been reconciled to create a distinctive and systematic mystical philosophy, or theosophy. Certain of these later developments involve various esoteric doctrines. There is as well an important and extensive Iranian tradition in philosophy that comes to its fullest flower in the centuries after the death of Ibn Rushd and the decline of *falsafah* and that still flourishes today. Moreover, certain philosophers in this later Iranian tradition, and particularly Mīr Dāmād and Mullā Ṣadrā, must rank among the greatest and most creative intellects that Islam has produced.

The second general aspect of Arabic philosophy to be emphasized is its systematic and encyclopedic nature. Such thinkers as al-Fārābī or Ibn Sīnā (Avicenna) sought to encompass the entire world of knowledge of their time; they wrote not merely on such subjects as logic and metaphysics but on questions of natural science, statecraft, and music. This ambitious quest for universality and coherence is characteristic of the best and most profound philosophy in the *falsafah* tradition. Moreover, the tradition was cumulative, as in the West; that is, thinkers built upon, and took issue with, the arguments of their predecessors. This creates a linked chain of thought between al-Kindī, the first *faylasūf,* and Ibn Rushd, the last such thinker, and confers a kind of coherence upon the tradition that is also typical of other indigenous Islamic disciplines, such as grammar or disputation or theology. In the West, one thinker such as Montaigne may provoke a development in a later thinker such as Pascal, and their "dialogue" over the span of centuries represents the confrontation of two extraordinary minds. Within the Islamic realm, by contrast, with its highly developed commentary tradition and its reliance on a personal conferring of legitimacy by a teacher to a student, the process is less centered on extraordinary individual minds, though these are important, than on a transmission and tradition of reasoning that is the product of many minds.

To understand the emergence of the *falsafah* tradition, moreover, it is essential to realize that a vigorous and productive form of dialectical reasoning already existed within Islam. From an extremely early period, as we have noted, Muslims came into contact with spokesmen of other faiths, and especially representatives of Christianity and Judaism. Contacts, often disputational, between faiths impelled Muslims to develop effective tools and skills of argumentation and persuasion. In addition, the very fact that the Qur'ān and the Sunnah left certain questions open inevitably prompted theological speculation. Questions of interpretation abounded, not surprisingly in view of the sporadic and rapturous nature of the Qur'ānic revelation. Simultaneously, an exceedingly intricate and forceful body of theoretical and practical jurisprudence was taking shape, in which the role of independent reasoning would assume a problematic character. Some jurists admitted human reason as one "root" of law; others rejected, or minimized, its role.

What is important for our purposes is that such fundamental notions as reason came under scrutiny from an early date. Echoes of this early concern would be heard throughout Islamic history, most conspicuously in the disputes over the primacy of "reason" and "tradition" (in Arabic, *'aql* and *naql*, respectively), which persisted for centuries and preoccupied philosophers inescapably. For if all truth has been revealed by revelation and is comprised within a valid tradition of precept and example, what possible role can the unaided human intellect play in ascertaining the truth? And such statements as that of al-Kindī, for example, that the object of philosophy must be to determine "the true nature of things" would be provocative to more traditionally minded Muslims: Was not the true nature of things made plain in God's own word embodied in the scripture?

Theology and jurisprudence were significant, if often ignored, parallel disciplines to *falsafah*. Grammar too played an important role. One of the most impressive contributions of native Arab thinkers was in fact the elaboration of a corpus of grammatical and linguistic thought that came to dwell not merely on the morphology and syntax of the Arabic language but on the very nature of human language itself.

These are ancillary matters and rarely, if ever, mentioned by the philosophers as such; nevertheless, such "Islamic sciences" as theology, jurisprudence, and grammar were intertwined and had numerous points of juncture. Within the discussions of the philosophers themselves, furthermore, there exists an awareness of traditional concepts that they often seek to reconcile with the truths of reason and the inherited truths of the ancient Greek tradition.

It is true that the philosophers sometimes speak slightingly of the dialectical theologians, the *mutakallimun,* but the philosophers' forms of discourse are often influenced by dialectical theology, the *kalām.* More significantly, in later centuries, and after the selective assimilation of certain of the methods and tools of philosophy by the mystic al-Ghazālī, philosophy and theology come to be quite distinctively amalgamated in Islamic thought. We shall consider this distinctive synthesis at the end of this chapter.

Abū Yūsuf Ya'qūb ibn Isḥāq *al-Kindī* (ca. 800–866)

It may appear that Arabic philosophy sprang full-blown into existence in the person of al-Kindī,[4] who was born around 800 A.D., but this is misleading. Al-Kindī was born in Kufa, one of the early cantonment cities in southern Iraq established by the armies of conquest, and his father was for a time the Abbasid governor of Basra, another such garrison city. Both Kufa and Basra were places of intense and original intellectual activity by the time of al-Kindī's birth; this activity centered on a number of disciplines indigenous to Islamic culture, such as Arabic grammar, the explication of the Qur'ān, and the principles of law, all of which would have important consequences for philosophy. More significantly, both cities were hotbeds of theological speculation and disputation, dominated by the powerful movement known as the Mu'tazilites. Though the Mu'tazilites differed among themselves on any number of issues—there were many factions, each with its own leader and sharply defined theological agenda—the movement generally stressed the transcendent unity and the justice of God. A corollary of these principles was the tenaciously held Mu'tazilite view of the primacy of human reason.

It seems clear that al-Kindī had links with this movement. The fact that some Abbasid caliphs—and especially the caliph al-Ma'mūn—supported and endorsed Mu'tazilism as an official theology (and persecuted its critics, such as the traditionist Ibn Hanbal), and that al-Kindī himself enjoyed patronage under the same caliphs, suggests at least some congruence of views. In addition, Mu'tazilite notions frequently appear in al-Kindī's own works: For example, al-Kindī puts great emphasis on divine unity and on a repudiation of divine attributes; he also upholds the characteristic Mu'tazilite view that this universe is optimal in all respects, a position that can be traced back philosophically to Plato's *Timaeus.* Perhaps most important, al-Kindī repeatedly underlines the indispensable role of intellect, and this hallowed position of the intellect is especially consonant with the Mu'tazilite worldview.

Furthermore, we know that when official protection of the Mu'tazilites came to an end, in the caliphate of al-Mutawakkil (reigned 847–861), al-Kindī also fell into disfavor; according to one account, the caliph even had him flogged.

The link with the Mu'tazilites is significant because it underscores an important aspect of al-Kindī's thought. Unlike later philosophers in the *falsafah* tradition, al-Kindī explicitly upheld a belief in the creation of the world from nothing. Moreover, he constantly sought a way to reconcile the truths revealed by religion with the truths available to the unaided human intellect. For al-Kindī, there was an ultimate convergence of both in a single truth. As a result, despite all his immersion in Greek thought, al-Kindī is a particularly Islamic figure, seeking to assimilate the wisdom and methodology of the past with the revelation of scripture. This attempt will occupy other Arabic philosophers, but none perhaps will be as consistent and as explicit as al-Kindī in the attempt.

Al-Kindī is representative in other ways. His approach to knowledge is universal and comprehensive, and he himself is a kind of Islamic "Renaissance man." His interests and expertise thus included not only philosophy, but mathematics, astronomy and astrology, medicine, politics, meteorology, theology, and music, as well as such applied crafts as the making of glass, jewelry, and armor. Later Arabic philosophers will also display this universal curiosity and competence, in addition to an amazing output. Some 242 individual writings are attributed to al-Kindī, of which only about forty survive today. These interests, of course, were not all theoretical; al-Kindī's livelihood depended on many of them. Indeed, the patronage he enjoyed at the Abbasid court depended more probably on his skill in astrology than on his philosophical acumen (though it should be noted that the caliphs were themselves keenly interested in philosophical, theological, and scientific questions). Al-Kindī regarded astrology as an exact science, and even sought to determine the future duration of the "empire of the Arabs." He predicted that the empire would last another 693 years and found this result to be consistent with scriptural predictions.[5]

Al-Kindī is a pivotal figure in Arabic philosophy. On the one hand, he looks backward to his predecessors among the ancients, and especially Aristotle, with a genuine reverence. On the other hand, he looks forward; one of his chief undertakings was the attempt to forge a new philosophical vocabulary, an attempt that would be superseded and refined by later philosophers. In all his endeavors, his final criterion is *al-ḥaqq*—Arabic for "the truth"—and so he states, "We should not be ashamed to acknowledge truth from whatever source it comes to us, even if it is brought to us by former generations and foreign peoples. For him who seeks the truth there is nothing of higher value than truth itself."[6]

In a little book of definitions of philosophical terms, al-Kindī wrote that philosophy, in addition to being the "love of wisdom," as its Greek name denotes, is "comparable to divine activity to the extent of man's capacity."[7] This definition, which goes back to Plato and was especially popular among the later Neoplatonists, illustrates how al-Kindī attempts to coordinate Greek thought with Islamic understanding. He explains that what the ancients meant by this was that man should be "perfected in virtue." In other words, to avoid any overt comparison between God and man, al-Kindī places his emphasis on human activity, especially such activities as awareness of death. This is a philosophical task par excellence since it is a twofold activity, involving not only awareness of the soul's inevitable relinquishment of the body but the philosopher's goal of mastering and deadening the passions, which are at war with reason. Philosophy is thus, for al-Kindī, ultimately "man's knowledge of himself."[8]

To philosophize is to ascertain the causes of things. To know the cause of something is to understand it. Following Aristotle, al-Kindī distinguishes four causes, which are themselves four objects of knowledge: the "whether?" of something, that is, does it exist; the "what?" of something, that is, what it is; the "which?" of a thing, that is, the specific category into which it falls; and the "why?" or the ultimate purpose of a thing. This hearkens back to Aristotle's *Physics* with its enumeration of material, formal, efficient, and final causes.[9]

In attempting to grapple with these notions, al-Kindī must devise new terms, for philosophical terminology had not by his time been fully formulated, let alone codified. Sometimes he falls back on archaic terms in Arabic to render such concepts as "existence" and "nonexistence," and at other times he invents new words, such as the verbal forms *hawwā* and *tahawwā* for "to bring into being," with the literal sense of to cause its "itsness" *(huwīya)*. It is interesting to see this early philosopher struggle to express ideas previously unknown. Al-Kindī was an ardent advocate of translation from the Greek into Arabic and even commissioned some translations; thus, he is reported to have had part of Aristotle's *Metaphysics* translated by one Astāt (Eustathius) into Arabic, as well as the so-called *Theology of Aristotle* (in reality, a compendium of excerpts from Plotinus).

For al-Kindī, existence falls into two broad realms: the realm of nature and of physical things, which is characterized by movement; and the realm above natural beings, which is characterized by immobility. The first realm is the material, moving, created world; the second is the immaterial and immovable divine realm. The first is the subject of natural inquiry; the second the subject of "first philosophy," the study of first causes, or metaphysics.

Furthermore, in discussing the nature of action and of agency, al-Kindī distinguishes between true agency, which is the prerogative of God alone—in al-Kindī's terminology, God is "The One, The Real"—and the apparent agency of all other beings, which is action only in a metaphorical sense. As with the theologians, for al-Kindī, God is the sole agent. At the same time, however, al-Kindī, unlike many of the theologians, accepts secondary causation. The divine action is exemplified particularly in the act of creation, which entails the creation of existing things out of non-existence (in Arabic, *ibdā'*); all other action is merely the result of cause and effect.

Later Arabic philosophers will accept the ancient Greek philosophical notion of an eternal universe, but al-Kindī explicitly rejects this. At the same time, he also accepts the reality of bodily resurrection and of miracles—articles of Islamic faith but stumbling blocks for later philosophers. Al-Kindī accepts a universe of emanation that is clearly indebted to later Neoplatonic philosophers. According to this scheme of reality, there are hierarchies of Intelligences. From the First Intelligence, itself dependent on the prior act of Divine Will, further Intelligences emanate in strict hierarchical order down to the lowest level, the sphere beneath the moon, our sublunary level. This ancient philosophical cosmogony will be extensively elaborated by later Arabic philosophers.

In his view of "The One, The Real," or God, al-Kindī also shows an indebtedness to earlier Greek, and perhaps even Christian, thinkers (such as John Philoponus). It is typical of this approach to discuss ultimate reality purely in terms of what it is not, that is, by means of a negative, or apophatic, approach. Thus, in his important treatise "On First Philosophy," al-Kindī states:

> The True One, therefore, has neither matter, form, quantity, quality, or relation, is not described by any of the remaining intelligible things, and has neither genus/specific difference, individual property, common accident or movement; and it is not described by any of the things which are denied to be one in truth. It is, accordingly, pure and simple unity, i.e., (having) nothing other than unity, while every other one is multiple.[10]

Al-Kindī died in approximately 866 A.D., in poverty, obscurity, and official disfavor. He left several important students and disciples: the astrologer Abū Mash'ar al-Balkhī and the philosophers Abū Zayd Balkhī and Aḥmad ibn Ṭayyib al-Sarakhsī (833–899). Like al-Kindī, al-Sarakhsī for a time enjoyed the patronage of the Abbasid caliph al-Mu'tadid but eventually fell into disfavor and was executed. Unfortunately, the work of al-Sarakhsī, al-Kindī's most important follower, is lost.

Abū Bakr Muḥammad ibn Zakarīyā' *al-Rāzī* (865–ca. 925)

Al-Rāzī's fame and the survival of his works rest on his reputation as a physician. As a philosopher, he stood outside the main Arabic tradition and provoked controversy and condemnation; indeed, much of his most provocative philosophical work has been preserved only in the refutations of his adversaries.

As his name indicates, al-Rāzī was born in Rayy, a town close to present-day Teheran, in Iran, around 865 A.D. We know little of his early life and education. According to some reports, he was fond of music and played the lute, but this may be simply an extrapolation from the high place al-Rāzī accords to music in his philosophy. His training in medicine and in science must have been thorough, for he rose at an early age— some say, around the age of thirty—to be director of the hospital at Rayy; he later headed the hospital at Baghdad.

It is clear from his writings, in philosophy as well as in medicine, that al-Rāzī was extremely knowledgeable in ancient Greek and in earlier Islamic authorities; allusions to and citations from Plato, Aristotle, Alexander of Aphrodisias, John Philoponus, Hippocrates, and Galen are frequent in his treatises. At the same time, however, al-Rāzī was unusually independent in his thinking. He never hesitates to advance his own opinion if he concludes that an earlier authority is mistaken. His great compendium of medicine, known in Arabic as *al-Hāwī*, was translated into Latin under the title *Continens* and was known to generations of physicians, including Vesalius, in the West. To the Latin Middle Ages, al-Rāzī was known as Rhazes.

As a philosopher, al-Rāzī is an outsider in many respects to the Arabic tradition. For one thing, he explicitly declares himself a follower of Plato, and rejects much of Aristotle; for al-Rāzī, Socrates is the model of the philosopher, and he refers to him as "Socrates, our *imām*" (leader), while he calls Plato the "*shaykh* of philosophers," that is, the master. Moreover, certain of his views show direct affinities with such Greek thinkers as Democritus and Epicurus.

Al-Rāzī is an Arabic Platonist not only in his respect for Plato and Socrates as philosophers but in his adoption of certain characteristic Platonic notions, which are, however, deeply tinged with Neoplatonic thought, especially that of Proclus. Al-Rāzī seems to have known well the works of Proclus in translation. For example, al-Rāzī accepts the Platonic tripartite division of the human soul into (1) the "divine, rational soul"; (2) "the animal, irascible soul"; and (3) the "appetitive, growing, vegetative soul."[11] Furthermore, al-Rāzī rejected the notion of the creation of the world from nothing, but accepted a view of matter as eternal; the creator thus becomes a kind of demiurge and, like the demiurge in Plato's *Timaeus*, the creator constructs a world from preexistent matter in the "highest perfection."[12]

Furthermore, as we have already seen in al-Rāzī's praise of reason at the beginning of this chapter, he regarded the human intellect as the indispensable instrument for the determination of truth. This primacy of intellect had two important consequences in al-Rāzī's worldview. First, reason took precedence over prophetic revelation, and al-Rāzī refused to credit the prophets of established religions, including Judaism and Christianity but also Islam itself, with any preeminence in knowledge. Second, al-Rāzī held that the use of the intellect was a great equalizer among people; he rejected the notion of an elite with special and privileged insights. Any human being had access to the truth through the use of reason. As he wrote:

> Whoever makes an effort and busies himself with study and research has set out on the way of truth. Indeed, the souls of men can be purified from the mud and darkness of this world and saved for the world to come only by the study of philosophy.[13]

Such a position brought al-Rāzī into direct conflict both with representatives of mainstream Islam and with those sects, such as the Ismailis, for whom the esoteric teachings of an imam, and a hierarchy of initiates, were fundamental. Some of the principal attacks on al-Rāzī, in fact, were launched by his fellow townsman, the Ismaili Abū Hātim al-Rāzī.

Another distinctive position of al-Rāzī is that philosophy entails a total way of life. Indeed, he wrote a book called "The Philosophical Life," and the word he uses for "life" connotes an exemplary life; it is a word usually associated with the life of the prophet Muhammad in early biographies. For al-Rāzī, the life of philosophy alone permits human beings to integrate knowledge and action into a single whole. Philosophy enables people to avoid the "evil codes and laws" that certain religions impose and that lead to destruction and confusion. Like al-Kindī before him, al-Rāzī espouses the old Neoplatonic notion that through philosophy, human beings come to resemble God to the extent of their capacities. But for al-Rāzī, this meant that humans should be "knowing and just and compassionate," as God is.

Somewhat surprisingly, al-Rāzī appears to have believed in a form of transmigration of souls, or metempsychosis. Thus, in a discussion of the sufferings of animals, he finds justification for the slaughter of domestic animals only in the possibility that their souls may be released into higher forms.

In some hostile accounts of his thought, al-Rāzī is credited with a belief in five "eternal principles." These are the Creator, the Universal Soul, Matter, Absolute Time, and Absolute Space. Al-Rāzī's discussion of time, in particular, with his distinction between "measured" and "unmeasured" time, suggests links both with the Neoplatonic thinker Proclus and with pre-Islamic Zoroastrian doctrines.

Finally, al-Rāzī is notable for another, less easily demonstrated characteristic. In his writings, even those that are fragmentary, a highly distinctive and individual voice comes through; he allows himself the occasional personal comment, as when he notes that although he had written almost two hundred works, he wrote nothing on mathematics, not because he was incapable of doing so, but because he deliberately chose not to. His "Philosophical Life" is also a kind of autobiography and he reveals details about himself in a way that makes him real to the reader, even more than a thousand years after his death. The philosophical autobiography is a form that Ibn Sīnā, and al-Ghazālī after him would make their own as well. Al-Rāzī's autobiography gives us a vivid portrait of a Socrates in Arabic form.

Abū Naṣr *al-Fārābī* (died ca. 950)

Though al-Fārābī is one of the greatest Arab thinkers, perhaps even the very greatest, little is known of his life. He was born in Turkestan and was himself of Turkish stock; his father was possibly a member of the caliph's Turkish guard. He spent most of his life in Baghdad, where he came into fruitful contact with members of the Christian Aristotelian school of philosophy. His teacher is reputed to have been the Nestorian Christian Yuḥannā ibn Haylān and he may have known the famous translator and commentator Abū Bishr Mattā ibn Yūnus as well. In 942, he was invited to the court of the Hamdanid ruler Sayf al-Dawlah and spent the last years of his life in Aleppo. He died around 950 at a ripe old age.

In the Islamic tradition, al-Fārābī is known as "the second teacher," second only to Aristotle, the "first teacher." This title reflects the high esteem accorded to al-Fārābī, but it also accentuates the continuity that is felt to exist between the ancient Greek philosopher and the medieval Islamic philosopher. In part, this is due to al-Fārābī's close attention to the Aristotelian tradition, as mediated by late Greek and early Christian Aristotelians. Much of al-Fārābī's writing consists of commentaries on Aristotelian works. For example, al-Fārābī composed commentaries on all the works in the *Organon,* which included not merely the logical works but the *Rhetorics* and *Poetics* as well, in accord with the late Greek tradition. He also commented on Aristotle's *Physics,* his *Meteorology,* and portions of the *Nicomachean Ethics.*

For al-Fārābī, however, Plato was important as well and, again like his late Greek predecessors, he attempted to reconcile the two ancient masters in his *Harmony Between the Views of Plato and Aristotle.* But al-Fārābī did not merely parrot the opinions of the ancients, following Aristotle in one view and Plato in another. Rather, he strove to make philosophy his own in a particularly thorough way. Thus, while he commented on Aristotelian treatises in logic, he also sought to assimilate Aristotelian logic within an Arabic context. This introduction of Aristotelian logic was an undertaking with immense and far-reaching consequences. Reliance on Aristotelian logic was also controversial. It was controversial not only because it was the invention of a pre-Islamic (that is, pagan) thinker, and a non-Muslim to boot, but also because it seemed to provide a form of intellectual autonomy independent of revealed truth. If truth can be determined by means of syllogism, what need is there of prophecy or of revelation? The story of the introduction of logic within the Islamic world is long and complicated. Al-Fārābī is probably the thinker who did the most to acclimatize Aristotelian logic, and especially syllogistic, in an Arabic milieu. He accomplished this by original treatises as well as by commentaries.

Over one hundred works, in all branches of knowledge, are commonly ascribed to al-Fārābī. He wrote important works on the classification of the sciences, on physics, metaphysics, ethics, politics, and music. In some polemical works, now lost, al-Fārābī attacked the views of al-Rāzī, who, as we have seen, argued that the world was created in time from preexistent matter, a view rejected by al-Fārābī.

Perhaps the most interesting and valuable of al-Fārābī's works, for a modern reader, is his great, systematic treatise entitled *On the Principles of the Views of the Inhabitants of the Virtuous City.* In this work, influenced by Plato, al-Fārābī sets out not merely to describe the "virtuous city" (or "the best state," as it may be rendered), but to locate human existence within the cosmos. For al-Fārābī, existence is hierarchical and symmetrical, and this structure of existence is mirrored in the order and structure of the book itself. Thus, the work begins with a discussion of the First Cause, from whom all existence emanates, and proceeds downward through eleven levels of existence to the sublunary world and the elements themselves, matter and form, and the heavenly bodies. Al-Fārābī then moves into a discussion of man, various human faculties, from the "nutritive" to the "rational," and the human body itself, and he concludes with a discourse on human reason and knowledge. The third section of the work deals with human society and government; al-Fārābī discusses the ideal ruler and the ideal city, or state; he concludes with the wicked and erring cities.

In this scheme of things, all that exists emanates in strict hierarchies from one level of existence to the next:

The substance of the First is a substance from which every existent emanates, however it may be, whether perfect or deficient. But the substance of the First is also such that all the existents, when they emanate from it, are arranged in an order of rank, and that every existent gets its allotted share and rank of existence from it. It starts with the most perfect existent and is followed by something a little less perfect than it. Afterwards it is followed successively by more and more deficient existents until the final stage of being is reached beyond which no existence whatsoever is possible. . . . Inasmuch as the substance of the First is a substance from which all the existents emanate, . . . it is generous, and its generosity is in its substance; and inasmuch as all the existents receive their order of rank from it, . . . the First is just.[14]

This First Cause, who is generous and just, has its origins in Greek thought, and yet accords with Qur'ānic teachings. For al-Fārābī, the First

Cause is the summit of existence, uncaused, self-subsistent, unmoved, intrinsically perfect; even so, the lower levels of existence mirror its perfection. The human soul and the human body are also governed hierarchically: In the body, the heart rules and is followed by the brain, under which all other organs are subordinated. Likewise, human society is arranged in orders of perfection:

> The excellent city resembles the perfect and healthy body, all of whose limbs cooperate to make the life of the animal perfect and to preserve it in this state. Now the limbs and organs of the body are different and their natural endowments and faculties are unequal in excellence. . . . The same holds good in the case of the city. Its parts are different by nature, and their natural dispositions are unequal in excellence: there is in it a man who is the ruler, and there are others whose ranks are close to the ruler. . . . Below them are people who perform their actions in accordance with the aims of those people; they are in the second rank. Below them in turn are people who perform their actions according to the aims of the people mentioned in the second instance, and the parts of the city continue to be arranged in this way, until eventually parts are reached which perform their actions according to the aims of others, while there do not exist any people who perform their actions according to their aims; these, then, are . . . in the lowest rank and at the bottom of the scale.[15]

The ruler of this excellent city stands in relation to his subjects as the First Cause stands in relation to all other existents. The order of existence is thus not only hierarchical but microcosmic: Each order of being is such that it mirrors a higher order and is itself reflected in a lower. The ruler of the virtuous city is a Platonic philosopher-king but with a distinctly Islamic cast: Thus, he will be physically strong as well as quick to understand; he possesses a retentive memory; he is endowed with eloquence; he is honest, abstemious, proud, and honorable; he will be unconcerned with money; be just and opposed to injustice; show himself resolute, determined, and courageous. Ultimately, he should be one to whom God has granted revelation, one in whom practical and theoretical reasoning are reconciled. For al-Fārābī, the intellect and reason remain the decisive instruments for the discernment of truth and are preeminent in the virtuous ruler. Prophecy is a necessary component of human perfection, but, for al-Fārābī, it remains decidedly secondary to reason.

Al-Fārābī's most illustrious pupil was the Christian Aristotelian philosopher Yaḥyā Ibn 'Adī (died 972), but his work influenced every later Arab philosopher, and remains important today.

Abū 'Alī *Ibn Sīnā* (Avicenna; 980–1037)

Ibn Sīnā—or Avicenna, as he was known to the Latin West—was perhaps the greatest, and certainly the most influential, Islamic philosopher. His life is rather well documented. He himself left a detailed account of his life up to the age of thirty, and his friend and disciple al-Jūzjānī wrote a biography of him. As a government official for most of his career, as well as an illustrious physician, he passed much of his life in the public eye.

Ibn Sīnā was born in 980 in the northwest province of Iran known as Khurasan, and Persian was his first language; later he would write a number of important works in Persian. His father was a government official and Ibn Sīnā enjoyed a comfortable childhood and youth. As a child, Ibn Sīnā was exposed to the teachings of Ismaili propagandists who influenced his father, and though Ibn Sīnā refused to accept Ismaili views, he seems to have been influenced by them himself. He received an excellent education and became especially adept in the study of jurisprudence, an exercise that may have sharpened his extraordinary talent in logic. Ibn Sīnā describes his early education in his autobiography. Modesty is not much in evidence. Thus, he notes that by the age of fourteen he had surpassed all his teachers and even found himself explaining the principles of logic to his instructor. In medicine as well as in natural science, he was self-taught; as he casually remarks, "Medicine is not a difficult science, and naturally I excelled in it in a very short time."[16]

Because of his skill in medicine, Ibn Sīnā began to enjoy the patronage of the Samanid princes and was granted access to their library. Still in his adolescence, Ibn Sīnā became absorbed in philosophy. He read the *Metaphysics* of Aristotle but was baffled. The work so mystified him that he eventually read it forty times and committed it to memory. One day, in a bookseller's, he came across a cheap copy of al-Fārābī's commentary on the *Metaphysics* and after reading this, for the first time, an understanding of the text dawned on him.

The anecdote is indicative, in a small way, of the importance that not only Aristotle but also al-Fārābī would have for Ibn Sīnā. Indeed, it might be said that Ibn Sīnā's thought is ultimately an immense elaboration of the implications of al-Fārābī's thought, itself constructed on Aristotelian, Platonic, and Neoplatonic foundations.

Ibn Sīnā led an unusually active career in the service of various princes and potentates, sometimes in an administrative capacity, sometimes as an astronomer or natural scientist, and most often as a physician. His fame as a doctor almost eclipses his standing as a philosopher. His great compendium of medicine known as *al-Qānūn fi'l-ṭibb*, or the *Canon of Medicine*, was for centuries the authoritative work in both the Islamic world and the West. (Indeed, the first Arabic book printed in the West was Ibn Sīnā's *Qānūn*, printed in Rome in 1593.) Ibn Sīnā's activity as a physician and official left him little time for writing. Almost all of his work was in fact accomplished at night, when he could dictate to his secretary. When he grew tired, he would drink a glass of wine to stimulate himself. In this way, he composed some 276 works, an enormous output, on every aspect of medicine, natural science, logic and philosophy, as well as on music, philology, and the "Islamic sciences" such as Qur'ānic explication and mysticism.

Ibn Sīnā was a man of prodigious, larger-than-life accomplishments, and he was a man of strong appetites as well. His death came about from an attack of colic, which his indulgence in sexual activity worsened. As his disciple remarked, "The Master was powerful in all his faculties, and he was especially strong sexually; this indeed was a prevailing passion with him, and he indulged it to such an extent that his constitution was affected."[17] Ibn Sīnā died in 1037, at about the age of fifty-seven.

Because certain key works of Ibn Sīnā have been lost, it is not possible to give a complete account of his thought. His great work, entitled in Arabic *al-Shifā'*, is a huge compendium, or summa, of philosophical knowledge, comprising logic and syllogistic, natural science, and metaphysics, but it is not, and was not intended to be, an original work of philosophy. The title means *The Healing,* and suggests the emphasis that Ibn Sīnā, physician as well as philosopher, placed on philosophy. Such claims would anger later opponents of Ibn Sīnā and of philosophy generally, such as the great mystic al-Ghazālī. The presumption that philosophy might offer some healing for the soul appeared to displace religion and was controversial.

At the same time, however, it must be noted that Ibn Sīnā was himself a deeply religious thinker. Indeed, in some ways, he is the prototype of a very characteristically Islamic figure: the pious, even mystical, rationalist.

For Ibn Sīnā, all being falls into two categories: necessary being and contingent being. Only God is Necessary Being. In such a necessary being, essence—what God is—and existence—that God is—are not separate; for if existence were to be added to God's essence, this would imply some multiplicity within his being, and that would diminish his unity. Essence and existence are one in the Necessary Being. All other beings, by contrast, are contingent; this means that all beings that are not necessary beings owe their existence to something outside themselves. A contingent being may exist or not exist, whereas a necessary being cannot not exist.

The Necessary Being—in Arabic, *wājib al-wujūd*—is also characterized as pure thought, or pure thinking, itself. If reason and intellect represent the supreme faculties, reason and intellect must characterize the supremely necessary and perfect being in a preeminent fashion. And it is the very act of intellect through which the Necessary Being becomes the originator of all that exists. The age-old problem of the derivation of a multiplicity from One is resolved for Ibn Sīnā in the emanation of existence from the Necessary Being: How can an entity perfectly one and uncompounded, without the shadow of multiplicity within itself, bring forth the profusion of entities in the created universe? From a religious viewpoint, the solution is that God created all that exists, instantaneously and out of nothing, by His mere command. From a philosophical standpoint, however, this is absurd.

For Ibn Sīnā, the Necessary Being by its quintessential activity of thought emanates a First Intelligence and further intelligences, and further levels of existence emanate or flow forth from these ranked intelligences, down to the sphere "beneath the moon" of our earthly existence. Existence is bestowed on contingent beings ultimately then by the Necessary Being in a kind of involuntary procession. This aspect of Ibn Sīnā's thought would offend theologians, for it seemed to reduce God to a mere, helpless automaton of His own will, unable not to create. For the theologians, by contrast, God was to be characterized by absolutely unlimited power, and could have refused to create the world at all, or could have created an entirely different universe, as He pleased.

Still, there is a reciprocity in Ibn Sīnā's thought, for creatures are drawn by impulses and inner emotions of love and longing for the source of their being. The term Ibn Sīnā uses is in Arabic *'ishq,* a word that denotes an intense and passionate feeling of love. Ibn Sīnā's concentrated focus on being, on existence itself, in its most universal aspect, earned him the sobriquet of the "philosopher of being." As such, he was of the utmost importance not only for later Islamic thinkers but for Western theologians and philosophers as well. The impact of his thought is clearly visible, for example, throughout the work of Thomas Aquinas, and Ibn Sīnā's distinction between essence and existence would have a significant history in later Western thought.

In the Islamic world, Ibn Sīnā's influence is impossible to exaggerate. His influence is perceptible not only in philosophy itself and in medicine but in some very distinctive Islamic modes of thought that later centuries would develop, especially a kind of mystical philosophic theology that would be prevalent throughout the Islamic world. Much of this tradition owes its impetus to various esoteric and mystical treatises that Ibn Sīnā wrote in both Persian and Arabic.

Abū al-Walīd *Ibn Rushd* (Averroes; 1126–1198)

With Ibn Rushd, or Averroes, as he was known to the Latin Middle Ages, we come to the virtual end of the Arabic *falsafah* tradition. At the same time, the entire focus of Arabic philosophy shifts from its traditional centers in the eastern Islamic world—especially, Iran, Iraq, and Syria—to Spain and North Africa. Spain had been settled by Muslim invaders from 710 on, and after the rise of the Abbasid dynasty in 750, the successors of the vanquished Umayyad empire took refuge in Spain, or al-Andalus, as it was known in Arabic, and continued there for some three hundred years. A sophisticated and distinctive Spanish Islamic culture developed and took root. Many of the most original Arabic poets, prose writers, theologians, historians, and legal scholars, as well as philosophers, came from Islamic Spain. Among philosophers, there were such figures as Ibn Bājjah in the eleventh century and Ibn Ṭufayl, an older friend and colleague of Ibn Rushd.

Ibn Rushd was a member of a prestigious family in Cordoba. Both his grandfather and his father had been judges, or *qāḍī*s, with his grandfather serving as both *qāḍī* and *imam* of the Great Mosque of Cordoba. Ibn Rushd was born in Cordoba in 1126 and received a thorough education in Islamic law as well as in other traditional disciplines. He was also formally schooled in medicine and practiced as a physician, like al-Rāzī and Ibn Sīnā before him. Though in the West Ibn Rushd is known principally for his commentaries on Aristotle—Dante refers to him in the *Inferno* as "Averroes who made the great commentary"—he was actually a universal figure, learned in numerous disciplines, not only law and medicine and philosophy but astronomy, physics, and other natural sciences. Thus, in 1153, Ibn Rushd pursued astronomical observation in Marrakesh, even discovering a new star. Later, he served as physician to the Almohad ruler Abū Yaʻqūb Yūsuf. Finally, he received the position of chief *qāḍī* of Cordoba. In all these activities, his intense work as a commentator and original philosopher continued. He died in 1198 in Marrakesh. The great Andalusian mystic Ibn al-ʻArabī was present at his funeral. Later, Ibn Rushd's body was conveyed to Cordoba for reburial in his native land; according to legend, the weight of his body on the back of the mule that carried him had to be counterbalanced by the weight of his books—an extravagant way of emphasizing his productivity!

Ibn Rushd's philosophical work centers on a number of commentaries on Aristotelian treatises, and on a small but important group of original compositions, most of them dating from the six-year period from 1174 to 1180. Ibn Rushd prepared commentaries of varying lengths on many Aristotelian works, including an extensive commentary on the *Metaphysics;* he also wrote a commentary on Plato's *Republic.* Certain of these works survive only in their Latin or Hebrew versions today, or in garbled renditions that make an exact reconstruction of his thought difficult.

Of Ibn Rushd's original works, perhaps the most significant is his famous *Tahāfut al-tahāfut,* somewhat opaquely translated as *The Incoherence of the Incoherence.* The Latin translation is better: *Destructio destructionis,* or *The Destruction of the Destruction.* The title refers to the attack on philosophy, and especially the philosophy of Ibn Sīnā, that the great religious thinker Abū Ḥāmid al-Ghazālī (died 1111) had launched under the name of *Tahāfut al-falāsifah.* Ibn Rushd's response is an attempt both to refute al-Ghazālī and to rescue Aristotle from the interpretations of Ibn Sīnā. In part, Ibn Rushd's defense of philosophy consists in showing that Ibn Sīnā and al-Fārābī before him had obscured Aristotle's true thought.

In his critique of philosophy, al-Ghazālī had singled out a number of theses that he considered false and heretical, among them the philosophers' doctrine of the eternity of the world. It is sometimes said that al-Ghazālī's work effected the decline of philosophy in the Islamic world, but this is incorrect. Perhaps its main force lay in al-Ghazālī's use of the methods of philosophy against philosophy, for al-Ghazālī not only attacked philosophy but appropriated those aspects of it that he could use in his own eclectic mystical theology.

Much of Ibn Rushd's rebuttal turns on the question of the eternity of the world. For Ibn Rushd, the universe is an eternal creation. Moreover, the world does not result from some form of emanation from the One; indeed, Ibn Rushd rejects the ancient notion that from the one, only one can proceed, a notion at the heart of Ibn Sīnā's cosmology. Furthermore, the God of Ibn Rushd is more directly involved as agent in the created universe, in contrast to the remote and transcendent divinity of Ibn Sīnā. It is through His will, rather than through some involuntary necessity of His nature, that God creates, according to Ibn Rushd. So, too, on the question of God's knowledge of particulars, which Ibn Sīnā had denied, Ibn Rushd affirms that God does know particulars, but in a way different from our knowledge of them.

Ibn Rushd held that reason and revelation are ultimately compatible. Indeed, in one work, he argues that the Qur'ān not only permits but encourages the use of intellectual speculation, and he cites Qur'ānic verses in evidence. But strict demonstration, in a rigorous logical fashion, may be unsuitable for some. Individual differences of temperament and of intelligence, as well as of education, account for the various ways in which people acquire the truth. In fact, it is wrong for those with specialized knowledge to divulge their findings to the untutored, who will be incapable of understanding them and who may be damaged by them. (Indeed, Ibn Rushd criticizes al-Ghazālī for making known certain esoteric truths to the wider public.) The use of demonstrative reasoning and of apodictic truth is reserved for those with the appropriate training. For others, the techniques of rhetoric or of poetry may be more apt. This line of reasoning, which was long established within Islam, held sway in any number of disciplines and was commonplace in mysticism: Knowledge was many-layered and intricate; it could not be merely disclosed, but depended upon training, apprenticeship, and initiation. For Ibn Rushd, logic is such a preparation for philosophy, and while it finally agrees with the truths of revelation, logic must be used judiciously.

The tradition of Arabic philosophy that begins with al-Kindī and culminates in Ibn Rushd did not die out, but was transformed in sometimes unexpected ways in later centuries. The tension inherent in this *falsafah* tradition derives from its scrupulous attention to the methods and insights of the ancient philosophers within a quite different, indeed alien, milieu. Like their counterparts among Jewish and Christian philosophers, Arab philosophers felt a profound affinity with ancient thought, and they acted not only as transmitters of this thought but as original minds working within a continuous tradition, as though ancient philosophy had been reincarnated in them. At the same time, as for the most part believing Muslims, they were compelled to find ways to integrate this "barbarian wisdom" into an Islamic worldview. Later thinkers would create new syntheses, in which the philosophy of Ibn Sīnā was combined with mystical or theosophical illumination. In theology, too, the philosophical tradition, including the use of Aristotelian logic, came to hold an honored place. The great theological compendia of later centuries derive much of their special quality of reasoning from these earlier philosophers, even when the theologians most emphatically rejected the philosophers' underlying positions. Even such a critic of philosophy as al-Ghazālī was himself thoroughly permeated with its style of thought. Ibn Rushd left no disciples and no pupils, but the tradition of Arabic philosophy has continued, often in novel disguises, to the present time.

Notes

1. Al-Rāzī, *Rasā'il falsafīyah/Opera philosophica*, ed. Paul Kraus (Cairo, 1939), pp. 17–18 (my translation).
2. E. Gibbon, *The Decline and Fall of the Roman Empire* (New York: Modern Library, n.d.), Vol. 3, p. 223.
3. The *mu'allaqāt*, or "suspended odes," of pre-Islamic Arabia were so called, according to legend, because they were written in gold letters and suspended before the Ka'ba in Mecca (my translation).
4. The name *al-Kindī* indicates his affiliation with the important South Arabian tribe of Kindah. Because of this distinctly Arab background, al-Kindī is often known as "the philosopher of the Arabs."
5. See Richard Walzer, *Greek into Arabic* (Oxford: Bruno Cassirer, 1962), p. 199.
6. Trans. R. Walzer, *Greek into Arabic*, p. 12. See also A. Ivry, *Al-Kindī's Metaphysics* (Albany: SUNY Press, 1974), p. 58.
7. Al-Kindī, *Rasā'il al-Kindī al-falsafīyah*, ed. M. Abū Riḍā (Cairo, 1950), Vol. 1, p. 172.
8. Al-Kindī, *Rasā'il*, Vol. I, p. 173.
9. See Aristotle, *Physics* II, 3 (195a).
10. Al-Kindī, "On First Philosophy," trans. A. Ivry in *Al-Kindī's Metaphysics*, p. 112. Al-Kindī is here denying all of the predictable categories, such as "genus" (e.g., "animal" is the genus of a human being) and "specific difference" (e.g., "reasonable" would be the specific difference of a human being); "accident" denotes such characteristics as "whiteness" or "corpulence," and so forth.
11. Al-Rāzī, *Rasā'il falsafīyah*, ed. Kraus, p. 27.
12. Ibid., p. 195.
13. Trans. R. Walzer, *Greek into Arabic*, p. 16.

14. Trans. Richard Walzer, *Al-Farabi on the Perfect State* (Oxford, 1985), pp. 95–96.

15. Walzer, op. cit., pp. 231–33.

16. Trans. A. J. Arberry, *Avicenna on Theology* (London, 1951), pp. 10–11. See also William E. Gohlman, *The Life of Ibn Sina* (Albany, 1974), pp. 25–27.

17. Arberry, op. cit., p. 22.

6

Persian Philosophy

Homayoon Sepasi-Tehrani and Janet Flesch

When, with the discovery of "new worlds" and new "scientific" principles of government, modern Europeans began their own difficult investigations into the question of national character, the Persian legacy was
well noted. Montesquieu, in his famous *Persian Letters,* has his character
Pico explain, "[I]f [in Paris] someone chances to inform them that I was
a Persian, I soon heard a murmur all around me: 'Ah! Indeed! He is a
Persian? How extraordinary! How can anyone be a Persian?' " Persian
thinkers from the ninth to the twentieth centuries were far ahead of their
European counterparts in the search for the foundation of their national
character, and Persian culture since Islam still has a flavor uniquely its
own, ironically distinguished in part by its very self-consciousness as a
culture. To consider seriously the question of what it means to be Persian
is our first goal in the following survey. Our hope is that these considerations may provoke yet another question: How can anyone be of any
culture at all?

One often finds among thinkers more familiar in the West themes
reminiscent of Persian thought; however, little attempt has yet been made
in the United States or Europe to gather together all its disparate strands.
In this essay, we will offer a brief (and we hope, tantalizing) overview of
Persian thought over the whole course of its history. We believe that by
reengaging our philosophical dialogue with Persia, we may better approach the questions of our common human experience, particularly the
questions of culture and political tolerance that confront us today.

Persian History

The geographical area under focus here is known today, as it was in
ancient times, as Iran.[1] Although its borders have been redefined many

times over its long history, Iran may be roughly described as stretching west to east from the Fertile Crescent (the Tigris and Euphrates valleys, where it is said that "culture" first began) to the Indus River (in what is today Pakistan), and north to south from the Caspian Sea to the Persian Gulf. Iran is both geographically and culturally the meeting place of the Orient and the Occident, bearing witness—sometimes bittersweet in its testimony—to their indissoluble interdependence. Down to the late twentieth century, Iran has retained its integrity as being neither East nor West, steadfastly refusing to be allied either with the Soviets or with Western Europe and the United States. Persian philosophy, then, poses an interesting challenge to the facile distinctions people tend to make between Eastern and Western worldviews. It is not easily fitted into the convenient explanatory categories, often used by university departments, of "Oriental Studies" or Western "Philosophy."²

The original Iranians were Indo-European (or Indo-Iranian or Aryan) tribespeople who moved in neolithic times from western Europe onto the Iranian Plateau. There they found the indigenous Elamites. The first Iranian nation, composed of Aryans and Elamites, was the Median, which ruled over several smaller kingdoms, including Persia and Anshan. These two kingdoms were ruled by different branches of the family of Achaemenes. By 539 B.C., Cyrus II, king of Anshan, had taken over the whole Median kingdom, plus Assyria, Babylonia, and Lydia (in Asia Minor).

This first Persian Empire of the Achaemenians of the line of Cyrus (including Darius and his son, Xerxes, of Persia) was the birthplace of what we would call Persian culture. Its legacy included the Iranian religion, Zoroastrianism, the first and perhaps the most influential of the world's revealed religions. The ancient Greek historian Herodotus wrote of the Persians that they were taught "to mount the horse, to draw the bow, and to speak the truth," crediting his enemies with combining their military skill with a devotion to justice and wisdom. This ancient Persian conception of virtue—including its powerful and puzzling combination of subtle grace and harshness—is the Persians' bequest to succeeding generations of Iranians.

The Achaemenid Empire finally fell, along with most of the ancient world, to Alexander the Great of Macedonia during the 330s B.C. After Alexander's death in 323 B.C., his empire was divided among his Greek generals. Persia was given to Seleucus, who turned an already oversized piece of the Greek pie into an enormous and long-lived dynasty. The Seleucids ruled Iran for Greece with relative stability through the middle of the second century B.C. The Parthians, from the north, who had never been under Greek rule, were the most powerful of the various challengers to Seleucid rule. The Parthians eventually became the overlords of more than half the Seleucid domain, strongly reasserting a native power in the region. The Parthian empire stood until the second century A.D., throughout the rise of the Roman Empire, and was Rome's principal opponent until its own demise.

In 224 A.D., the Persian king overthrew the Parthian monarchy. The Sassanid dynasty he founded established the so-called second Persian Empire, which rivaled the Byzantines throughout the early Christian era. The Sassanids unified and nationalized social and religious institutions, often with a strong arm. They collected and organized the traces of the scripture and practice of Zoroastrianism, which had become the state religion. Out of political desire to unify their rule over a nation that had become factionalized, they tried to define the Persian character and to reconstruct its cultural "roots," making them, in a sense, the first "cultural anthropologists." As in our own day, unification was not achieved without opposition, and the Sassanids were very severe toward heresy against Zoroastrianism and dissent from Sassanid rule. Among the "heretical" religions were Manichaeism, which exercised a tremendous influence on the major world religions, and Mazdakism, a protocommunist doctrine. Although Zoroastrianism was not the only religion to perceive these heresies as a threat, it was the Sassanians who executed both Mani and Mazdak.

In the early 600s, the prophet Muhammad began teaching in Mecca, Arabia. Most of what we today call the Middle East, including Iran, was conquered by his followers for Islam during the first half of the seventh century A.D. The Iranian region was ruled with only local resistance as a set of principalities under the Muslim Umayyad and Abbasid caliphates, from neighboring Arab countries, until the thirteenth century. Most Iranians have been devoted Moslems ever since; and so it might seem that Iran had been an easy conquest for Islam. During the seventh to ninth "centuries of silence," however, tremendous political upheaval, in which few found time to write, only masqueraded as passive submission. In reality, the region was wracked. Rulers and landowners, secure in their positions under Islam, were converted quickly. The lower classes and smaller communities, however, had more invested in local traditions, including Zoroastrianism. They were often converted only through violent oppression. The Arab conquest of Iran and the Iranian devotion to Islam in which it resulted were gained with much more conflict and at much greater cost than might appear to be the case, even to contemporary Iranians, who have settled into a vision of their own ancestors as having been ripe for Islam.

Since the ninth century, Persians have struggled continuously for integrity in the face of ethnic and religious diversity and foreign rule. With the whole Middle East by then awash in Islam, national identities were translated from historical and territorial terms into those of religious dogma. Political-religious power circulated primarily among Arab, Persian, and Turkish Muslims. For the next five hundred years, the identification of Persian thought is less a matter of delineating the body of ideas that originated in the Iranian Plateau than it is a matter of tracing the sympathies and influences of various (mostly Islamic) sects. Sectarian groups included "Twelver," or "Imami," Shi'ites, who believed that the twelve Imams, male descendants of Muhammad's cousin and son-in-law, Ali, had a "divine" right to the leadership of Islam; and Sufis, or Islamic mystics.

The High Middle Ages in Persia, as in most of Europe and Asia, was a period of great turmoil and tenacity of belief, but also of creative thought and heated debate. Dynasties rose and fell, ruling over Persia piecemeal and often claiming religious or caliphal authority for political conquest. In both their poetic and theological literature, medieval Iranians celebrated the relentless honesty, wily strategy, and distinguished comportment of the Achaemenians, by now the bench marks of Persian thinking.

Three centuries' worth of attempts at independent Persian rule culminated in 1501, when the Sufi orders, which had flourished in the preceding countries, provided the support necessary for the establishment of the Safavid dynasty, which claimed a lineage from the twelfth Imam and instituted Twelver Shi'ism as the state religion. Esfahān, the Safavid center, was the "Florence of the East," hosting European visitors and the discourse between their "age of enlightenment" and Persian classicism. Over the two hundred years of Safavid rule, Persia gained a worldwide reputation as a cultural and political hub. During the eighteenth century, however, two short-lived dynasties and an interregnum of decentralization disrupted Persian efforts at autonomy and unity. When the Turkish/Afghani Mohammad Khan Qajar was crowned *shahenshah* of Persia's Qajar dynasty in their new capital of Tehran in 1796, the world was a very different place from what it had been during the earlier Persian empires, and Persia had a very different place in it.

Iran under the Qajars, like so much of the world in the nineteenth century, was no longer valued for its commercial and cultural affluence but purely for its geographically strategic position. The British sought alliance with Iran as a buffer against a Russian invasion of India, but reneged when their promised support was needed. Czarist Russia, a progressively ambitious empire, took Iranian territory. With the discovery of oil and the establishment of the Anglo-Persian Oil Company in 1908, Iran became politically and economically dependent on the world powers. Britain and Russia invaded Iran during World War I. At the war's close, Iran and many of its Middle Eastern neighbors were parceled out by the victors, and Iran was practically given to the British.

In 1921, Reza Khan, the son of a Persian farmer, took Iran by coup d'état. Five years later, he crowned himself Shahenshah Reza Pahlavi in a pitiful, poorly documented attempt to associate the new Pahlavi dynasty with the ancient golden age. Reza Shah pursued a policy of modernization, which in essence meant only Westernization. He instituted a whirlwind industrialization and enforced separation of church and state.[3]

In 1941, the Allies occupied Iran and forced the abdication of Reza Shah in favor of his son, Mohammad Reza Pahlavi. But Mohammad Reza Shah, now under the patronage of the Americans and the British, followed the same policies as had his father. His "modern," "Western" policies could not accommodate all the disparate interests of his subjects. Devoted Muslims felt betrayed by the secular government. Farmers were displaced and confused by a hasty, poorly planned policy of industrialization and oil production. Urban youth, born disinherited by Persian tradition, were despondent under the Pahlavis. The unity, identity, and recognition that Persians had so long sought came to seem like dreams from which they had been violently awakened—or like dreams that only violence could again make real.

Resistance to the shah, seeking every avenue of expression, culminated in the 1978 Iranian revolution. After the defeat of the shah, the various revolutionary groups whose shared wish was for a "genuinely Iranian" government were gathered under the umbrella of the Islamic Republic, which still claims to fulfill that wish. Ayatollah Khomeini, an outspoken opponent of the shah and a Shi'ite leader, returned triumphantly from exile to lead it. Khomeini's government detached Iran from the world powers, making and breaking alliances according to its own interests. Dissent, however, is still widespread and without legal recourse.

We might describe Persian history as an ongoing dialectic between an antiauthoritarianism by which Persian culture disassociates itself from exogenous orders and an authoritarianism by which it establishes a rigid indigenous order. The Persian virtues so long ago noted by Herodotus have reappeared in various forms as ideals of Persian culture. Notably, a cosmopolitan and universalist character has strengthened Iran in both peace and war. Throughout 1,300 years of internal conflict and only occasionally broken foreign rule, however, Persians have acquired a characteristic penchant for satire, secrecy, irony, and indirectness. Persian writers still wield their language as cunningly as their ancestors did the bow.

Persian Thought in Pre-Islamic Times

Of the religions, or systems of thought, devised by the Persians before the Arab conquest, Zoroastrianism was by far the most important and long-lasting.

Zoroastrianism

Zoroastrianism is one of the most profound and influential systems of belief ever to have existed. "Some knowledge of the teachings of Zoroaster," writes Mary Boyce, a prominant scholar of Persiana, "is needed by every serious student of world religions. . . . [It is] the oldest of the revealed world religions, and it has probably had more influence on mankind, directly or indirectly, than any other single faith." Although it is practiced today by only a tiny community, recurrent interest in Zoroastrianism and the recognizable traces of its influence in Judaism, Christianity, and Islam make the study of Zoroastrianism a vital and provocative task for anyone in serious pursuit of answers to the fundamental questions of existence.[4]

The Zoroastrian Scriptures

The *Zend-Avesta,*[5] the holy book of Zoroastrianism, was first brought to modern Europe in 1764, and various copies and editions of it have been the subjects of scholarly analysis ever since.[6] Unfortunately, none of the available scholarship can tell us with certainty what the original Zoroastrians believed or practiced, nor which Zoroastrian beliefs date from the Sassanian Empire and which from pre-Sassanian periods in Persian history. The *Avesta* consisted originally of twenty-one books, of which only one, the *Videvdat* (or *Antidemonic Law*, a book of doctrine), has come down to us in its entirety. Much of our knowledge of the religion comes from the extensive commentary, theology, and scriptural interpretation of the Sassanian priests, most of which was actually completed after the Arab conquest.[7]

Zoroastrianism derives its name from its prophet, Zoroaster (more properly, Zarathustra), who, most scholars now agree, lived and preached in the late seventh and early sixth centuries B.C. Like any prophet, Zarathustra is believed to have received direct revelation from his God, called Ahura Mazda. Zarathustra's claim to divine authority was a fortunate defense for his religious teachings, which were in radical disagreement with those of his contemporaries. Zarathustra proclaimed a monotheistic religion amidst a thriving polytheism. The ancient Indo-Iranians who lived in Iran before Zarathustra's time apparently worshiped two types of deity: *daevas* (or *devas*) and *ahuras* (or *asuras*). Zarathustra denounced the worship of the daevas, and venerated but one of the ahuras, Ahura Mazda, or "Wise Lord."

After fleeing his homeland and after years of wandering, he took refuge under the patronage of a king, Vishtaspa, in northeastern Iran. In the *Gathas* (the oldest section of the *Avesta*), he sings, "To what land to turn; aye, whither turning shall I go?" (*Y* XLVI: 1) The opening passages of the *Gathas* describe with great sensitivity the confusing and complicated, desperate and delicate, uncertain but inviolate, relation between man, nature, and God. They preach free and responsible moral choice in the face of the suffering and injustice that afflict mortal life. We adopt the view of some contemporary scholars that the Zorastrianism of the *Gathas* is a metaphysical monism. In other words, it expresses the belief that there is only one God, the creator of everything that exists. At the same time, the *Gathas* express a moral dualism. In other words, they hold that human beings—and, in fact, all of sentient creation—are capable of doing both good and evil.

The Pantheon

Existence, as described in the earliest scripture, is a pantheon of interdependent entities, each with a distinct character and a distinct role to play in the drama of history. Ahura Mazda, the Lord, created by thought and from nothing all that exists, in seven steps or stages. First, He created—through his Spenta Mainyush (the "Holy" or "Beneficent Spirit")—six other, lower divinities, called the Amesha Spentas. They became Ahura Mazda's helpers in the creation of the natural world. The process of creation culminates, at the seventh step, in the creation of material things. The Amesha Spentas are persons, both one with Ahura Mazda and distinguishable from Him. They are described as "aspects" of Him, but they are lesser gods, not mere metaphors or symbols. Each represents one of the good characteristics of the all-good Ahura Mazda, personifying one of His attributes.

Through the Amesha Spenta Vohu Manah ("Good Mind" or "Good Purpose"), each individual instantiates the good, or right. Allegiance to the Amesha Spenta Asha Vahista ("Righteousness" or "Truth") distinguishes the devoted worshiper of Mazda from the adherents of immoral religions. Together with Ahura Mazda, their sustainer and Lord, the Amesha Spentas create the rest of the world. Every aspect of nature is associated with its own divinity, the Amesha Spenta who shares its unique character. There is a spiritual unity and yet a real distinction between creator and creature, where again the aspects of the material world represent, but are not merely a metaphor for, the divine aspects of God. Thus:

The divinity or natural entity:		shares the characteristic of:	with:
Ahura Mazda (Wise Lord)		Free will	Man
Vohu Manah		Good thinking, Good purpose	The Cow
Asha	The	Righteousness, Truth	Fire
Khshathra Vairya	Amesha	Kingdom, Dominion, Metals	The Sky
Armaiti	Spentas	Rightmindedness, Devotion	The Earth
Haurvatat		Health	Water
Ameretat		Long life	Plants

The vibrancy and appeal of Zoroastrian metaphysics comes partly from the rationality and naturalism of these representations. Water does indeed maintain health, refreshing and restoring the creatures of the hot, dry, Iranian Plateau; the plants do indeed sustain us. The cow is our ward and partner in the work of sustaining life, which is our good purpose here on earth. Finally, man, the only intelligent creature, is alone capable of making a deliberate and reasoned choice of good, as God does and directs His creatures to do. Fire (and the Sun, its most powerful creature) pervades all things, and is the cause and source of all activity. As the source of change, it is the source also of order and measure, of conflict and resolution, of sight, and thus of righteousness and truth.

Because each of the Amesha Spentas is associated with its special natural creation, worship is therefore as much of these natural entities as of their supernatural creator. The proper worship of fire, the natural entity representative of Asha, was in particular the cardinal duty of Zoroastrians. In fact, in their own time, Zoroastrians were referred to as fire worshipers. "And we pray likewise for Thy Fire, O Ahura! . . . in many wonderful ways our help . . ." (Y XXXIV: 4).

Moral Dualism

Early Zoroastrianism is most fundamentally a moral doctrine. Everything that exists, spiritual and especially material creation, engages in spiritual activity, inspired by moral sensibility and purposefulness. Zarathustra's original revelation, in fact, could be described as the awakening of righteous indignation:

> Unto you (O Ahura and Asha!) the Soul of the Kine (our sacred herds and folk) cried aloud: For whom did ye create me, and by whom did ye fashion me? On me comes the assault of wrath, and of violent power, the blow of desolation, audacious insolence, and thievish might. (Y XXIX: 1–5)

The soul of the ox, in grief over its perennial mistreatment, asks Ahura Mazda, much as Job asks God, to explain this injustice and to protect the ox from it. Ahura Mazda answers:

> [A]sk[ing] of Righteousness: How (was) thy guardian for the Kine (appointed) by thee when, as having power (over all her fate), ye made her? . . . Whom did ye select as her (life's) master who might hurl back the fury of the wicked?

Asha ("Righteousness"), disconcerted, says he has found no one. Zarathustra takes the initiative on behalf of the ox; and recognizing his worthiness, God names Zarathustra its guardian.

This religion, then, is founded on the initial recognition of evil. It asks, in other words, what can explain the existence of evil if God is all-good and all-powerful. Zarathustra's response to the classical and always compelling question of the meaning and origin of evil may still be considered quite satisfying.

In original Zoroastrianism, Ahura Mazda is fully—but only indirectly—responsible for both good and evil. Ahura Mazda alone and out of nothing creates everything that exists, but He instills in each of his creatures the tendency toward either good or evil, as well as the ability to act in accordance with that tendency. The Amesha Spentas having been created by Ahura Mazda through his "Holy Spirit," Spenta Mainyush, Spenta Mainyush must therefore have been created prior to the other Amesha Spentas. Indeed, according to scripture, he was created first—along with his twin, Angra Mainyush (the "Destructive Spirit"). Ahura Mazda's original creation of just these two spirits marks a duality second only in priority to the one God.

> Thus are the primeval spirits who as a pair (combining their opposite strivings), and (yet each) independent in his action, have been famed (of old). (They are) a better thing, they two, and a worse, as to thought, word, and as to deed. And between these two let the wisely acting choose right. (*Y* XLV: 2)

In this way, the spiritually endowed natural world is set against itself, like two armies in an eternal battle between good and evil. Everything that exists freely chooses its allegiance. This expression of Angra Mainyush's free yet nonetheless characteristic choice of evil is the birth of evil, and its forms are deceit, destructiveness, and death. A Zoroastrian, a follower of Mazda, is a soldier for the good creation. He or she fights valiantly for Truth, Creation, and Life, against the Lie, Destruction, and Death, through a threefold duty of "good thoughts, good words, good deeds."

There is implicit in the *Gathas* the belief that there will be ultimately an end to the war in which the "Good Creation" will be victorious. This will be the final "death of Death," the end of all destruction, and happy immortality for everything that cleaves to truth and righteousness. At the end of time as we know it, the righteous will be led by Zoroaster himself across the "Judgment Bridge" of Ahura Mazda to eternal blessings.

The Political Significance of Zarathustra's Teaching

Zarathustra's doctrine was politically radical. The society into which Zarathustra was born was only loosely organized politically, the people being a mostly nomadic, polytheistic people who practiced animal sacrifice. With the domestication of horses and the invention of the horse-drawn chariot, many of the Indo-Iranians turned progressively from a settled, agricultural way of life to a more socially disintegrated, warlike one. Small, settled communities and herds were regularly ravaged by their warlike neighbors.

Zarathustra's revelation was not just a sectarian dogma, but a moral challenge to the followers of the established religion. The Indo-Iranians, by worshiping multiple gods, of whom many (the daevas) were no less warlike than human beings, were "pretending," in a sense, that violent beings and the death and destruction they wrought were worthy of emulation and worship. Zarathustra—himself a priest of the old religion—denounced them as "followers of the Lie," at the same time calling the worshipers of Mazda *ashavans,* or "followers of the Truth" (Asha).

The followers of the ancient religion, Zarathustra claimed, worshiped with indiscriminate prayers and to no good purpose. They sacrificed cattle "in an ill-considered manner, impulsively, or at any time when [they] feel . . . a sharp urge," and distributed the meat to laymen who did not understand its sacredness. The carelessness of these sacrifices may have been attributable to the orgiastic manner in which they were performed. The Indo-Iranian rituals included imbibing the juice of the intoxicating *haoma* plant, which they worshiped as a god. Zarathustra disavowed the drinking of the *haoma,* or at least its use in the sacrifice. Although it is not clear that he disavowed animal sacrifice, Zarathustra did champion the settled agricultural life of the farmer and shepherd together with the responsibility for treating cattle well. A "right worshiper" freely chose to respect life in all its forms—human, animal, and plant—and thus to will an equitable social order establishing the unity and long life of an agricultural community.

> Yea, he who, as ruler, treats no coming applicant with injury, as a good citizen (or nobly wise) in sacred vow and duty, and living righteously in every covenant, . . . let him (this righteous judge) declare (vengeance) to that (hostile) lord, (my) kinsman. (*Y* XLVI: 5).

The Magians

The Achaemenian kings of the first Persian Empire do not appear to have venerated Zarathustra as the prophet and sole authority of their religion. They subscribed to a modified form of Zoroastrianism implemented by the Magi. The Magi were members of a priestly caste who had retained their position since Indo-Iranian times. Magian Zoroastrianism is similar in spirit and in its essential tenets to original Zoroastrianism. However, the Magian religion reinstituted considerable doctrine from the old Indo-Iranian religion, including some of the old gods.

The god Mithra was one of the most important gods in the earlier, Indo-Iranian pantheon. His name literally means "contract." This, added to his standard epithet, "the lord of wide pastures," would imply that Mithra is the protector of the members of the Mazdayasnian community. But he is also represented as a violent god who devastates his enemies: "[He] with Manly Courage, smites the foe in battle, and does not think he has smitten him . . . till he has smitten away the marrow and the column of life" (*Mihir Yt* XVII: 71). His readmission to the pantheon means the incorporation of some violent sentiments into Zoroastrian worship and seems to favor more purely political alliances than those espoused by the prophet originally.[8]

Mithra, in his new, exalted position, is joined by Sraosha ("Obedience") and Rashnu ("Genius of Truth," "Judge"), who appeared in the earlier liturgy, but as lesser divinities. In the later scripture, the three of them are constantly together, a team of warriors against the "lying parties to the contract." "Mithra strikes fear into them; Rashnu strikes a counterfear into them; the holy Sraosha blows them away from every side . . ." (*Mihir Yt* IX: 41). Mithra, Sraosha, the "fiend-smiting," the "Incarnate Word," and Rashnu, the "best killer," the "best doer of justice" (*Srosh Yt Hadhokht* I: 1, V: 18; *Rashn Yt* I: 7–8) are now worshiped with a sacrifice formerly withheld from any but Ahura Mazda. Interestingly, this sacrifice is a *haoma* sacrifice. Quite inconsistently with the Gathic teachings of the prophet, *haoma* is welcomed back into the Zoroastrian pantheon and venerated by the Magians as a god.

Verethragna ("Victory"), Vayu ("the god of the winds"), and Khwarenah ("Glory," or "Well-Being") were also added to the pantheon after the prophet's death. They, too, brought more of a fighting spirit to Zoroastrianism, which by then was the religion of a great empire. Verethragna, "the best armed of the heavenly gods," arms Zarathustra with virility, strength, eyesight, sturdiness, and health. Vayu seems to have maintained the petulant moral ambivalence by which he was characterized in the Indo-Iranian religion, and in his case the Zoroastrian worshiper must specify the part of his character worthy of veneration: "To this part of thee do we sacrifice, O Vayu! that belongs to the Good Spirit" (*Ram Yt* XI: 57). This practice foreshadows still further changes in the liturgy. Khwarenah ("Kingly Glory") is the spiritual quality with which all great human achievements are endowed. Through its own Khwarenah, every individual, every household, every community, and every country achieves its ultimate fulfillment.

In Magian Zoroastrianism we also find the reintroduction of the Fravashis, spirits that "belong to" particular individuals, not unlike individual souls as envisioned by some religions, but here personified as divinities. These "souls of the dead" belong not just to human beings but also to the gods and natural entities, connoting less the idea of souls than of guardian angels. They are the perfections of spirits and the helpers of God. Their scriptural hymn delineates the great heroes of Persian history, including the Amesha Spentas, Mithra, Sraosha, Rashnu, and Ahura Mazda himself. Thus, the Fravashis link the gods to the heroes, original creation to human creation, and myth to history.

This link is made by Ahura Mazda at the request of the Fravashis, in the person of Gaya Maretan, the human prototype or "primal man," "who first listened unto the thought and teaching of Ahura Mazda; of whom Ahura formed the race of Aryan nations, the seed of Aryan nations" (*Farvardin Yt* XXIV: 87). Gaya Maretan marks the beginning of history, the beginning of time as we understand it. Our time is the "mixed state" in which God's primordial creation, which is completely good, battles the evil forces of Angra Mainyush.

The Saoshyant is the savior[9] who will be born of Zarathustra's seed (his third son) at the end of this "mixed" millennium. He will beckon the Final Judgment, wherein the souls of the dead will be purified by fire and rejoin their bodies to enjoy an everlastingly good material existence in Heaven.

The introduction of these gods into the Magian religion after the prophet's death represented a threat to the Zoroastrian beliefs in the omnipotence of Ahura Mazda and the strict moral alliances of natural entities. Vayu, for instance, does not seem to be subject to God in the same way as every other creature, and the association of Mithra with Light implies that the created world is not divided by moral choice alone but also by natural kind—light and dark—and so suggests an incipient metaphysical dualism. These changes in the tone of the religion laid the groundwork for later developments in Zoroastrianism under the Sassanians.

The Zoroastrianisms of Sassanian Times

Little is known of the precise course that Zoroastrianism followed during the years of Greek and Parthian rule in Persia. However, by the time the Sassanians came to power in the third century A.D., several different sectarian Mazdaisms had developed and none of them corresponded precisely to the religion of Achaemenian times. Political competition with Rome and Byzantium compelled the Sassanian kings to unify Iran under a state religion, for which purpose they made efforts to reconstruct a standarized Zoroastrianism. Their achievement, however, was somewhat inconsistent and inauthentic. Their fragmented collection of scripture showed Greek, Indian, and anachronistic Sassanian influences, and uniformity of worship was attained only through the violent persecution of unorthodox practice.

Over the unrecorded centuries of Seleucid and Parthian rule, Ahura Mazda (whose name over the intervening period had been shortened to Ohrmazd) had become irreversibly identified with Spenta Mainyush, the "Good Spirit." He had also become more closely associated with Light, in addition to His Truth, Life, and Goodness. Angra Mainyush (now Ahriman) was therefore conceived as equal and opposite to Ohrmazd, and taken to represent Darkness in addition to Deceit, Death, and Destruction.

His identification with Spenta Mainyush devalued Ohrmazd and limited the metaphysics of the religion. The earlier, elegant, monist response to the question of evil was no longer possible. The Ahura Mazda of the early parts of the *Avesta* was powerful enough to have created a mixed world whose creatures could freely choose to be evil or good. The Ohrmazd of the ninth-century texts (although still officially omnipotent) apparently could create only Good and Light. With these new conceptions of God and of Ahriman, Zoroastrianism offered several different solutions to the problem of evil. In fact, the variety of Zoroastrian sects may be differentiated according to their accounts of the origin of evil.

The official doctrine of the Sassanian high priests was thoroughly—that is, metaphysically as well as ethically—dualist. God, in this new conception, was limited in His power by Ahriman, the principle of Darkness and Evil. The story of the good and evil twins was now interpreted in such a way that Ohrmazd/Spenta Mainyush and Ahriman were de facto two opposing first principles. In this conception, they jointly create the "mixed time," which is the natural world as we know it. Ohrmazd creates everything that is good, and Ahriman everything that is evil. Yet despite Ahriman's more powerful position in the pantheon, technically he was still the weaker force and would be vanquished at the end of this time by a now somewhat contrivedly omnipotent Ohrmazd.

Zurvanism

This explanation of evil, however, was not the only one made possible by the identification of Ohrmazd with Spenta Mainyush. It was probably not even the most popular theological solution of the period, but rather the one chosen as the most efficacious for the Sassanians' reunification project. It is likely that some form of Zurvanism was actually the more prevalent version of Zoroastrianism before the various Sassanian reforms, and afterwards Zurvanism was orthodoxy's most threatening heresy.

Zurvanism may be differentiated from other forms of Zoroastrianism by its explanation of evil, which was a very reasonable one, considering the conditions into which the religion had fallen. Because Ohrmazd's identification with Spenta Mainyush was by this time irremediable, the Mazdean dualist position just described necessarily implied that Ohrmazd had created his own twin brother. Taken seriously and literally, however, this does not make sense. The Zurvanites therefore claimed, on the contrary, that the primordial twins must have had a common parent, whom they called Zurvan Akarana ("Infinite Time"), taking the scripture's allusion to the "beginning of time" literally.

The concept of Zurvan restored a balance between monism and dualism. The pairs—Life and Death, Truth and the Lie, Good and Evil, and now Light and Darkness—could now be differentiated from each other by or in the One: Infinite Time. The Zurvanite Ohrmazd, however, is no longer this one creator. Now identified with one of the twins, Ohrmazd must be a created being. He is limited both in time and by his twin and equal, Ahriman. The Zurvanite claim that Time, rather than God, was the true first principle, then, alienated Zurvanites from the orthodox. They maintained God's goodness and unity at the cost of His omnipotence and omniscience.

Zurvanism's new monism gave it a darker tone than that of orthodoxy. Because the Zurvanites maintained that "nothing could come from nothing," they had to claim that the seeds of evil existed prior to the birth of the twins, in Infinite Time. In the Zurvanite version of creation, Zurvan performs the sacrifice for a thousand years, in the hope of having a son. In the anxiousness of waiting, Zurvan comes to doubt his ability to create. Thus, within the heart of Zurvan, even before the birth, there are two competing characters: the hope and the doubt. Ohrmazd is the child of Zurvan's hopeful sacrifice, Ahriman of his despondent doubt. Since evil originates prior to both twins, Ahriman's power must be equal, rather than just opposed, to Ohrmazd's. Thus, Ohrmazd's victory at the end of time was not so clearly ensured. Zurvanism's emphasis on the concept of the infinity of time also contributes to its darkness. For Zarathustra, the finite world with its temporal battlefield and material weapons is Ahura Mazda's most powerful creation, a glorious abundance of life; for Zurvanism, it is a fleeting and distressing period in the immensity of Time.

There were sectarian differences even within the basic Zurvanite position, however, that diverged still further from Zoroastrian orthodoxy. Some Zurvanites denied the most essential of Zoroastrian credos, the belief in the freedom of the human will. They claimed that finite and mortal human beings had no power to change the progress of infinite time; their actions were necessitated by Zurvan. Because humans did not have the choice of doing otherwise, human moral actions did not merit God's good judgment. Thus these Zurvanites also denied that Ahura Mazda rewarded moral action and punished evil. Other, Aristotelian Zurvanites conceived of the infinite as uninformed matter. This sect not only denied that Ohrmazd was all-powerful but also that He was immaterial, and because of this they were the most strongly persecuted of the Zurvanite sects.

Despite its persecution, it is likely that early Zurvanism was as popular as Mazdean orthodoxy, and that it held an audience right down to Islamic times. Certain originally Zurvanite tenets have left a clear impression on history's image of Zoroastrianism. Zurvanism's claim, however, that God was created, and its even more unorthodox sectarian claims against freedom of the will, just rewards and punishments, and God's immateriality, were considered heretical by all the powerful clergies—Mazdean, Christian, and, later, Manichaean and Muslim as well. In the end, Zurvanism was completely vanquished by its persecutors. The Zurvanites, however, raised a theological question that would plague Persian thought up to the present day: the question of whether reason, revelation, or tradition was the best path to the truth. The grating conflict between what was considered "Persian" and what "non-Persian" authority, first raised in Iran by the Zurvanites, marks Persian thought forever afterward.

Manichaeism

One of the most interesting moments in the history of Persian ideas is the emergence of the far-reaching and influential religion of Manichaeism. Its founder and prophet, Mani, was born in Babylon in 216 A.D. of noble Parthian parents. Mani began proselytizing in 240 A.D. while traveling in northwest India. Later, he succeeded in converting two brothers who were well placed at the Sassanian court, and so gained a sympathetic hearing from King Shapur I. Despite his initial successes, his fortunes began to turn with the ascendancy to the throne of Bahram I, under whose rule Mani was imprisoned and executed.

Manichaeism is the only religion preaching universal redemption to have come out of the Near Eastern Gnostic tradition and flourished. It was syncretistic of Christianity and Zoroastrianism, and it stressed the notions of purity and pollution. Mani and his followers wrote and preached in many different languages and adopted different vocabularies depending on the religious sympathies of the audience they hoped to convert. In the service of propagating the religion, the Manichaean deities were given a variety of pseudonyms. On account of the adaptability of its rhetoric, Manichaeism was a seductive faith that seemed to subsume and improve on the offerings of every other religion of the time.

Manichaeism is deeply rooted in the pessimistic spirit of Zurvanism and in the dualism of Sassanian Zoroastrianism. However, it furnishes its own unique and ingenious response to the questions, focal here as elsewhere, of evil and of man's responsibility for it. Manichaeism admits of two fundamental primordial principles: Light and Darkness. The Realm of Light is orderly, intelligent, and spiritual, and is presided over by the good principle, called Father of Greatness (who, when Mani was preaching at the Sassanian court, he named Zurvan). The Kingdom of Darkness, on the other hand, is ruled by unregulated passion and lust. Consequently, it is chaotic, disorderly, and material. For the Manichaeans, matter is a part of the Evil existence. It inhibits, or consumes, Light.

Compared with the stern war story of Zoroastrianism, the Manichaean cosmogony is a melodrama. The two principles, Light and Darkness, were originally separated and had distinct boundaries. Ruled by lust and with no intelligence or order to control them, the motion of the demons of the Realm of Darkness is random. Thus, some overstep the boundaries of Light. Lustful and aggressive creatures that they are, they are immediately infatuated with the Light, and they plan to invade it. The Evil Principle of Manichaeism, then, is capable not just of volition but also of thought. In thinking, therefore, men may participate in evil as well as in good. The human role here is desperate, not noble. The souls of men, according to Manichaean doctrine, are helpless by themselves. Though of divine origin, their material existence imprisons them within the walls of evil. Human beings are morally vulnerable, unable to trust even their own thoughts.

To protect Paradise, the Father of Greatness calls forth a succession of beings, something like the Zoroastrian Amesha Spentas, culminating with the Primal Man, who battles the invading demons. The Primal Man is defeated and taken into captivity, where he is devoured by the demons. In this event, Light and Darkness mix. The "mixed" time here is not just a battle, but a demoralizing attempt to recover from utter defeat.

The Primal Man is not in a position to effect recovery by himself. He is not able to take the moral initiative, but only to Answer the Call of morality (two new deities). He must respond through an apprehension of *nous,* which is made available to him by the child of Call and Answer. Without *nous,* he is helpless before the demons of Darkness.

Light plays a vital role in this moral struggle. "Good" or "redemption" is defined in terms of a quantity of Light, which is immaterial. "Evil" is defined in terms of a quantity of Darkness, of which matter is comprised. Manichaeism, then, gives as great a weight to the metaphysical principles of Light and Darkness as to the moral principles of Good and Evil. Further, it complicates the Zoroastrian notions of human alliances. Human beings must now fight against material existence rather than with it—hence the more desperate and hopeless tone of Manichaeism as compared with the other revealed religions.

Few religions offer so sympathetic an understanding of the despair and irony with which material existence is infused, or so compelling a version of "fire and brimstone." In Manichaeism, embodied humanity is of demonic origins and is the last best hope of Evil in its eternal quest to dominate and imprison Light. This is the result of human procreation, which actually prolongs the captivity of the Light particles within material entities. Far from the humanistic and life-affirming optimism of Zoroastrianism, the Manichaean sees human life as inherently evil. On the other hand, demonic as humans may be in their embodiment, they also have a divine essence, because their souls, inherited from the Primal Man, are made by the Father of Greatness. Redemption is possible.

If human beings are to be liberated from Darkness, however, they must be informed about their divine origins, and become one with *nous.* There have been three prophets, according to Mani, who have been illumined by *nous:* Zarathustra, Buddha, and Jesus. Mani claimed to be the culmination of this line of illuminative prophecy, and he expected his followers to refrain from the activities of their dark nature and from harming the light particles already imprisoned here on earth.

Manichaeans were forbidden to kill any living creatures or to eat meat.

This was not because animals were considered rational and divine, as is argued in some defenses of vegetarianism. Rather animals, according to Mani, are darker and placed lower on the hierarchy of being than are vegetables. They are therefore contaminants. Manichaeans were also prohibited from forgetting their divine origins by drinking wine; from harming plants by working in the fields; and from perpetuating the imprisonment of light within the confines of their bodies through sexual intercourse. These precepts are known as the three seals "of the Mouth, Hand, and Heart," as they are restrictions against certain types of food, work, and love. Taken to their logical conclusion, these Manichaean strictures encourage humanity gradually to die off from lack of food and diminishing population. The separation of Light from Darkness will thus approach completion and call forth the future time. There will be a great war, a judgment day, and a second coming of Jesus, and Darkness will be sealed in a pit for eternity.

Manichaeism was the most persecuted and, so we may assume, the most popular of Christian heresies. It spread rather rapidly in Persia and abroad because of its relentless appeal to reason and its ability to incorporate borrowings from other religions. It survived the great Sassanian persecutions and retained a following in the West until the sixth century. Manichaeism crossed over the boundaries between the various churches to give meaningful answers to eternal human concerns about our darker nature, espousing the only moral doctrine that would follow reasonably from them.

Mazdakism

Around the turn of the fifth and sixth centuries A.D., Persia witnessed the emergence, consolidation, and brutal persecution of a revolutionary, protocommunist doctrine—Mazdakism. Named after its chief advocate, Mazdak Bamdadan, Mazdakism was a Gnostic doctrine based, like Manichaeism and Zurvanism, on the dualism of Light and Darkness.

Mazdakism is consistently more materialist than the Persian religions that preceded it. At the beginning of time, according to Mazdakite doctrine, there were three substances: Water, Earth, and Fire. Out of their mingling, two Cosmic Managers emerged, one of Good and one of Evil. Without denying the existence of spiritual qualities, Mazdakites claimed that the origin of all things was material, or physical. The three physical substances, Earth, Water, and Fire, rather than one immaterial God, are the fountain from which Good and Evil spring. The Cosmic Managers originally oversaw distinct territories. Mazdakites believed that their mixture, the mixture of Good and Evil, came about through sheer coincidence. However, only the Light, or Good, principle of Mazdakism is wise and endowed with consciousness. The Dark, or Evil, principle is blind, ignorant, and without volition. Thus, despite the seeming similarity to Manichaean dualism, Mazdakite doctrine is hopeful that through rationality we will be able to overcome evil.

According to some Arab accounts, the Mazdakites' "object of worship" sits on a throne like an ancient monarch. He orders the world from an aloof distance, through four spiritual powers, with their Seven Viziers and Twelve Spiritual Forces. Each of these nineteen "helpers" is named by a Persian word. Anyone in whom these four, seven, and twelve qualities are embodied will himself become "godly." This perfect man is exempt from participation in the religious rituals. Such a person, of course, will no longer be subject to any authority other than his own knowledge of the good. This antiauthoritarianism, added to the earthly materialism of their cosmology, marked Mazdakites as politically rebellious as well as religiously heretical.

Mazdakites were known for their concern with distributive justice. Their doctrine stipulated that the resources provided by the earth were intended to be utilized collectively. Human needs, the Mazdakites claimed, could and should be met in a cooperative manner, without recourse to violence, competition, or the domination of any one individual over any other. Evil disrupted this proper process by instigating in people a blind, irrational passion to own property and an equally blind sexual desire such that men would be enticed by the prospect of dominating their mates. Thus, 1,200 years before the German philosopher Karl Marx offered a similar argument, the Mazdakites pinpointed the ownership of private property as the "origin of evil."

Here, as in Zoroastrianism, evil is thought to originate in an alliance of the human being with the evil principle. Unlike Zoroastrian ethics, however, the Mazdakites believed that human choice is free only when it is allied with the Good. The evil human being gives in to lust and, like the evil principle itself, loses the power of volition. Mazdakite ethics promoted free and rational containment of the demons of Wrath, Envy, Vengeance, Need, and Covetousness. To behave rightly was to properly distribute the earthly goods the ownership and domination of which tempted individuals to evil. The human good was to lead a noncompetitive life based on kindness, hospitality, egalitarianism, and fraternity. Thus the primary tenet of Mazdakite moral doctrine was the abolition of private property, which, under the prevailing social structure, included land, wealth, family, and women. Needless to say, Mazdakite ethics, like the communistic ethics they foreshadowed, were unpopular with the wealthy and powerful governments of their time.

Manichaeism and Mazdakism had diametrically opposed ethical beliefs, and both were rightly considered heretical by late Zoroastrian orthodoxy. Nonetheless they can be said to share with each other and with the original Zoroastrianism a sense of righteous indignation over the divisions within the community and the aggression of the more powerful against the weaker.

Persian Post-Islamic Thought

The philosphical trends between the Arab conquest of Iran and the Safavid dynasty can only very awkwardly be discussed in terms of national or geographic origin. There was tremendous mobility both of individuals and of ideas over the entire region. Under the caliphate, a great number of small dynasties rose, flourished, and fell. Each house patronized its own scholars, artists, and theologians, each of whom had his own ideas to promote and many of whom worked at more than one court. Similarly, the intellectual disciplines of this period cannot easily be categorized. In Islam, most theological considerations have direct political application, and most political decisions are justified theologically. Islamic dicta are so much involved in practical affairs that almost any artistic theme or scholarly project had religious and political significance.

It must be noted, however, that Islamic culture was indelibly marked by the pre-Islamic political organization and intellectual activity of Persia. Political and military leadership remained largely in the hands of Arabs and Turks; but the right-hand men—local governors, scholars, secretaries, viziers, advisers, laureates, and philosophers—were very often Persian. In this way, the intellectual tone of Islam, particularly under the Abbasid caliphate, grew progressively "Iran-ized" and Persian literature progressively "Islam-ized." "Persian Islamic" thought, then, is probably most easily defined retrospectively. Today, for instance, Iran is a Shi'ite state that projects an image of Shi'ism as both the more true and the more Persian of Islamic doctrines. Shi'ism in itself, however, is no more nor less Iranian than other Islamic sects. Rather, Shi'ism is "Iranian" in the sense that the development of Shi'ism played an important role in the development of autonomy in modern Iran. Using this retrospective method, then, we will look at the important sectarian ideologies that contributed to the modern self-concept of Iranian Islam.

The *Umma*

The prophet of Islam, Muhammad, received his first revelations from Allah in the year 610 A.D., in Mecca, Arabia, and they continued throughout his life. The texts of these revelations were copied down according to Muhammad's order and compose the Muslim scripture, the Qu'ran.

The Arab society of the time consisted of extended families, or clans, within which there were tremendous loyalty and cohesion, but between which there were few ties at all. The moral or social unit was the family, not the individual. In Mecca and other centers, however, members of different nomadic Arab families could meet together. There, too, Arabs interacted with representatives of the powerful Sassanian and Byzantine empires, and with their monotheistic Christian, Jewish, and Zoroastrian views.

Muhammad's revelations conferred upon him the mission of unifying the disparate Arab families into a nation by redirecting their familial loyalties toward the one proper object of faith, Allah. Among other things, this was achieved through a redefinition of the concept of justice in terms of personal responsibility. Despite its clear designation of the Arabs as a "chosen" people, the faith is also for the ears of Christians and Jews, and the "final" comment from the Judeo-Christian God is "Noah prayed to us, . . . Abraham was of the self-same faith. . . . We gave him Isaac, . . . We also sent forth Elias. . . . Lot, too was an apostle, . . . Jonah, too. . . ." (37). The unification of the Arabs, then, is but the first step in the mission of spreading to everyone the One True faith.

The charismatic presence of the prophet delayed recognition of the many philosophical problems inherent in the Islamic mission. In 622 he took his small following to Medina, where they built their support into the first Islamic community—the *umma*. The Islamic calendar begins with the *hijra,* or migration, to Medina and the establishment there of a community of the faith. The *umma* served under the political and military leadership of Muhammad, whose authority came directly from God. These original Muslims were certain that their actions were just, that their policies were rational, and that they knew God's law. When in 632 the prophet died, however, leaving no heir and no instructions on how to choose his successor, the community was at a loss for answers to fundamental philosophical questions concerning justice, truth, and God's will.

Abu Bakr, Muhammad's father-in-law and close friend, was elected caliph, the successor of the prophet. He was nominated by the "companions" (Muhammad's circle of close associates), and his succession was ratified by the community as a whole. Abu Bakr designated his successor to be 'Umar, who also had his appointment ratified. After 'Umar's death in 644, an appointed council elected 'Uthman to succeed him. Thus, no clear precedent was set for choosing the Islamic leadership. The universalism of the Qur'an and *hadith* (the sayings of the prophet) conflicted with the Arab particularism of the new covenant.[10] Questions about the treatment of non-Arab Muslims, the expansion of the empire, and the authority of caliphs all aroused dissent within the *umma*. The resulting disenfranchisement and factionalization within Islam raised questions about the ability of human beings to understand and institute Allah's will.

Disputes came to a head in 656 with 'Uthman's murder. Ali, Muhammad's son-in-law and cousin, was elected to replace him, but he had to defend his right to succession militarily. A wartime judicial council ruled 'Uthman's murder unjustified and Ali's election illegitimate. 'Uthman's cousin Mu'wayia declared himself caliph and set a precedent for hereditary succession to the caliphate. The 'Umayyads (the family of 'Uthman and Mu'wayia) ruled until 750. Their policies favored the familial, or Arab, notion of the *umma* The Abbasid family then usurped the caliphate and ruled Islam until the Mongol conquest. They favored a more universalist interpretation of the *umma,* but were inconsistent in their policies.

Thus, it became apparent in the first four caliphates that interpretations of Allah's instructions differed widely, that human leadership was not always trustworthy, and that the consequences of building an Islamic empire were of mixed value. Differing interests fell out along religious sectarian lines, and disputes within the Islamic world took on the character of philosophical debate.

Early Islamic Philosophy

Because the primary authority on all questions is scripture, Islamic philosophy begins with the study of Qu'ranic law, or *shari'a.* Early scholarly interest, particularly in moral and legal matters, also focused on the *hadith* (the prophet's sayings and works). These studies, through early and ongoing debate, endeavored to establish the relative authority of the individual versus that of the *umma.*

There were many different sects within Islam, and each maintained a long list of tenets. We will focus here on just the few that play a role in the evolution of contemporary Persian thought, and on those of their tenets that are most crucial to the issue of establishing authority over Qur'anic interpretation.

The Kharij'ites

The first Islamic group to develop a sectarian doctrine were the Kharij'ites (or "secessionists"), who originally supported Ali's claim to the caliphate. They defended the doctrine of freedom of the will and so of the individual's responsibility for his or her actions. Their strong sense of responsibility brought the Kharij'ites to turn against Ali when he consented to negotiate with his enemies, whose sinfulness proved them not to be true Muslims. Their belief in Ali's resultant sinfulness justified their murder of him.

The Mu'tazilites

Calling themselves the "People of Justice and Unity," the Mu'tazilites believed fundamentally and unquestioningly that Allah is Just and that

Allah is One. This could be understood, they claimed, in the "ordinary," human rational way. Allah could not intend the Qu'ran as a guide for human action and yet have a "different" and "inscrutable" meaning for its terms.

The Mu'tazilites claimed that an individual is responsible for his or her own actions. For instance, a child is not responsible for adherence to the faith if he or she was born Muslim. Unless the individual chose the faith, Allah would not be just, as we understand the word, in rewarding him or her for being faithful. For human beings to be responsible for their actions, they must act freely. Genuine freedom, however, must be the power to do both good and evil. Human action, therefore, causes evil, and God rightly condemns the person who sins. Mu'tazilite doctrine, then, affirmed belief in the freedom of the human will, and was also thoroughly "rationalist." The application of reason, called the *kalam,* they claimed, was the proper way to approach religious questions.

Orthodox Christian theology, with which the Mu'tazilites were familiar, had it that Christ was the Word of God, uncreated and coeternal with the Father. Application of this claim to Islam would imply that the Qu'ran, the Word of Allah, was coeternal with Him and uncreated, a part of God Himself. But the Mu'tazilites claimed that this was inconsistent with God's Unity. To be genuinely One, Allah must be indivisible. But the Qu'ran (even the words themselves, irrespective of the written text) is distinguishable from God. Hence, the Qur'an must be created. It is part of the natural mechanism of the created world, which Allah sets in motion and which free individuals mold, rightly or wrongly, to their ends. God's justice, power, knowledge, and compassion, however, cannot be created things, even though there are separate names for them in the Qur'an. If they were, then Allah could be understood "piecemeal," as sometimes exhibiting one attribute, sometimes another. But this would be impossible if He is One. Allah's attributes are of His essence. They cannot be subject to human will, like created things.

Mu'tazilite doctrine derogates revelation as a means to understanding Allah's truth. Their claim that scripture is created and subject to rational interpretation meant that authority in matters of law, morality, and politics rested in the *kalam,* not in the caliph, the scholars' assertions, or the literal word of the Qu'ran.

The Ash'arites

Al-Ash'ari (ca. 873–941) led a conservative reaction against the Mu'tazilites, and the school that followed him set the tone for succeeding Islamic theological debate. Al-Ash'ari was determined to defend the authority of revelation and of the literal Qur'an. But he was not content merely to assert the truth of Qur'anic passages. Whenever possible, al-Ash'ari gave a reasonable account of how the literal word of scripture could be true. For the Ash'arites, then, both reason and revelation were appropriate to the understanding of Allah, but the authority of revelation, as given in scripture, "trumped" that of reason. They availed themselves of the rational method of the Mu'tazilites, but only as a secondary tool.

The Ash'arites took a position between determinism—the belief that God is responsible for all actions, including human ones, and that therefore human beings are not free—and belief in freedom of the human will. They claimed that God created everything, including human actions, but that humans acquire God's actions by making choices. Allah's actions are made directly by Him. Human actions are God's actions mediated by human choice. A human action is like a gift from Allah. One cannot give oneself one's own gift, but one can choose good gifts and refuse bad ones, and in that way can be said to deserve what one gets. In this way, God's rewards and punishments can be said to be just, yet God's omnipotence, as testified in scripture, can be consistent with His justice.

The Ash'arites believed that both the Qur'an and God's attributes were uncreated because it is stated in scripture that the Qur'an is God's own words. According to the Ash'arites, this must be accepted as true. Yet words on paper, like the words we speak, are material, mortal, and created things. In order to make consonant the conflicting testimonies of scripture and reason the Ash'arites distinguished between a word's meaning and its expression. A person's intention, for instance, can be expressed in different ways, in different languages, and so forth. The same is true for the Qur'an. Its Arabic words—the expression—are created and subject to change. The meaning, which is expressed in its text, however, is of the very essence of Allah, uncreated and eternal.

The Shi'ites

The Qur'an, among Shi'ites, is understood as only the written articulation of a divine message. According to the Shi'ites, however, it contains not just expression and meaning but also multiple levels of meaning. The *zaher* is the apparent or literal meaning, called *exoteric*. The *batin* is the hidden or secret meaning, called *esoteric*. *Shari'a* (legal studies) derive from study of the Qur'an's exoteric expression, or *zaher*, but the deeper spiritual message of scripture, the *batin,* remains veiled from those uninitiated in the Qur'anic mysteries. The *batin* cannot be understood by the usual human faculties of reason.

For the Shi'ites, the prophet's role in revelation was considered unique and inimitable by ordinary human beings. He united the exoteric meaning of scripture with its esoteric meaning. The Shi'ites believed that Muhammad was the last one in his "cycle of prophecy." Direct revelation is no longer possible; for us, a gulf forever separates the *batin* from the *zaher.* Only the imams, members of a new "cycle of sainthood," can render the esoteric meaning of scripture intelligible. The imams had unique qualities that distinguished them from ordinary Muslims. They were men of charismatic personality in whom the seemingly divergent aspects of political and spiritual authority were united. The Shi'ites traced the lineage of the imams through Muhammad's daughter, Fatimah, and recognized the authority of Ali to be the ruler of Islam.

Sectarian disputes within Shi'ism arose, however, over disagreements about the imams themselves. The most obvious disagreement regards the number of the imams. Thus the easiest categorization of Shi'ism is into "Twelvers," "Seveners," "Fivers," and "Fourers." Another way to distinguish Shi'ite sects is according to the relative importance that each attributed to the personal qualities of the imams. Each imam is an embodiment of "sainthood." In addition to his ability to interpret the *batin* from the *zaher,* he has an innate understanding of Muhammad's revelation, bringing together in his person the different levels of meaning of scripture. Shi'ite sects disagreed over the ratio in which these abilities were to be found in the imams and over their lineage from the prophet. The most important distinction in this regard falls between the Twelvers and the Seveners.

The Seveners, or Esmai'ilis, believed that the *batin* and the *haqiqa* (the inner truth revealed by it) were somewhat more important than the *zaher* and the *shari'a.* This gave Esmai'ilism an esoteric, or mystical, tone. The Esmai'ilis believed that Allah's creation was mediated by a series of "Intellects." The First Intellect created the Second, and the Second the Third, who, the Esmai'ilis claimed, was the Archetype, or Prototype, of Adam. In their version of the Fall, or the origin of evil, the Third Intellect is said to have sinned by forgetting his distance from Allah and believing himself to have direct knowledge of his maker. As a result of his forgetfulness, the Third Intellect is further distanced from the Creator, demoted to the rank of Tenth Intellect.

The world, according to the Esmai'ilis, is evolving through the Seven intermediate Intellects to a restoration of its original state and an immediate knowledge of God. The imams mediate between human reason—which directly knows only the *shari'a* and *zaher*—and God's truth, in the *haqiqa* and *batin.* Human beings can achieve knowledge of God only by recognizing and following the Seven imams. The *shari'a* and *zaher* give guidance to ordinary human beings. Knowledge of God, however, can actually transform the human being into a higher form, closer to the Creator.

The "Twelver" Shi'ites, on the other hand, gave equal weight to the legal *zaher/shari'a* and the mystical *batin/haqiqa.* They believed that not only sainthood but also infallibility distinguishes the imams from other Muslims. The infallibility of the imams, which qualifies them for both spiritual and political leadership, is not given to them by the endorsement of the *umma,* but by divine decree. According to the Twelvers, then, God intended the imams to outrank the caliph in all matters. The Twelvers adopted from the Sunnis the method of hermeneutic interpretation, by which they elicited the esoteric meaning from particular passages of scripture. Thus, they combined reason with faith in the infallible authority of the imams. Their method blossomed into a rich and colorful philosophical tradition whose influence can be seen well into the modern era.

Belief in the Mahdi, the hidden Twelfth Imam, is particularly characteristic of Twelver Shi'ism. Mahdi, the only child of the Eleventh Imam, is believed by Twelvers to be the Messiah. He is believed to have disappeared at a young age, and to exist in a state of occultation awaiting resurrection. In its present state, humanity can overcome its distance from God and its ignorance of His will only through the mediation of text, imam, and reason. The return of Mahdi, however, calling forth a universal judgment and a restoration of justice and peace, will restore to humanity the full meaning of the Qur'an through a definitive revelation.

The Peripatetic Schools and the Development of Islamic Theology

According to the Ash'arites and Shi'ites, humans can come closer to a divine knowledge by fully understanding scripture. For them, revelation was the primary authority in all matters, but reasoning about the dicta given through revelation was nonetheless worthwhile and obligatory. Although this stance set a standard for the justification of claims to authority in Islam, Islamic theology was nonetheless rich and diverse. Islamic thought went well beyond the political and epistemological questions of authority into metaphysical investigations of God, knowledge, and the structure of the universe. One branch of this development was largely influenced by, and debated with, the philosophies of the Greeks and the Christians. It could be referred to as a Western trend in Islam. Another branch showed influences of Zoroastrianism, Manichaeism, and Buddhism, and so could be called an Eastern trend.

The theological, or Western, trend really knew no geographical boundaries. However, the influence of Aristotle, which it shares with Jewish and Christian theologians, has tended to make this tradition more amenable to study in Western universities. The first great Islamic theologian of this tradition was al-Kindī (801–873), called "the Arab philosopher." Al-Kindi was influenced primarily by Aristotelian (or peripatetic) thought, which included Christian followers of Plato. Also of great importance in this tradition were al-Fārābī (870–950), a Persian, who stuck still closer to the works of Aristotle, and al-Rāzī, also a Persian, known in the West as Rhazes (865–925), and a critic of al-Fārābī.

Most Islamic philosophy was conducted under various Eastern and Western influences and involved in dialogue with thinkers of diverse backgrounds. Even Ibn-Sīnā, for instance, the Islamic theologian who is best known in the West, professed a Persian-influenced angelology and cosmogony. The Persian al-Ghazali (1058–1111), called "the Ornament of Faith" and the "Proof of Islam," ranks with Ibn-Sīnā as the most eminent of Islamic theologians. He engaged in vociferous debate with Aristotelians and others in the Western branch of Islamic thought, and yet his work was designed to give rigorous philosophical expression to the beliefs of the mystics—which derive their influence from what we might call an Eastern tradition. Until al-Ghazali, Islamic mysticism was taught almost exclusively through the personal practices of particular masters to their disciples. This methodology, combined with an antipathy for the Aristotelianism with which Westerners identified philosophy, has often kept this Eastern trend out of ongoing philosophical conversations with Europe.

Without doubt, the pinnacle of the development of the peripatetic trend was Ibn-Sīnā, known in the West as Avicenna (980–1037). Ibn-Sīnā was a theologian of tremendous depth, influenced by Neoplatonism as well as by Aristotelianism, and again a Persian. In the tradition set by the Ash'arites, Ibn-Sīnā attempted to harmonize the authority of reason with that of revelation. Ibn-Sīnā made a distinction, however, on which the later Persian thinkers discussed in this chapter rely, and so it will be helpful to outline it here. Any particular thing, he claimed, is to be understood as a combination of its essence—its nature or definitive feature—and its existence—its real content. God, Ibn-Sīnā claimed, gives real existence to the various essences. For particular things, then, existence is added, or secondary, to essence. In the universe as a whole, however, existence—God's existence—is prior to all created things.

The Western trend in Islamic theology is usually thought to have ended with the death of Ibn-Rushd in 1198. Exclusive focus on this tradition would leave little room for explaining the development of Islamic theology after his death. Therefore, we will concentrate here on the Eastern trends in Persian Islam, both to avoid duplication of the material in other chapters and to pick out adequately the influences from which modern Persian Islamic theology develops.

Sufism

The ecclesiastical world in which the epistemological and metaphysical debates just described had political significance grew progressively more wealthy and powerful as the Islamic empire expanded. The inevitable corruption and injustice in which this situation resulted was disillusioning to many Muslims. They felt that philosophical squabbles over abstract metaphysical issues led Muslims away from Allah and His moral dicta. The message of the Qur'an, in the opinion of these critics, was lost among the endless arguments as to its interpretation, and among those who clung to these interpretations in order to justify their political power. Hence, individual Muslims from different walks of life began to renounce this world and its earthy trials and joys in order to find God. In this, they echoed the hermitage tradition of Manichaean and Christian mystics. These Muslim mystics eventually distinguished themselves as a group, called the Sufis, because of the coarse woolen (or *suf*) garments that some wore, reminiscent of the Christian monks' hair shirts.

Sufi philosophy is ahistorical. It does not represent an ongoing "conversation" through which a body of knowledge has been built. Rather, Sufism is a "way of being" whose theological doctrines were for some Sufis best put in terms of Shi'ism, and for others in terms of Sunnism, reflecting the same degree of diversity that exists in the region as a whole. It is difficult, therefore, either to give a history of Sufism or to trace its cultural influences. Nonetheless, its Persian influence cannot be ignored. Manichaeism is the most consistent philosophical basis for the Sufis' asceticism (the stringency of Sufi asceticism is not adequately explained by reference to Christian influences; only Manichaeism's identification of evil with matter matches it) and Iranian religious practice shows a marked Sufi influence. Given the diversity of Sufisms, the fickleness of its theological alliances, and its intimate, interpersonal method of teaching, a full exposition is impossible. Here we will braid together a discussion of the theologies allied with Sufism with a description of some of its practices and literature.

The Sufis' esoteric version of Islam followed the Shi'ite epistemology in the belief that the Qur'anic text contained not just expression and meaning but different levels of meaning, *zaher* and *batin*. The unlock the mysteries of the Qur'an, however, Sufis considered it essential that one rely not only on the mediation of the imams but directly on the grace of God. Only by God's grace could one have the "veil"—which keeps a human soul from the knowledge of God—removed from one's heart.

Sufism's emphasis is primarily moral and practical. Sufis believe, like other Muslims, that God is One and that God creates everything that exists. For the Sufis, however, this means that God is central to the existence of every created thing. Everything other than God emanates from God and is of God. Sufism is not pantheist, however; it does not think of God as the sum of all that exists, but rather as the One Truth of which everything that exists is only an indication. God and He alone is real, and everything else is an illusion, a veil that obscures the divine meaning hidden behind created things. Through *qalb* ("heart") a person becomes capable of finding this hidden meaning, which is God. To succeed in finding God, it is essential that one perfect one's spirit or cleanse one's heart.

Most Sufis believe that spiritual perfection is achieved in stages. The stage of *shari'a*—ordinary obedience to the Islamic law—is a prelude to the higher stage of mystical experience, the "path." At this higher stage, the Sufi lives in poverty, renouncing the world and its physical attractions; the Sufi suppresses desire and will in anticipation of achieving union with the One. The next stage is that of "gnosis," in which it becomes possible for the Sufi, having rid himself or herself of will or ego, to attain isolated moments of unity with the One. These are supreme moments of ecstasy, and the dream of everyone who embarks upon the Sufi path. It is only in the stage of unity with the One that it becomes possible to know the full, hidden truth, or *haqiqa*. It is so beautiful that the Sufi loses all desire to be a self, or ego, distinguishable from this One. The Sufi's only wish at this moment is to disappear, to enter the last stage, *fana* ("vanishing" or "annihilation"), and to be absorbed completely and eternally into God.

Abu al-Mughith Hussayb ibn-Mansur, known as al-Hallaj, is said to have uttered his famous cry, "Ana al haq!" ("I am God!"), during this stage of ecstasy. He was put to death as a heretic for this outbreak in 922. The Sufis, however, believe his remark to be extremely pious. The Sufi poet Rumi interprets al-Hallaj in one of his discourses:

> Some men reckon it as a great pretension; but "I am God" is in fact a great humility. The man who says, "I am the servant of God" asserts that two exist, one himself and the other God. But he who says, "I am God" has naughted himself and cast himself to the winds. He says, "I am God": that is, "I am not, He is all, nothing has existence but God, I am pure non-entity, I am nothing." In this the humility is greater.

This idea of communion with God in the state of ecstasy later became the basis of the Illuminationist, or Ishraqi, school of Persian philosophy, founded by the Sufi sheikh al-Suhrawardi. He was also executed for heresy, in approximately 1191, and is more often called "al-Maghtul" ("the assassinated"). Suhrawardi expounded a metaphysics based on a mystic epistemology. He attempted to engage and better the discursive method of the peripatetics with the "Oriental wisdom." In fact, he used a linguistic connection between the concept of "Eastern-ness" *(mashriq)* and that of "wisdom," or "light" or "illumination" *(ishraq)*. Both words are derived from *sharq,* meaning "the sunrise." Suhrawardi and his followers claimed that Light was the foundation of all existence. Knowledge of the truth, therefore, was achieved through an intuition of Light— an "illumination." He called the mystic stages a "trip to the East" whose final destination was beyond the world of material things. The "Occident," from which one embarks upon the mystic journey, is the world of matter, darkness, and illusion. The "Orient" proper is beyond the material world. It is the realm of light and the home of the archangels.

Suhrawardi considered the discursive reasoning and logical categorization of Peripateticism to be an important stage in the mystic's aquisition of knowledge. He attempted to reconcile the mystic's belief in the personal transmission of knowledge from master to disciple with the

philosopher's belief in discourse and study, claiming that the most knowledgeable men attained perfection in both "philosophy" and "gnosis."
Suhrawardi believed that illumination was transmitted along two historical
lines, the Greek and the Persian. He believed that his own role was to
reunify the Zoroastrian wisdom with the Platonic, in Islam.

Suhrawardi accepted the essence/existence distinction of Ibn-Sīnā, but
he rejected Ibn-Sīnā's claim that existence is prior to essence. For
Suhrawardi, the essence of any particular thing, its definitive characteristic, is just a higher, or more "luminous," level of its existence, and God
is the highest essence of all. For God, or Pure Light, the distinction
between existence and essence vanishes. God, or Pure Light, is the
primary existence *and* essence. Suhrawardi claimed that there are degrees
of existence which differ according to their illumination. Matter is responsible for the obstruction of light, which is darkness.

For Suhrawardi, the term *reflection* has the dual meaning of "mirror-
ing" and "thinking." Light that reflects itself is akin to consciousness.
God, the angels, the archetypes, and the human soul are lights of this
kind, called "incorporeal" lights. Fire and the stars are unconscious and
need another to reflect upon them. They are called "accidental" lights.
The bodies of natural things are inanimate and ignorant. They obstruct
light. Through the reflection, or intellection, of each angelic effusion upon
God, a new effusion is created. Each is illumined both directly by God
and indirectly by Him through its predecessor. Each successive effusion
of light dominates, or illumines, the next effusion below. Sadly, though,
it also veils or obstructs the direct illumination of God from its subordinate. Each effusion is therefore dependent upon its superior, and its
attitude toward its superiors is love. Creation or illumination, like the
birth of a child, is achieved through a combination of the masculine
"movement through nature"—the effusion of a subordinate light—and
the feminine "movement through love"—reflection upon the superior
light.

The notion of love is central to Sufism generally. Love of God is an
effort on the part of the lover to join with that which creates him or her
as a lover, to join with the beautiful, the beloved. Love is the epistemological principle that joins the Sufi to the wisdom that is God, in his or
her single-minded effort along the path of enlightenment. Love is also
understood by the Sufi, however, as a metaphysical principle. The will of
God to create could be understood, according to the Sufi, only as a
gracious love, an overflowing of His abundant divinity into the forms of
created things. This overflow, however, is a devolution, a "sending
away." God's love is like a beautiful woman who inspires a lover only to
spurn him, or a mother who gives birth to a son only to send him on his
own way.

In the light of this pervasive notion of love, it is not surprising that
Sufis like al-Hallaj would put forth a rereading of the sin of the "fallen

Angel"—*Iblis,* or Satan. He attributes Satan's fall not to Satan's arrogance but to his inability to compromise his love of God; he is the epitome of the failed lover:

> When it was said to Satan, "Venerate Adam!" he spoke these words to God: "How can it any longer be owed to you if I must now adore Adam?—"I am going to torture you forever."—"Yes."—"Then your glance toward me will help me bear the vision of my punishment! Do as you wish with me."

This vision of the Angel, "fallen away" from God and seeking reunion even at the risk of death, reechoes the Manichaean and Zoroastrian explanations of evil. In this Sufi account, an all-good God devolves into a dark, material existence. In Sufi practice, however, this separation from God is keenly felt and motivates the Sufi to embark on the path of love. The path is an evolution through the stages to reunion with God. The Sufi stages are developments in enlightenment or knowledge. They fulfill God's desire to be known by appreciating His graciousness and His beauty. Thus, the stages are ever more "truthful" reflections of God's own love. Since the desire to join with the beloved is a guide to action, we can say that love is the basis of Sufi morality.

The indirect medium of poetry rather than direct philosophical prose was often the forum for the Sufi message. Its effect is like the indirect vision of a face in a mirror as opposed to a direct glance at it. Certain romantic metaphors have been so often repeated in Sufi poetry that their interpretation is unequivocal; their religious significance is just short of their literal meaning. Allah is universally represented as the beloved, the beautiful. The beloved's beauty, and the lover's nearness to her, are most often represented in visual terms—her radiance and his longing glance. Beauty is described as light, and the knowledge acquired by the lover's closeness to her as vision. One of the richest and most lavish of the visual romantic metaphors is of God's creation as a hall of mirrors. God's and the humans' souls are figured as mirrors of each other. An example from the poet Hashimi gives an entire cosmology in romantic verse:

> . . . So fond was he
> Of his own beauty that he wished no
> bliss
> But to admire himself unceasingly
> As with a hundred eyes. So, to that end
> He set out to construct a palace . . .
> . . . .
> . . . last and most important he
> Himself set out with all his skill to make
> The interior of his castle one vast hall
> Of mirrors . . .

Another image of love, recurrent to the point of cliché, is of a flame—to which of course a moth is passionately drawn and from which it takes sustenance. One erotic and multifaceted visual metaphor is the image of the beloved's hair, flowing over her face, obscuring the lover's vision. Like the woman's hair, all nature images play the role of intermediaries, mediating between the Divine Beloved and the human lover. The beauty of the flowers, the countryside, the water and the air are small in comparison to that of their maker. Nonetheless they stir the passions of the seeker after wisdom. They, like Suhrawardi's angels, at the same time both obscure and reveal God to the human understanding. 'Attar (d. approx. 1230) reflected: "In the way of love there must be knowledge and ignorance/so I have become both a dullard and a sage."

Some romantic themes stray further from the visual metaphor. Drunkenness, for the Sufi, is the most common and compelling image for the stage of ecstasy, and religiously toned images of wine and intoxication practically identify Sufi poetry. Further, the "way" of nature, the path of all God's creatures toward Him through love, is dialectical, because it proceeds through conflict—the imbalance and rebalance of good and evil, of mystical and physical desire, of nearness to God and distance from Him. On the one hand, this dialectical movement symbolizes the overcoming of "illusion" by truth, but, on the other, it symbolizes God's justice.

Classical Persian poetry, a tremendous literary achievement by any standards, was well read in Europe, where its themes were sometimes appropriated. For the Sufi, however, love had a religious significance that did not accompany the poetry to the West. The goal of the Sufi is union with the One, but the secular romantic can never bridge the spiritual distance between lover and beloved. Sadly, this secular reading seems to be the preference of modern Persian poets, who have accommodated with Sufi images of the beloved into a whole literary tradition in which women figure as cruel, aloof, narcissistic, and masochistic. The growing secularism of the readings given to the classical Persian poets both by modern Persians and by European romantics may in part be responsible for a certain chauvinism some find in them today.

Sufi poetry also makes allusions of political import. Sufis believe that the Qur'anic truth to which humans have access is both revealed and hidden in its text. Only those who have achieved the very highest stages are capable of uncovering its hidden meaning. Accordingly, the Sufi poems often include biographical notes on particular Sufi masters. The masters do not expound principles; rather, they exemplify the virtues and stages of enlightenment. The poets' patrons were Muslim kings who sought power and glory, and political attention for their courts. Under these circumstances it was necessary that the poems include emphatic praise for the patron. With their mastery of irony and inscrutability, however, the poets couched political commentary and criticism in their panegyrics. One can imagine how well the rhetoric of lover and beloved would lend itself to the praises of a vain monarch. Yet one can equally well imagine how ambivalent would be the Sufi's opinion of even the best king's earthly rule.

The Safavid Era and the Reintroduction to Europe

The Sufi followings grew progressively strong and popular, but they remained for the most part unaffiliated with the philosophical schools. These schools continued into the Safavid era (1502–1736) to teach the peripatetic tradition and to debate the authority of reason versus that of revelation. The important School of Esfahān concentrated on Shi'ite theology. It produced one of the most important philosophers of later Islam, Mulla Sadra (approx. 1571–1641). In a philosophy of astonishing depth, Sadra again took on the challenge of integrating the so-called Western categories and discursive technique with Islamic mysticism. He remains one of the central figures in Persian and Shi'ite theology. Sadra's coherent synthesis of the seemingly opposing schools of Peripateticism and Illuminationism has been compared with that of the eighteenth-century German philosopher Immanuel Kant.

In regard to the question of authority, Sadra in essence claimed, and quite effectively demonstrated, that discursive reasoning, revelation, and mystical illumination are consonant with each other and mutually dependent. He claimed that the esoteric meanings of the *hadiths* corresponded with the gnosis achieved by the prepared soul of the mystic. Both revelation and illumination, Sadra claimed, were fully rational in their content and so could be rationally argued and demonstrated. His method, then, combined literary, or symbolic, interpretation of scripture with the logic of the ancient Greeks and the defense of mystical experience.

Sadra reasserted the priority of existence over essence. He claimed, however, that all existence was fundamentally One. God does not give a distinct existence to each essence. Like the Illuminationists, Sadra claimed that existence in its most pure and intense degree is God, and that existence manifests itself, like light spilling out from its source, in lesser and lesser degrees of intensity. For Sadra, however, each particular thing just manifested God's existence in a limited form. For instance, when the light of a lamp falls onto a chair, the light is broken from an undifferentiated flow into "pieces"—the lighted surface of the chair, the light that continues past its edges, and the shadow behind it. In the same way, God's Being flows "into" things themselves, and their essences limit His singular existence. The mind abstracts ideas of these limits upon God's existence, and calls them "essences," but these human ideas are not the real essences of things. The real essences of things are not mere human ideas, and God's real existence is unlimited; therefore neither can be comprehended in its entirety by the human mind. Through mystical transcendence, however, the human soul can join with its true essence, in the divine realm.

Persia was reunified independently of Arab Islam by the Safavids in the sixteenth century. The Safavid dynasty championed Twelver Shi'ism and declared it the national religion. Theological schools focused on Shi'ism. European contact with Iran expanded. The British Empire had increasing colonial designs on India, and used Iran as buffer against the growing threats by its main rivals, Russia and France.

Some Iranians became infatuated with the idea of progress, resuscitated perhaps from the eschatologies of Zoroastrianism and Manichaeism, and of which the version presented by their Enlightenment European visitors reminded them. The notion suggested to them that Persia's ancient glory could be reproduced on the foundation of scientific principles. This created a seemingly immeasurable rift between religious and secular intellectuals. Their debates were further complicated by the profundity of the various new philosophical methods that arose from the intermingling with Europe. The French was the most attractive of the European traditions in Iran. In the nineteenth century, secular philosophy in Persia, which gathered force outside the Shi'ite schools, initially concentrated on the study of the French positivists. In the twentieth century, positivism and its derivations were taught in the state universities, and French existentialists are still widely read among Persian intellectuals.

On the other hand, a segment of Persian intellectuals, motivated by a distaste for European liberalism, embraced Marxist philosophy in its Soviet form. Persian Marxism did little more initially than mimic Soviet philosophical theories. More recently, however, Iran has identified itself more and more as a Third World nation and has better adapted Marxism to its own political circumstances. Marxism was influential in the intellectual development of the young Persians whose revolutionary parties rose against the shah in 1978.

The nationalization of Shi'ism in the sixteenth century gave a new and distinctly Persian focus to Islamic theological debates. The Twelvers claimed that the Mahdi was still alive and had sole authority to lead Islam. Thus, the Shi'ites tried to establish the beneficiary of the imam's trust—a person of "true opinion"—to rule in his stead. A group of ecclesiastical authorities, called the *Mujtahed,* or "religious scholars," was already in place in the Persian theological seminaries. They considered themselves most qualified to interpret the law, using the philosophical methods in which they were schooled, called usul (and their epistemological school Usuli). The usul method combined "reasoning about the Islamic law" with "consensus" among the Mujtahed, and so their claims to ecclesiastical authority were based on reason and professional qualification.

Needless to say, the Usulis faced opposition, not only from the secular political influences of Europe, but also from Shi'ite thinkers of a more egalitarian bent. The main opposition to the Usuli school came from a group of Shi'ite theologians called the Akhbaris or "traditionalists." The Akhbaris claimed that usul was incompatible with the authority of the imam, and that that authority was therefore illegitimately usurped by the Mujtahed. The disappearance of the hidden Twelfth imam, they claimed, left Shi'ites to make do with the Qur'an and *hadith*.

The Usuli/Akhbari controversy spanned three centuries. Theological emphasis on the centrality of the imams, particularly that of the last hidden Mahdi, developed from the literalist interpretation of the Akhbaris. The Usulis provided philosophical justification for the growing authority of the Mujtahed. Ultimately, it was the Usuli position that dominated the intellectual scene in Iran. Dwindling opposition to the Mujtahed found its main expression in the Shaykhi schools. The Shaykhis deemphasized the literalist approach to scriptural interpretation in favor of an advanced metaphysical study. They claimed that the imam's existence was higher than that of the rest of God's creation. Shaykh Asha'i (1756–1825), the founder of the Shaykhi schools, claimed that the hidden imam existed in a transcendent, immaterial realm, and that knowledge of the imam's true opinion could be had only by entering this realm.

From the point of view of contemporary Iranian politics, the most important opposition to the Mujtahed was offered by the nineteenth-century religions of Babism and its descendant, Baha'ism. The founder of Babism claimed to be the *Bab,* or "gate," to the Imam. His student, Baha'i, later claimed to be the Mahdi himself. The return of the Messiah, the Baha'is claimed, brought with it a radically different concept of ecclesiastical authority.

Although Shaykhism and Baha'ism still retain followings today, by and large the rationalism and organization of the Mujtahed won the day. The Usulis established the strongest basis for an attack on the growing secularism that culminated in the Pahlavis. No one familiar with Iranian history would consider Khomeini, a high-ranking Mujtahed, an arbitrary or accidental choice for the leadership of the parties whose collaboration resulted in the downfall of the shah in 1979. Despite the failures of the Islamic Republic, it was a concrete result of ten centuries of Iranian attempts to establish an indigenous authority.

The issues involved in today's notions of sovereignty and pluralism are much more complicated than they were in Sassanian times. We can only speculate as to whether the Islamic Republic will give birth to as interesting and egalitarian an opposition as did the Sassanians to Mazdakism and Manichaeism. In today's politically, philosophically, and morally confusing world, however, we believe that the study of Iranian thought will help direct thinkers everywhere toward that region. Iran is likely to produce hard-fought, timely insights into the questions of identity and diversity.

We have characterized Persia's intellectual history since the ninth century as an ongoing dialectic between an antiauthoritarian pull away from other cultures and an authoritarian attempt to establish a culture of its own. Persia is one of the oldest civilizations in today's world; one would think, therefore, that the character of its people would be among the most clearly defined. But on the contrary, Persia's long survival as a culture has depended on the cosmopolitan interests of its thinkers and leaders and on the openness of its borders. Persia has always maintained a relationship with non-Persians, both within and outside the political boundaries of the country. It is only the tenor of that interaction which has flip-flopped between friendliness and aversion. In the past two centuries, political weakness has caused Iran to withdraw somewhat from intellectual intercourse with its neighbors and attempt to reconstruct an identity in contrast to them.

Notes

1. "In 1935 the Persian government requested countries with which it had diplomatic relations to call Persia 'Iran,' which is the name of the country in Persian. . . . 'Persia' is associated with a number of pleasing notions that in the main emphasize its cultural heritage. . . . 'Iran,' on the other hand, possesses none of these associations." Thus Eshan Yarshater, Kevorkian Professor of Iranian Studies at Columbia University, opens a "communication" to *Iranian Studies* XXII, 1 (1981). In this essay, we will use both names interchangeably in the hope of reuniting contemporary habit with historical connotations.
2. This refers to today's universities. European scholars of the nineteenth century and earlier had a deeply felt and respectful interest in other-than-Western cultures that seems to have been abandoned by most contemporary academicians and students. The European scholars were not without their biases, but the recent research conducted in the name of "multiculturalism" cannot guarantee retroactive justice to the cultures that are the objects of their studies—some of which, moreover, have been irreversibly changed already by "scholarly" attention. The proper spirit of philosophical inquiry is to temper personal interest with fairness. That is our intention here.
3. In the communication quoted, Yarshater continues, "The suggestion for the change is said to have come from the Persian ambassador to Germany, who had come under the influence of the Nazis. . . . Flattered, . . . the government fell into the trap." Shah Reza, in other words, was happy to oblige the Germans in their quest for a non-Semitic pedigree.
4. Zoroastrianism inspires recurrent popular interest in the West. Some of this interest is attributable to the popularity of Friedrich Nietzsche, whose most influential and cryptic book was *Thus Spake Zarathustra*. In order to ally the historical Zarathustra with his own protoexistentialist philosophy, however, Nietzsche would have had to change the prophet's character greatly. That he did so, and deliberately, is evident from his own evaluation of Zarathustra in *Ecce*

Homo, pp. 327–28 of the Vintage edition, translated by Walter Kaufmann, 1967: "I have not been asked, as I should have been asked, what the name of Zarathustra means in my mouth, the mouth of the first immoralist: for what constitutes the tremendous historical uniqueness of that Persian is just the opposite of this . . . [T]he self-overcoming of the moralist, into his opposite—into me—this is what the name of Zarathustra means in my mouth." The passage, of course, is not univocally interpretable.

In a similar vein, mythic notions of ancient Persia have recurrently influenced European art, philosophy, and literature. German nationalistic movements, seemingly interested in tracing a non-Semitic lineage for Germanic peoples, were interested in Zoroastrianism as well. In addition, the New Age movement has revived an interest in Gnosticism, which shows extensive Zoroastrian influence.

5. All passages from the Yasna are taken from the *Zend-Avesta,* Part III, translated by L. H. Mills, part of the series *The Sacred Books of the East,* ed. F. Max Muller (Greenwood Press, 1972; first published Oxford, 1887). All passages from the Yashts are taken from *Zend-Avesta,* Part II, translated by James Darmesteter, part of the series *The Sacred Books of the East,* ed. Max Muller (Delhi: Motilal Banarsidass, 1965; first published Oxford, 1883).

6. There is still a small community of practicing Zoroastrians, called the Parsees, in India, to which they fled some time after the Arab conquest (it was to them that Anquetil and his later colleagues traveled). Modern scholarly interpretations of the Avesta are based on linguistic comparisons of it to ancient Greek, Vedic, or cuneiform texts and on the observation of modern Parsee practices (although the modern Parsees reevaluated their own practices in the light of the findings of European Persian scholars who visited them).

7. Any study of Zoroastrian belief, as of any ancient text, must therefore be qualified by reference to a certain historical time period and certain passages of scripture. The dating and analysis of scripture, however, represent an ongoing and exceptionally complex scholarly task. Further, the texts, whose compilation is disorderly and heteronomous, are not apt to be very accommodating to it. Our treatment is entirely introductory: we by no means intend to enter into a debate about the dating of the texts.

8. For some 250 years, the Mithraic mysteries were popular in the Roman Empire, especially among the military. Although the name and era of the cult imply that it had traveled from Iran, the Roman cult, while resembling Zoroastrianism in some respects, was inconsistent with it. Recent scholarship has moved away from the thesis of an Iranian origin.

9. The Saoshyant is akin to a messiah, and his appearance in Zoroastrianism marks it as the first of the great religions to have a belief in salvation after death. Although this concept is central to Christianity the Persian concept is distinct in that the Saoshyant is the son of Zarathustra, not of Mazda. So, like all material creation, he is indirectly, not directly, created by God. Similarly, the salvation the Saoshyant offers is not the "life in death" of the Christians, but the death of death—everlasting material existence, a reunion of body with soul.

10. "Almost from the outset," states Ira Lapidus in *A History of Islamic Societies* (New York: Cambridge University Press, 1988), pp. 55–56, "the elite was divided among those who held a Muslim and those who held an Arab concept of the Caliphate. . . . Caliph 'Umar pursued an 'Islamic' policy. . . . ['Uthman] . . . favored . . . Meccan interests at the expense of the companions of the Prophet."

7

The Myth of Authenticity: Personhood, Traditional Culture, and African Philosophy*

Jacqueline Trimier

Give me back
my black dolls
so that I can play the games of my instincts
. . . .
I become myself once more
myself again
out of what I used to be
   once upon a time
      once without complexity
         once upon a time
when the hour of uprooting came

Will they never know the rancor in my heart
opened to the eye of my distrust too late
they did away with what was mine

from the poem "Limbé"
by Léon Damas

*In this chapter, most references appear within parentheses in the text. A few endnotes appear immediately following the text. For complete information on both the internal references and the works cited in the notes, see the bibliography at the end of this chapter.

Every culture has a concept of personhood that defines what it is to be a human being. As the African-Caribbean poet Léon Damas so vividly tells us, African culture too possesses a concept of personhood, sewing the body, face, and hair into a "black doll"—a symbol of African personhood, self, and identity. Personhood poses and answers several fundamental questions: What is a person? How are persons related to one another? What happens to persons at death? Are persons individual substances or manifestations of a cosmic process? What is a person's relationship to his/her body, society, culture, environment, and history?

Questions like these, embedded in a culture's worldviews, naturally attract the philosopher's interest. A rich vein of philosophically relevant and provocative worldviews underpin any culture. Philosophy mines and extracts these deposits and raises them to systematic contemplation and critique. Often, traditional African cultures, mainly oral cultures, fascinate the philosopher. In an oral culture, the continued retelling of legends, myths, and folklore transmits and preserves the cultural worldview. Usually, the Western social sciences—particularly anthropology and ethnology—have provided the only written accounts of oral cultures. Thus, African philosophers, when interested in aspects of traditional culture like personhood, must rely on these collected data.

Adopting the Western theological definition of the word *person,* social scientists sometimes study personhood by probing a culture's religious system (Middleton, p. 492). In the long Christian tradition, culminating, perhaps, in Descartes, a "person" is presumed to be a rational, individual, indivisible substance (Cartry, p. 19). Accordingly, Western social scientists have attempted to understand personhood in non-Western cultures by defining the nature of this substance in a person. Among the many cultures in sub-Saharan black Africa, the Yoruba of Nigeria create personhood through their religion. Although African religions are far from homogeneous, animism—the belief that a spiritual power, psychic force, dynamism, or life force pervades all animate and inanimate things—characterizes many African religions including the Yoruba's. Such a power or force distributes itself among a cosmological hierarchy made up of a Supreme Being at the top, followed by lesser gods, dead ancestors, natural forces (the power in rain, rivers, stones, and so forth), earthly kings and chiefs, and human beings (Parrinder, pp. 20–28).

The "Black Soul," Colonialism, and Authenticity

Léon Damas's poem,[1] quoted earlier, introduces further concerns. African philosopher M. A. Makinde, using Yoruba personhood as an example, states that personhood is "perhaps the most important aspect of African philosophical thought . . ." (Makinde, 1988, p. 4). Indeed, traditional culture in general, but personhood in particular, seems to dominate most anthologies and periodicals on African philosophy.[2] One immediately asks: Why, among so many ideas in African philosophy, would personhood be the *most* important? Moreover, why do African philosophers privilege traditional culture in African philosophy? The answers to these questions can undoubtedly be found in Africa's post-colonial reality.

When we think of modern-day Africa, a legion of dismally familiar facts swarm in our heads like a plague of locusts. Africa's economy—afflicted by a foreign debt of $270 million ("Gulf," p. 6) and a total gross domestic product the size of Belgium's (Barnett, p. 45)—forces us to conclude that "were the whole continent to disappear beneath the sea—South Africa aside—the world economy would hardly be disturbed" (Barnett, p. 46). AIDS, having reached epidemic proportions in Africa, "will be the leading cause of death among adults in sub-Saharan Africa within the next 25 years . . ." (Prentice, p. 7c). Throwing fuel on an already raging fire, recent "First World" developments—the liberation of Eastern Europe, the breakup of the Soviet Union, the end of the Cold War, and the emergence of a European Common Market in 1992—have diverted global attention from the world's neediest countries. Increasingly, Africa risks being sucked into a black hole of marginalization, completely alienated from the dawning "New World Order."

The continuing colonial legacy, many believe, helped cause Africa's Pandora's box of problems. In "Limbé," a Creole word meaning "spleen" or "the blues," Damas mourns the loss of an indigenous culture that colonialism destroyed often beyond recognition and grieves for the violent clash between traditional African culture and modern Western culture. Damas, like many other people of African descent, understood that the West had robbed him of his African identity—his "black dolls." In his book *The Souls of Black Folk*, W. E. B. DuBois articulates the African-American's dilemma of being both "African" and "American," the same dilemma the African wrestles with in being both "African," and "Western": "One ever feels his twoness,—an American, a Negro; two souls, two thoughts, two unreconciled strivings; two warring ideals in one dark body, whose dogged strength alone keeps it from being torn asunder" (DuBois, p. 17).

To resist colonialism, African nationalism demanded a complete independence from Western political, economic, intellectual, and cultural hegemony. Perhaps the best known and most controversial nationalist ideology is that which espoused negritude. As an extreme form of nationalism, negritude is a doctrine of authenticity, described wonderfully in "Limbé." Damas's "black dolls" are the "games of his instincts." Clearly, the poem links the notion of an instinctual, inherent, natural, and unchanging essence to an indigenous African culture. Damas, therefore, explains authenticity's main ingredient as an inward essence, instinct, or soul manifesting itself externally in precolonial black African culture. A "black soul" creates "black dolls"; race as a biological given determines a black African cultural identity; authentic culture is traditional culture. Consequently, many African intellectuals want to use traditional culture to construct authentically African academic disciplines, with their own concepts, language, and paradigms. In particular, African philosophers yearn for an *authentic* African philosophy, with "African philosophy" often being synonymous with traditional cultural worldviews. With race as the point of departure, cultural authenticity constitutes philosophical authenticity.

Yet many African intellectuals vehemently attack the idea of cultural and philosophical authenticity because the concept of race as a biological determinant is a Western myth used to colonize Africans. Should valid nationalist aims become embroiled with "authenticity," such critics argue, Africans will only further enslave themselves to neocolonialism. Writes Abiola Irele about negritude and authentic African culture: "A myth of Africa developed in consequence out of . . . *negritude,* which involved a glorification of the African past and a nostalgia for the imaginary beauty and harmony of traditional society" (Irele, 1965a, p. 509). Similarly, Paulin Hountondji passionately believes that if authentic African culture is mythology, then so too is authentic African philosophy: "African philosophy, such as it has so far been defined in most of the works dealing with Africa, is nothing but a myth" (Hountondji, 1974, p. 1). To these critics, categories like "African essence," "African philosophy," "race," "traditional culture," and "Africa" are only neocolonialist fictions.

Personhood as the Nexus of Cultural and Philosophical Authenticity

Within the colonialist/neocolonialist context, personhood's centrality in African philosophy reflects the wish for cultural and philosophical authenticity. This is not surprising; personhood, as we have seen, can readily be used to create ideologies of cultural and philosophical authenticity. For instance, personhood and negritude explicate two different aspects of the same subject: personal identity. Personhood merely defines identity, while negritude, by introducing race, shows whether this identity is "authentic" or "inauthentic." The African philosopher, in turn, can build the foundations of an authentic philosophy from an authentic cultural identity. Personhood, in which the problems of traditional African culture, African philosophy, and negritude as an ideology of authenticity converge, vibrates with a multitude of tensions. To make this knot of tensions understandable, I will describe Yoruba personhood as an example of personhood in traditional Africa, explain how race forms authenticity, and then evaluate authenticity.

Personhood in Traditional African Culture

As in many African societies, religion is the most important aspect of Yoruba culture:

> The keynote of their life is their religion. In all things, they are religious. Religion forms the foundation and the all-governing principle of life for them. . . . the full responsibility of all the affairs of life belongs to the Deity . . . man is in the hands of the Deity whose dictate is law . . .
> The religion of the Yoruba permeates their lives so much that it . . . forms the themes of songs, makes topics for minstrelsy, finds vehicles in myths, folktales, proverbs and sayings, and is the basis of philosophy. (Idowu, p. 5)

Yoruba Religion and Cosmology

Yoruba religion can be understood in the *Ifa* divination corpus. *Ifa* is a divination system in Yoruba religion that predicts the future. The oral literature of this system contains a series of 256 sections of poems each of which deals with a particular subject (disease, good, evil, and so forth). As divination system and literature, *Ifa* forms the basis of all Yoruba thought (Abimbola, 1976, pp. 26–27).

The Yoruba divide the world into earth *(aye)* and heaven *(orun)* (Abimbola, 1973, pp. 74–76). Earth is the realm of human beings, witches, animals, birds, insects, rivers, and hills, whereas heaven is the spiritual domain of the Supreme Creator *(Olodumare)*, the lesser gods and spirits *(orisa)*, and the ancestors *(oku-orun)*. These heavenly and earthly beings form the universal hierarchy:

> *Olodumare* (Almighty God)
> *Orisa* (divinities)
> *Oku-orun* (ancestors)
> *Oba* (king)
> *Baálè* (village and town heads)
> *Baálé* (household heads)
> *Agba* (elders)
> *Omode* (children and young people)

As the Supreme Being, *Olodumare* possesses many attributes distinguishing him from other beings in the cosmos (Idowu, pp. 38–47). He is the creator who made heaven and earth. He is the king who has authority over all heavenly and earthly beings. He is omnipotent, being the most powerful being in the universe. He is all-wise, all-knowing, and all-seeing, attributes expressed in a popular Yoruba song: *Kil' e nse ni bekulu t oju Olorun o to?*—"Whatever do you do in concealment that Olorun's eyes do not reach?'' He is the judge who controls people's destinies, judges people's characters, and punishes people for moral offenses. He is immortal, called by the Yoruba *Oyigiyigi Ota Aiku,* ''The Mighty, Immovable Rock that never dies.'' Finally, He is holy, having unique qualities that others do not possess.

Although *Olodumare* permeates all of Yoruba life, the Yoruba see Him as too removed from everyday affairs and too holy to be worshiped directly. Thus, *Olodumare*'s very nature as the Supreme God necessitates the presence of other gods whom people can worship to secure their physical, spiritual, and mental welfare. These other gods, serving as *Olodumare*'s deputies, are the *orisa* (Lucas, pp. 45–46). Intermediaries between humans and *Olodumare,* each *orisa* has a particular responsibility. Special religious cults have been created to worship particular divinities. *Orisanla* (the creation god) is responsible for molding human beings. *Orunmila* (the god of wisdom) uses wisdom to interpret the past, present, and future. *Ogun* (the iron god) is charged with responsibility for war and heroic exploits. *Esu* (the trickster god) uses divine power to protect or punish human beings and gods according to their conformity to or abandonment of the divine will. Although there are hundreds of other deities, the *orisa* just mentioned are the most important because they hold most of the power and control over human beings (Abimbola, 1973, p. 74).

The ancestors *(oku-orun)* also live in heaven, but they intervene directly in human, earthly affairs. At death, every adult automatically becomes an ancestor and a small *orisa* to his or her family and lineage. Ancestors help the living by acting as intermediaries between them and the other *orisas.* Thus, they must be worshiped and sacrifices made to honor them (Abimbola, 1973, p. 75). This heavenly-earthly role of the ancestors is perhaps the single most important ingredient in understanding the spiritual framework within which even the most mundane activities obtain their meaning.

The king *(oba)* lives on earth, where he rules supreme over his subjects, but because kings are descended from the great mythical king Oduduwa, they have divine power. Sometimes the king is thought of as an *orisa* in his own right (Abimbola, 1973, p. 76). Although the king is associated with spirituality, he still has responsibilities in earthly society that are as secular as those of any American president or governor—conducting foreign affairs, administering justice, settling disputes, and keeping the peace (Fadipe, pp. 203–7). In this capacity, the kings are assisted by many town and village heads *(baálè),* who in turn are assisted by the lineage or family heads *(baálé).*

The *baálé* is the oldest male member of the family compound, a collection of apartments for individual families who are each part of an extended family through patrilineage (Fadipe, pp. 97–98). As head of the lineage and family, the *baálé* preserves peace, discipline, and solidarity within his compound (Fadipe, pp. 105–10). The *baálé* makes decisions and takes them to the elders *(agba)* for final approval. The children and young people *(omode)* have no lineage authority, and if they die before becoming elders, they cannot become ancestors after death. Therefore, they occupy the lowest place in the cosmological hierarchy (Abimbola, 1973, p. 76).

The Elements of Personhood

The Yoruba believe that a person consists of a physical element, or body *(ara)*, and three spiritual elements—the soul *(emi)*, legs *(ese)*, and inner head *(ori)*. These spiritual elements have physical counterparts: The *emi* rests in the breath, the *ese* rests in the legs, and the *ori* rests in the head. *Ifa* myths explain these elements of personhood (Abimbola, 1973, pp. 76–77).

One myth tells how the body was created. *Olodumare* gave *Orisanla* the responsibility for molding bodies from clay. He is responsible for molding both normal people and people with deformities, like hunchbacks and albinos. The deformed are banished from their own lineage households and are denied the opportunities given to people in the hierarchical system. Yet *Orisanla* takes care of these deformed people, allows them to live in his shrine, and makes them a part of his religious and domestic staff (Abimbola, 1973, p. 77).

According to the creation myth, after *Orisanla* molds the body from clay, *Olodumare* breathes the soul or "divine breath" *(emi)* into the body. This act makes an individual a proper person by giving life and being to the body. Every individual with the divine breath has the hope of enjoying the good things in life such as money, houses, wives, and children (Abimbola, 1973, pp. 77–78).

In addition, the Yoruba believe in multiple souls in which each individual has three separate souls (Bascom, 1960). The breath *(emi)* resides in the lungs and chest. The shadow *(ojiji)* is a "cast," like the skin shed by a snake, that only follows the body. Finally, the ancestral guardian soul *(eleda, olori)* exists in the head, associated with individual destiny and reincarnation. William Bascom succinctly explains the differences among the three souls:

> One can see the shadow, and hear and feel the breath, but no one sees, hears, or feels the ancestral guardian. The breath is sustained by the food which the individual himself eats; the shadow is without substance and requires no nourishment; but the ancestral guardian must occasionally be fed through sacrifices known as "feeding the head" (ibo-(o)ri). (Bascom, 1960, p. 401)

The Yoruba offer different and sometimes contradictory explanations of the three souls. For example, people variously identify the ancestral guardian soul with the head, the thumbs, the big toes, the crown, the forehead, and the occiput. Some, however, view these as distinct souls. Others believe that the ancestral guardian soul controls the three parts of the head. Many think that the big toes and thumbs are separate ancestral guardian souls. Still others imply that the stomach is the seat of the ancestral guardian soul. Underlying these differences is a distinctive pattern: Each part of the body is personified as a separate soul. The forehead controls luck. The crown protects against evil. The occiput guards the rear and the past, while the big toes signal good or evil lying ahead. The breath, the "vital force," gives the power of speech and makes one work. The shadow follows the body throughout life. The stomach oversees the personality or character. Finally, the head governs intelligence (Bascom, 1960, 407–11).

Perhaps the most important element of personhood is the *ori,* or "inner head" (Abimbola, 1976, pp. 116–17; 1973, pp. 79–80). In Yoruba thought, the *ori* determines one's fate, and contrary to most accounts of destiny, an individual actually chooses his or her own *ori.* In a creation myth, *Ajala,* the "potter of heads," provides each body with a head. Before a person arrives on earth, he or she must go to the house of *Ajala* to choose a head. To make matters more complicated, *Ajala* has a reputation for being irresponsible and careless. As a result, he molds many bad heads; he forgets to fire some, misshapes others, and burns still others. Because he owes money to many people, *Ajala* commonly hides in the ceiling to avoid creditors and neglects some of the heads he has put on the fire, leaving them to burn.

Thus, the choice of a destiny is fraught with dangers and uncertainties. *Ajala* molds many bad heads and only a few good ones. When a person gets to *Ajala's* storehouse of heads, he or she does not know which heads are bad or good; all people choose heads in ignorance. If a person picks a bad head, he or she is doomed to failure in life. Before a person reaches earth with a body, head, and soul, rain can erode an imperfectly made head. As a result, on earth, hard work would be useless because all of one's energy must be used to repair the damaged, useless head. Yet choosing a good head destines one to a prosperous life. With hard work, he or she will surely be successful, since little or no energy need be expended on costly head repairs. Because the life one leads depends on the head one chooses, the Yoruba call a prosperous person *Olori rere* ("one who possesses a good *ori*") and a failure *Olori buruki* ("one who possesses a bad *ori*"). According to the Yoruba song, "What the *ori* comes to fulfil/It cannot but fulfil it" (Idowu, p. 171).

A Yoruba saying explains:

> He who is wise
> Is made wise by his Ori.
> He who is not wise

Is made more foolish than a piece of yam by
his Ori. (Abimbola, 1976, p. 114)

Not only is *ori* a component of the person; it is also the name of an *orisa* who represents individual and personal interests. Other *orisa* represent clan and lineage interests, but *Ori* is every individual's personal god. If one ever needs anything, he or she should approach *Ori* first by sacrifice. When a person consults *Ifa*, he or she is, in fact, trying to determine the wishes of his or her own personal *Ori*. Thus, *Ifa* is an intermediary between people's desires and *Ori*. Even the gods have their own personal *Ori* whom they must consult through *Ifa* (Abimbola, 1976, pp. 114–15).

Although one's destiny is fixed by the choice of an *ori*, a person must work hard to realize a good *ori*'s success or to avert a bad *ori*'s misfortune. Legs *(ese)*, symbolizing power and activity, enable a person to realize whatever has been ordained by his or her choice of an *ori*. *Ori* cannot function without *ese*'s aid. A story tells of the day when all the heads gathered together to deliberate on something they wanted to do. Yet they did not invite *Ese* to the meeting and so no one could execute the plans:

> All heads called themselves together.
> But they did not invite Legs.
> Esu said: "Since you do not invite Legs,
> We will see how you will bring your
> deliberations to success."
> Their meeting ended in a quarrel.
> They then sent for Legs.
> It was then that their deliberations became
> successful. (Abimbola, 1976, p. 149)

Nevertheless, the Yoruba still believe and act as though destiny *can* be altered in various ways, and they accept this contradiction without question: "They offer neither explanation nor rationalisation about it" (Idowu, p. 183). A particular *ori* can be changed in several ways (Idowu, pp. 173–83).

Orunmila, as the oracle divinity, is universally worshiped by the Yoruba people. *Olodumare* gives *Orunmila* special wisdom so that he can represent Him on earth in matters concerning destiny. Only *Orunmila* witnesses the choice of an *ori;* therefore, only he can alter destiny. Because he knows all the secrets of man's being, he can prescribe solutions to any bad occurrence. With this unique knowledge, *Orunmila* pleads with *Olodumare* on behalf of humans to avert or rectify unhappy situations. Thus, many human beings and gods readily worship the cult of *Orunmila* (Idowu, pp. 76–77).

Discovering whether the *ori* one has chosen is good or bad can also alter destiny. When a child is three days old, an oracle is consulted to find out what type of child it is, what things are taboo to it, and what things should be done to preserve a good destiny or change a bad one. People also consult the oracle during a crisis in their lives so that appropriate measures can be taken in response. For instance, when an oracle prophesies death during an illness, a substitutionary sacrifice is offered to counteract a bad destiny's influence.

A destiny can be changed—usually for the worse—through "the Children of the World" *(Omo Araiye),* various evil forces *(Elenini),* and a guardian angel *(enikeji).* The Children of the World are witches who possess the world's evil powers. Both the Children of the World and other evil forces wage war against anyone not conforming to their standards, spreading unbridled destruction. A person's guardian angel is thought to lend a person things that make his or her life possible on earth. Thus, an *enikeji* must be appeased with regular offerings. If he is not happy, he will take half of a person's possessions.

Finally, a person's own character *(iwa)* can affect an *ori.* The Yoruba feel that character is important because it differentiates a person from an animal. The Yoruba call a person of good character *omoluwabi* (a person "who behaves as a well-born") and a person of bad character *enia-k'enia* ("a mere caricature of a person, a reprobate") (Idowu, p. 154). Impatience and rashness, especially, can ruin a good *ori.* A small amount of human responsibility is necessary to bring to fruition a good *ori;* a good destiny without a good character can cause a bad life.

Death and Personhood

Beliefs about death function prominently in Yoruba personhood. Death, like life, is predetermined; each individual has a time when he or she must die. At death, the body rots away, but the soul (or multiple souls) and "inner head" continue to function in the afterlife. Death is not a final resting place but a transition into a heavenly and divine world. Personhood does not stop with death. The Yoruba say: "The world is a foreign land./Heaven is home" (Awolalu, p. 37). The importance of an afterlife in Yoruba thought is reflected in various beliefs and practices such as burial rites, the existence of two heavens, ancestor worship, and reincarnation.

In preparation for burial, the body is thoroughly washed and dressed in white, men's hair is shaved, and women's hair is plaited. Buried with the body are things the person needed in life that can aid him or her on the journey to heaven and in the afterlife; for instance, a yam meal placed at the foot of the bier nourishes the deceased. The dead's family erect a shrine to communicate with the dead. Oral and material messages are given to the dead to give to others in heaven (Idowu, pp. 190–91; Awolalu, pp. 34–35).

Idowu stresses that the Yoruba do not have a theory of reincarnation in the "classical" sense of a soul's being reborn into another body, as if to start life over anew. Instead, the Yoruba believe in an afterlife, "partial reincarnation," through which the living and the dead communicate. For example, the dead can "reincarnate" in grandchildren and great-grand-children, recognized in the names often given to children—for instance, *Babatunde* ("father returns") and *Yetunde* ("mother returns"). One can see the identity of the reincarnated ancestor through physical resem-blances, similarities in character or behavior, through dreams in which the ancestor has returned, and through *Ifa* divination on the newborn child or mother. Yet this is only a partial reincarnation because the deceased still lives in the afterlife (Idowu, pp. 194–96; Bascom, 1969, p. 71).

With multiple souls, the ancestor guardian soul, the shadow, and the breath are all "reincarnated" into a new body. Yet other Yoruba individ-uals maintain that only the ancestral guardian soul receives a new body, new breath, and a new destiny at rebirth. The shadow and the breath remain in heaven to help the deities protect the living. Yet, from this contradiction, Bascom concludes that all individuals are the reincarnation of an ancestor, having the ancestral guardian soul. In addition, an individual is almost always reborn into his or her own clan, making the guardian soul that of a patrilineal ancestor (Bascom, 1960, p. 406).

After death, souls can live in one of two heavens: the "Good *Orun*" ("White *Orun*" or "Our Father's *Orun*") or the "Bad *Orun*" ("*Orun* of the Potsherds") (Bascom, 1960, p. 406; Idowu, pp. 196–201). Olodumare decides who goes to which heaven based on one's actions on earth. In the good heaven, the dead live happily with relatives and friends who have died before them. Life in the good heaven magnifies life on earth; it is an "enlarged copy" of all the good things that have happened in the former life. Consequently, those with good *oris* and good character are rewarded in the afterlife by being surrounded by friends and relatives. In the good heaven, as well, the air is fresh, everything is good, wrongs are righted, and losses are restored. Souls stay in the good heaven until they are reincarnated in another body and can resume life on earth.

On the other hand, the bad heaven is a dreary place, worse than the worst places on earth. The potsherd is a place where broken pots are thrown. The phrase "Heaven of the Potsherds" indicates that the bad heaven is a "celestial rubbish heap" where broken things can never be repaired. Here, the souls in the bad heaven are totally lost and, therefore, can never be reborn or reincarnated. Those who have been cruel, wicked, or guilty of murder, assault, theft, slander, or the use of bad magic or who have harmed people in other ways are punished by being sent to the bad heaven. Hot like a pepper, the bad heaven punishes people by making them walk in the hot midday sun. In addition to evil people, suicides cannot be reincarnated, being forever "broken." In renouncing earth, they do not live in either heaven, but become evil spirits that cling to treetops like bats or butterflies.

Every adult who dies becomes an *orisa* to his or her own family. Ancestor worship maintains lineage responsibilities and relationships among living and dead family members (Awolalu, p. 36; Abimbola, 1973, pp. 75–76 and 78; Idowu, pp. 191–92). The dead continue to hold the position, status, or authority they had when they were alive. As *orisa,* ancestors have limitless powers and capabilities to influence the living. To keep ancestors happy and in good favor, the living must regularly worship them. A passage from *Ifa* illustrates the permanent relationship between the dead ancestors and the living family:

> If one has a problem,
> One should take it to one's ancestors.
> He shall protect you;
> One's dead father never fails to protect one.
> She shall protect you;
> One's dead mother never fails to protect one.
> (Abimbola, 1976, p. 157)

Yoruba Personhood After Colonialism

In the seventeenth century, Islam and Christianity came to Yorubaland, and the Yoruba religion thereafter underwent extensive assimilation into both religions. For instance, the 1952 census counted four-fifths of the Yoruba provinces as being either Muslim or Christian (Eades, p. 118). Yet, as J. S. Eades writes, the indigenous religion survived, though somewhat changed by contact with Christianity and Islam: "The Yoruba have succeeded in adapting the world religions to meet their needs, while at the same time retaining their own cultural identity to a remarkable extent. . . . [R]eligious institutions and beliefs . . . still show many continuities with the past" (Eades, p. 143).

Many examples of this blending exist. Often, the Bible would be reconciled with *Ifa,* and Christ would be added to the Yoruba pantheon. Typically, only those aspects of Islam and Christianity that were compatible with Yoruba belief were adopted. For instance, *Olodumare* became God or Allah; *Esu* became the devil; the *orisas* became archangels; and passages from the Bible or the Koran replaced Yoruba *Ifa* verses (Eades, p. 143). David Laitin shares his personal observations of an Anglican church service:

> In the Anglican church that I attended (and all churches I visited were similar in this regard), the organist plays a Yamaha organ with a mambo beat, and

he is surrounded by a coterie of "talking drums." As the *egbe* [church societies] members move to the altar to be blessed, they swing their hips and dance as they would in a traditional festival. (Laitin, p. 85)

Not surprisingly, Islam and Christianity deeply influenced the Yoruba understanding of personhood. Barry Hallen's interview with Yoruba theologians "demonstrated considerable ideological adjustment." A Yoruba theologian suggested to Hallen that one's soul could be resurrected. Hallen then asked if this idea came from the Bible, and the theologian answered yes. When Hallen wanted to focus the discussion on Yoruba traditional ideas, the theologian replied that " 'there is little difference . . . It is those who are wise before the Bible came, they are also the same set of people who believe in the Bible.' " The theologian admitted that these changes originated with Christianity (Laitin, p. 139).

Playing with Black Dolls: Cultural and Philosophical Authenticity

Imagine a seven-year-old black girl named Karen. One day near Christmas, she threw her doll collection in the trash and demanded of her parents: "I want a black doll for Christmas! I'm tired of white dolls!" Karen simply wanted a doll that resembled her "curly-haired, dark-skinned, broad-nosed blackness." An easy wish for Santa Claus to fulfill? Hardly! At the toy store, the shelves groaned under the weight of all kinds of dolls—Barbie, Betsy Wetsy, china, Cabbage Patch. But their fair skins and rosy cheeks were not what Karen sought. With the thoroughness of bloodhounds, Karen's parents frantically searched for a black doll in time for Christmas. They knew that positive self-esteem for a black girl is crucial in a world that values only a certain kind of beauty. On Christmas, Karen's parents, burdened by guilt, surrounded the tree with extra presents to make up for the absence of The Ultimate Gift. Karen held back the tears as she opened each box, always to find books, candy, games, but never a black doll.

Karen's dilemma mirrors the whole crisis of authenticity in colonial and postcolonial Africa. As Karen's story shows, authenticity has two main characteristics: essence and value. Essence is "that which is most irreducible, unchanging, and therefore constitutive of a given person or thing" (Fuss, p. 2). Essence is the "whatness" that distinguishes one thing from another. Take a banana, for example. A banana's essence, differentiating it from, say, an orange, is its yellow color, half-moon shape, and waxy peel. Or the example of Karen's doll. The black doll has several characteristics—hair, skin color, facial characteristics—giving it an authentic "blackness." This essence contains a value judgment: Something authentic is good because it is real, genuine, or original, whereas something inauthentic is bad because it is false, corrupt, or tainted. Picture an antique furniture collector who covets an eighteenth-century American four-poster bed but loathes the tacky copies of it in department store catalogs. Karen hated her old white dolls because they did not conform to an authentic blackness.

Using these two basic characteristics, colonialism based authenticity on race. Racial biology marked an irreducible, natural, and unchanging essence: The external biological reality of "blackness" indicated an internal essence distinguishing it from "whiteness." Whiteness was valued while blackness was denigrated. Colonialism, as we shall soon see, oppressed people using this simple logic of biological/racial authenticity. At the same time, Africans also employed race, finding for themselves an authentic cultural personhood with which to attack colonialism.

Colonialism and the Creation of a Black African Authenticity

To justify the colonization of Africa for its raw materials, European intellectuals created a body of ideas concerning the essence of African peoples. Ethnology and anthropology, particularly, provided colonialism with its theoretical underpinnings. Reaching its nadir in the late eighteenth and early nineteenth centuries, anthropology generally regarded African people, culture, and history in terms of French scholar Lucien Levy-Bruhl's racial opposition of the black African's "primitive" or "prelogical" mind to the white European's "civilized" mind. White European essence meant superiority, humanity, modernity, civilization, logicality, rationality, Judeo-Christianity, and science, whereas the black African essence meant inferiority, inhumanity, backwardness, the traditional, savagery, illogicality, barbarism, irrationality, paganism, and mysticism (Irele, 1983, pp. 12–15; Zahar, pp. 18–25; Mudimbe, 1988, p. 64). Essentially, racism maintained the colonial system:

> The most characteristic feature of the colonial situation is racism, which underpins ideologically the division of society into "human beings" and "natives" caused by the colonial process of production. . . . Racism endows the colonial system with cohesion. (Zahar, p. 19)

To guard against revolts, colonialism brutally executed a program of acculturation in which European civilization was the standard against which all non-European civilizations had to measure themselves. This systematic acculturation attempted to erase and suppress the indigenous cultures by imposing European culture throughout Africa, establishing groups of "little Europes" (Serequeberhan, p. 8) where Africans became "Greco-Latin Negroes" (Sartre, p. 8). Colonialism completely alienated Africans from their historical and cultural identity—colonized people despised their own culture, but idolized their oppressor's culture:

If he is overwhelmed to such a degree by the wish to be white, it is because he lives in a society that makes his inferiority complex possible, in a society that derives its stability from the perpetuation of this complex, in a society that proclaims the superiority of one race. (Fanon, 1967, p. 100)

Nineteenth-century romanticism challenged the privileging of reason and objectivity and instead found value in the exotic, sensual, subjective, and irrational—fire melted ice. Reflecting this new attitude, anthropology stopped denigrating Africa and celebrated its supposed uniqueness. Instead of characterizing Africa as essentially inferior and primitive, anthropology glorified the apparently emotional, mystical, and intuitive nature of African cultures. Encouraged by this romanticism, African intellectuals rebelled against colonialism's racial ideology. Many nationalistic movements developed to express a renewal, rebirth, and redefinition of a lost African essence (Kesteloot, pp. 93–102).

This nationalistic spirit manifested itself in three different ways. Political nationalism asserted the rights of Africans to found independent nations from colonial territories. A political agenda often included the rediscovery and reassertion of an essential cultural pride. Therefore, political nationalism has mostly mirrored, if not intertwined with, cultural nationalism (Irele, 1965, p. 321). Such cultural and political nationalism formed the theoretical and methodological background of all African intellectual activity. An intellectual nationalism, throughout all academic disciplines, focused on a regained precolonial Africa (Wauthier, pp. 21–22). Because Western intellectuals have produced almost all the knowledge about Africa, intellectual nationalism demands that the African scholar begin to control the production of knowledge about Africa and to insert an African intellectual presence in international scholarship (Irele, 1991, p. 64).

The most systematic attempt at redefining this African essence occurred in 1934, when a group of African students living in France, including Léopold Sédar Senghor, Aimé Césaire, and Léon Damas—all poets, formed the negritude movement. Thomas Melone articulates their new attitude:

Negro consciousness flowered the day the Negro refused to consider the West as the fountain of life and the source of everything that is beautiful. Negritude blossomed the day that the policy of assimilation . . . caused him to create his own gods and enact his own laws . . . Instead of becoming assimilated, he assimilated. (Melone, p. 177)

Negritude transformed mere nationalist pride into a complex doctrine of authenticity. In the words of one of its founding fathers, Léopold Sédar Senghor, negritude is "nothing other than the authenticity of Negroes . . ." (Senghor, 1976, p. 82, my translation). The relationship between nationalism in general and authenticity is like the difference between a pin prick and a knife cut: a difference in degree or intensity of the same pain. The presence of a "black soul" or "black essence" makes authenticity more extreme than nationalism.

The spirit of negritude survives today, in the 1990s, particularly in the form of cultural authenticity and intellectual authenticity. Many people still desire to reclaim a cultural authenticity that rests on traditional African culture. Depending on cultural authenticity for its impetus, intellectual authenticity believes that for a particular discipline to be uniquely "African" in subject matter, methodology, and theory, it must devote itself to studying traditional African culture. In the past thirty years, the quest for intellectual authenticity has been particularly intense in the discipline of philosophy. Paulin Hountondji explains this link between cultural and philosophical authenticity:

> In this quest, we find the same preoccupation as in the negritude movement—a passionate search for the identity that was denied by the colonizer—but now there is the underlying idea that one of the elements of the cultural identity is precisely "philosophy," the idea that every culture rests on a specific, permanent, metaphysical substratum. (Hountondji, 1991, p. 116)

Cultural Authenticity

To rediscover a lost identity, cultural authenticity asks and answers the following questions: What is an African? How does one speak of him or her and for what purpose? Where and how can one gain the knowledge of his or her being? How does one define this very being, and to what authority does one turn for possible answers (Mudimbe 1988, p. 153)? Negritude answers these questions by appealing to a black soul or black essence, constructing cultural authenticity from two components, objective and subjective.

Objectively, negritude is the ensemble of economic and political, intellectual and moral, artistic and social values that all black people throughout the world (in the Americas, Asia, and the Caribbean) share (Senghor, 1977, p. 270). Objective negritude gives black people a sense of community (Senghor, 1976, p. 83). Moreover, this ensemble of values is to be found in traditional, precolonial culture, prompting Senghor to describe negritude as a return to the sources (Senghor, 1976, p. 83). Thus, African culture, to be authentic culture, has characteristics like mysticism, intuitiveness, and spirituality. By returning to these roots, one finds his or her authentic, collective cultural identity.

Subjectively, negritude is the active manner by which each black person in the world embodies and asserts these cultural values (Senghor, 1976, p. 83). In other words, this "manner" is the black essence, described by Senghor as both a physiopsychology and an emotional quality. Senghor emphasizes that a certain "psychological and physiological makeup of each race" (Senghor, 1962, p. 7) expresses a culture's material, objective reality: "The physio-psychology of the African explains his metaphysics, and consequently his social life" (Senghor, 1965, p. 36). Senghor also explicitly describes "l'âme nègre" (the black soul) in terms of emotion (Senghor, 1964, pp. 23–25). Emotion "explains all the cultural values of the African negro: religion, social structures, art and literature, and above all, the genius of their languages" (Senghor, 1962, p. 15). In an emotional frenzy of sensuality, rhythm, and spirituality, black people experience "the seizure of the whole being, consciousness and body, the indeterminate world" (Senghor, 1965, p. 34). Senghor further uses emotion to underscore differences between black essence and white essence, shown in his famous statement: "Emotion is Negro, as reason is Hellenic" (Senghor, 1964, p. 24).

Such assertions prompt Abiola Irele to conclude that subjective negritude creates and manifests itself as objective negritude: Culture is "primordially" determined by an original, internal black essence (Irele, 1977, pp. 3–5). The subjective element—the collective racial soul and essence—determines a collective black culture. Race marks an inherent nature. Black essence produces black culture.

Philosophical Authenticity

Since the 1960s, questions about philosophical authenticity have dominated African philosophical discourse: What importance does race have in philosophy? What is "African" about African philosophy and how does it differ from Western philosophy? What does not count as authentically African philosophy? What does it mean to philosophize as an African and as a black person?[3] Contemporary African philosophy tries to answer these questions in two ways by dividing itself into two large groups (Mudimbe, 1983, pp. 138–47). One group, ethnophilosophy, answers the questions by using authentic African culture to form authentic African philosophy (Mudimbe, 1983, pp. 142–43; 1988, pp. 135–53).

The term *ethnophilosophy* originally referred to Placide Tempels's book *Bantu Philosophy*, published in 1945, which explored Bantu thought. As a Belgian missionary, Tempels's main concern was to civilize Africans by assimilating them to Christianity. Thus, he needed to understand Bantu people to better acculturate them. In his civilizing mission, Tempels believed that he had uncovered a Bantu philosophy that had five main points. First, the Bantu have a systematic, rational, and logical fund of worldviews constituting their philosophical knowledge. Second, the primary philosophical category of Bantu philosophy is force, demonstrating a dynamic and vitalist conception of the universe. Third, being is force; vital forces classify and order all beings in the universe in a strict cosmological hierarchy of mineral, vegetable, animal, human, ancestral, and divine. Fourth, Bantu philosophy can be properly analyzed and understood not by the Bantu themselves but only by Westerners in a Western philosophical framework. Nature can be made explicit only when Westerners interpret it in a Western conceptual framework. Finally, the characterizations of Bantu philosophy as a primitive or native philosophy describe philosophy in all non-Western societies.

Inaugurated by Tempels's work, ethnophilosophy—combining the disciplines of ethnology, anthropology, and philosophy—assumes that traditional African cultures have a unique essence that separates them from Western culture. Therefore, ethnophilosophy's sole aim is to uncover and document this authentic essence. Ethnophilosophy, explicitly using the colonial dichotomy, wanted to show that Africa in fact had a uniquely "African and black" philosophy, which differed from "Western and white" philosophy. As an authentic philosophy, ethnophilosophy takes from traditional culture its own philosophical language and concepts, like *ori, ara, ese,* and *emi.* From this perspective, African philosophy has several characteristics. Whereas Western philosophy has individuals called philosophers, African philosophy has no individual philosophers because it is a "group," "folk," or "collective" philosophy that is shared by all members of a culture. Another unique feature of African philosophy is its emotive, intuitive, and spiritual quality, as opposed to Western philosophy, which is rational and systematic.

Tempels's successors can be divided into three groups. The first, closer to Tempels's method and theory, engages in ethnographic description and exegesis, using anthropological analysis as a model. Another group creates African philosophy in terms of Aristotelian and Thomist categories. Finally, the last group identifies a unique African philosophy by sifting through ethnographic and anthropological documentation of myths, folklore, and stories. All three share Tempels's original project of isolating a black African essence and differ only in their theoretical considerations.

Breaking the Black Dolls, But Playing with the Pieces: A Critique of Cultural and Philosophical Authenticity

Karen, needless to say, cried for days because she didn't unwrap a black doll from under the Christmas tree. Her parents tried to sew a doll from cotton and felt. But they weren't especially talented, and the finished product resembled a misshapen hippo more than a person. Then, one day, Karen's parents thought of the perfect solution: buy a white doll and dye it black! So they bought Karen a very expensive doll and baptized it in a sinkful of a cinnamon brown liquid. An ecstatic Karen played with the doll constantly, but after a couple of days the doll fell apart at the seams: The paint of her eyes and mouth flaked, the stuffing bulged out, and the limbs were hanging by frayed threads. Unfortunately, the dye, too strong for the fabric, eroded the doll, leaving it in a bundle of tatters in Karen's hands.

The fate of Karen's doll—of Damas's doll—parallels the fate of cultural and philosophical authenticity under criticism: Its very underpinnings and foundations fall apart because they are illegitimate and false. Race as biology, the backbone of authentic African culture and philosophy, is a myth established by Western discourse that African intellectuals unwittingly adapted. When Africans unthinkingly appropriate Western categories—the way Karen used a white doll to create a sense of blackness—everything falls apart.

Yet race, African culture, and African philosophy are also realities as well as myths. Paulin Hountondji explains the logic of this contradiction in his wish to speak of an "African philosophy, myth *and* reality" instead of an "African philosophy, myth *or* reality": "[t]he concept of 'African philosophy' is, on certain conditions and only on those conditions, a meaningful and therefore legitimate concept . . . but on any other conditions and any other context, an unthinkable and properly mythological concept" (Hountondji, 1974, p. 1). Because race has always created African culture, African philosophy is a reality. Although Karen's doll may fall apart when it tries to conform to an otherwise "white" situation, Karen can still use the scraps of material for something else; extra cotton stuffing, yarn, and fabric can make a wonderful blanket!

Cultural and Philosophical Authenticity as Racial Myth

In *The Invention of Africa,* V. Y. Mudimbe reviews the many religious, anthropological, scientific, and historical Western discourses that have tried to understand and define Africa. The implications he draws are clear. Because the West for the most part created and controlled knowledge about Africa, it is the West that invented Africa. Africa, as a body of knowledge, is a Western concept. The West, by studying Africa, projected Western ideas, hopes, and fears onto an African terrain. Like a movie, Western discourse on Africa projects distorted images of Africa. In this sense, Africa is the West's "dirty little movie."

In fact, the main criticism of negritude as a doctrine of authenticity is that it only reverses the colonialist myth of Africa without challenging its foundations. Senghor simply and uncritically accepts the European dichotomy, not realizing that even though he accepts its more favorable aspects, he never challenges its basic assumptions and foundations. What the European said was bad about Africa, Senghor exalted to resist the colonial ideology. This reversal is inevitable because negritude must "rely on the methods of colonialist ideology to react against it; even in the act of negating colonialism it reproduces its feathers" (Zahar, p. 67). By adopting anthropology's idea, negritude at its very inception was flawed, as René Depestre notes: " '[T]he original sin of negritude . . . come(s) from the spirit that made it possible: anthropology' " (Mudimbe, 1988, p. 87).

Depending explicitly on negritude, the ethnophilosophers only reverse but do not question the colonial ideology's foundations. Paulin Hountondji scathingly criticizes negritude as an "ethnopsychology concerned essentially with defining the 'Negro soul' . . . *ethnopsychology* always betrays the ambition to become an *ethnophilosophy*" (Hountondji, 1983, p. 194). Critics generally attack ethnophilosophy because it mythologizes African culture. The supposed "unanimity" and "collectiveness" of African philosophy "is an illusion consistent with the vision of anthropologists and ethnologists alike of 'African village unanimity' and with their hankering for the 'unique spectacle of a society without conflict, division, or dissonance' " (Owomoyela, p. 158). Claiming the collectiveness of African culture and philosophy implies that Africans are primitive and simple.

Because African authenticity simply appropriates mythology to counter a colonialist mythology, it duplicates several dangerous, yet inevitable results: fetishism, overcompensation, conservatism. Like the colonialist aim, authenticity is politically conservative because its glorification of a lost, past culture only avoids present problems. Traditional culture becomes so romanticized and mystified in the past that it remains completely isolated from modern economic and political realities (Hountondji, 1983, p. 160). Particularly with ethnophilosophy, Tempels simply wanted to understand the "uniqueness" of the African essence in order to better colonize Africans. As Frantz Fanon remarks sarcastically: "I admit that all the proofs of a wonderful Songhai civilization will not change the fact that today the Songhais are underfed and illiterate, thrown between sky and water with empty heads and empty eyes" (Fanon, 1963, p. 209).

Also, cultural and philosophical authenticity appeals to the African intellectual's taste for exotic cultural fetishes. Alienated from their culture by a total assimilation of Western values, African intellectuals, like their European counterparts, view African culture as a group of empty symbols, a "stock of particularisms" (Fanon, 1963, p. 223). Fanon writes with a sneer that in the intellectual's banal search for exoticism, the "sari becomes sacred, and shoes that come from Paris or Italy are left off in favor of pampooties" (Fanon, 1963, p. 221). Kwasi Wiredu sums up the problem:

> African nationalists in search of an African identity, Afro-Americans in search of their African roots, and Western foreigners in search of exotic diversion—all demand an African philosophy different from Western philosophy, even if it means the familiar witches' brew. (Wiredu, p. 46)

This second problem is linked to the last. Like colonialist ideology, cultural and philosophical authenticity is addressed to a European public. Authenticity of any type never targets an African audience, but always a Western audience: "[E]very attempt at systematizing the world-views of a dominated people is necessarily destined for a foreign public and intended to fuel an ideological debate which is centered *elsewhere*—in the ruling classes of the dominant society" (Hountondji, 1983, p. 49). The black intellectual is simply a white European in blackface, performing an academic minstrel show to display that he or she too can engage in intellectual discourse. Thus, negritude is a childish reaction of overcompensation to patronizing white Europeans.

Authenticity's reversal left unquestioned the basic foundation of Western colonial discourse: the concept of race. Now, we will focus more closely on some of the specific problems presupposed in the critique of authenticity as a mythology—on what is meant by the pernicious phrase "traditional black African culture." The study of racial/biological purity was once a large part of Western anthropology. This "scientific" racism tried to prove that race was a biological concept creating essential differences among people. Science, particularly in the nineteenth and twentieth centuries, defined racial essence by comparing the sizes and shapes of the brain, cranium, genitalia, and so forth. Such "research" proved the inferiority of black people. For instance, the nineteenth-century naturalist Baron Cuvier concluded that the black complexion, woolly hair, compressed cranium, flat nose, projection of the lower parts of the face, and thick lips of the "Negro race" "evidently approximate it to the monkey tribe: the hordes of which it consists have always remained in the most complete state of barbarism" (Bernal, p. 241). Yet race as biology has long been proved to be steeped more in ideological motivations than in facts: "Every reputable biologist will agree that human genetic variability between the populations of Africa or Europe or Asia is not much greater than that within those populations" (Appiah, p. 21). But if race is not a matter of anatomical or morphological differences, then what is meant by race?

Henry Louis Gates, Jr., maintains that race is not a thing, but "a metaphor for something else and not an essence or thing in itself" (Gates, 1986, p. 402). Throughout its history, the term has taken on many arbitrary meanings, serving as a metaphor for everything from skin color, intelligence, culture, and history to economic status and morality. For instance, in the United States specifically, the drug problem and poverty are both associated with black people to such an extent that "blackness" means being poor and having a drug problem. "Race" has meant so many things as a metaphor that it "means" nothing at all—like pants labeled "one size fits all," which never fit any one person "correctly" because they try to fit everyone correctly. Indeed, "race" turns out to be the various human forces that create a certain metaphor of race to suit a particular historical, cultural, economic, social, and political situation. In other words, "race" does not point to an unchanging essence, but to a changing human situation.

When "race" is mythologized, race-based history and culture do not grow, change, and develop. As Ahmeed Sekou Touré emphatically states, " 'there is no black culture, nor white culture, nor yellow culture . . . Negritude is thus a false concept, an irrationality based on racial discrimination' " (Lindfors, p. 6). History and culture become fossilized, Paulin Hountondji writes: "By dint of trying to defend our civilizations at all costs, we have petrified, mummified them" (Hountondji, 1983, p. 50). We can see the falseness of the phrase "traditional black African culture" in several ways.

For instance, much scholarship is only beginning to admit (and there is a long way to go) that contact between Greece and Egypt flourished during ancient times, providing some of the basic foundations of Greek civilization and, therefore, of so-called Western civilization:

> the Ancient Greeks, though proud of themselves and their . . . accomplishments, did not see their political institutions, science, philosophy or religion as original. Instead they derived them—through the early colonization and later study by Greeks abroad—from the East in general and Egypt in particular. (Bernal, p. 120)

"West" and "Africa" do not point to some "essential" Westernness or Africanness. Without a notion of racial culture, what the "West" is or what "Africa" is remains highly ambiguous. Neither European nor African civilization is "a closed system of values" but rather the product of "the creative tensions which underlie them." Thus "Africa" and the "West" can be spoken of only as geographic labels instead of as authentic essences (Hountondji, 1983, pp. 160–61).

Another way that race has distorted the idea of African culture is by homogenizing all people of African descent, inside and outside Africa. "Africa" is not a singular, homogeneous culture, but a *continent* with many nations, cultures, languages, and religions. To homogenize Africa is to shave off its diversity so that it can fit neatly in the anthropological box. As Frantz Fanon writes, culture is primarily *national,* defined by the particular nation's historical, economic, and political situation: "[E]very culture is first and foremost national, and . . . the problems which kept Richard Wright or Langston Hughes on the alert were fundamentally different from those which might confront Leopold Senghor or Jomo Kenyatta" (Fanon, 1963, p. 216). African-American poet Langston Hughes expresses his impatience with those of his patrons who insisted that he write poetry in a "primitive" African mode:

> I was only an American Negro—who had loved the surface of Africa and the rhythms of Africa—but I was not Africa. I was Chicago and Kansas City and Broadway and Harlem. . . . (Mphahlele, p. 51)

Moreover, the only thing that black people throughout the diaspora share is the historical, political, and economic reality of racism. If culture is "racially" determined at all, it unites blacks around the world in their common marginality, in their, as James Baldwin puts it, "unutterably painful relation to the white world" (Gérard, p. 34).

Often, authenticity encourages a selective view of the past. The past is synonymous with paradise, perfection, harmony, unsullied by encounters with the West. Yet, as Kwame Nkrumah writes, not everything about Africa was wonderful:

> The truth remains, however, that before colonization . . . Africans were prepared to sell, often for no more than thirty pieces of silver, fellow tribesmen and even members of the same "extended" family and clan. Colonialism deserves to be blamed for many events in Africa, but surely it was not preceded by an African Golden Age or paradise. A return to the precolonial African society is evidently not worthy of the ingenuity and efforts of the people. (Schall, p. 6)

In addition, the binary of "tradition" versus "modern" is based on a false view of history. Kwasi Wiredu effectively dismantles the binary of traditional versus modern by looking at Western "modernity." Western society still explains phenomena by appealing to spirits and mysticism. Witchcraft, astrology, the Tooth Fairy—very present in contemporary Western society among the mass population—would be called "traditional" if they were found in a nonwhite and non-Western society. Anthropologists and ethnologists characterize Africa as traditional and the West as modern only because "they have . . . apparently been unfamiliar with the folk thought of their own culture" (Wiredu, p. 38).

African Culture and Philosophy as a Racial Reality

Yet "race," "black culture," and "black history" are still living realities. "Race" still operates to create concrete and material realities in the world; political, economic, social, and cultural forces exist to give "race" a certain metaphorical meaning in a given situation (Fuss, p. 92). Just because "race" may be a fiction does not mean that people are not oppressed because of their skin color. Similarly, culture and history, unshackled by the fossilization of biological race, are organic and changing entities. Thus, the word *race* and phrases assuming race like *traditional black African culture* should always be placed within quotation marks to signal their mystification (LaCapra, p. 1). Such words and phrases, having no real meaning, are convenient fictions needed to talk about certain real ideas.

African philosophy is also a reality because the culture, history, and racial situation in which it was constructed is a reality. African philosophy, like all philosophy, addresses the racial, historical, and cultural reality surrounding it. The second group in contemporary African philosophy addresses this "nonauthentic" African reality by criticizing philosophical authenticity and by searching for new territory to study. As Theophilus Okere writes, expressing the group's spirit, the background of an African philosopher

> need not be the fossilized, unadulterated past. The black African philosopher is not to become a cultural historian . . . or a curator of the ethnic museum, jealously guarding the purity of ancestral heritage and protecting it from the adulterating encroachments of time and evolution . . . Background for a black African philosopher certainly means traditional institutions, symbols, and values, but also the often violent culture contact that was the colonial experience and its aftermath. It means the present-day reality. (Okere, p. 121)

In particular, this group seeks a new, nonanthropological way for philosophy to study African history and culture. African philosophers see the rich and varied ideas in their indigenous cultures, as we have seen with the Yoruba concept of personhood, and do not want to ignore what is in their own backyard: "The prospects of an original African contribution to knowledge become even more distinct when we consider that the fund of positive knowledge available to our traditional societies has yet to be seriously investigated and made available to the world" (Irele, 1991, p. 68). Instead of creating an authentic African philosophy, this group wants to contribute an African orientation to the discipline of philosophy. This means using the best from all philosophical traditions (including the West's) and applying them to an African context to subvert Western philosophy and to redefine the historicocultural horizon of Africa—what Tsenay Serequeberhan calls "an indigenizing appropriation" of other traditions (Serequeberhan, p. 23).

One way in which African philosophers are trying to reevaluate African culture and history is through the use of hermeneutics. Associated mainly with such Western philosophers as Martin Heidegger, Hans Georg Gadamer, and Paul Ricoeur, hermeneutics is the theory and methodology of interpretation.[4] African hermeneutics, therefore, tries to reinterpret African culture and history, to recapture them from Western interpretations. By understanding fully the relationship between the past and the present, "African" culture and "Western" culture, hermeneutics provides "the subject matter, the problematics, and its very own philosophical course" for contemporary African philosophy (Okolo, p. 207).

As Theophilus Okere explains, hermeneutics as a method interprets the signs and symbols embedded in a culture's institutions and ideas to uncover the hidden meaning behind the overt symbols and signs themselves. For example, a hermeneutical interpretation of Yoruba culture would consist in interpreting the symbols of such Yoruba institutions and ideas as the *ori* or the cosmological hierarchy. Okere writes: "African cultures have their own symbols pregnant with meaning. A reflection on these symbols with a view to making the implicit meanings explicit would constitute African philosophy" (Okere, p. 115). The move from implicit to explicit occurs in three steps: *reading,* which surveys the various myths, institutions, and their cultural symbols; *retake,* which subjects these facts to rigorous philosophical reflection; and *arbitration,* which tries to find a solution to the resulting conflict of interpretations between the symbol's apparent meaning and its hidden meaning (Ngoma, p. 156).

In his essay "Traditions and Destiny: Horizons of an African Hermeneutics," Okonda Okolo argues that only hermeneutics can reappropriate African history by understanding the relationship between the past, the present, and the future. First, reappropriating African history means knowing the meaning of "tradition." The past, never locked away in a vacuum, always creates the present, which in turn creates the future. In this sense, tradition, being a reflection of the past from the present, is an invention of the past *and* the present. The past can be seen only in terms of the present. Take the example of a person who as a small child has had the traumatic experience of almost drowning in a pool; the person might, as an adult, view swimming pools with an intense alarm because the past experience interpreted the present. Thus, Okolo describes this interplay between past, present, and future as "a tradition-in-becoming" (Okolo, p. 204).

A second proposition for African hermeneutics would be that interpretation is never objective, unbiased, or neutral; it always comes out of a particular cultural, political, economic, and social situation. Anthropology especially has shown us this: It received its power to create pictures of Africa because it claimed that anthropology was a "universal" discipline, able to present knowledge neutrally about any culture. Yet, as we have seen, anthropology could understand non-Western cultures only from within its own point of view. In this way, history is his-*story,* a human narrative and not an empirical fact.

Finally, African hermeneutics means understanding the practical and political role it can play in the present and concrete situation of Africa's postcolonial struggle against forms of oppression: "Praxis unleashes the hermeneutical process and gives it an orientation. Hermeneutics, in turn, offers praxis a cultural self-identity necessary for ideological combat" (Okolo, p. 208).

But, like all realities, African philosophy in its new, "nonauthentic" relationship to culture and history is also faced with certain problems. If Africa is an "invention" of the West and the Western discourses on Africa have been largely biased and false, how can one expect that the critical use of Western philosophy will result in anything different? As V. Y. Mudimbe writes: "The main problem concerning the being of African discourse remains one of the transference of methods and their cultural integration in Africa" (Mudimbe, 1988, p. 183). Many would immediately argue that by appropriating Western discourse, one automatically reappropriates the discourse of colonialism because, in Audre Lorde's famous words, "the master's tools will never dismantle the master's house" (Stephan and Gilman, p. 87). Let's take Yoruba personhood as an example. Wouldn't the very concept of "person," a Western concept in itself, result in a faulty interpretation? If knowledge comes from a particular context, can Western philosophy grafted onto Yoruba culture give credible knowledge about the Yoruba? Is hermeneutics, a distinctly Western discipline, cross-cultural? Can hermeneutics—which emphasizes analyzing the symbols embedded in written language—be applied to oral cultures?

Perhaps this dilemma can be expressed by another question: Can one ever break away completely from the "family" one is born into? One may try to create a new personality and life-style away from one's family, but the fact of one's family heritage cannot somehow be erased, forgotten, or negated to "start all over again." The Argentine philosopher Enrique Dussel, in creating a philosophy of liberation for the oppressed of the world, expresses the impossibility of escaping the conceptual language and ideas in which we have been reared:

> It [a philosophy of liberation] sets out, of course, from the periphery [marginalized non-Western world] but for the most part uses the language of the center [the West]. It could not do so otherwise. The slave, in revolt, uses the master's language. (Dussel, p. viii)

The only way that African philosophy can use Western discourse is actively and hypercritically to appropriate its methods for the purpose of simultaneously subverting Western philosophy and developing an African orientation to philosophy. Tsenay Serequeberhan calls this twofold goal of African philosophy a "deconstructive and reconstructive challenge": deconstructive because it must expose the ethnocentrism of Western discourse, and reconstructive because it must mend the "historico-cultural possibilities of the broken African heritage" (Serequeberhan, p. 22). If the "West" is not inherently some monolithic tradition, then it should have space within itself to allow the marginalized to use it. Only by accepting one's place in the family can one know its secrets in order to challenge it and appropriate it. This maneuvering within Western discourse "means using the most sophisticated critical theories and methods available to reappropriate and to define our own 'colonial' discourses" (Gates, 1986, p. 14). Paulin Hountondji echoes this: "It is not by skirting round, and still less by ignoring, the international philosophical heritage that we shall really philosophize, but by absorbing it in order to transcend it" (Hountondji, 1983, p. 72). To use Western discourse in this twofold way will ensure that African philosophy does not simply "substitute one mode of neocolonialism for another" (Gates, 1986, p. 15).

Fun and games . . .

That's what all kids want. Karen quickly recovered from her disappointment over not getting a black doll. She tired of waiting for what she could never have. Mounds of Christmas gifts—hardly touched in her sulk—now attracted her. No longer playing games of instinct, Karen joyfully played with all the other games and toys at her disposal—video games, coloring books, kaleidoscopes, watercolors, a chemistry set, puzzles. Playing any games to suit their fancy gives Africans and their philosophy the ability to assert an innovative presence on the scholarly scene. As culture and history—ever in flux—are continuously in the making, African philosophy is a reality and yet at the same time still to be discovered. It is *this* game, this playful spirit, that will take Africa not backward but forward into the twenty-first century.

Notes

1. Damas, in Kesteloot, pp. 131–33.
2. One periodical in particular, *Second Order,* is saturated with articles on traditional culture.
3. The current debates in African philosophy address two related problems. In this chapter, I want to address the problem of *philosophical authenticity* and its relationship to cultural authenticity. Yet a part of the debates—though tangential to our purposes—asks questions about what is and is not *authentically philosophical.* For more on this aspect of the debates in African philosophy, see *African Philosophy in the Present Situation of Africa,* ed. Alwin Diemer (Wiesbaden: Franz Steiner Verlag, 1987); Henri Maurier, "Do We Have an African Philosophy?" in Richard A. Wright (ed.), *African Philosophy,* 3d ed. (New York: University Press of America); and Paulin Hountondji, "African Philosophy: Myth and Reality," *Thought and Practice* 1 (1974).
4. For the background on hermeneutics in Western philosophy, see Joseph Bleicher, *Contemporary Hermeneutics* (New York: Routledge and Kegan Paul, 1980); Kurt Mueller-Vollmer (ed.), *The Hermeneutics Reader* (New York: Continuum, 1989); and Roy J. Howard, *Three Faces of Hermeneutics* (Berkeley: University of California Press, 1982).

Glossary of Yoruba Terms

Agba: elders in the cosmological hierarchy.

Ajala: the heavenly potter of heads; an individual goes to his storehouse to choose an *ori* for his or her life on earth.

Ara: the body; the physical element of a person.

Aye: the earth, the physical realm in the cosmological hierarchy.

Baálè: village and town heads in the cosmological hierarchy.

Baálé: household heads in the cosmological hierarchy.

Eleda, Olori: the ancestral guardian soul.

Elenini: evil forces who can spoil a person's good destiny.

Emi: the soul, spirit, or "divine breath"; the spiritual element of a person.

Enikeji: guardian angels who can spoil a person's destiny.

Ese: the legs; the spiritual element of a person.

Ifa: the Yoruba divination system; the oral literature of the divination system.

Iwa: the character of a person, which can influence his or her destiny.

Oba: king in the cosmological hierarchy.

Ojiji: shadow, one of many multiple souls in Yoruba personhood.

Oku-Orun: ancestors in the cosmological hierarchy.

Olodumare: Supreme Creator in the cosmological hierarchy; also called *Olorun*.

Omo Araiye: the "Children of the World," evil beings who can spoil a person's destiny.

Omode: children in the cosmological hierarchy.

Ori: the inner head; the spiritual element of personhood controlling destiny; the divinity responsible for individual and personal concerns.

Orisa: lesser gods and spirits in the cosmological hierarchy.

Orisanla: the god of creation who molds the body from clay.

Orun: heaven; the spiritual realm of the cosmological hierarchy.

Orunmila: the god of wisdom who can influence destiny.

Bibliography

Abimbola, Wande. *Ifa: An Exposition of Ifa Literary Corpus*. Ibadan: Oxford University Press Nigeria, 1976.
———. "The Yoruba Concept of Human Personality." In *La Notion de Personne en Afrique Noire*. Edited by Colloques Internationaux du Centre National de la Recherche Scientifique. Paris: Centre National de la Recherche Scientifique, 1973, Pp. 73–89.
Appiah, Anthony. "The Uncompleted Argument: DuBois and the Illusion of

Race." In *"Race," Writing, and Difference*. Edited by Henry Louis Gates, Jr. Chicago: University of Chicago Press, 1986. Pp. 21–37.

Awolalu, J Omosade. "The Yoruba Philosophy of Life." *Présence Africaine* 73 (1970): 20–38.

Barnett, Richard. "But What About Africa?" *Harper's Magazine*, May 1990, pp. 43–51.

Bascom, William. "Yoruba Concepts of the Soul." In *Men and Cultures. Selected Papers of the Fifth International Congress of Anthropological and Ethnological Sciences*. Philadelphia: University of Pennsylvania Press, 1960. Pp. 401–411.

————. *The Yoruba of Southwestern Nigeria*. New York: Holt, Rinehart, and Winston, 1969.

Bernal, Martin. *Black Athena*. New Brunswick, N.J.: Rutgers University Press, 1987.

Bodrunin, P. O. "The Question of African Philosophy." In *African Philosophy: The Essential Readings*. Edited by Tsenay Serequeberhan. New York: Paragon House, 1991. Pp. 63–86.

Cartry, M. "Introduction." In *La Notion de Personne en Afrique Noire*. Edited by Colloques Internationaux du Centre National de la Recherche Scientifique. Paris: Centre National de la Recherche Scientifique, 1973. Pp. 15–31.

DuBois, W. E. B. *The Souls of Black Folk*. Greenwich, Conn.: Fawcett Publications, 1961.

Dussel, Enrique. *Philosophy of Liberation*. Maryknoll, N.Y.: Orbis Books, 1985.

Eades, J. S. *The Yoruba Today*. Cambridge: Cambridge University Press, 1980.

Fadipe, N. A. *The Sociology of the Yoruba*. Ibadan: Ibadan University Press, 1970.

Fanon, Frantz. *Black Skins, White Masks*. Translated by Charles Lam Markmann. New York: Grove Press, 1967.

————. *The Wretched of the Earth*. Translated by Constance Farrington. New York: Grove Press, 1963.

Fuss, Diana. *Essentially Speaking*. New York: Routledge, Chapman and Hall, 1989.

Gates, Henry Louis, Jr. "Talkin' That Talk." In *"Race," Writing, and Difference*. Edited by Henry Louis Gates, Jr. Chicago: University of Chicago Press, 1986. Pp. 402–9.

————. "Writing, 'Race,' and the Difference It Makes." In *"Race," Writing, and Difference*. Edited by Henry Louis Gates, Jr. Chicago: University of Chicago Press, 1986a. Pp. 1–20.

Gérard, Albert. "Historical Origins and Literary Destiny of Negritude." *Diogenes* 48 (1964): 14–37.

"The Gulf Crisis: Is This the Third World's War?" *Africa Report*, March-April 1991, pp. 5–6.

Hountondji, Paulin. *African Philosophy: Myth and Reality*. Translated by Henri Evans. London: Hutchinson University Library for Africa, 1983.

————. "African Philosophy: Myth and Reality." *Thought and Practice* 1, no. 2 (1974): 1–16.

——. "African Philosophy: Myth and Reality." In *African Philosophy: The Essential Readings*. Edited by Tsenay Serequeberhan. New York: Paragon House, 1991. Pp. 111–31.

Idowu, E. B. *Olodumare: God in Yoruba Belief*. New York: Longmans, 1962.

Irele, Abiola. "The African Scholar." *Transition* 51 (1991): 56–69.

——. "Introduction." In *African Philosophy: Myth and Reality* by Paulin Hountondji. Translated by Henri Evans. London: Hutchinson University Library for Africa, 1983. Pp. 7–30.

——. "Negritude of Black Cultural Nationalism." *Journal of Modern African Studies* 3, no. 3 (1965): 321–48.

——. "Negritude—Literature and Ideology." *Journal of Modern African Studies* 3, no. 4 (1965a): 499–526.

——. "Negritude—Philosophy of African Being." *Nigeria Magazine* 122/123 (1977): 1–13.

Kesteloot, Lilyan. *Black Writers in French: A Literary History of Negritude*. Translated by Ellen Conroy Kennedy. Philadelphia: Temple University Press, 1974.

Lacapra, Dominick. Editor. *The Bounds of Race*. Ithaca: Cornell University Press, 1991.

Laitin, David D. *Hegemony and Culture: Politics and Religious Change Among the Yoruba*. Chicago: University of Chicago Press, 1986.

Lindfors, Bernth. "Anti-negritude in Algiers." *Africa Today* 17, no. 1 (1970): 5–7.

Lucas, J. O. *The Religion of the Yoruba*. Lagos: CMS Bookshop, 1948.

Makinde, M. Akin. *African Philosophy, Culture, and Traditional Medicine*. Athens: Ohio University Press, 1988.

Melone, Thomas. "The Theme of Negritude and its Literary Problems." *Présence Africaine* 20, no. 48 (1963): 166–81.

Middleton, John. "The Concept of the Person Among the Lugbara of Uganda." In *La Notion de Personne en Afrique Noire*. Edited by Colloques Internationaux du Centre National de la Recherche Scientifique. Paris: Centre National de la Recherche Scientifique, 1973. Pp. 491–506.

Mphahlele, Ezekiel. *The African Image*. London: Faber and Faber, 1974.

Mudimbe, V. Y. "African Philosophy as an Ideological Practice: The Case of French-Speaking Africa." *African Studies Review* 26, nos. 3/4 (September/December 1983): 133–54.

——. *The Invention of Africa: Gnosis, Philosophy, and the Order of Knowledge*. Bloomington: Indiana University Press, 1988.

Ngoma-Binda. "Pour une orientation authentique de la philosophie en Afrique: l'herméneutique." *Zaire-Afrique* 17 (1977): 143–58.

Okere, Theophilus. *African Philosophy: A Historico-Hermeneutical Investigation of the Conditions of Its Possibility*. New York: University Press of America, 1983.

Okolo, Okonda. "Tradition and Destiny: Horizons of an African Philosophical

Hermeneutics." In *African Philosophy: The Essential Readings*. Edited by Tsenay Serequeberhan. New York: Paragon House, 1991. Pp. 201–210.

Owomoyela, Oyenka. "Africa and the Imperative of Philosophy: A Skeptical Consideration." In *African Philosophy: The Essential Readings*. Edited by Tsenay Serequeberhan. New York: Paragon House, 1991. Pp. 156–86.

Parrinder, Geoffrey. *African Traditional Religion*. London: Hutchinson's University Library, 1954.

Prentice, Thomson. "Birth control vaccine tested." *The Times*, February 18, 1991, p. 7c.

Sartre, Jean-Paul. "Preface." *The Wretched of the Earth* by Frantz Fanon. Translated by Constance Farrington. New York: Grove Press, 1963. Pp. 7–31.

Schall, James. "Excursus III: Problems in African Political Philosophy." *World View* 18, no. 9 (1975), 6–8.

Senghor, L. S. "Authenticité et Négritude." *Zaire Afrique* 102 (1976): 81–86.

———. *Liberté I: Négritude et Humanisme*. Paris: Editions du Seuil, 1964.

———. *Liberté III: Négritude et Civilisation de l'Universal*. Paris: Editions du Seuil, 1977.

———. "On Negrohood: Psychology of the African Negro." *Diogenes* 37 (1962): 1–15.

———. *Prose and Poetry*. Translated by Clive Wake and John Reed. London: Oxford University Press, 1965.

Serequeberhan, Tsenay. "African Philosophy: The Point in Question." *African Philosophy: The Essential Readings*. New York: Paragon House, 1991. Pp. 3–28.

Stephan, Nancy Leys, and Sander L. Gilman. "Appropriating the Idioms of Science: The Rejection of Scientific Racism." In *The Bounds of Race*. Edited by Dominick LaCapra. Ithaca: Cornell University Press. Pp. 72–103.

Wauthier, Claude. *The Literature and Thought of Modern Africa*. Washington, D.C.: Three Continents Press, 1979.

Wiredu, Kwasi. *Philosophy and an African Culture*. Cambridge: Cambridge University Press, 1980.

Zahar, Renate. *Frantz Fanon: Colonialism and Alienation*. Translated by Willfried F. Feuser. New York: Monthly Review Press, 1974.

Introductory Texts in African Philosophy

I. General Survey

Wright, Richard. *African Philosophy: An Introduction*. Washington, D.C.: University Press of America, 1984.

Hountondji, Paulin. *African Philosophy: Myth and Reality*. Bloomington: Indiana University Press, 1983.

Makinde, M. Akin. *African Philosophy, Culture, and Traditional Medicine*. Athens: Ohio University Press, 1988.

Diemer, Alwin. *Symposium on Philosophy in the Present Situation of Africa.* Wiesbaden: Franz Steiner Verlag, 1981.
Mudimbe, V. Y. *The Invention of Africa.* Bloomington: Indiana University Press, 1988.
Oruka, H. Odera. "African Philosophy: An Introduction." *Second Order: An African Journal of Philosophy* VII, nos. 1 and 2 (1978): 112–16.
Conradie, Anna-Louize. "Africa." In *Handbook of World Philosophy.* Edited by John R. Burr. Westport, Conn.: Greenwood Press, 1980.
Wiredu, Kwasi. *Philosophy and an African Culture.* Cambridge: Cambridge University Press, 1980.
Kruks, S. "African Philosophy: An Introduction to the Main Philosophical Trends in Contemporary Africa." *Africa* 52, no. 4 (1982): 103.

II. Ancient Africa and Ancient Greek Philosophy

Sumner, Claude. *Ethiopian Philosophy.* Addis-Ababa: Central Printing Press, 1974.
Bernal, Martin. *Black Athena.* New Brunswick, N.J.: Rutgers University Press, 1987.
Olela, Henry. *From Ancient Africa to Ancient Greece: An Introduction to the History of Philosophy.* Atlanta: Black Heritage Foundation, 1981.
Philip, Edward. "Can Ancient Egyptian Thought Be Regarded As the Basis of African Philosophy?" *Second Order* 3 (1974).

III. Ethnophilosophy

Tempels, Placide. *Bantu Philosophy.* Paris: Présence Africaine, 1963.
Mbiti, John. *African Religions and Philosophy.* New York: Anchor, 1970.
Senghor, Léopold Sédar. *On African Socialism.* Translated by Mercer Cook. New York: Praeger, 1964.
———. "On Negrohood: Psychology of the African Negro." *Diogenes* 37 (1962): 1–15.
———. *Prose and Poetry.* London: Oxford University Press, 1965.
Irele, Abiola. "Negritude—Philosophy of African Being." *Nigeria Magazine* 122/123 (1977): 1–13.

IV. Social and Political Philosophy

Nkrumah, Kwame. *Consciencism.* New York: Monthly Review Press, 1964.
Padmore, George. *Pan-Africanism or Communism.* New York: Doubleday, 1971.
Nyerere, Julius. *Freedom and Socialism.* Oxford: Oxford University Press, 1968.
Fanon, Frantz. *The Wretched of the Earth.* New York: Grove Press, 1974.
———. *Toward the African Revolution.* New York: Grove Press, 1967.

V. Philosophical Sagacity

Hallen, Barry. "Phenomenology and the Exposition of African Traditional Thought." *Second Order* 5, no. 2 (1976): 45–65.

————. "A Philosopher's Approach to Traditional Culture." *Theoria to Theory* 9, no. 4 (1975).

Horton, Robin. "Traditional Thought and the Emerging African Philosophy Department: A Comment on the Current Debate." *Second Order* 6 (1976).

Gyekye, Kwame. *An Essay on African Thought—The Akan Conceptual Scheme*. Cambridge: Cambridge University Press, 1987.

VI. Professional/Synthetic Current

Okere, Theophilus. *African Philosophy: A Historico-Hermeneutical Investigation of the Conditions of Its Possibility*. New York: University Press of America, 1983.

8

Indian Philosophies

Stephen H. Phillips

In 1930, Mahatma Gandhi set out with seventy-eight followers from Sabarmati Ashram to walk 241 miles to the sea. His purpose was to make salt in defiance of a British government ban. It was not a violent act, but it would undermine the legitimacy of the British Empire. Local salt production, the British feared, would allow evasion of a salt tax considered essential to government revenues. Gandhi, on the other hand, saw the salt tax as a crime against the poor, a final proof that the British, despite repeated pledges of good faith, could not be trusted to act in the interests of common people. The British had ruled India for more than a hundred years, and had no intention of letting this "jewel in the crown" of their empire pass from their hands. Gandhi, on the other hand, had taken a vow never again to return to his home at the Sabarmati Ashram until India had won self-rule. The Mahatma, who would become regarded as the father of the Indian nation and the first great Asian and African anticolonialist, insisted on "holding fast to the truth," *satyagraha,* the byword of the civil disobedience movement he was about to launch. Gandhi had preached all his adult life the virtue of "noninjury," *ahiṃsā,* and had shaped his own conduct by that ideal, as had generations of Jain, Buddhist, and Hindu saints before him. Echoing ancient spiritual disciplines, he urged no violence against the British but rather "soul force." As he walked barefoot along the hot, dusty roads, hundreds of villagers joined him. After breaking the law, he was joined by thousands upon thousands from all over the vast Indian subcontinent who followed his nonviolent but very effective example. British authority was shaken, and independence became inevitable.

But what is India, and what was the culture from which Gandhi gathered strength to galvanize millions to confront and best the mighty British, at the time the most powerful imperial nation on earth? Postcolonial India is now one of the great Third World countries, but this demeaning phrase hides a long history that precedes that of the West by centuries. Indeed, Indians were highly literate, with institutions of law and civil society, producing masterpieces of philosophy, when the English were still barbarians. India had an enormously rich philosophical tradition when European philosophy was in its infancy. Only the Chinese can claim as long an unbroken tradition as that of the philosophy preserved in the Indian intellectual language of Sanskrit. And whereas Chinese philosophy is predominantly social, ethical, and political (at least until the advent of Buddhism, a cultural import from India), all the fundamental questions are addressed in Indian philosophy and readdressed in a dozen major schools and by hundreds and hundreds of individual writers. Philosophic works in India stretch from the mystic proclamations of ancient gurus as early as 1000 B.C.E. through the sermons of the Buddha (500 B.C.E.) and polemics of Buddhist skeptics (100 C.E.–600) and idealists (200–900) to the enormous refinements of the New Logic (1300–1850 +), with thousands of texts in between. The New Logic school alone presents achievements in the philosophy of language and cognition that are so subtle that at most a handful of modern scholars have so far achieved anything comparable to a traditional pundit's command of the system (Skt: *paṇḍita,* literally "learned"). The culture of the South Asian subcontinent—the land from the mountains of Afghanistan in the west to the Himalayas in the east and including all of what are now Pakistan, India, Bangladesh, and Nepal—produced a philosophical tradition of enormous diversity, power, and profundity, from which moderns like Gandhi could draw. What the British by and large did not understand—but we shall try to—is the richness of a heritage of wisdom preserved in India through three thousand years.

The principal philosophies of India and the South Asian subcontinent include, on the one hand, religious and mystical worldviews oriented to an otherworldly good—that is, "salvation," "enlightenment," or "liberation"—and, on the other hand, less esoteric systems of analysis and speculation, systems that focus on language and the concerns of day-to-day life. In the modern period, philosophy is done in the universities, where there is a global perspective and much influence from the West. There the religious and mystical systems no longer dominate Indian thought as they once did. But in earlier periods, even the more earthbound thinkers concerned primarily with issues in the philosophy of everyday life address religious and mystical concerns, if only to attack the positions of others. First we shall survey, briefly, the periods of Indian philosophy. Then we shall look at both the mystical "enlightenment theories" and the logic-minded philosophies of language and sense perception. In conclusion, I make a general statement about the relevance of the views originating in the subcontinent for our global age today.

A Brief History of Indian Philosophy

It is convenient to divide the history of Indian philosophy into four periods: (1) the Vedic and Upanishadic, (2) the epic (or early classical), (3) the classical (proper), and (4) the modern. It is necessary to have some appreciation of the continuity and conflicts of these periods to have any overview of Indian philosophic thought.

The Veda and Upanishads

The oldest documents of Indian thought are the Veda, "Revealed Knowledge," comprising poems and hymns to various gods. The Veda defines much subsequent Indian culture, though it is only the first of thousands of texts. The Veda is composed in Sanskrit, and Sanskrit becomes the intellectual language of both the ancient (ca. 1500–500 B.C.E.) and classical (ca. 500 B.C.E.–1800+ C.E.) civilization. (In this broader division, the epic period of philosophy is included as the earliest subdivision of the classical.) Sanskrit is an Indo-European language with close affinities to Greek and Latin. (English also belongs to this family.) The Veda was composed by people who called themselves Āryans, in Sanskrit a word meaning "high-minded" and "noble." Āryan tribes began to invade the Indian subcontinent as early as 1500 B.C.E. The composition of the poems and hymns that make up the Veda stretched over several generations, beginning as early as 1200 B.C.E. Four collections were made: Thus people say there are four Vedas (occasionally three). The four as a group came to be viewed as sacred in classical Hinduism, the revealed Veda.

Some Vedic hymns and poems have philosophic themes that are important in later periods. For example, we find expressed in the Veda a "henotheism" that is key to classical Hindu theology. This is the idea that one God takes many forms, that although men and women worship several different gods and goddesses, it is really one Supreme Being they all revere. Nowadays in India it is commonly held that the different temples and sects and gods and goddesses—Vishnu the Protector, Krishna the Divine Man, Shiva the Destroyer with his consort Parvati, the terrible Kali with her necklace of human heads, Ganesh with his elephant's body, Saraswati the goddess of learning—are all faces and manifestations of one supreme God. *Ŗg Veda* 1.164.46 reads: "What the sages call diversely Agni [the god of fire], Yama [Death], Mātariśvan [the lord of the winds] is just one Supreme."

Also in the Veda are numerous cosmogonies, stories about creation and the origins of things. Skepticism is in a few places expressed about the possibility of such explanations. For example, one hymn tells us that we cannot discover the All-Maker, for he is hidden. But positive theories seem to win the day. "On the navel of the Unborn was set the One on whom all creatures rest," this same hymn also says (*Rg Veda* 10.82). Another hymn states that against a backdrop of neither Being nor Nonbeing, "That One by force of heat came into being" (*Rg Veda* 10.129), and still another finds the origin of this world in a sacrifice of a cosmic Person (*Rg Veda* 10.90).

Hints of mysticism are present in the Veda. The belief that important alterations of consciousness occur through shamanic practices—involving *soma,* a mushroom-made potion with psychoactive effects, or induced by heat-boxes or sweat-houses thought to be purificational, or asceticism and early forms of yoga such as *prāṇāyāma,* "breath-control"—can be discerned in the texts. Several scholars claim to find a shamanism throughout Vedic culture, and this is most probably a forerunner of later Indian mystical views.

The breadth and importance of certain Vedic conceptions notwithstanding, the poems of the Veda tend to be about the activities of various gods. Indra, the god of rain and thunder, helps the poet's tribe defeat its enemies. The god Soma brings poetic inspiration, and Agni, Fire, brings the riches of heaven to earth. The Veda often presents beautifully phrased and rhythmic pleas for divine aid or riches or love, and the philosophy in them is usually only implicit.

Vedic culture extended over many centuries, from about 1500 to 900 or 800 B.C.E. Vedic literature is a testament to the literary sensibilities of an early civilization, one deemed by later Hindu romantics a lost golden age. But it is with the Upanishads, the "secret doctrines" of a subsequent era, that Indian philosophy is most decisively launched. So-called "early Upanishads" dominate the late ancient period and are key to the emergence of the classical philosophies of India. Indeed, several modern Indian philosophers also champion ideas first formulated in the ancient Upanishads.

In the sequence of the centuries, however, what is most important about the early Upanishads (from ca. 800 to ca. 300 B.C.E.) is that they represent a break with the earlier literature in the freeing of an abstract intellect from myth and ritual. The Upanishads are little concerned with the gods hymned in the Veda, but report, instead, free-thinking arguments. One Upanishad recounts the sage Yājñavalkya's winning first a hundred, then a thousand, cows in the court of King Janaka in reward for his skill in metaphysical debate. Yājñavalkya successfully challenges the ideas of a series of opponents.

Attention to evidence is not nearly as pronounced and standardized in the Upanishads as it comes to be in the classical period, but the reasoning is sometimes sharp and the questioning penetrating, revealing conceptual impossibilities. The content of the Upanishads is decidedly mystical, and thus only the mystically oriented of the classical philosophies have an unmediated dependence on the Upanishads, though all later Indian philosophies are in some way indebted to the early Upanishads. The Upanishads declare the way to knowledge or "realization" of *brahman*. Brahman is the Absolute, the Ground of Being, or God. And such realization of Brahman, "Brahman-knowledge" (Skt: *brahma-vidyā*), becomes the goal of many of the numerous Indian mystic sects that have flourished in the subcontinent.

Finally a word about the term *Vedānta*: The Upanishads came to be called Vedānta because they were in time appended to the collections of poems known as the Veda; literally, the word in Sanskrit means "the end of the Veda." On another interpretation, the Upanishads are Vedānta because they reveal the mystical secret of the earlier sacred texts. In the classical period of Indian philosophy—more than a millennium after the composition of the oldest Upanishads—Vedānta became the name of a family of schools basing their views explicitly on an interpretation of the Upanishads. In a philosophic context, to refer to one or another of these schools has come to be the primary usage. We shall discuss the classical schools of Vedānta in a later section.

The Epic Period

Beginning as early as the fifth century B.C.E., wandering minstrels and poets began the composition of what was to become the "Great Indian Epic," the *Mahābhārata*. This text of over 100,000 verses about a war and the adventures of five brothers leading one side was compiled, edited, and amended over the next six or seven centuries until it reached the form in which we know it today. (Some changes occurred even later: Texts were copied on palm leaves, which soon aged, and copiers sometimes edited.) Amidst great battle scenes in the long poem are dialogues about what one should believe about God and creation, and a wide range of abstract interests are taken up: Many of the philosophies of the classical period proper are expressed in a discernible "seed" form in the epic.

Of special note is the dialogue between Krishna and Arjuna known as the *Bhagavad-Gītā*. This is a portion of the epic in which Krishna reveals himself as "God incarnate." The *Gītā* is a philosophic poem that has immense importance with Hinduism. We shall review the thought of the *Gītā* in the section entitled "Vedāntic theism." The *Gītā,* and other passages in the Great Epic as well, develop ideas of the early Upanishads, the original "Vedānta."

Also noteworthy concerning the epic period is that a "Hindu" social order of caste and occupational mores calcifies during this time. Caste is a perplexing subject, particularly in relation to the history of the religion now called Hinduism.

Indeed, before proceeding further, we must ask what Hinduism is and give some thought to just what is meant by the term. From one perspective, the words *Hindu* and *Hinduism* should not be used in discussing the ancient and classical Indian civilizations. Their current usage derives from a contrast of Hinduism with Islam and the coming to India of Muslims, who arrived in large numbers (and armies!) only late in classical times. The word *Hindu* seems first to have been used by Arab traders of the ninth and tenth centuries to designate any person who lived near the Indus River. *Hindustan* came to be the Arabic word for greater India, and from Arabic to pass into wider usage. What best distinguishes Hinduism is only a certain difficult-to-define unity of culture in the Indian subcontinent before the Muslim invasion (ca. 1100 +, earlier in the Sind and Punjab), including but hardly limited to the social practices of caste. But for present purposes, what I shall mean by "Hinduism" in this essay may be described as an umbrella religion with precisely two key characteristics: (1) a claim of adherence to the Veda or Vedic traditions (including of course Vedānta) and (2) an endorsement of a certain social order including practices of caste. So characterized, Hinduism has emerged by the time of the Great Epic.

It bears stressing that there is no one set or system of beliefs that can be said to be Hindu. Some Hindus are theists; some are not. Some believe in a personal salvation; others do not. I repeat, Hinduism is defined not by beliefs but by a social structure including caste (although some today have rejected caste), along with reverence for the Veda. And it is the epic period when the characteristic Hindu patterns of society become established. The Great Epic reflects an intricate but settled organization of society. Marriage in the epic, for example, is in all but rare instances arranged by a boy's or a girl's parents, a practice that continues among Hindus today. And priests, called Brahmins, enjoy special privileges. A social hierarchy fixed by birth becomes established.

Buddhism also originated in the epic period. The Buddha was an actual person who lived in the sixth century B.C.E. He preached a goal of a supreme personal good, namely enlightenment, *nirvāṇa,* comparable to the "Brahman-knowledge" of Upanishadic philosophy. The Buddha was born Siddhārtha Gautama of the Śākya clan, a prince in India (or perhaps what is now southern Nepal), in the Gangetic valley, near the year 560 B.C.E.

The Buddha did not himself write anything. Records of his teachings and sermons were kept by his disciples, and probably in the midst of the reign of the Buddhist emperor Aśoka in the third century B.C.E. an enormous canon of literature sacred to "Southern" Buddhists was compiled (in the contemporary world, Southern Buddhists are in Sri Lanka, Burma, Thailand, and elsewhere in Southeast Asia). "Northern" Buddhists (in Nepal. Tibet, China, Korea, Japan) recognize a distinct literature as sacred, though they do not entirely reject the teachings of the Southern canon.

Indian Buddhism flourished for some seventeen centuries before succumbing to the intolerance of India's Islamic conquerors, and it matured in India for some seven or eight centuries before becoming prominent in the courts of China. Buddhist thinkers were great innovators in many areas of philosophy, including logic, the theory of knowledge and justification for what we believe, the assumptions implicit in everyday speech, and causal reasoning.

Mahāvīra, who was roughly contemporary with the Buddha, founded Jainism, another religion and religious philosophy that originated in the epic period. Jainism is also concerned with "enlightenment" or "liberation." Though not historically as prominent as some of its rivals, it has an enormous literature, and its defenders in the classical period were among the most astute philosophic minds.

Mahāvīra and the Buddha rejected the validity of caste as a principle of social order. This is important in differentiating Jainism and Buddhism as "non-Hindu."

Classical Indian Philosophy

The formation of the great schools or systems of philosophy occurs in the epic period. Unfortunately, we have little direct record of the debates and efforts of the highly creative intelligences responsible for the wide-ranging explanations—of the world and its ground, of the human in relation to nature and God, of the meaning of existence, and of details of perceptual experience and practices of everyday life—that make up the six or seven earliest of the major philosophies of classical India, the great schools. The work of the earliest system makers has become inseparable from centuries of later interpretation and advocacy. We know what we know about the formation of these schools primarily through (1) their embeddedness in epic poetry and various religious genres and (2) reconstruction based on later texts that are expressly philosophic.

But within the first two centuries of the Common Era, philosophy in India makes another quantum leap, this one captured in texts expressly devoted to philosophy and exposition of the worldviews. The second jump centers on argument, both elaborate patterns of argumentation and the metaissue of what counts as good and bad reasoning. Argument and defense of positions appear in earlier literature, but there is no real science of debate nor at all the attention to minute details of reasoning—what precisely follows from what and why—that becomes the obsession by the middle of the classical age. The systems formulated as world explanations in the epic period are defended by increasingly intricate strategies.

The pivotal figure in the second revolution is the Buddhist philosopher Nāgārjuna, who lived in the second century C.E. Nāgārjuna is bent upon establishing that our everyday world, naively assumed to be real and captured by the words we use in ordinary discourse, is not in fact real. Nāgārjuna's fame as a philosopher derives from the penetrating questions he put to all the schools of his time, Buddhist and non-Buddhist, and indeed to much common, nonscholastic opinion. His questions were presumed to expose inadequacies in all familiar theories, with the result that (according to his followers) one would lose faith in intellectual cogitations and learn to intuit the real nature of what is, presumed to be inexpressible in words in a direct fashion. A large part of the reaction to Nāgārjuna was that advocates of positive world explanations rethought their views and concocted elaborate defenses against his attacks.

It is also around the time of Nāgārjuna that the *sūtra* texts of the earliest schools appear in their final forms. The Sanskrit word *sūtra* means literally "thread" and by extension an "aphorism" that captures in a most succinct statement a philosophic tenet. The *sūtra* texts of individual schools are systematic expressions of entire worldviews. Thus we see that many of the great Indian schools find their earliest expression about the time of Nāgārjuna's revolution (that is, 100+ C.E.) and that their separate literatures begin to take shape. What we now see as the distinctively philosophic genres do not emerge, that is to say, until the time of the conceptual revolution centering on argument, although there are in the Upanishads, the Great Epic, and elsewhere expressions of many central positions. The *sūtra* period is, then, a time of final systematization organized around reasons and arguments. In sections to follow, we shall survey the major schools of philosophy, many of which, in sum, are first written up as systems and expressly defended close to the time of Nāgārjuna.

There are no gaps in the "professional" philosophy expressed in Sanskrit that thus begins early in the Common Era and extends into the modern period, though in the past two centuries Sanskrit has waned as a medium for original philosophic efforts. Schools do have their moments, their times of flourishing and periods of decline, but Indian philosophy as a whole continually advances, that is, becomes increasingly refined as later thinkers profit from the work of their predecessors. There may be two or three individuals whose brilliance is so outstanding that it is legitimate to say that none of their followers surpass them—perhaps the subtle Buddhist Idealist of the seventh century, Dharmakīrti, or the great Advaita Vedāntin, Śaṅkara, of the eighth century, or the astute New Logician, Gaṅgeśa, of the fourteenth. But philosophic reasoning and reflection as a whole can only be said to advance—both in overall sophistication of argument and in the volume and scope of new texts that are innovative, though it may be argued that for sheer creativity the early classical period of the Buddha, Mahāvīra, and the Great Epic remains unsurpassed. The number of titles grows almost exponentially from the time of Nāgārjuna, reflecting advances in argument and an expanse of philosophic concern (probably the increased numbers of philosophers also had something to do with the phenomenon). There is one unbroken tradition of philosophy in Sanskrit, and later thinkers studied and responded to the arguments of those who came before them.

Buddhist philosophers have their heydey in the earlier centuries, and there is a sharp decline in Buddhist textual productivity in the ninth and tenth centuries. Original Buddhist philosophic writing practically disappears by the fourteenth. Some scholars say that the Buddhists' thunder was stolen by the school of Advaita Vedānta, which came into prominence with Śaṅkara in the eighth century and which remains prominent to this day. This school is also referred to as "Illusionism" and in its argumentative pose took over many of the ploys of Nāgārjuna. In the late classical period, theistic Vedānta is also a major movement, and there is much disputation with followers of Śaṅkara over how to interpret the Upanishads. The Vedāntic theists have a loose alliance with a school known as Logic. Debates between the Logicians, who are realists about the objects of experience, and the Illusionists become prominent in the late classical age. (See the Glossary of Sanskrit Terms in Appendix B, page 258, for brief characterizations of the important classical schools.)

The Modern Period

Although thought transcends culture, philosophy is not immune from political events and social upheaval and change. We can easily imagine—indeed there is considerable evidence—that from the earliest times the philosophers of the Indian subcontinent were largely dependent for their daily subsistence upon the munificence of kings and princes. Perhaps there were also gifts from wealthy merchants to the philosophers' monastic orders, many of the great writers having lived as monks. Success in live debates held in a king's court could mean the flourishing of a school, with money for time to reflect and to support students, while defeat could mean not just intellectual embarrassment but loss of livelihood and young followers to keep the philosophy current. Thus the Islamic conquest of much of northern India—which occurred gradually, in waves, from the eleventh century to the height of Moghul rule in the fifteenth—had a large impact on the philosophy of the subcontinent. Admittedly, there are authors, such as the great Logician Gaṅgeśa (ca. 1325), who seem unaware of a Muslim presence, so thoroughly absorbed are they in the Sanskrit tradition. Yet many historians believe that the coming of Islam played a large role in the demise of Indian Buddhism, as the conquest meant the closing of Buddhist universities and a general disappearance of funds.

Indian theistic philosophies, by contrast, prospered under some of the Muslim rulers. Syncretisms emerged, though new Sanskrit theistic works remained focused predominantly on the Upanishads and other earlier Sanskrit texts. In south India, Sanskrit traditions continued little disturbed. But even there things changed with the coming of the Europeans and, in particular, the British.

The British came to India late in the seventeenth century to make money in trade, but they found a Moghul empire in decline along with a general political fragmentation, and their greed was soon matched by a lust for power. During the eighteenth century through various deals, subterfuge, and superior technology, they consolidated a large sphere of influence, with entire principalities under their direct administration and others administered indirectly (a weak maharaja paid respect in title only). The nineteenth and early twentieth centuries represent the period of the British Raj. In 1832, it was decreed that henceforth the medium of instruction in schools receiving government funds would be English exlusively; instruction in Persian (the language of the Moghuls) or in Sanskrit would not be supported.

Much traditional education was unaffected by this. Many Sanskrit pundits belonged to healthy traditions that relied on the wealth of native merchants and other prosperous non-Englishmen. But the culture of the Indian subcontinent changed, heavily influenced by the West. Conflicts of culture became manifest in many ways, from styles of dress and diet to language, education, and religion. Indians went to universities in England, and there emerged a new class of intellectuals and philosophers, Indians expressing their views in English. Many great figures of modern Indian thought—even those reviving traditional views such as Ram Mohan Roy, Vivekananda, Aurobindo, and Gandhi—wrote primarily in English.

India became independent in 1947 (the new nation smaller by the simultaneous creation of the Muslim state Pakistan by partition), but the legacy of the British survives, particularly in education. Though in primary and secondary schools the various regional vernaculars—Hindi, Gujarati, Bengali, Marathi, Tamil, Telegu, Malayalam, and others—are the principal media of instruction, India has a university system like that of the West, with English predominant. And the professionals who staff the departments of philosophy espouse the whole range of modern (and postmodern!) positions current in Europe and the United States. But the classical traditions have lived on, especially with traditional pundits, and the classical schools appear now to be having an increased influence within academia. In the last section, I address some of the issues of this interaction, as well as the question of the contemporary relevance of the ancient and classical views.

Yoga and "Analysis"

Now we turn to the individual philosophies of ancient and classical India. Some of these differ from one another broadly by approach and interest. Presuppositions vary widely too—amidst intricate commonalities framing issues and intellectual movements. The philosophy of India is extremely complex and multidimensional.

But no issue is more important throughout the long history of Indian philosophy than the nature and possibility of the individual's own best interest, his or her *summum bonum*. The question of what is the "supreme personal good" (Skt: *parama-puruṣa-artha*), in the phrase philosophers used to discuss competing positions, could not be ignored. Nirvāṇa, enlightenment, liberation, supreme bliss, a life in heaven with the gods—these were among a variety of mystical and religious conceptions competing for people's allegiance. Whole philosophies, worldviews, grew up around the differing conceptions of personal salvation. I call philosophies of this type "enlightenment theories." These theories are invariably implemented by teachings about self-transformative practices, a path to enlightenment, a yoga—that is, a "way" (Skt: *marga*).

Then in distinction to the enlightenment theories are philosophic efforts devoted to trying to understand the activities of everyday life. Some philosophers attack problems apart from religious interests. "How do we know anything? How do we know, for example, that the pot there on the table is a pot? What allows us to use any word for what there is, the pot or anything else? How can we ever mean what we say?" These are some of the questions asked.

The enlightenment theorists also have views on matters to which their own mystical orientation is irrelevant: Great advances are made in logic, for instance, among Buddhist theorists. But the Buddhists and all who are engaged with the personal goal try above all to articulate what makes enlightenment possible. Thus they see as central to the philosopher's task the spelling out of the relation of Nirvāṇa, Brahman, God—things considered mystically revealed—to things of the everyday world. Since a mystical orientation is somewhat more pronounced in the older period than in the philosophy of the later classical age, we shall look first at enlightenment theories—specifically Yoga and "Analysis"—that are first expressed in the Great Epic and other early protophilosophic literature and are systematized much later in expressly philosophic texts. ("Analysis" is better known by its Sanskrit name, Sāṃkhya.)

Yoga—understood in its common anglicized usage as meditation and various somatic practices—was current in India at least from the time of the Great Indian Epic and probably as early as the eighth century B.C.E. The Sanskrit word *yoga* occurs roughly in this sense in some of the early Upanishads (for example, *Kaṭha* 6.11). Practices aimed at a transformation of consciousness may indeed predate the invasion of the tribes who spoke Sanskrit, the Āryans, as some archaeological evidence suggests. But systems of philosophy explaining how such a transformation is possible appeared later. These schools took it as their task to relate the idea of the personal transformation to a way of looking at the world. The Yoga philosophy and the Sāṃkhya, "Analysis," are schools or world-views of this type. They are similar in their overall outlook, and we shall review them together, focusing rather arbitrarily primarily on the Yoga school.

The *Yoga-sūtra* is the central Yoga text. It is part handbook on practices of yoga (a "how-to book"), part mystic psychology, and part metaphysics. The teachings about yogic practices may be the most important dimension of the text. It is, after all, much more as "yoga," understood as a system of physical exercise, than as "Yoga" (with a capital *Y*), as a philosophy, that the word is best known throughout the world today. But it is the metaphysics, and secondarily the psychological conceptions—the abstract ideas of the text—that give the Yoga philosophy defined by or rooted in this *sūtra* text its distinctness and unity. The Yoga school does not speak for all yoga proponents, all the advocates and practitioners. The Yoga school is one prominent philosophy associated with yogic practices. There are others, for example, all Buddhist schools, because all Buddhism incorporates practices mentioned in the *Yoga-sūtra* into its practical side.

The Yoga worldview is a dualism of nature and individual consciousness. The individual achieves enlightenment when the individual consciousness breaks away from nature to stand alone, resplendent in a self-absorbed trance. This dualistic view centered on an idea of an individual supreme good in turn shapes practice and the psychological concepts expressed in the *Yoga-sūtra* and other texts.

There are four distinct types of yogic practice mentioned in the *Yoga-sūtra*: (1) effort at emotional disengagement from the world; (2) concentration on "God" as the archetypal liberated yogin; (3) discipline of purifying action, including the study of philosophy; and (4) somatic discipline consisting of stretching exercises, breath control, and immobile meditation and closed-eye trance. Important psychological notions, for example, that there are "subliminal impulses" (Skt: *vāsanā* or *karma*) that need to be controlled, are associated with these practices. "Mental silence"—the quieting of the inner voice of thought and emotion—is the most important of these psychological notions, and *yoga* is defined early in the text simply as mental silence (Skt: *citta-vṛtti-nirodha,* literally "cessation of the fluctuations of mentality"). Nevertheless, it is above all the dualism of nature and consciousness that unifies the ideas of Yoga as a systematic philosophy.

According to this worldview, in reality there is no connection between consciousness and the world. There are many consciousnesses, but they are related to one another only through a general *illusion* of embodiment or involvement with nature. In "liberation" (Skt: *mukti*), a person comes to see himself as how he really is, namely, as a pure consciousness self-rapt, blissful in himself, and unaware of anything other than himself alone. (We could equally well say *herself*, for sex is not a real feature of a person but a false identification with nature like everything concerning bodies.) The *Yoga-sūtra* calls this state "independence" as well as "liberation," an independence from all the appearances of the world.

Presumably, the notion of individuals existing entirely absorbed in a state of self-bliss was meant to explain how a certain mystic trance could occur. But as a world explanation, the view does not work; for what explains the original illusion? Further, how is it possible that we are ever at any time aware of objects in nature, and how is it that we can even seem to act in the world? Consciousness and nature are in reality absolutely distinct. Also, if consciousness is so wonderful, as the text attests, how can it be so stupid as to lose itself in nature? These were common criticisms voiced by proponents of other classical schools. The Yoga school in later writings makes some effort to solve these problems. But it fails, it seems. The school loses prominence as philosophy progresses in classical times.

The Sāṃkhya worldview is similar to Yoga. There is a similar conception of a supreme personal good. But *Sāṃkhya* means "Analysis," and the method endorsed in this school to realize the supreme personal good is analysis of the principles of nature, of which twenty-four dominant principles (or "realities," Skt: *tattva*) are identified. In this way, an individual cognizer would be better able to disengage from nature in a mystic trance. Such intellectual discipline is thought to aid a psychological process of wholesale disidentification. Listed are "gross elements" (air, fire, water, and so on), "subtle elements," and organs of action and knowledge. There is also an overlying system of natural "qualities" presented. These are "strands" or "threads" (Skt: *guṇa*), of which all nature is composed, a strand of (a) light, (b) activity and passion, and (c) inertia and darkness. The Sāṃkhya system practically disappears from the philosophic scene over time, apparently because its "analysis" of nature was felt to be inadequate.

Despite the conceptual failings in both the Yoga and the Sāṃkhya systems—which their classical adversaries delighted in pointing out—the practices that motivate these views may well be valuable, as philosophers of various persuasions in both classical and modern times have insisted. Let me make a rather bold comparison. The Greek philosopher Socrates is not remembered so much for his particular opinions as for teaching us to question all views. He teaches the value of keeping one's distance from ideas for which no good reasons are apparent, and establishes tough scrutiny of claims as a philosophic norm. The methods intellectualized in Yoga—and in Sāṃkhya, too—are methods of disidentification and, so to say, psychological distancing that are more radical than the intellectual distancing taught by Socrates. Supposedly, we can refuse to identify with thoughts that "cross our minds" but also with our own sense experience, emotions, memories, and subconscient dispositions to action. There can be no doubt that the practices bring increased personal power within each of these spheres, great self-control, and a leverage over psychological movements similar to what Socrates taught that we can achieve over opinions we have inherited. Surely these are important matters, however badly they may have been handled conceptually by the Yoga and Sāṃkhya philosophies.

Early Buddhism

Others conceived of a supreme personal good differently. The Buddha said it was *nirvāṇa,* an "extinction" or "blowing out" of suffering and desire.

The Buddha lived in the sixth century B.C.E. in the Gangetic valley in what is now Nepal. He was born Siddhārtha Gautama, a prince of the Śākya clan. As a young man, the "Buddha-to-be" led a life of pleasure and enjoyment in his father's palace, according to a popular version of his life. His father encouraged him in this because of a prophecy that the young Siddhārtha would become a religious mendicant. The prince's father tried to protect him from the sight of anything unpleasant or evil. Once when his father was away from the palace, the prince ventured out into the world accompanied by an adviser. He encountered first a diseased person, then an old person wrinkled and decrepit, and then a corpse. Inquiring about each of these "three evils" in turn, he was told that everyone was subject to them. Then the prince declared his former life of pleasure meaningless and set out to find the source of evil and the power to uproot it. After an arduous ordeal of personal inspection, meditation, and transformation of desire, he became "awakened," "enlightened" (Skt: *buddha*), and began a long career of teaching and directing disciples to the transformation that he had experienced.

At the center of the teaching are the "Four Noble Truths": (1) All is suffering; (2) suffering has a cause, namely desire (or attachment); (3) by uprooting the cause, there is an end to suffering in the bliss of Nirvāṇa; and (4) the way to this is the Eightfold Noble Path—right understanding, right thought, right speech, right action, right livelihood, right effort, right mindfulness, and right meditation. The Four Noble Truths are the central teaching of Early Buddhism, but, as we shall see both in this and in later sections, Buddhist philosophy expands in many directions.

As mentioned earlier, Buddhism divides into Southern and Northern traditions with distinct literatures. The oldest sections of the Southern canon include what scholars consider to be actual sermons of the Buddha. The term *Early Buddhism* is used to refer to the doctrines proclaimed in these sermons and in the Southern canon generally.

In addition to the Four Noble Truths, important doctrines proclaimed in the Southern canon include (a) the causal interdependence of things, (b) the insubstantiality and phenomenal nature of things as mere groups of qualities or states of consciousness (Skt: *dharma*), and (c) the insubstantiality of the self or soul—there is "no soul" according to the Buddha. The Buddha seems to have seen false identification with the body, mind, emotions, and desires as the prime obstacle to spiritual accomplishment. Much thought and elaboration in later years were directed to an analysis of the apparent person as a "bundle" of states or qualities.

But more than any metaphysical teaching, the Buddha of Early Buddhism emphasizes the practice of meditation and compassion. Indeed, anti-intellectualism becomes a prominent theme in later Mahāyāna Buddhist writing, in particular with Nāgārjuna.

Jainism

Vardhamāna Mahāvīra, the founder of Jainism, lived in the sixth century B.C.E.; he was roughly contemporary with the Buddha. Mahāvīra is also known as "the Jina," the Victor (over passion). There is some evidence that Mahāvīra's followers merged with another group to establish the religion of the Jina. Jains and Buddhists disavow all explicit allegiance to Vedic traditions and do not practice caste.

Like the scriptures of Early Buddhism, the Jain canon is immense. And most Jain teachings are similarly focused on a path to enlightenment, with a variety of theories put forth to support practice concepts.

Of all the early Indian systems organized around a mystical *summum bonum,* Jain philosophy is the most renowned for having an ethical commitment to the value of life. Jains are vegetarians; moreover, Jain monks have been known to wear masks so that their breathing will not cause injury to insects. Regarding even vegetable life as sentient, some Jain monks have starved themselves to death to prevent injury to others. Noninjury (Skt: *ahiṃsā*), an ideal popularized in modern times by Mahatma Gandhi, as was noted, was propagated in ancient and classical India foremost by Jains. Noninjury was also taught by Buddhists, whose views on many counts are close to the Jains'.

The noninjury teaching finds articulate justification in early Jain texts. Noninjury is defended by an idea of equality in soul. Everything that is conscious hates injury, and so anyone realizing that others are like himself in being conscious and hating all forms of personal injury should also realize that refraining from committing injury to others should be practiced at all times.

Noninjury is a universally prescribed moral dictum. But in the details of ethical precepts, Jain monks and nuns, on the one hand, and laypersons, on the other, are said to have duties that differ. Not only asceticism but prescribed "reflections"—for example, on the impermanence of things, on human helplessness, and on the difficulty of enlightenment—mark the life of nuns and monks. Householders desist from dishonest business practices, lying, illicit sexual relations, and so forth, but do not aspire to "liberation" in this lifetime. As with Buddhist and other early Indian enlightenment theories, rebirth is presupposed. Jains believe that only the enlightened are liberated, that is, not reborn.

Jain thinkers are partners to the philosophical discussions of all periods of the classical civilization. Early Jain cosmology, however, stands by itself. A testament to human imaginative capacities working from the premise that everything is alive, the cosmology had little influence outside the Jain community. (Fantastical beings are proposed, beings made of water, of earth, and so on.) But in metaphysics, later Jain thinkers became especially famous throughout the philosophic world for propagating two engaging metaphilosophical positions, "nonabsolutism" and "maybe-ism." The two may be seen as an extension of the noninjury ethic into the area of philosophic polemics. Jains declare that no metaphysical claim should be taken as absolutely true. Every view represents only one perspective among many. Further, every view should be regarded as right *maybe*. There is at least a grain of truth in every position, and the modality of the *maybe* directs the intelligence to find and appreciate what is correct in what an opponent is saying. Indeed, though not all are Jains, there are no absolute opponents, none that need simply to be intellectually vanquished and their views discarded. All have a perspective, and none has the entire truth.

Such attitudes made some Jain writers great reporters of philosophic debates in that they presented the positions of all parties fairly. Sometimes within other schools, opponents' positions are misrepresented and ridiculed, but never in Jain texts. Jains are among the best historians of Indian philosophy.

A common criticism of the Jain metaphysics of nonabsolutism to be found among philosophers of other schools is that the position is self-contradictory. "Nonabsolutism" is proposed as absolutely true. Its content, however, denies what it asserts, that is, when it is applied to itself. No self-contradictory position should be espoused, say the critics of the Jain philosophy. Jain defenders respond that "nonabsolutism" is not one position among rivals, but rather an overview of all of the views that take themselves to be contenders for metaphysical truth.

Mahāyāna Buddhist Philosophies

Buddhist Mystic Skepticism

As mentioned, what becomes Northern Buddhism, a movement known as Mahāyāna, should not be said to reject the teachings of the Southern canon; the division is not really a schism. Nevertheless, there are doctrinal differences between Northern and Southern Buddhists. Notably, there occurred a split early in Buddhism concerning how the goal of Buddhist practice should be conceived. According to a school known as Theravāda—and Southern Buddhism in general—the "saint" (Skt: *arhat*) loses all individual personality in a universal impersonal, unconceptualizable bliss and awareness that somehow (*how* cannot be said) underlie all appearance. By contrast, according to Mahāyāna, a personal salvation without regard for others is to be eschewed. No one has reached the truest supreme good until every sentient being is freed from suffering and spiritual ignorance. This core Mahāyāna doctrine is reflected in a well-known vow repeated each day by the devout. The Buddha, Mahāyānins say, could have lost himself in a total Nirvāṇa, but refused and turned back out of compassion to help the world.

Early Buddhist writings also indicate that there were disputes as to how to understand the aggregate of "elements" or "qualities" that the Buddha had taught make up an apparent person and are to be transcended to achieve the supreme good. A doctrine of no real self (Skt: *anātman*) appears in the sermon portion of the Southern canon, and some Buddhist thinkers believed that the components of the false appearance of self could be identified and analyzed, as was noted in the section on Early Buddhism. Thus they attempted to provide comprehensive lists of these components, that is, of qualities and their groupings. And they engaged in an analysis of phenomena—somewhat in the fashion of Sāṃkhya but with more sophistication and often with great effort to refrain from viewing things as in any way elements existing *apart from* consciousness.

But it was pretty widely recognized, if not always explicitly acknowledged, that the Buddha himself had considered similar intellectual activity counterproductive. There are famous fables in which he asks, "When your house is on fire, is it wise to discourse on the nature of fire? No, it is wise to put the fire out. When shot with an arrow, would you discourse on the nature of arrows, or pull the arrow out?" The implication is that we are ablaze with suffering, and need not discourse on its nature but rather should do something, principally meditating and acting with compassion, to put the suffering out.

Nāgārjuna, the founder of Buddhist Mystic Skepticism or Mādhyamika (the school of the "Middle Way" or "in balance"), was a reformer. He found the intellectualizing tendencies of his contemporaries, with their lists of qualities and aggregates that make up the apparent person, to stray from the practical end that he saw as the true message of the Buddha. Nāgārjuna identifies paradoxes, contradictions, and impossibilities in the positions of the quarreling schools of Buddhist interpretation, and indeed in non-Buddhist positions. He was apparently motivated in this by a sense of the goal of the Buddhist path as a practical end to which thought and mind have no direct access.

Nāgārjuna's fame as a philosopher rests with the difficult questions he raised, and not only for Buddhist theorists but for many others as well. As I noted in reviewing the philosophic history of the subcontinent, Nāgārjuna sparked an intellectual revolution by being such a brilliant anti-intellectual, by drawing attention to subtle problems of conception.

For example, against those of the (Hindu) "Logic" school who proposed that in debate one should argue on the basis of justification, viewed by the Logicians as (a) sense experience, (b) inferential reasoning, (c) analogical identification, and (d) the testimony of experts, Nāgārjuna asks, "What justifies the justifiers?" He examines several answers, but finds none satisfactory and suggests that none could be satisfactory because each answer raises the question of what justifies it. The Logician upholder of justifiers is thus faced with an infinite regress, with a task of justifying justifiers that cannot be accomplished. Nāgārjuna concludes here—and with other insoluble problems he purports to reveal—that one should give up such futile intellectualizing and aim at a mystic transformation instead.

Some moderns try to see in Nāgārjuna's attacks on others' views a champion of "relativism" as understood in our "postmodern" times. But despite the fervor of his anti-intellectualist streak, Nāgārjuna remains first and foremost a Buddhist, intent on a mystic self-transformation. What is paramount to Nāgārjuna is to develop the six virtues, or "perfections" (Skt: *pāramitā*), of the living enlightened, the Bodhisattva.

In India at Nāgārjuna's time, the two principal branches of later Buddhism were not, apparently, so well defined. Nevertheless, Nāgārjuna does espouse the doctrine of the Bodhisattva, and this doctrine marks the chief point of difference between the tradition of the North and that of the South. As noted, in Early Buddhism and Southern Buddhism generally, the goal is to achieve a personal salvation in Nirvāṇa. But for Nāgārjuna, it was problematic whether an individual could achieve a complete extinction of personality, for everything is interconnected. One can read Nāgārjuna as trying to say this without saying it directly: The interdependence of everything has to be experientially realized. All things arise in interdependence, and no one is entirely enlightened until everyone is.

Nāgārjuna's Mādhyamika school was prominent for many centuries from the beginning of the classical period. His followers continued to provoke responses within the philosophies of other camps by their penetrating questioning.

Buddhist Idealism

Despite Nāgārjuna's efforts and the efforts of his disciples, Buddhist speculation does not cease. Within Mahāyāna, the most noteworthy example of renewed theorizing is the school of Buddhist Idealism, called Yogācāra. The motivation of this development seems to be at least in part the following (religious) response to Nāgārjuna. Not every element of our ordinary life should be considered illusory or intellectually problematic, because then there would be no possibility of a living Nirvāṇa experience. But the Buddha's testimony that there is such a possibility is reliable. If this is to be a real possibility for everyone, as the Buddha teaches, then there must be some element of our ordinary existence that may serve as transition to Nirvāṇa experience. The Buddhist Idealists claim that this element is pure, immediate awareness (Skt: *vijñapti*). The Buddhist Idealists accepted the dialectic of Nāgārjuna only to an extent: An imputation of reality and externality to objects apart from experience is considered problematic, but not immediate awareness itself.

The Buddhist Idealists also try to show how our ordinary experience can be explained. Thus they take up the project of Buddhist "theodicy" to explain why we do not ordinarily experience Nirvāṇa. They apparently feel that we should so experience it—Nirvāṇa is seen as the "natural state"—and propound a doctrine of "mind alone." This doctrine is taken to mean that immediate awareness is by nature nothing but the luminous Nirvāṇic meditation, with an affective or emotional side blissful, free of desire, and full of compassion for all, as exemplified in the life of the Buddha. The problem is then to explain not this original and healthy state but deviation from it. To this end, the Buddhist Idealists posit a beginningless "storehouse consciousness" (Skt: *ālayavijñāna*) consisting of numberless subliminal urges and memory impressions. The arising of these urges deforms awareness yet accounts for our ordinary experience.

The Buddhist Idealists face a difficulty in the apparent intersubjectivity of the world. We seem to see the same trees, flowers, and furniture of external objects. Now, accounting for this by a *common* "storehouse" may work, but it seems a cumbersome conception. Would it not be better, simpler, that is—the rival Hindu school of Logic asks—to admit that there are objects independent of consciousness, external to us, and real even when no one is aware of them? Such a realist conception seems closed to the Buddhists because of their religious commitments as Mahāyānins: Everyone and everything is interconnected, and someday we shall all pass together into the final Bliss.

Some later Buddhist Idealists put the storehouse conception on a back burner to focus on questions of logic and the theory of knowledge and justification. These Buddhist Idealists are sometimes called Buddhist Logicians. The most eminent among them were Dharmakīrti (ca. 600) and his predecessor, Dignāga (ca. 450).

Dignāga in his late work turns his attention almost exclusively to questions about how we know anything and the means whereby we know what we know or, we might say, are justified in our beliefs. He argues that there are only two "means to true belief," or "justifiers" (Skt: *pramāṇa*), namely (1) sensation and (2) inference. He then defines and elaborates their nature at length.

Dignāga's most lasting fame is due to his formalization of rules of inference. He is a key figure in the development of Indian logic. On sensation, Dignāga remains more closely allied to the Buddhist Idealist camp than does his successor Dharmakīrti. Although Dignāga claims that his epistemological theory holds up whether one regards the objects known as "external" or as "internal," he takes a phenomenalist view of illusion: False perceptual beliefs (such as "This is a snake" when in reality the object is a rope) do not result from error in sensation but from error in intellectual judgment. Illusions are not perceptual errors but rather misinterpretations of data infallibly presented. This view has a clear affinity with other Buddhist Idealist tenets: All immediate awareness is in its true nature the Supreme Reality such as was discovered by the Buddha in Nirvāṇa experience. It is then the perversions of thought (misinterpretation) and desire that prevent us from realizing this. Dignāga defines sensation as "free from conceptualization" and views it as always in itself reliable.

Dharmakīrti takes a different view: Sensation is not always reliable. In some circumstances—such as having hepatitis and seeing white objects as yellow, or traveling on a ship and seeing stationary objects as moving—sense presentations are not to be trusted, and the judgments that would express them (for example, "That is yellow") are false. Thus some illusions occur not because of misinterpretation but because of something wrong in the causal nexus that results in sensation (having hepatitis, for instance). Dharmakīrti is, like Dignāga, concerned chiefly with issues of epistemology and logic, but he incorporates these areas of theory all within an understanding of what a real object is to which causal notions are central.

Anything real has "causal efficacy," while something unreal, say the horn of a hare, has none. The purpose of philosophy, says Dharmakīrti, is to investigate human cognition because successful action is invariably preceded by right cognition. If we successfully milk Bessie and make butter, we have rightly cognized that Bessie is a milkcow, that milk churned turns into butter, and so on. Right cognition, or "knowledge," arises within a causal nexus that includes both an object's effect on us (for example, our sight of Bessie) and our action in the world (for example, milking her). Dharmakīrti views certain types of inference as having causal underpinnings. When, for example, we reason from the sight of smoke rising from a hill that there must be a fire there, the inference we make is based on the causal relation of smoke and fire. Similarly, when we do not see an elephant in the room and infer that none is present, we are reasoning based on a causal relation: Were an elephant nearby, we would necessarily perceive it (so long as we were not blind). There are also inferences based on natural classifications, such as "Bessie is a cow and therefore an animal." But much meaningful inferential knowledge—"meaningful" because it helps us get what we want—is based on relations of effect and cause.

There are many additional positions taken by Dharmakīrti, and several arguments, that hold great interest for philosophers of all places and times: his "proof" that all things are momentary, for example. This Buddhist Idealist is one of the great minds of Indian civilization, and of all civilization for that matter. But let us close our introductory study by asking how it is that Dharmakīrti is to be counted a *Buddhist* philosopher, and not simply a philosopher *tout court*. What is it about his epistemology and causal understanding of objects that ties in with Buddhist doctrines? Is his religious faith separate from his philosophic reflection?

The answer lies in Dharmakīrti's understanding of the Four Noble Truths. Dharmakīrti views a human being as an active creature, one who acts to attain objects of desire. The Second Noble Truth is that suffering has its origin in desire, and the third that the uprooting of desire is the end of suffering and the attainment of Nirvāṇa. When Dharmakīrti analyzes right cognition and talks about effects and causes within the world, he is presupposing a worldly perspective conditioned by desire and suffering. Thus his position is mediated by his further contention that it is possible to transform desire back into a pristine state of compassion, as we follow the Buddhist Way. That transformation would eliminate the essential precondition of worldly activity, namely desire for certain results of action. Thus Dharmakīrti's upholding of a possible suspension of desire-provoked activity gives his philosophy "two tiers," one world-oriented and one not. Then in a brilliant twist of unification, his final defense of both is their reputed usefulness for attaining what *should* be a person's number-one desire, namely, the experience of Nirvāṇa, the supreme good.

Vedānta

Advaita Vedānta

Vedānta, as mentioned in the survey of Indian philosophy, is a school of philosophy with several distinct branches. Followers of one brand of

Vedānta quarrel with followers of another. But from a distance, the branches fall into two principal groups: (1) Advaita monism and (2) Upanishadic theism, or Vedāntic theism. Recall that the term *vedānta* is originally an epithet for the Upanishads, and comes later to be the name of the schools that expressly embrace Upanishadic views.

The most significant difference of interpretation among Vedāntins is whether the "Absolute" (*brahman*) declared in the Upanishads should be understood as "God" or not. The theists see a Creator loosing forth a real world, and sustaining it by an act of will at every moment. Advaita Vedāntins, in contrast, see Brahman as transcendent to worldly form and individuation: The world—with regard to Brahman—is a "cosmic illusion" (Skt: *māyā*).

Several other issues relate to this difference in conception of Brahman, preeminently how the supreme personal good is to be understood. For Vedāntins in general, this is *brahma-vidyā,* "knowledge or realization of Brahman," but the term does not have the same meaning for Advaitins and theists. Advaitins, or "Nondualists" (Skt: *advaita* = nondualism), hold that the "self" (Skt: *ātman*) of everyone is in reality nothing other than Brahman, and that in the mystical "knowledge of Brahman" there is known only the One, the Sole True Existent, whose nature is perfect Being, Consciousness, and Bliss. Vedāntic theists, by contrast, hold that the individual and God are in many ways distinct. In the "supreme knowledge," the Absolute cannot be known in precisely the fashion that God knows God, for an individual knower is not entirely identical with his or her Creator and Ground.

Advaita philosophers try to make hay out of the occurrence of perceptual illusion, such as the appearance of a rope as a snake and mother-of-pearl as silver. They argue that in the mystical realization of Brahman, ordinary perceptions of the world are *sublated,* that is, revealed as illusory. There is nothing real but Brahman, and insofar as one perceives things as distinct or separate from Brahman one perceives illusorily. One follows a "path"—according to some, a "yoga"—to transcend ordinary perceptions and live in the true consciousness that reveals Brahman. The Upanishadic declarations that Brahman is the Real, the "One without a second," inspire a person to follow a path to make this an immediate experience (Skt: *brahma-sākṣātkāra* = to be immediately Brahman-aware).

In other words, Advaitins argue that illusions and corrections of illusions show the possibility that knowledge of Brahman could sublate the world and reveal it to be illusory, as the correcting perception of a rope shows the snake to be illusory. The Upanishads teach us that this is not merely a possibility but a fact.

In trying to assess the Advaita claims, one must observe the depth of the sublatability argument. The Western philosopher Descartes shows this when he asks, "Is there any presentation of experience that could not possibly be deceptive?'' He decides that a powerful demon *could* be deceiving him with each and every one. The Advaitins argue similarly that all the presentations of experience *can* be sublated, that is, revealed to be illusory like the false presentation of a snake in the correcting experience of a rope. And like Descartes, they hold that only ''self-consciousness'' is *un*sublatable. But unlike Descartes, they believe that I-consciousness is really nothing but Brahman-consciousness and that when the full splendor of this dawns, one is liberated, saved, having achieved the supreme personal good.

It is not made clear, however, that Brahman-awareness could not itself be sublated, at least as the Advaitins understand ''sublation'' (Skt: *bādha*). Central to the Advaita polemic seems to be an understanding of the cognition that corrects a perceptual illusion as simply a cognition that *follows* the illusory presentation with a different content, for example, of a rope instead of a snake. So why could not Brahman-cognition be followed by a fuller experience of the world? (Variations on this objection date all the way back to the Sermons of the Buddha.) Why could not a mystic ''come back'' to the world after a trance of self-absorption? Would not this show the world to be real?

The history of Advaita Vedānta, however, is not confined only to the sublation argument. Advaita Vedānta presents in fact a surprisingly rich and resilient tradition, making a variety of contributions to the march of Indian philosophy. There are three or four important subschools. There is also in the later classical period the emergence of a dialectical Advaita. Advaitin skeptics rehearse Nāgārjuna-like arguments against the realist school of Logic. We shall review the Advaita dialectic in the section devoted to the Logic worldview.

Upanishadic Theism

Vedāntins who interpret the Upanishads theistically—as teaching that Brahman is ''God,'' the Creator and Supreme Knower of a real world— share several positions with Advaitins. (The terms *brahman,* the ''Absolute,'' and *īśvara,* ''God,'' are used by the theists interchangeably.) One important commonality that distinguishes Vedāntic theism from Western varieties is a doctrine of Brahman as the world's material cause. Not positively every theistic Vedāntin holds this, but most do. ''From nothing, comes nothing,'' they reason (following *Chāndogya Upaniṣad* 6.2.1–2). Therefore in creating the world, Brahman creates out of Brahman's own substance: The world is a ''self-manifestation'' of God. From the perspective of ''stuff,'' the Advaitins are right, the Vedāntic theists say: There is nothing other than Brahman. But Brahman has two natures: (1) God as God is in God's self, which is God's necessary and essential nature, and (2) God as God self-manifests in the world, ''names and forms'' (Skt:

nāma-rūpa) that are real but contingent and inessential. Brahman is the "Inner Controller," who dwells in everything finite and sustains and directs the world from within, but who in a supreme unmanifest "self-existence" is infinite and transcendent over all names and forms.

These views are taken to be revealed in the Upanishads, and other theistic texts are often said simply to reiterate the vision. But the history of theistic Vedānta is not only long and complex, there are a variety of texts that come to be as important as the Upanishads. For a prime example, a portion of the Great Epic known as the *Bhagavad-Gītā* comes to be, within some theistic sects, as important as or more important than the Upanishads.

There is a crisis depicted in the *Gītā* that is principally ethical, but the solution that is proposed by Krishna, an "incarnation of God" (Skt: *avatāra*), is a "spiritual discipline" or yoga. Thus is consummated a marriage between highest self-interest and ethical duty that is typical of almost all Indian mysticism (a similar point could be made with regard to Buddhists or Jains and Advaitins as well): One has to behave ethically to advance along a path to the *summum bonum,* and by advancing, one's behavior naturally becomes more ethical, it is claimed. The Buddhists say that by exercising compassion one advances toward enlightenment, and by advancing toward enlightenment one cannot help but act out of compassion. Krishna teaches Arjuna, his interlocutor in the *Gītā,* that by striving to be aware of God he will be led to do the right thing in battle, and by doing the right thing he will progress toward "God-awareness."

Also in the *Gītā,* the Indian theist theory of the *avatāra* is put forth. This is the idea of a special "Divine Descent" into finite form to uphold a moral order and to direct the world in the right ways. The Avatar is an embodied individual conscious of being a manifestation of God and sharing in God's awareness, power, and native delight. In a sense, all individuals can be avatars; maintaining a living awareness of God, sharing in God's bliss, and so on constitute the goal of the person or the supreme personal good as conceived by Vedāntic theists. But the difference between the proper avatars and you and me is that Krishna, Rama, Jesus (according to some modern eclectics), and others never lose the awareness of their essential divinity, we have to do yoga or follow a guru to overcome our "spiritual ignorance" (Skt: *avidyā*).

Later theists teach that the way to mystical realization is not meditation or the more ascetic practices associated with the *Yoga-sūtra* and Buddhist disciplines, but rather par excellence something much simpler, namely *bhakti,* "love" and "devotion" to God. The *bhakti* teaching goes back to the *Gītā,* but it becomes the rage in much later centuries, flowering in the late classical age. The whole world is God's play (Skt: *līlā*), say the theistic Vedāntins; and through love of God and worship and devotion, we are eventually to realize this and find in every experience the embrace of a Divine Lover. Vedāntic theists from the classical age into the modern conceive of the supreme personal good as a spiritual act of lovemaking. The twentieth-century "neo-Vedāntin" Aurobindo, writing in English, says, "To commit adultery with God is the perfect experience for which the world was created" (Sri Aurobindo, "Thoughts and Aphorisms," *Sri Aurobindo Birth Centenary Library* [Pondicherry: Sri Aurobindo Ashram Trust, 1973], vol. 17, p. 129).

Vedāntic theists of course face many difficult conceptual problems, some of which are similar to those faced by theists in the West. For example, there is the problem of evil. It is reported that the Buddha himself rejected the notion of God precisely because of clear examples of evil—pain, suffering, and death. Could God have prevented evil? Then God is not worthy of *bhakti*. Does God wish to prevent evil but is incapable of doing so? Then God does not seem to be "God" as conceived in the Upanishads. There would be a greater power.

Within Vedāntic camps, one finds three types of response, which are often combined. First, it is said that without evil we would not be motivated to find and know God in a supreme mystical experience (Skt: *brahma-vidyā*). Second, it is said that at bottom it is only God who suffers evil in that we are all "manifestations" of God and God is the one ultimate "Self" of all experience. Brahman permits suffering and pain just for the kick of it, so to say, as part of the "play" that is Brahman's dawdling in the finite. In other words, evil adds increased diversity to God's "inessential" experience, that is, to God's experience as the likes of you and me. Third, it is argued that without evil or at least its possibility, this world would not be possible. Finitude (or some other intrinsic feature of the ways things are with us here) entails evil, it is claimed, and this world is valuable so Brahman creates it anyway. Buddhists, in particular, find these responses inadequate, and their attacks are carried on by Advaita Vedāntins in the late classical age.

Counterbalancing the difficulties of satisfactorily explaining God and God's relation to the world, the Vedāntic theists urge that there are the plain facts of mystical experience revealing God. But, of course, Buddhists claim to found their teachings on the revelations of a mystical experience, and Advaitins (and Jains and others) do too. So can an "argument from mystical experience" show the theists to be correct?— or the Buddhists? or the Advaitins? and so on? This is a complex question about which there is much disagreement. But it is noteworthy how prominent such an argument is in the Indian context—with variations according to what is believed revealed.

"Exegesis"

Dominant in many regions and periods of civilization in the Indian subcontinent and along many dimensions of culture were conservative

Brahmins, the priests and intellectuals of Hinduism, or, more precisely, of Brahminism, the highbrow religion of Vedic interpretation and defense of caste. What today we call Hinduism had and still has little unity; worship of popular gods and goddesses was socially at a great remove from the exegetical enterprises of the high-caste priests. These did not view the lower classes as fit to read their sacred texts. As noted, Jains and Buddhists rejected caste as well as the Brahmins' Veda, although many Jain and Buddhist philosophers were themselves converts from the Brahminical caste.

Proponents of the classical school Mīmāṃsā, "Exegesis," were conservatives among the conservative. The Exegetes were most concerned with the proper interpretation of the texts they viewed as revealed, the Veda and its appendages. They were particularly concerned with questions of *dharma*, "right practice," which they understood chiefly as the performance of certain rituals. But some Exegetes were interested in the philosophical topics debated in rival schools and worked out theories of their own on many issues. This expansion occurs over several centuries, paralleling the development of Buddhist and Jain philosophy and of other less conservative Hindu schools.

The Exegetes' root text is the *Mīmāṃsā-sūtra* (ca. 100 C.E.). There the broad lines of an approach to the Vedic revelation are laid down. This text itself does not contain much philosophy other than theorizing about linguistic meaning. But in some commentaries on it, there are discourses on many of the issues—the self and self-awareness, the reality of the external world, justification and canons of debate and argument, rebirth and the possibility of liberation and enlightenment—that are the concerns of philosophers.

The Exegetes are realists: The objects of consciousness exist independently of our perceptions. Thus they are motivated to direct arguments against Buddhist positions in particular. On several issues, they are allied with the Logic school.

But the philosophic activity notwithstanding, even the greatest theorists—such as Kumārila (ca. 650) and his student Prabhākara (ca. 700)—were preoccupied with interpretations of the right way to perform certain rituals. Apparently, there were hot disputes about some of these. There is a legend that Prabhākara was asked to declare on the occasion of his teacher's death whether the cremation rites should be performed according to his teacher's views or his own. When he replied his teacher's, Kumārila, who had been feigning death out of frustration in not convincing his prime pupil, rose up to declare victory. Prabhākara replied that he was not defeated so long as the two of them were still alive.

Ceremonies at a cremation or burial were performed by Brahmins, for which they were paid in cash or barter. The Brahmins enjoyed other social privileges as well, and were beneficiaries (along with two other "twice born" or high castes) of the caste system. Caste is perpetuated by marriage, and there are strict regulations on who can marry whom. Caste is fixed at birth and cannot be altered. In rebirth, one is likely to change station according to the merits and demerits accumulated in this and past lifetimes. This picture is propagated by the Exegetes in the classical period. Much of it is challenged in sects of modern Hinduism, but there remain conservative circles where caste distinctions are still observed as sacred law.

The Materialist Skeptics

Whereas, as we have seen, many of the classical philosophers of the subcontinent declare a "supreme personal good" to be the central conception of their worldviews, few authors explicitly say that their philosophy is *non*-teleological in this sense. But with the Cārvāka school—the "Materialist Skeptics"—opposition to all the teleological views is most vividly explicit. This school is also known as Lokāyata, literally "those attached to the ways of the world."

Cārvāka philosophers were materialists in the sense that they believed that physical matter is the only reality. They maintained that we can know only what we perceive through our senses, which is limited to physical things. Thus they were motivated to attack the religious positions prominent in their time. However, the concepts of nonphysical things like the soul were not their primary target, but rather the validity of inference. The Materialists rejected inference, and for this reason they were commonly referred to as skeptics.

To elaborate, the Cārvākas attack ideas of an immortal soul, rebirth, God, a mystical enlightenment or liberation, and other notions by first arguing that inferential reasoning cannot establish anything. That is to say, by showing that inference is unreliable whatever the topic, these skeptics would strip away all excesses of belief beyond the simple facts of pleasure and pain and the body. The body exists in an inexplicable material world.

Opponents retort that the Cārvāka attack is self-defeating, for it utilizes the very processes of thinking that it aims to show invalid. The Cārvāka response is that the burden of proof is on the other side.

Cārvāka philosophers provoke innovations in the theories of their rivals; they assume a historical position like that of Nāgārjuna and his Mādhyamika followers, although the Cārvākas have no truck with the discipline of the Middle Way. The Cārvākas are also good at poking fun at the pious and the religiously pretentious. Ridicule in their hands is as effective a tool as argument. For example, Cārvākas are reported as asking why, if, as the Brahmins and Exegetes asserted, the soul of the beast slain in a religious sacrifice goes to heaven, does the sacrificer not offer up his own father.

There has come down to us only one complete text belonging to this school, but there are quotations attributed to Cārvākas within the works of philosophers opposed to the Skeptics' views. In fact, Cārvākas are so often mentioned that it seems right to suppose that there were many more of their persuasion than the fact of the survival of a single text would suggest by itself. In ancient and classical times, manuscripts were written on dried palm leaves, and had to be recopied about every century or so not to be lost. That Cārvāka texts have been lost may be due to the nature of Cārvāka positions: With skeptical arguments and antireligious views, copying texts perhaps did not seem so imperative as with a great guru proclaiming a "supreme personal good."

Atomism and Realist "Logic"

Our introductory survey of classical Indian philosophies closes with the views of Atomism (Vaiśeṣika) and Logic (Nyāya). The two schools were unified by Udayana (ca. 1000) as "Nyāya," though Naiyāyikas ("Logicians") before him had accepted, at least implicitly, key Vaiśeṣika positions. Here I shall consider the unified school and follow the practice, post-Udayana, of referring to it simply as Logic (Nyāya).

Nyāya is in effect a nonteleological worldview, in the sense explained previously, although at least lip service is usually paid to the importance of various *summum bonum* conceptions—with particular ideas of "enlightenment" and "liberation" sometimes explicitly embraced, especially in the early period. Still, the philosophers of this school seem to lose interest in the topic. One should not think that even the late Logicians are opposed to the various traditional views of enlightenment or liberation, but rather that they are not eager to dispute them, being absorbed in other concerns. However, in some instances, a firm commitment to a *realism* about the objects of perception (including "qualities" and "class concepts," as will be explained) does set the Logicians in evident opposition to and controversy with philosophers of mystic camps. Debate between Logicians and dialectical Advaita Vedāntins becomes heated in the late classical age.

According to scholars with a sympathy for current analytic philosophy, the Nyāya system is the outstanding achievement of Indian classical reflection. Clearly there is much coalescence with the logic, epistemology, ontology, and philosophy of language that has dominated the Anglo-American tradition for almost the entire twentieth century. Some scholars see these coalescences as a refutation of the relativism and antirationalism of those who see Western traditions as incurably ethnocentric. Such judgments are likely premature. Nevertheless, with its amazing breadth of doctrine, its longevity (more than eighteen centuries), and its increasing refinement over the years—including innovations in logic, epistemology, ontology, the philosophy of language, rational theology, rhetoric, and informal logic—Logic-Atomism (Nyāya-Vaiśeṣika) is indeed a multi-dimensional worldview, a system unparalleled, I confess I agree, for its completeness in its native context (only Dharmakīrti's Buddhist Logic and late Mīmāṃsā show nearly the same breadth and refinement). But it is also the school that, *except* among professional scholars of Indian systems, is probably the least well known.

The *Vaiśeṣika-sūtra* is the earliest text (ca. 100 C.E.), though the *Nyāya-sūtra* is also quite old (ca. 150). On both these "root texts," extensive commentaries were written until late in the classical age. The commentaries reflect the movements and concerns of a wide range of philosophic efforts of their individual times: Dignāga's innovations in logic, Dharmakīrti's criterion for the real, errors in Mīmāṃsaka views, and so on. Though, as indicated, we shall look at the Logicians' positions as they had evolved by the middle and late periods, from Udayana (ca. 1000) and later, let me stress that some of these have *not* changed much from the original articulations of the *Nyāya-sūtra* or *Vaiśeṣika-sūtra*. Other positions are greatly refined, or are simply absent from those early texts.

Let us begin with the more distinctively Vaiśeṣika side of the combined school; namely, the theory of "categories" or "types of things to which words refer" (Skt: *padārtha*). When we talk about things, refer to them, point them out, describe them and say what they are like, what in general are we talking about, and what are the ways available to us to say anything about them at all? The answer—which becomes greatly elaborated—is that most generally there seem to be three basic types of existent: (1) substances, noncomposite substances such as the atoms of fire, earth, water, and so on, and composite substances such as rocks, trees, houses, and individuals we know like Devadatta; (2) qualities, such as color, size, weight, and shape, which, although they always appear *in* or qualifying particular substances, do seem to be a radically different kind of thing (the Buddhists vehemently dispute this position); and (3) motions, such as moving straight ahead, upward, and so on. Though motions are like qualities in that they appear in individual substances, they have causal effects that qualities by themselves do not have, bringing about conjunctions and disjunctions, for example.

Now these three may be the most general types of thing that we talk about. But there must be other categories as well, things that do not "exist" in the way substances, qualities, and motions do, but that do certain work for us when we say anything. For example, when we say "This pot is blue," the pot is a substance and blue is a quality. But what does *is* mean? Another way of asking the same question is to say, "What relates the blue to the pot?" The answer the realist Logicians give is that it is (4) "inherence" (*samavāya*), a special ontic glue that binds qualities to substances, likewise motions, and we may even say that substances inhere in other substances. A piece of cloth inheres in its threads, and the threads in what make them up, all the way down to the atoms. So substances also inhere in substances. The pile of rice inheres in the individual grains.

But that's not all we talk about, or implicitly assume, when we say certain things. There are also (5) universals; otherwise we would not be able to identify the categories identified so far (more precisely, the first three), since we are dealing in generalities. When we talk about substances as a *padārtha* ("category"), we are talking about substances in general, not just a collection of pots, pieces of cloth, and so on. Also, when we say "Bessie is a cow," we mean the same thing as when we say "Bessie has cowness." (The abstraction generators in Sanskrit, chiefly the suffixes "*-tva*" and "*-tā*," have the same meaning as "-ness" and "-hood" in English. They are used in analysis to identify the generality of an expression.) Universals inhere in substances, qualities, and motions, but not in inherence or in universals; otherwise there would be an "infinite regress" (Skt: *anavasthā*). The topic of universals, or class concepts, is much debated, particularly with Buddhists. The Logicians are not platonists—there are no uninstanced universals dwelling apart from the individuals that are their instances—but universals are a separate category, and thus in a sense a separate real. They are directly given in perception insofar as their instances are perceived—according to Logicians of all periods. Indeed, we come to know individuals only through the general, repeatable characteristics they present. Substances, qualities, and motions are, in contrast, individuals. Inherence is repeatable, according to most; some very late Logicians see inherence as infinitely particular, different with every two *relata* related.

Another basic category is (6) the "individualizer" (Skt: *viśeṣa*). No scholar has given a convincing justification for the inclusion of this, and not even the classical defenders of the system pay much attention to it. In the earliest texts, individualizers seem to be considered simply as correlate to universals, and thus, together, a species-genus relation. Later, the reason for positing individualizers as a separate type of thing appears to be that otherwise individual atoms all of the same type (water, for example) would be identical; maybe a better translation of *viśeṣa* would be "numeralizer" (the difficult problem of how atoms were thought of in relation to time and space is involved in this question of interpretation).

Finally, we need the category of (7) "absence," or "negative facts," for how else would it be possible to deny anything? When we say that there is not an elephant in the room, what do we mean except that there is an absence of an elephant here, or that the statement "There is an elephant in the room" is false? We do make denials, and this category explains how it is possible that we do, Nyāya-Vaiśeṣika claims.

With this "ontology" as background, many Logicians concern themselves principally with issues in the theory of knowledge. They identify and elaborate four "justifiers" or "means to true belief" (Skt: *pramāṇa*): (1) perception, (2) inference, (3) analogical acquisition of vocabulary, and (4) expert testimony. The nature and scope of the first two of these four absorb much more reflection in the texts than the last two, with the views of others, such as the Buddhists, contended.

Expert testimony is defended as irreducible to perception and inference (unlike, for example, personal memory). An example would be that when I tell you something you did not before know, for example, that I have a dog named Malone, you know it through my testimony insofar as I am an *āpta*, an "authority" on the subject. The question is then what in general makes a person an expert. The answer usually given is that it is, first, knowing and, second, having no reason to lie or mislead. (Advaitins such as Śrīharṣa attack this as circular and begging the question.)

The stock example of analogical acquisition of vocabulary is a person, P, being told that a *gavaya* (a kind of water buffalo) is like a cow except in certain specified respects. When encountering the creature, P is able to identify it and use its conventional name through the analogical understanding P acquired. There is some dispute as to whether this "means of knowledge" is reducible to the other three, but let us move on to other topics central to the Realist tribe.

No position is more central in the late period than the nature and scope of inference. But because the issues and discussion are quite technical, we must be content with only a broad outline. According to Nyāya, any good inference must have premises that are themselves justified. The Logicians do not distinguish between a formally "valid" deductive argument (which may or may not contain premises known to be false) and deductive arguments that are "cogent" (with no unjustified premises and no errors in the logic). Though the theory abstracts from all actual employment, it is held that any good inference has to have a conclusion about the real world, a conclusion, that is, that should be believed because the premises should be believed (for whatever different reasons) and because a rule of inference is correctly used. Here is an example of inference:

(0) There is fire on yonder hill. (The conclusion to be proved. How? Because:)

(1) There is smoke rising from it. (We are justified in believing this because we *see* the smoke. And:)

(2) Wherever there's smoke, there's fire. (We are justified in believing this because of wide experience of positive correlations such as of smoke and fire in the kitchens of our own homes, and negative correlations such as of the absence of smoke on a lake where there is an absence of fire. And:)

(3) This smoke-possessing hill is an example of the "wherever" of the general rule, "Wherever . . ." (Therefore:)
(4) There is fire on yonder hill.

It is a mistake to say, as some modern scholars have said, that this logic is only "inductive." No, it is deductive, in the sense that the premises guarantee the conclusion—albeit the premises are arrived at inductively. Indeed, *the* crucial premise in an inference is that expressing a "pervasion" (Skt: *vyāpti*) between two things, *x* and *y*—in the example above, premise (2), which is known through wide experience. Pervasions or concomitances are of different sorts, but they obtain in nature, such as that between the smoke-possessing and the fire-possessing. Regarding precisely how these relations that underpin inferences are known, the Logicians both develop a "logic of discovery" concerning causal relations and defend views about universals being directly perceived.

The Advaitin Śrīharṣa (ca. 1150)—and other Advaitins later on—abuse the Logician understanding of a "cognition," a theory crucial to much of the entire Nyāya philosophy. One line of his criticism goes like this:

> You Logicians say that each and every cognition, even the simplist, has a so-called logical structure, which can be analyzed. So when I point to the pot and say "pot," this is, according to you, just shorthand for "This thing presented in perception has potness." And you would go on to argue that the particular is given in perception, and the "potness" as well. But what about the "has"? You say it reflects inherence—potness inheres in the pot—but what a peculiar notion! What is its source? Not perception: no person not already confused by your theories ever says he perceives an inherence. If you say "inference," that won't do, because . . . [and Śrīharṣa here gives seven or eight refutations matching what he takes to be all the available avenues of response]. And there are other problems as well. What are you going to say when I inquire about the meaning of your reply, "This potness-exhibiting-thing *has* inherence as the exhibitor." What could the "has" mean here? And if you tell me, I'll have another question about the "has" of your reply (or about whatever connector you try to use). I am sorry, but there is no way I (or anyone else!) can understand what you insist on trying to say. Probably it would be best that you not try to say it; keep quiet with your convoluted cogitations and contemplate Brahman instead!

The "New Logicians"—that is, as explained in the history section, those advocates of the combined Nyāya-Vaiśeṣika school beginning with Gaṅgeśa (ca. 1300) who rethink all the old theories under the force of Śrīharṣa's onslaught—make here an ingenious response. They admit that with any cognition there is something that is necessarily unsaid and implicit only. What is cognized is verbalizable except in this part. And even this, the "mode" of the cognitive episode, can by reflection be made explicit and can be expressed in a corresponding statement one level up. But the cognition and statement whereby *it* would be expressed would have another element that would necessarily be only implicit. "We Logicians will play this game as long as you like. There may be a regress that in principle cannot have an end. But so what? By reflection, we can identify all that in any particular case we need to explain what we mean." (Gadādhara in the seventeenth century is especially good in elaborating this answer.) Of course, it is dubious that Śrīharṣa would be convinced. Surely several Advaitin followers of his are unswayed.

Finally, the Logicians at times devote themselves to trying to prove the existence of God. For the most part, or at least in most periods, these philosophers are theists, with much in common with the Vedāntic theists already discussed. But "mystical experience" and the revelations of the Upanishads are not so much the Logicians' avowed reasons for their theistic views, unlike what the theistic Vedāntins claim; rather the Logicians say that it is "rational" considerations that ground their belief in God—such as, "How do you explain otherwise the fact that the world appears designed?" Moreover, the Logician theists seem more "inclusivist" than their Vedāntic counterparts. For example, the great Udayana opens a long work devoted exclusively to the case for God with the claim that what each and every individual sect sees as the Supreme (Brahman with the Advaitins, the unattached "pure conscious being" with the Yogins, the Buddha in his Bliss with the Buddhists, and so on) is nothing other than the One God whose existence he, on other grounds, is about to prove. Many of the arguments advanced are similar to arguments found in the history of Western rational theology, but some are peculiar to the Indian context.

Rhetoric—including informal logic (with lists of commonly committed fallacies and analyses of why they are erroneous) along with the presuppositions of conversation and debate—is another rich area of Nyāya reflection. Here the Logicians anticipate much recent work in semantics and the philosophy of language. But with this, as with several other areas that are addressed by proponents of the system, I must refer readers to the Guide to Further Reading at the end of this chapter.

The Contemporary Relevance of Indian Philosophies

A leading twentieth-century Anglo-American philosopher writes, "The history of philosophy is the *lingua franca* which makes communication between philosophers, at least of different points of view, possible" (Wilfred Sellars, *Science and Metaphysics* [London, Routledge & Kegan Paul, 1968], p. 1). Most probably he has in mind the traditions of philosophy preserved in Greek, Latin, German, French, and English and perhaps two or three other languages, all Western. But of course, the history of philosophy is much broader, as this volume amply attests. Still, the point is a good one. Contemporary philosophy uses the ideas wrought in the past as the currency of present business, as the tools of ongoing discussion and debate. Even someone advancing an entirely original position on an issue that is itself new perforce draws on an understanding of the history of philosophy to express it and to argue in its defense. A much more diverse tool kit containing implements forged in a *world* history will be carried by the philosophy professionals of the future. Philosophy has a world history, and it is inevitable that it will become better known. At present, the prime relevance of the ancient and classical philosophies of the South Asian subcontinent is probably just their part in the broad history of philosophy worldwide. Many academics in the United States and Europe and around the globe simply have not been exposed to traditions of critical thought, argument, and speculation other than those preserved in the languages of the West. In the future, I expect that the Indian schools will be studied the world over and that the issues and positions that exercised the great minds of the Indian past will be valued resources for continuing research and debate.

So, standing as we are at the doorway of a much larger mansion and storehouse of treasures of philosophic effort than anyone anywhere imagined a century ago, I hesitate now to specify areas and achievements within the long and complex history of views and arguments first expressed in Sanskrit that hold out special relevance for contemporary philosophic inquiry. The deep channels of the history of philosophy are formed by the responses of new generations of philosophers to earlier work, that is to say, by the value, the insights and errors, the relevance and irrelevance that fresh thought finds in the philosophy it inherits. It is not for me to dictate what in the Indian traditions is or is not really valuable for current philosophy of language, for example, but rather for the experts in that field once they become apprised of the achievements in the area that are preserved in Sanskrit. The same holds for other individual specializations of contemporary philosophy, where others may speak with far more authority than I. My hope is that the experts can be encouraged to look at the available translations of Sanskrit works that seem relevant. Of course, this process does not move quickly. And it is probably necessary that Sanskrit and other non-Western traditions of philosophy become part of the standard graduate and undergraduate curricula so that future experts will by their basic training know where there are veins to mine. Also, there must be further efforts of translation and exposition of the great works of the past. Efforts not just of scholarship but of defense and championing some of these views are probably necessary before the classical philosophies of the Indian subcontinent can take their rightful place in the global arena. Aristotle would not be widely read today were it not for those who, agreeing with much that he held, championed his views in languages other than Greek in extremely different circumstances and times.

On this last score, much of promise is astir among academics who have learned Sanskrit and who have also mastered much on the contemporary global scene. There are, for example, several first-rate contemporary philosophers, principally of Indian origin, who not only use ideas of classical Nyāya (Logic) to illumine difficult problems of contemporary concern (particularly in logic, epistemology, and ontology, long-standing strengths of Nyāya) but who also directly defend certain Nyāya views. Doubtless, the next few decades will produce more.

Now it seems particularly imperative that such stout bridging between the classical and the modern be built on Indian soil because there and only there are located the centers of traditional Sanskrit learning and the pundits who during the transition to our global society have played—and are playing—the most crucial role in keeping the classical philosophies alive. Traditional punditry seems an endangered occupation, threatened by currents of globalization—economic, linguistic, educational—different from expanding philosophic sensibilities. (To wit, according to some reports, the pundits, or traditional scholars, are experiencing increasing difficulty in attracting young people of ability because of the more lucrative career opportunities in business, medicine, and so forth that are open these days.) Fortunately, much fruitful interaction with academics is occurring within India today. We can only hope that the trend will quicken, prosper, and continue for a century or more.

With the religious and mystical philosophies of ancient and classical India, there are additional factors to consider and other forces at work. Practices of yoga and spiritual disciplines pioneered in India have proliferated at amazing rates in the past few decades throughout the world. And within the subcontinent, traditional religion—with its mix of myth, superstition, *and* profound philosophy—continues to flourish. Probably there is much too much superstition in the religious practices of many in India today, and probably trends of modernization and increasing educational opportunities for the urban poor and in the villages will have effects similar to what they have had in, for example, European societies. But probably what is truly valuable will survive. And I dare say—agreeing with the great figures of what has been called a "Hindu Renaissance"— that the traditional emphasis on an "inner life" can bear the full brunt of the ax of modernity pruning away the superstitions of the past. The extraordinary personal powers and psychological discoveries apparently made possible through yoga and meditation wear on their face great allure, and could conceivably appear more attractive as there becomes less and less to discover about the laws and makeup of the physical world.

This does not mean that the classical philosophies that champion and defend mysticism have to be accepted in their classical forms. No, like all views, their motivations have to be rethought, their claims revised, and their concerns widened and supplemented by other areas of philosophy and science. But revamped and redressed for a new age with wider horizons, the philosophies of a "supreme personal good"—or new philosophies that draw upon them without flying any of the old flags—may well have an important place in the future philosophical world. The day of dogmatic advocacy is passing, though obviously lingering longer in some places than in others. But not everything in traditional religion and spirituality need depend on an unthinking allegiance to survive. For example, in modern Japan, Kitaro Nishida, Keiji Nishitani, Masao Abe, and others of the "Kyoto School" have brought to new life, in a world of global ideas and the triumph of science, Zen and many of the views, perspectives, and practices forged in traditions of Zen. In India, Swami Vivekananda (1863–1902) and Sri Aurobindo (1872–1950) are two "folk Vedāntins" who have no strict allegiance to a school of classical philosophy, though they draw on the Upanishads and other works influenced by yogic mysticism and India's spiritual heritage. Neither of them was a professional academic, but especially with Aurobindo there is a great depth of integration of modern ideas within a philosophy that is oriented by a perception of the value of mystic pursuits. Then there are also innumerable modern academics who present variations on and sophisticated defenses of Advaita. So long as yoga and meditative practices flourish, philosophies that connect them intellectually with other areas of life and human concern will flourish. Again, like all inherited theories, the old mystical worldviews cannot enter the new age unchanged. But yoga and concrete "self-transformative" practices give these views resilience and motivate fresh efforts to keep them current at least in broad outline. No one has been able to explain consciousness and will and all that has to do with the "inner" side of life on strictly materialist suppositions. Thus there is room for continuing efforts to achieve an adequate "spiritual" worldview. Surely the ideas hammered out in the ancient and classical Indian traditions would be important resources here.

APPENDIX A: Guide to Sanskrit Pronunciation

This guide is written for native speakers of English within North America. Closely similar sounds are suggested. A more precise pronunciation guide may be found in any of the many Sanskrit readers and grammars, for example, William Dwight Whitney, *Sanskrit Grammar* (Cambridge, Mass., 1889), pp. 10–26.

N.B. By convention, the names of the consonants add an *a* (Sanskrit *a*) in pronunciation. Thus *y* is pronounced *ya* (like *yu* in *yummy*). Vowels, in contrast, are pronounced exactly as written. Note also that each vowel corresponds to only one sound, unlike in English. With a few exceptions, this is true of consonants as well.

Vowels (omitting two that rarely occur):
a   like *o* in *mother*
ā   like *a* in *father*
i   like *ey* in *pulley*
ī   exactly like Sanskrit *i* except voiced longer: like *ee* in *treed*
u   like *oo* in *moon*
ū   same *oo* sound voiced longer
ṛ   like *rea* in *really* (pronounced while turning the tip of the tongue up
    to touch the palate)
e   like *a* in *crazy*
ai like *i* in *mine*
o   like *o* in *go*
au like *ow* in *cow*

Semivowels (best understood as a particular class of consonants):
y   like *y* in *yummy*
r   like *r* in *rum*
l   like *l* in *love*
v   like *v* in *rover*

Consonants:

Guttural class:
k   like *c* in *cup*
kh exactly like *k* in Sanskrit except aspirated, that is, breath out, as
    with *Kate*
g   like *g* in *gun*
gh another aspirate, same principle as with *kh, g* while breathing out
ṅ   like *n* in *trunk* except more guttural

Palatal class:
c   like *ch* in *chump*
ch another aspirate, same principle
j   like *j* in *jump*
jh aspirated *j*, like *jay*
ñ   like *n* in *canyon*

Lingual class:
ṭ   There is no English equivalent: a *t* sound (as in *tough*), but with the
    tip of the tongue touching the roof of the mouth
ṭh aspirated *ṭ*
ḍ   like *d* in *dump*, but "lingualized" as with *ṭ*
ḍh aspirated *ḍ*
ṇ   lingualized *n* sound

Dental class:
t   like *t* in *tough*
th aspirated *t* (*not* like *th* in *thumb*)

d   like *d* in *done*
dh   aspirated *d*
n   like *n* in *nut*

Labial class:
p   like *p* in *pun*
ph   aspirated *p* (*not* like *ph* in *philosophy*), like *pin*
b   like *b* in *bus*
bh   aspirated *b*
m   like *m* in *mumps*

Sibilants:
ś   like *sh* in *shove*
ṣ   lingualized *sh* sound
s   like *s* in *sun*

And in a class alone:
h   like *h* in *hundred*

Special characters and sounds:
ḥ   "Visarga": calls for breath following a vowel. For example, '*duḥkha*'
     ("pain") is pronounced *du* and then breath (very short) and then
     kha
ṃ   This is shorthand for all nasals, the particular type determined by
     the class of the following consonant. For example, the *ṃ* in
     '*sāṃkhya*' ("analysis") is equivalent to *ṅ*, since *kh* belongs to the
     guttural class. (Do not try to remember this rule; just nasalize.)

APPENDIX B: Glossary of Sanskrit Terms

This glossary is limited to Sanskrit terms—including names of schools
or movements—mentioned in this introductory survey. For a much more
complete glossary, consult John Grimes, *A Concise Dictionary of Indian
Philosophy* (Albany: SUNY, 1989). For a chronology of persons and texts
mentioned, see Appendix C.

Religious and Philosophic Schools and Movements

Advaita Vedānta   One of the most prominent schools of classical
                           philosophy, an Upanishadic monism ("all is
                           brahman," including especially the seemingly
                           individual consciousness or self); sometimes
                           called Illusionism because of its claim that all
                           appearance of fundamental diversity is illu-
                           sory.

Brāhminism	A prominent Indian religion that centers on rituals and liturgies performed by priests called Brāhmins, who are the highest of four principal Hindu castes.
Buddhism	A world religion founded by Siddhārtha Gautama (the Buddha, or the "Awakened One"), who taught that a supreme felicity and end to suffering occur in a special experience termed *nirvāṇa,* along with the "way" to attain it.
Cārvāka	A materialist and skeptical school also known as Lokāyata, "those who follow the way of the world."
Jainism	An ancient Indian religion founded by Mahāvīra, ca. 500 B.C.E., who, like the Buddha, taught a philosophy of a "supreme personal good."
Mādhyamika	The school of philosophic Buddhism founded by Nāgārjuna; sometimes called Buddhist Mysticism or Buddhist Absolutism.
Mahāyāna	Northern Buddhism, the "Great Vehicle."
Mīmāṃsā	"Exegesis," the classical school most closely tied to Brāhminism.
Navya-Nyāya	"New Logic," the revolutionary Realism of Gaṅgeśa (ca. 1300) and his followers.
Nyāya	"Logic," the Realist school prominent throughout the classical period, combined with Vaiśeṣika in the later centuries; focused on issues in epistemology but took positions on a wide range of philosophic topics; proponents are called Naiyāyikas.
Sāṃkhya	"Analysis," an early school of Indian philosophy concerned with achieving a "supreme personal good" through psychological disidentification.
Theistic Vedānta	Any of several schools of classical Vedānta espousing a concept of God (*īśvara*), and usually grounding their outlook in teachings of the *Bhagavadgītā* as well as various Upanishads.
Theravāda	"The Doctrine of the (Buddhist) Elders," an early school of philosophic Buddhism, appearing in the Southern canon.
Vaiśeṣika	"Atomism," a classical philosophy focusing on ontological issues ("What kinds of things are there?") and defending a realist view of mate-

	rial things as composed of atoms; later combined with Nyāya.
Vedānta	Originally an epithet for the Upanishads; in the classical period, any of several schools defending Upanishadic views, e.g., Advaita and Theistic Vedānta.
Yoga	A classical philosophy of a "supreme personal good" much like Sāṃkhya but proposing various exercises of "self-discipline" (i.e., *yoga*) as the means thereto.
Yogācāra	"Buddhist Idealism" conveniently divided into (A) Early and (B) Late, or Buddhist Logic: Buddhist Logicians (Dignāga, Dharmakīrti, and their followers) propose a much more advanced epistemology concerning worldly knowledge and are less concerned with the concept of a "storehouse consciousness" than are their Early Yogācāra predecessors.

Terms

ahiṃsā	noninjury.
ālayavijñāna	"storehouse consciousness"; a principal concept in early Yogācāra.
anātman	"no self," or "no soul"; an important Buddhist doctrine.
anavasthā	"infinite regress"; a mark of conceptual inadequacy according to some classical philosophers.
āpta	an expert; a person whose testimony is reliable.
arhat	the "saint" who, according to Theravāda Buddhism, has realized Nirvāṇa.
ārya	noble, high-minded; a term used by Sanskrit-speaking tribes invading the subcontinent in the second millennium B.C.E. to refer to themselves.
āsana	various stretching exercises taught as part of some disciplines of *yoga*.
ātman	self or soul; the Upanishadic term for an individual's true or most basic consciousness.
avatāra	Divine Incarnation.
avidyā	spiritual ignorance; in much Vedānta, lack of direct awareness of *brahman* or God.

bādha	experiential "sublation," as a veridical perception of a rope correcting an illusory perception of a snake.
bodhisattva	the enlightened being who turns back from an utter extinction of personality in the bliss of a final Nirvāṇa out of compassion for every sentient being; a key concept of Mahāyāna.
brahman	the "Absolute"; the key concept of the Upanishads according to a prominent group of commentators.
brahma-sākṣātkāra	immediate awareness of the Absolute; a synonym, according to some, for *brahmavidyā*.
brahma-vidyā	knowledge of the Absolute (or of God).
buddha	the awakened; an epithet of Siddhārtha Gautama, the founder of Buddhism, after his enlightenment.
citta-vṛtti-nirodha	cessation of the fluctuations of mentality; the definition of *yoga* given by the *Yoga-sūtra*.
dharma	(1) right living, right religious practice; (2) quality or state of consciousness.
guṇa	strand of nature; there are three of these according to Sāṃkhya: (1) light and intelligence, (2) activity and passion, and (3) inertia and darkness.
karma	"action"; psychological disposition to act in a certain manner accrued through previous actions; habit.
īśvara	God.
jīvan-mukti	"living liberation"; a person's knowledge of the Absolute or God, and "liberation" from all entanglement in the world while alive, according to some schools of Vedānta.
līlā	play, divine play; a prominent concept in theistic Vedānta understood to capture God's relation to the world.
marga	a path or way deemed to lead to a person's greatest good.
māyā	illusion, cosmic illusion.
mukti	liberation, salvation.
nāma-rūpa	"name and form"; individuation.
nirvāṇa	extinction (of suffering); enlightenment.
padārtha	category, "type of thing to which words refer"; a central Vaiśeṣika concept.
parama-puruṣa-artha	supreme personal good.

pāramitā	perfection; there are six moral and spiritual perfections exhibited by a Bodhisattva, according to Mahāyāna Buddhism.
prakṛti	Nature; a principal Sāṃkhya concept.
pramāṇa	justifier, means to true belief.
prāṇāyāma	breath control.
puruṣa	"individual conscious being" according to both Sāṃkhya and Yoga.
ṛta	the cosmic "Law" or "Order"; a Vedic concept.
saccidānanda	(Absolute) Existence-Consciousness-Bliss, a popular Vedāntic characterization of *brahman*.
samādhi	mystic or yogic trance.
samavāya	inherence; an important category for Nyāya-Vaiśeṣika.
satyagraha	"holding fast to the truth"; the byword of Mahatma Gandhi's civil disobedience movement.
śiṣya	student.
soma	a psychotropic plant used in shamanic practices during Vedic times.
sūtra	literally "thread"; a philosophic aphorism.
tattva	principle of being or reality; there are twenty-four of these according to Sāṃkhya.
vāsanā	subliminal impulses, karma.
vijñapti-mātra	"consciousness only"; the central doctrine of Early Yogācāra Buddhism.
viśeṣa	individualizer or numeralizer; the Vaiśeṣika concept of that which differentiates atoms of the same type (e.g., water).
vyāpti	pervasion, invariable concomitance; a factual relation that grounds inference according to Nyāya.
yoga	self-discipline.

APPENDIX C: A Chronology of Selected Works and Authors

Ṛg Veda   1200–900 B.C.E.
                                   (excluding the 10th book)

N.B. Individual Indian authors of the past two millennia can usually be dated accurately to within a century. But many Indian texts, especially of the older period, have undergone layer upon layer of expansion and revision; in such cases the *termini a quo et ad quem* must be very widely spaced.

Early Upanishads	800–300 B.C.E.
Middle and late Upanishads	ca. 300 B.C.E.–1500 C.E.
The Buddha (Siddhārtha Gautama)	ca. 500 B.C.E.
Mahāvīra (founder of Jainism)	ca. 500 B.C.E.
Southern Buddhist Canon	ca. 300–200 B.C.E.
Mahābhārata (the "Great Indian Epic"):	
earliest portion	ca. 500 B.C.E.
latest portion	400+ C.E.
Bhagavadgītā	
earliest portion	200 B.C.E.
latest portion	400 C.E.
Prajñāpāramitā	100 B.C.E.–800 C.E.
(Mahāyāna "scriptures")	
Mimāṃsāsūtra	200 B.C.E.–200 C.E.
Brahmasūtra	200 B.C.E.–200 C.E.
Vaiśeṣikasūtra	ca. 100 C.E.
Nāgārjuna (Mādhyamika)	150 C.E.
Nyāyasūtra	ca. 200
Yogasūtra	300–400 (final redaction)
Asaṅga (early Yogācāra)	fl. 350 (?)
Vasubandhu (early Yogācāra)	fl. 360
Sāṃkhyakārikā	ca. 375
Vātsyāyana (Nyāya)	fl. 410
Dignāga (Buddhist Logic)	ca. 550
Dharmakīrti (Buddhist Logic)	fl. 625
Kumārila (Mīmāṃsā)	fl. 660
Prabhākara (Mīmāṃsā)	fl. 700
Śaṅkara (Advaita)	ca. 700–750
Jayarāśi (Cārvāka)	ca. 750
Vācaspati Miśra (chiefly Advaita and Nyāya)	fl. 960
Udayana (Nyāya-Vaiśeṣika)	975–1050
Śrīharṣa (Advaita)	ca. 1150
Gaṅgeśa (Navya-Nyāya)	fl. 1325
Vardhamāna (Navya-Nyāya)	fl. 1360
Raghunātha Śiromaṇi (Navya-Nyāya)	ca. 1500
Madhusūdana Sarasvatī (Advaita)	ca. 1600
Gadādhara (Navya-Nyāya)	ca. 1650
Vivekananda	1863–1902
Gandhi	1869–1948
Aurobindo	1872–1950

Guide to Further Reading

Dasgupta, Suredranath. *A History of Indian Philosophy*. 5 vols. Cambridge: Cambridge University Press, 1922+; Delhi: Motilal Banarsidass,

1975 + . This remains one of the best surveys of classical Indian philosophies, though the later volumes are disproportionately concerned with late religious philosophies, with Navya-Nyāya given short shrift. Vol. I is particularly useful as a general survey of the principal schools. Dasgupta is a master not only of the classical philosophies but of fluid English prose.

Deutsch, Eliot. *Advaita Vedānta: A Philosophic Reconstruction.* Honolulu: East-West Center Press, 1969. An excellent introduction to the principal themes and arguments of Advaita, this book achieves a remarkable overview given its brevity (119 pages).

Eliade, Mircea. *Yoga: Immortality and Freedom.* Princeton, N.J.: Princeton University Press, 1969. This is a sympathetic survey of Yoga philosophy as well as of the influence of yogic psychology and techniques on other schools. It may also be the best overall introduction to Indian mysticism.

Koller, John. *The Indian Way.* Albany: SUNY Press, 1982. Koller focuses on the religious philosophies, providing context in social practices at some cost to doctrinal details. This is almost as much an introduction to Indian religions as it is to the philosophies, though doctrines are Koller's chief concern. The book could be used in a course on world religions for high school seniors.

Matilal, B. K. *Perception.* Oxford: Oxford University Press, 1986; Delhi: Motilal Banarsidass, 1987. Matilal commands the traditions of Western philosophy as well as of Indian philosophy to an extraordinary degree. In this book, he mounts a sophisticated defense of key classical Naiyāyika positions in epistemology, ontology, and philosophy of language. Though it is not a book for a beginner, any serious student of the issues that Nyāya addresses should read it. It presupposes no familiarity with either Sanskrit or Indian traditions.

Murti, T.V.R. *The Central Philosophy of Buddhism.* A highly influential study of Buddhist Mādhyamika, this book focuses on both the religious, or mystical, dimension of Nāgārjuna's thought and his philosophic "dialectic." In the final part (out of three), Murti makes comparisons with prominent Western philosophies and defends the Mādhyamika system against objections.

Potter, Karl. Series Editor (as well as volume editor for Volumes I, II, and III). *Encyclopedia of Indian Philosophies.* Princeton, N.J.: Princeton University Press; Delhi: Motilal Banarsidass, 1970 + . Four volumes of this watershed project have so far appeared. Vol. I: *Bibliography.* This is *the* most indispensable work for research on Indian philosophies. Vol. II: *Indian Metaphysics and Epistemology: The Tradition of Nyāya-Vaiśeṣika up to Gaṅgeśa.* Potter's long introduction is written for students of philosophy in general and not for the specialist. But the summaries of classical works appearing in the second part (some written by Potter but most by other scholars) presuppose in many instances a thorough familiarity with the classical philosophic scene. Vol. III: *Advaita Vedānta through Śaṅkara and His Pupils.* Potter has himself written most of the summaries here, as well as another long and illuminating introduction. Vol. IV: *Sāṃkhya,* ed. Gerald Larson and Ram Shankar Bhattacharya. Larson's introduction is both lucid and thorough. The summaries are in some cases extensive.

Potter, Karl. *Guide to Indian Philosophy.* Boston: G. K. Hall, 1988. This book comprises a much more complete and detailed "Guide to Further Reading" than is provided here. Potter includes scholarly articles, translations, and books of criticism and interpretation in his purview. This is a book that would prove particularly useful to instructors, but the characterizations that Potter provides are accessible to beginning readers as well.

Radhakrishnan, Sarvepalli, and Charles A. Moore. Editors. *A Source Book in Indian Philosophy.* Princeton, N.J.: Princeton University Press, 1957. Unfortunately, this is the only collection of translations ranging widely over the schools of classical philosophy. Thus it is practically an essential text for beginning students who want to go beyond the secondary material to the original works. The book also includes selections from the modern thinkers Radhakrishnan and Aurobindo. The translations are on the whole good, but the introductions the editors provide are sometimes too brief and even—though only very occasionally—misleading.

Raju, P. T. *Structural Depths of Indian Philosophy.* Albany: SUNY Press, 1985. As a wide-ranging, readable, and reflective introduction to Indian philosophies, this book rivals Dasgupta's volumes. Informed by recent scholarship, it is—despite its relative brevity—in several instances an advance.

Warder, A. K. *Indian Buddhism.* Delhi: Motilal Banarsidass, 1970. This has become in effect *the* standard introductory work on Indian Buddhist philosophies as well as on the history of Buddhism within the subcontinent.

9

Esoteric Philosophy

Robert A. McDermott

Like other chapters in this book, this chapter sounds a minor note, a counterposition, an alternative perspective, a philosophically unorthodox point of view relative to the contents of most introductory philosophy texts. And, like the other chapters, this minor status relative to modern Western philosophical orthodoxy is not intended to mean lower or less: In its own right, *esoteric* is a worthy adjective, indicating a more difficult and more specialized kind of philosophy than the usual "phil 101" fare. By definition, esoteric means knowledge available only to a small group of initiated seekers, and consequently regarded as *secret*.

Whereas most, if not all, philosophy courses emphasize critical thinking about large fundamental questions concerning knowledge and truth, human nature and morality, God and religion, history and society, a course or text in esoteric philosophy would invite the student to consider a change in thinking, and a change in character, as a way to attain a deeper kind of knowledge. This is not a boast: Philosophers who do not study or teach esoteric philosophy choose not to do so because they are convinced that ordinary philosophy goes as deep as it is reasonable to go—and beyond that lies neither truth nor meaning, but only confusion and danger.

In addition to its risky and controversial attempt to begin where ordinary philosophy leaves off, this chapter on esoteric philosophy is slightly more unusual than the chapters on the philosophies of Africa, China, or India in that esoteric philosophy does not reside exclusively, or even primarily, within a particular culture. Esoteric philosophy is to be found as a minority presence in all, or nearly all, cultures, from ancient to contemporary times. This chapter will focus on the esoteric in the history of Western philosophy, but it could be written equally well with respect to any of the other philosophical traditions under discussion here.

Given that it is transcultural, we might imagine esoteric philosophy to be a subdiscipline such as ethics, aesthetics, or the philosophy of religion, but again esoteric philosophy is an exception: It is not so much a discipline within philosophy—such as ethics and political philosophy—as it is a different kind of philosophy. A philosopher, Plato, for instance, can philosophize esoterically at one moment and exoterically at another; his philosophy can be part esoteric, part exoteric.

An analogy might be: Esotericism is to philosophy as mysticism—the immediate experience of a divine unifying presence—is to religion. For the mystic, and for most students and followers of various mystics, mysticism is the essential center of religion; for most people in religion, however, mystics and their mysticism are entirely "other," out of reach and unintelligible. Similarly, for the esoteric philosopher, and student thereof, the esoteric is what it is "really about," the only reliable source of knowledge and truth, of which all other knowledge is but a pale reflection. Most authors of philosophy books as well as professors and students—though decidedly more professors than students—regard esoteric philosophy as unreliable and unscientific and, therefore, not representative of true knowledge.

By including a chapter on esoteric philosophy, this book is in effect saying that we need to study not only the philosophies of other cultures but also another *kind* of philosophy, one that builds on different assumptions and experiences and uses a method different from that used in modern Western philosophies. As we will see, esoteric philosophy is in important respects closer to the values and methods of other philosophies, the so-called non-Western philosophies. Although this chapter will focus on esoteric philosophy as we find it in the West, in the end we will look at the relationships, by way of comparisons, between Western esotericism and the philosophies presented in the other chapters, all of which are concerned with exoteric materials, exoterically presented.

One of the most important tasks in philosophy is defining the key terms and then working them until they take on a certain energy of their own. In the *Oxford English Dictionary, esoteric* is defined as follows:

> Of philosophical doctrines, treatises, modes of speech, etc.: designed for, or appropriate to, an inner life of advanced or privileged disciples; communicated to, or intelligible by, the initiated exclusively. Hence the disciples: Belonging to the inner circle, admitted to the esoteric teaching. Opposed to exoteric.

This same authoritative dictionary also indicates that in ordinary conversation, *esoteric* means "obscure." So, in their letter inviting the authors of this book to write for college students, the editors urged us to avoid esoteric vocabulary. In this sentence, *esoteric* is used in a new, more popular meaning—"highly technical." In effect, the editors are saying: "Don't use vocabulary familiar only to those 'initiated' into the 'secrets' of esoteric philosophical terminology."

At the outset of this chapter, readers might want to ask the editors of this book, and me, as author of this chapter, how we intend to present a nonesoteric, nonsecret, and nontechnical exposition of esoteric philosophy! The answer must be that this chapter is a pointing. It is like a book about music; it can lead the reader to, and a little bit through, music, but it cannot supply the music. It says: Try to go beyond your ordinary thinking; try to imagine what Plato saw; and try to transform your thinking into a kind of intellectual "seeing."

As should be expected, I deal here for the most part with the advantages of esoteric philosophy, but the disadvantages must also be acknowledged and evaluated. Obviously, few if any of us would be studying philosophy if the only method were the esoteric. A book such as *From Africa to Zen* would be inconceivable if that were the case. The only philosophy that would be taught anywhere in the world would be the philosophy of the master philosopher, the philosophical sage, the guru, the spiritual-philosophical master. Not only would there be no books presenting a variety of philosophical teachings; there would be no philosophy books at all!

This book is an example of exotericism in that it aims to bring philosophical teachings to the largest possible number of readers, probably few of whom will strive to develop the kind of receptive consciousness that was once required of all those who heard the teachings here summarized. Yet it represents a dramatic exception to virtually all other introductions to philosophy precisely in that it presents philosophical traditions that still honor the esoteric dimension. More than any other tradition, the Western identifies philosophy with the exoteric, with reason, with argument, with democratic inquiry—and with the exclusion of the esoteric.

All the other traditions presented in this book—at least to the extent that they have not succumbed to the approach of philosophy characteristic of the West—include teachers, schools, and practices that are closer to the method of Pythagoras than to that of Aristotle. All the philosophical traditions outside the Greek, particularly the Aristotelian model, include some amount of the esoteric and some recognition of the significant, and perhaps essential, relation between philosophy and inner schooling.

What difference would it make if the authors of the chapters in this book were known to have received such a training? For a standard chapter on nonesoteric Western philosophy, a philosophic author would be expected to be trained in the history of philosophy and in philosophical thinking, with little regard for his or her inner life or spiritual discipline. For standard Western philosophy, whether oriented toward historical or contemporary questions, there is simply no room for the kind of esoteric training given to the students of Pythagoras, the sixth-century-B.C. mathematician and spiritual teacher.

True esoteric teachers revealed their teachings only to students who would understand and respect them. It was to protect the purity of the teachings that esoteric teachers carefully screened their students and did not teach them in advance of their capacity to understand and use practices and ideas that were known to be transformative. Esoteric teachers were convinced that uninitiated students—or, in modern times, the general reader—would use presumably profound teachings for selfish or ignorant purposes. This is exactly what has happened: Despite the efforts of these teachers, and no doubt the vast majority of their students, esoteric teachings, particularly in the present century, have been rendered exoteric.

The democratic impulse has prevailed. And this, of course, has mostly been a great contribution to individual and cultural growth: Had the esoteric not given way to the exoteric, most of us would know nothing about the esoteric. And, since at one time all philosophy was esoteric, were it not for the development of the exoteric, we would not know any philosophy at all, either esoteric or exoteric. By traveling, in effect, from esoteric to exoteric, philosophy is now in a position to view, from an exotic vantage point, the widest possible range of exoteric philosophies—all the ideas that, since Aristotle, have been in principle (though obviously not in fact) available to everyone. (Because of the greater availability of higher education, it is safe to estimate that more people have studied Plato and Aristotle in the United States over the past fifty years than in the entire world during the previous twenty-three centuries.)

The way to the esoteric is partly through the exoteric. Anyone who is willing to read, listen to, and think about philosophical ideas can then decide to look beyond, or behind, the exoteric to the esoteric, to the teachings recently made available even though intended for a privileged few. While we should be amazed, and perhaps grateful, that profound teachings once jealously guarded and available only at the expense of great personal sacrifice are now blithely summarized in college textbooks, we need to admit a negative side of this radically new opportunity: because of the democratization and popularization process, what we and other unschooled students know of the esoteric—for example, the contents of this chapter—is almost certainly thin and corrupt compared with the original, undiluted esoteric teachings.

We can be grateful to know something, however secondhand, of the great teachings of the Indian *rsis,* African and Native American shamans, Taoist healers, and other esoteric teacher-practitioners who have been published and popularized for the first time in the past half century, but this democratization has also had the expected, and perhaps necessary, result—widespread misinterpretation, misrepresentation, confusion, dissolution of the teachings, and prejudicial ridicule. The esoteric invites ridicule as well as suspicion and skepticism because, from the vantage point of the exoteric, and the ideal of the exoteric, there is something wrong about communicating truth to a privileged few. But if there is something really demanding about philosophy, so that truth comes only to those who serve it by personal effort, discipline, and sacrifice, then a survey by an outsider cannot claim to offer anything like a true account. This chapter is in trouble from the outset because there is something inherently wrong about an admittedly exoteric account of esoteric philosophy. I repeat, this can only be a pointing.

While these references to special states of consciousness might seem alienating to our democratic and homogenized understanding of teaching, learning, and truth, except for the philosophical tradition that began in classical Greece and has flourished over the past three centuries in the West, almost all philosophy has been built on this model. The persuasive (not to mention political and economic) power of the West, however, has resulted in the reduction and near elimination of the esoteric dimensions of non-Western philosophies. In fact, it is misleading to use the term *philosophy* for the wisdom traditions of the cultures discussed in this book. We can, of course, define the term as we wish, but it cannot be used univocally for the teachings of these cultures and the teachings of the modern West.

Because very few professors of philosophy are informed as to the esoteric methods of the transmission of wisdom in the premodern West, most tend to miss the uniqueness of modern Western thinking. Professors and students in philosophy courses throughout Europe and the English-speaking world seem not to question the limiting of philosophy to the exoteric. It is almost true that this limiting has not been seriously questioned since the time of Plato. This is not quite true, however, in that some of the great philosophers of the Jewish, Christian, and Muslim cultures should be regarded as esoteric thinkers, as should some modern Western thinkers.

The identification of philosophy with the exoteric leads to the elimination of esoteric thinkers from the ranks of philosophers. Increasingly, the same process of creating and re-creating a core, or canon, of philosophers according to the philosophically correct definition of philosophy as exclusively exoteric has been under way, in diverse ways and for different lengths of time, in the cultures represented in this book. This process, which has been extremely complex and controversial, represents the full range of influences that fall under the label *Westernization*—that is, from colonialization to democratization.

Esoteric and Exoteric in Greek Philosophy

As with most new directions and disputes in Western philosophy, Socrates, Plato, and Aristotle serve as precedents. In this case, we can best begin with Aristotle, who organized the field and the method of philosophy. Aristotle was the first to divide his philosophy into esoteric and exoteric. By *exoteric* he meant popular and nontechnical; by *esoteric* he presumably meant the kind of knowledge attained in mystery centers by special training, and thereafter intelligible only to the initiated few. In his philosophy, Aristotle neglected the esoteric completely, concentrating solely on the exoteric.

Because the West has followed Aristotle in omitting the esoteric, only a minority of philosophers are conscious of, or interested in, what Aristotle ignored. There are, however, texts that can be read either esoterically or exoterically, the most vivid and influential of which is Plato's Allegory of the Cave. This allegory has served as an archetypal image (original creative expression) of the esoteric consciousness in the West (albeit one that is usually read without much attention to its esoteric quality). It is here quoted in its entirety from *The Republic* because it is so revealing not only of Plato's thought, and of Platonism in the West (particular Christianity), but equally of our own thinking. Is this the way we understand our mentality? Are we ordinarily separated from Knowledge and Reality, and do we need to ascend to another level of experience? Is there a "cave" and an ascent? (In this passage Socrates is the speaker.)

ALLEGORY OF THE CAVE (*Republic* VII: 514a–517e)

514   Next, said I, compare our nature in respect of education and its lack to such an experience as this. Picture men dwelling in a sort of subterranean cavern with a long entrance open to the light on its entire width. Conceive them as having their legs and necks fettered from childhood, so that they remain in

b   the same spot, able to look forward only, and prevented by the fetters from turning their heads. Picture further the light from a fire burning higher up and at a distance behind them, and between the fire and the prisoners and above them a road along which a low wall has been built, as the exhibitors of puppet shows have partitions before the men themselves, above which they show the puppets.

All that I see, he said.

See also, then, men carrying past the wall implements of all kinds that rise

c   above the wall, and human images and shapes of animals as well, wrought in
515   stone and wood and every material, some of these bearers presumably speaking and others silent.

A strange image you speak of, he said, and strange prisoners.

Like to us, I said. For, to begin with, tell me do you think that these men would have seen anything of themselves or of one another except the shadows cast from the fire on the wall of the cave that fronted them?

b   How could they, he said, if they were compelled to hold their heads unmoved through life?

And again, would not the same be true of the objects carried past them? Surely.

If then they were able to talk to one another, do you not think that they would suppose that in naming the things that they saw they were naming the passing objects?

Necessarily.

And if their prison had an echo from the wall opposite them, when one of the passers-by uttered a sound, do you think that they would suppose anything else than the passing shadow to be the speaker?

By Zeus, I do not, said he.

Then in every way such prisoners would deem reality to be nothing else   c than the shadows of the artificial objects.

Quite inevitably, he said.

Consider, then, what would be the manner of the release and healing from these bonds and this folly if in the course of nature something of this sort should happen to them. When one was freed from his fetters and compelled to stand up suddenly and turn his head around and walk and to lift up his eyes to the light, and in doing all this felt pain and, because of the dazzle and glitter of the light, was unable to discern the objects whose shadows he formerly saw, what do you suppose would be his answer if someone told him that what he had seen before was all a cheat and an illusion, but that   d now, being nearer to reality and turned toward more real things, he saw more truly? And if also one should point out to him each of the passing objects and constrain him by questions to say what it is, do you not think that he would be at a loss and that he would regard what he formerly saw as more real than the things now pointed out to him?

Far more real, he said.

And if he were compelled to look at the light itself, would not that pain his   e eyes, and would he not turn away and flee to those things which he is able to discern and regard them as in very deed more clear and exact than the objects pointed out?

It is so, he said.

And if, said I, someone should drag him thence by force up the ascent which is rough and steep, and not let him go before he had drawn him out into the light of the sun, do you not think that he would find it painful to be so haled along, and would chafe at it, and when he came out into the light,   516 that his eyes would be filled with its beams so that he would not be able to see even one of the things that we call real?

Why, no, not immediately, he said.

Then there would be need of habituation, I take it, to enable him to see the things higher up. And at first he would most easily discern the shadows and, after that, the likenesses or reflections in water of men and other things, and later, the things themselves, and from these he would go on to contemplate the appearances in the heavens and heaven itself, more easily by night,   b looking at the light of the stars and the moon, than by day the sun and the sun's light.

Of course.

And so, finally, I suppose, he would be able to look upon the sun itself and see its true nature, not by reflections in water or phantasms of it in an alien setting, but in and by itself in its own place.

Necessarily, he said.

And at this point he would infer and conclude that this it is that provides

the seasons and the courses of the year and presides over all things in the
c   visible region, and is in some sort the cause of all these things that they had
seen.

Obviously, he said, that would be the next step.

Well then, if he recalled to mind his first habitation and what passed for
wisdom there, and his fellow bondsmen, do you not think that he would
count himself happy in the change and pity them?

He would indeed.

And if there had been honors and commendations among them which they
bestowed on one another and prizes for the man who is quickest to make out
the shadows as they pass and best able to remember their customary
d   precedences, sequences, and coexistences, and so most successful in guess-
ing at what was to come, do you think he would be very keen about such
rewards, and that he would envy and emulate those who were honored by
these prisoners and lorded it among them, or that he would feel with Homer
and greatly prefer while living on earth to be serf of another, a landless man,
and endure anything rather than opine with them and live that life?

e   Yes, he said, I think that he would choose to endure anything rather than
such a life.

And consider this also, said I. If such a one should go down again and
take his old place would he not get his eyes full of darkness, thus suddenly
coming out of the sunlight?

He would indeed.

517   Now if he should be required to contend with these perpetual prisoners in
'evaluating' these shadows while his vision was still dim and before his eyes
were accustomed to the dark—and this time required for habituation would
not be very short—would he not provoke laughter, and would it not be said
of him that he had returned from his journey aloft with his eyes ruined and
that it was not worth while even to attempt the ascent? And if it were
possible to lay hands on and to kill the man who tried to release them and
lead them up, would they not kill him?

They certainly would, he said.

This image then, dear Glaucon, we must apply as a whole to all that has
b   been said, likening the region revealed through sight to the habitation of the
prison, and the light of the fire in it to the power of the sun. And if you
assume that the ascent and the contemplation of the things above is the
soul's ascension to the intelligible region, you will not miss my surmise,
since that is what you desire to hear. But God knows whether it is true. But,
at any rate, my dream as it appears to me is that in the region of the known
the last thing to be seen and hardly seen is the idea of good, and that when
c   seen it must needs point us to the conclusion that this is indeed the cause for
all things of all that is right and beautiful, giving birth in the visible world to
light, and the author of light and itself in the intelligible world being the
authentic source of truth and reason, and that anyone who is to act wisely in
private or public must have caught sight of this.

I concur, he said, so far as I am able.

Come then, I said, and join me in this further thought, and do not be
surprised that those who have attained to this height are not willing to
occupy themselves with the affairs of men, but their souls ever feel the

upward urge and the yearning for that sojourn above. For this, I take it, is d
likely if in this point too the likness of our image holds.

Yes, it is likely.

And again, do you think it at all strange, said I, if a man returning from
divine contemplations to the petty miseries of men cuts a sorry figure and
appears most ridiculous, if, while still blinking through the gloom, and before
he has become sufficiently accustomed to the environing darkness, he is
compelled in courtrooms or elsewhere to contend about the shadows of
justice or the images that cast the shadows and to wrangle in debate about e
the notions of these things in the minds of those who have never seen justice
itself?

A person who was dragged up and out of the cave would find the light
blinding, but a person who trained properly would be ready for the light
(or Light). In this same work, *The Republic,* Plato indicates clearly that
progress in philosophy, or preparing to know-see, preparing for insight,
would require fifteen years of mathematical training, and that both
mathematics and philosophy would require a very exacting way of life.
Plato almost certainly spent some years training in centers influenced by
Pythagoras, and never lost his conviction that philosophic truth can be
attained only by a total, lifelong spiritual training.

Although most of the philosophy taught in this book, and discussed on
the basis of this book, is exoteric, Plato's allegory gives each reader an
opportunity to examine how far he or she wishes to go in search of an
alternative, and purportedly superior, way of knowing. Plato, in contrast
to Aristotle, intends his readers—or, more accurately, his listeners—to
experience an invitation to find ordinary consciousness stifling and un-
bearable. He in effect says, if you think that you are in a cave of
consciousness, in a blind alley of awareness, taking shadows for realities,
there is another reality, and a way to it. Further, Plato himself allows his
readers to believe that he is not speaking abstractly, or at secondhand,
but knows firsthand whereof he speaks:

One statement at any rate I can make in regard to all who have written or
who may write with a claim to knowledge of the subjects to which I devote
myself—no matter how they pretend to have acquired it, whether from my
instruction or from others or by their own discovery. Such writers can in my
opinion have no real acquaintance with the subject. I certainly have composed no work in regard to it, nor shall I ever do so in future, for there is no
way of putting it in words like other studies. Acquaintance with it must come
rather after a long period of attendance on instruction in the subject itself
and of close companionship, when, suddenly, like a blaze kindled by a
leaping spark, it is generated in the soul and at once becomes self-sustaining.

Besides, this at any rate I know, that if there were to be a treatise or a
lecture on this subject, I could do it best. I am also sure for that matter that
I should be very sorry to see such a treatise poorly written. If I thought it
possible to deal adequately with the subject in a treatise or a lecture for the

general public, what finer achievement would there have been in my life than to write a work of great benefit to mankind and to bring the nature of things to light for all men? I do not, however, think the attempt to tell mankind of these matters a good thing, except in the case of some few who are capable of discovering the truth for themselves with a little guidance. In the case of the rest, to do so would excite in some an unjustified contempt in a thoroughly offensive fashion, in others certain lofty and vain hopes, as if they had acquired some awesome lore. (Seventh Letter, 341c–342a)

To sum it all up in one word, natural intelligence and a good memory are equally powerless to aid the man who has not an inborn affinity with the subject. Without such endowments there is of course not the slightest possibility. Hence all who have no natural aptitude for and affinity with justice and all the other noble ideals, though in the study of other matters they may be both intelligent and retentive—all those too who have affinity but are stupid and unretentive—will never attain to an understanding of the most complete truth in regard to moral concepts. The study of virtue and vice must be accompanied by an inquiry into what is false and true of existence in general and must be carried on by constant practice throughout a long period, as I said in the beginning. Hardly after practicing detailed comparisons of names and definitions and visual and other sense perceptions, after scrutinizing them in benevolent disputation by the use of question and answer without jealousy, at last in a flash understanding of each blazes up, and the mind, as it exerts all its powers to the limit of human capacity, is flooded with light. (Seventh Letter, 344a–344b)

This is the characteristically Platonic—and esoteric—attitude and intent that does not find its way into the writings of Aristotle or into Western philosophy generally. Although some readers might find some of the discussions in this and similar books entirely too esoteric (technical, and as though intended for a privileged few), none of the material in this book is intentionally esoteric. Aristotle's philosophy is occasionally quite esoteric in its degree of technicality and in its appeal to only a small number of people favored with philosophic aptitude, but he clearly does not intend any part of his philosophy to be secret.

When Aristotle says that his philosophy is exoteric—that is, intended to be understood, at least in principle, by any and all readers—he has in mind a clear distinction between his way of doing philosophy and the way of some earlier philosophers, for example, Pythagoras, whose teachings were intended to be secret to all but his highly trained disciples. It is this kind of philosophy that is under discussion here—though, I hope, in a way that is no longer secret and not so technical that it cannot be understood, in principle, by beginning readers.

Although it is easy for us to agree that Aristotle was right to democratize philosophy, it might be worth asking whether there was something true and necessary in the Pythagorean training. Of course, it would be difficult for us to evaluate Pythagoras's method of training since philosophy has few if any examples of such special training, or special teachers capable of guiding such a training. Yet it is the task of this chapter to explore precisely this question—what, if anything, is there about philosophy that would benefit from a Pythagorean-style training, one that would proceed according to a strict hierarchy of esoteric schooling?

We have already pointed to the contrast between the exoteric philosophy of Aristotle and the partly esoteric philosophies of Pythagoras and Plato. By now we should understand that there is something wrong with the question "What did Pythagoras teach?" The question awaits the distinction—what Pythagoras really taught, that is, esoterically, and what he is exoterically reported to have taught. The exoteric in this case might be due to the passage of time and state of consciousness: A student might summarize exoterically what he had learned while he and Pythagoras shared an esoteric state of mind. (It would have been a "he" because we are told that only men were members of the esoteric schools, but this was so of exoteric schools as well. This may be shocking but not surprising considering that the women of Athens, the source of Western democracy, were not citizens.)

Or Pythagoras himself might have summarized in an exoteric state of mind, and for an exoteric purpose, an approach to or the implications of his esoteric teaching. But Pythagoras was a typical esoteric teacher in that he did not publicize his esoteric teachings. More to the point, even if his esoteric teachings had been widely publicized—even by Pythagoras himself—they would automatically have ceased to be esoteric. The link between ancient and contemporary interest in the esoteric is precisely this characteristic—the exceptional state of mind of the teacher and student. Aristotle's philosophy is not esoteric because he does not insist on a special state of consciousness necessary to hear and hold the truth that he seeks to communicate. Pythagoras, however, did insist on a specially achieved mental state that was presumably possible for students who followed his prescriptions for meditative thinking.

The entire process of replacing esoteric by exoteric philosophy in Greek civilization was realized within three generations—essentially by three astonishing thinkers. Aristotle represents the complete neglect within philosophy of esoteric methods and claims. But because he was a Greek of the fourth century B.C.—and for twenty years Plato's student—what Aristotle meant by exoteric is not at all what it means in the West of the late twentieth century. If we approach Aristotle's writings, as we typically do, we might miss the affinity between Aristotle the exoteric philosopher and the amount of esotericism that was an essential element in the achievements of all Greek genius, including the philosophy of Aristotle.

The habit of treating Socrates and Plato as though they were contemporary Western philosophers has been established by the texts for introductory philosophy courses used throughout the English-speaking world. As a senior professor and chair of a philosophy department in New York

City, each semester I observed beginning instructors in introductory philosophy courses striving to establish the contemporaneity of Socrates and Plato. Establishing the relevance of Socrates and Plato for those who are encountering them for the first time is made easier by a combination of introductory philosophy textbooks, some of Plato's own statements, and the cultural filters through which we see the past. (We should bear in mind that references to Socrates are references to the character in the dialogues written by his student Plato; Socrates, like Lao Tzu, Confucius, Krishna, Buddha, and Jesus, did not record his own thoughts, but had them recorded, more or less accurately, after his death.)

Students and professors alike find the Socrates and Plato they expect to find—typically, the first and second generation, respectively, of Western rationality. It is true that Socrates was a martyr for philosophy: He favored free inquiry against government-sponsored religious beliefs and practices. Perhaps more important, he examined attitudes and convictions that for his fellow citizens were too obvious to question. But what should we make of the fact that Socrates launched his lifelong career as a philosopher on the advice of an oracle? (An oracle, from the Latin *oraculum,* is a prayer or divine communication.) Or that throughout his life Socrates followed the advice of his *daimonion,* an inner voice that forbade him to perform certain contemplated actions. These nonrational factors in Socrates' life tend to be reduced to a literary or psychological device by modern interpreters, but it is clear from the text that both Socrates and Plato took them seriously as esoteric realities.

At his trial for impiety and corruption of the youth of Athens—obviously politically motivated charges—Socrates admitted that he had spent his life testing the oracle's statement that Socrates was the wisest of men. The oracle in question, one of the oldest and most famous in Greece, was the shrine of Apollo, the foremost of all Greek gods in relation to human affairs such as religion, law, and civilization. The pronouncements of Apollo were mediated, or channeled, by a woman called the Pythia. Apparently the Pythia communicated to a friend of Socrates, Chaerephon, while Socrates was not yet conscious of his philosophic mission, that Socrates was the wisest of men.

Socrates subsequently set out to disprove, or at least to test, this assertion. As is well known to all students of Western thought and culture, Socrates was at first bewildered by the oracular pronouncement because he was so aware of his ignorance concerning really important issues like virtue. In time, however, after entering into dialogue with those with reputations for wisdom, Socrates concluded that they did not really know the truth, and Socrates was alone in acknowledging that he did not really know.

Plato, who was in his early twenties when Socrates was tried and executed for not believing in the state religion, focused on the "really": If Socrates did not really know, who did, and how would one know if and when one were really to know? The task of knowing and of knowing whether we are really knowing (and not, like those who argued with Socrates, accepting opinions as though they were true knowledge) was given central place in Plato's brilliant and uniquely influential philosophy, but neither Socrates nor Plato turned their skillful skepticism on the oracle.

In addition to the fascinating question of the oracle and its importance in the career of the model for Western philosophers, there is also the question of Socrates' *diamonion,* or inner voice, which told Socrates what not to do. Some interpreters casually regard Socrates' *daimonion* as a kind of conscience, and some others maliciously regard it as a sign that Socrates was maladjusted, but in fact we are here confronting another sign that Socrates, whom the entire West claims as its first philosopher, was also involved with esoteric practices and teachings. Plato tells of Socrates' trances, in one of which he stood in a rapt mystical state for more than twenty-four hours. It is clear that Socrates was familiar with both Pythagorean initiation (mystery-schooling) and with the religious practices surrounding Orpheus.

As Socrates is the initiator, the archetypal or symbolic first example of the philosopher, his student Plato is the first creator of a full-scale philosophy. Plato's early works are referred to as Socratic because they concern, and are obviously influenced by, the life and ideals of Socrates. His middle dialogues are more ambitious, and as typified by the *Symposium* and *The Republic,* represent Plato's unsurpassed ability to combine speculative imagination with rigorous analysis and argument. In the third period, Plato's dialogues tend to be analytic and without the confident speculative power of his middle dialogues, but there in the third period we find *Timaeus,* with its mix of cosmology and myth.

The most dramatic evidence that Plato maintained a close relationship to the esoteric is provided by his many references to exceptional states of consciousness and to teachers who have benefited from such states, some of whom teach others how to achieve these unusual states of awareness. In the *Symposium,* for example, Socrates presents, with approval, a theory of beauty—or, more precisely, True Knowledge of the Idea of Beauty—that he learned from Diotima, a priestess who is clearly identified as an esoteric teacher. In *The Republic,* Plato separates human experience, or consciousness, into two levels: the lower level, concerned with ordinary states of mind, mostly with appearances, or sense perceptions of ordinary objects, and the upper level, concerned with True Knowledge of Reality. To move from the lower to the higher level would be like moving out of a cave, out of a world of shadows into the Light. In such a text as this, the mystical and esoteric finds one of its fullest and most influential expressions.

Although so brief a discussion as this cannot do justice either to esoteric philosophy or to the Greek philosophy, I hope that it has been able to depict Plato as a fascinating example of the way in which the esoteric and exoteric can be mixed, and the degree to which a perspective committed to the exoteric can miss the esoteric dimension of one of its most important representatives. It might also serve to establish a pattern of neglect with respect to the esoteric in other periods of Western philosophy. Esoteric philosophy is an unbroken tradition from the Egyptians, Hebrews, and Greeks through the Christian West and continuing to the present. Philosophy texts and courses nevertheless give the impression that all philosophy is exoteric, or, if a teaching, teacher, or idea is esoteric, then it is not philosophy.

This neglect of the esoteric did not happen all at once. The process that began with Aristotle continued to gain scope, depth, and confidence through the Christian centuries until in the modern West of the past three centuries, the esoteric has been excluded not only from philosophy but from knowledge and culture as well. If the story here told is accurate, then it would seem to be, as Shakespeare's Hamlet well stated, that

> There are more things in heaven and earth, Horatio,
> Than are dreamt of in your philosophy. (I: v. 166–67)

The more unusual things together with ordinary things from unusual perspectives are the special concern of esoteric philosophy.

Philosophy in the West took a decisive step with Aristotle's determination to focus on the logical and rational to the exclusion of the kind of knowledge attained in the mystery centers, but esoteric philosophy did not disappear. Rather, the impulse that led men to join the esoteric academy of Pythagoras was presumably the same as that which led seekers of spiritual wisdom in later centuries to join Christian monasteries, and in recent centuries to join communities guided by modern esoteric teachers. Although the content and methods of Greek mystery centers differ from those of medieval monasteries, and both differ from those of modern esoteric communities, the commonalities are important and revealing for our understanding of the history of Western thought and culture, and for our orientation.

Essentially, the Greek mystery center—of which that of Pythagoras was the best known—offered a comprehensive way of life, requiring a strict ascetic regimen, including a plain diet, sexual abstinence, exact meditation requirements, and model teachers who guided the seeker toward deeper insight into mathematics, music, and philosophy. As the example of the Pythagorean school clearly indicates, esoteric philosophy assumes a necessary relationship between various transformative disciplines and the attainment of deep knowledge. It assumes that such knowledge is attainable only by means of what is now referred to as an altered state of consciousness.

In effect, Socrates and Plato continued to regard such altered states as necessary for philosophic wisdom, whereas Aristotle, while insisting on contemplation as the highest level of thinking, nevertheless did not build on, or recommend, the practices developed in Greek mystery centers. But Platonism continued as an alternative to Aristotle's philosophy from their time to the present. It is sometimes claimed that all thinking people in the West fall into one of two types—Platonist or Aristotelian. But it must be admitted that Aristotelianism represents the kind of thinking that is more typically regarded as characteristically Western—that is, rational and, in recent centuries, rational-scientific.

This broad characterization is unfair to both Plato and Aristotle, but it does remind us of the competing qualities, not so much of the philosophies as such but of the "isms." Whereas the Aristotelian is closer to nature and the body, and to the facts of experience, the Platonic is identified with the pure form, with the ideal, and with the spiritual. This is significant for our focus on the esoteric because the Platonic tradition from Plato to the present has been identified with spiritual disciplines as ways to special knowledge. As is evident in the passages quoted from Plato's *Republic* and the Seventh Letter, the Platonic tradition calls for special disciplines that reportedly lead to special (particularly spiritual) knowledge. Special/spiritual knowledge is not ordinarily attainable except by a path of purification and meditative thinking.

Esotericism in the Christian West

During the centuries after Plato, this emphasis on purifactory and meditative exercises as a way to spiritual insight evolved both within religion, particularly Christianity, and as an alternative to religion. Within Judaism, Platonic philosophical ideas were developed by the Jewish philosopher Philo of Alexandria (15 B.C.–40 A.D.). Christian theologians began to develop a Christian Platonism as early as the mid-second century. St. Augustine (354–430) developed a full Platonic Christian theology, at the core of which is an essentially Platonic insistence on the superiority of the soul over the body, and the corresponding belief that the soul can be illumined directly by God.

The source of Augustine's Platonism was Plotinus, a non-Christian mystical philosopher. Plotinus represents a kind of pagan spirituality— *pagan,* in this context, meaning not belonging to an established religion. Because of its spiritual dimension, Platonism serves part of the function of religion. So does all esoteric philosophy in that it requires the kind of transformative discipline by which the seeker after wisdom strives to develop receptivity to divine knowledge. While philosophy as studied at the present time is ordinarily regarded as opposed to religion—and indeed generally is—it is not unusual to find a philosopher, particularly in the Platonic tradition, practicing philosophy in a way similar to how someone would practice religion. For such a person, Plotinus's non-Christian Greek mystical philosophy represents a kind of pagan, or secular, scripture.

During the Christian Middle Ages, from approximately the fifth to the fourteenth centuries, a series of Christian spiritual teachers and theologians developed Platonic thinking within the context of Christian revelation and medieval culture. Owing to the virtual monopoly on thinking and culture exercised by the Catholic church during these centuries, there were no major esoteric alternatives to the Christian Platonism within the Christian West. Platonism and the subsequent mystical Platonic philosophy of Plotinus were not tied to any religious orthodoxy even though they were appropriated by Jewish, Christian, and Muslim thinkers as theoretical supports for their religious worldviews.

What is lost in all this wrangling over orthodoxy and its habit of appropriating or suppressing is the ideal of philosophy in general, and of esoteric philosophy in particular: that the aim is to prepare oneself to receive the maximum amount, and purest version, of truth about reality of which we, in our mortal frame, are capable. It is worth studying the early centuries of the Christian West if for no other reason than to see something of how teachings considered to be spiritually profound and selfless can nevertheless get tangled in ideological and institutional prejudices. This is extremely important for us because we live in a time of intense ideological and institutional prejudice, one in which the disagreements between the presuppositions of esoteric and exoteric philosophies, as well as within these two kinds of philosophies, have led to the widespread conviction that no one really knows and that no one can know.

The intellectual climate in the contemporary West is similar to that of Socrates' time, when the Sophists (who were essentially lawyers—people paid to make the weaker argument appear the stronger) were in charge of truth. But do we have a Socrates or a Plato or an Aristotle to offset this sophistic relativism? Now that we have had a glimpse of Platonism and the general evolution of esoteric philosophy in Greek thought, and its complex evolution within the Christian West, how can we set about determining whether any of these worldviews is true? When we study this mix of thinking and practice generated by Platonic vision and Christian revelation, the first and most difficult task is to determine whether, or the extent to which, the unusual claims in this tradition are the result of actual, believable experience.

Do such ideas as those of the Trinity, the Ideas in/of God's mind, Truth and Light, grace and salvation come from esoteric practice and insight? To make this judgment fairly and reliably, we need to exercise a level or kind of insight similar to that exercised by the Christian Platonist. Or, if the Christian part of this combination proves to be an obstacle, we could try to glimpse something of what Plato or Plotinus saw: By working through their texts, we could try to ascend the ladder of knowledge and reality. And if the Christian part seems right, we might then follow Augustine in arguing that the Christian scriptures provide the missing piece in the Platonic vision, namely Christ, which, for the Christian, is the link between the spiritual ideal and the limitations of the physical.

The medieval Christian culture, however, regarded the spiritual and the ideal—the primary concerns of Platonism—as the first priority, and the material as of secondary value. The philosophy of Aristotle, with its attempt to bring spirit and matter into a closer, in fact indissoluble, conjunction, would have provided a helpful polarity for the otherworldliness of Christian Platonism, but the major texts of Aristotle were scarcely known during these centuries. Consequently, Platonism came to be the dominant teaching of the Christian Middle Ages, and, with the aura of orthodoxy bestowed by its intimate association with the increasingly powerful church, virtually eliminated all non-Christian esoteric teachings during these centuries. It was not until the forceful return of the texts of Aristotle that the Platonist grip was loosened.

One of the phenomena we will notice in this history is the way in which each teaching appears true in what it affirms but less convincing in what it rejects. So, we might want to conclude that Platonism is on to something true when it insists on the independent reality of Ideas, or Ideals, such as Truth, Beauty, Love, or Justice, but not convincing when it is stingy in assigning meaning to the physical world. All of the Platonic schools and texts, from Plato in the fourth century B.C. to Plotinus in the third century A.D., agree that Ideals (Truth, Beauty, and so on) are independent of the sense world, and are knowable directly by a nonsensory or intuitive mode of knowing.

The Christian Platonists were convinced that they were developing a balanced worldview that combined a full account of the divine reality with a rich account of the created world. The Platonic account of the Ideal, particularly the Idea of the Good, which Plato referred to as metaphorically as the Sun, the Source of Light and Insight, fit neatly with the Christian idea of God, the Creator and Provider of life. For the intellectually alert Christian of the early Middle Ages, Platonism and the philosophy of Plotinus (called Neoplatonism) provided additional support for the belief that the deeds, teachings, and status of Jesus Christ were not only experientially vivid but intelligible as well.

Christian Platonists also believed that, because they followed the transformative practices developed out of both Platonic and Christian traditions, they were capable of receiving, or discovering, whatever truth was available to an honestly striving seeker. They were very skilled at seeking, finding, and articulating a vast array of spiritually and philosophically efficacious ideas; they were also, perhaps predictably, less adept at appreciating the spiritual insights of others.

Christian Platonists of the Middle Ages regarded some esoteric teachings of the Greek mystery centers, such as Pythagoreanism, as compatible with Christian revelation, and they included them in orthodox Christian theology; other Greek esoteric teachings and practices, such as those of the Gnostics, were eventually, after several centuries of theological and institutional conflict, declared by the Christian winners to be heretical and were repressed. Platonism was able to be absorbed into orthodox Christianity because it lent itself to a systematic articulation. The Gnostics, by contrast, were inherently unorthodox, or antiorthodox, in their thinking.

In the early centuries after Christ, when the Christian church was involved in the complex task of defining its doctrines and establishing its practices, many Gnostics considered themselves Christians; almost certainly, many others would have wanted to be Christians, and would have been, had the church not been involved in a process of increased Romanization; that is, under the influence of Rome, the church entered a process of transforming itself into a law-giving, orthodox institution.

What happened to the Gnostics, and thereby to Gnosticism, is instructive for our present situation. If we do not look too closely, we might imagine that the kind of authority exercised by the Christian church does not exist in the democratic West, for example, northern Europe or the United States. In his *Adventures of Ideas,* Alfred North Whitehead, one of the truly wise philosophers of this century, observes that the present reign of scientific rationalism imposes an orthodoxy similar to that exercised by the medieval Christian church.

Fortunately the scholastic age of Alexandrian scholarship dominated Europe for centuries, and bestowed upon civilization priceless treasures of thought. It was an age of immense progress. But a scholarly age works within rigid limitations. Fortunately a revival of Hellenism overwhelmed the Hellenistic unity of the Middle Age. Plato arose as if from his tomb. Vagrant speculation and direct observation broke up the scholarly system. New interest, new Gods, prevailed. The new basis for thought was the report upon facts, directly observed, directly employed. Fortunately, in the subsidence of the Italian Renaissance of the fifteenth century, the drama of the transference of culture from Athens to Alexandria was again repeated. Europe gradually entered upon a new scholarly age. The modern historian appeared, the modern critical literature appeared, the modern man of science appeared, modern technology appeared. The old Egyptian metallurgists, the Semitic mathematicians and the mediaeval scholastics were avenged.

But modern scholarship and modern science reproduce the same limitations as dominated the bygone Hellenistic epoch, and the bygone Scholastic epoch. They canalize thought and observation within predetermined limits, based upon inadequate metaphysical assumptions dogmatically assumed. The modern assumptions differ from older assumptions, not wholly for the better. They exclude from rationalistic thought more of the final values of existence. The intimate timidity of professionalized scholarship circumscribes reason by reducing its topics to triviality, for example, to bare sensa and tautologies. It then frees itself from criticism by dogmatically handing over the remainder of experience to an animal faith or a religious mysticism, incapable of rationalization. The world will again sink into the boredom of a drab detail of rational thought, unless we retain in the sky some reflection of light from the sun of Hellenism.[1]

When we deal with the life of nature, however, we might find ourselves longing for the Aristotelian complement, for the other side of our nature— as the masculine and feminine in our natures, and our culture, each long for the other. Someone who is not ideally balanced will presumably stay with one "ism" to the exclusion of the other. But two dauntingly difficult problems will inevitably remain: (1) How balanced is the "ism" itself? Is Platonism, or Aristotelianism, balanced? And (2) In my approach to polarities such as mind/matter, natural/divine, individual/cultural, Truth/ experience, am I capable of a perspective that is balanced?

We might argue that the best way to join, or rejoin, the spiritual and the physical is to avoid the Platonic framework in order to develop a philosophy along the lines laid down by Aristotle. This is what the Christian monk Thomas Aquinas accomplished in the thirteenth century. Though seemingly incompatible with Christian revelation, Aristotle's philosophy was integrated by the patient genius of Aquinas. But Thomas Aquinas was himself a Christian Platonist when he set out on his radical task of reconciling Christian revelation and Christian theology, which was throughly Platonic, with the philosophy of Aristotle.

As a result of the Muslim conquest of Syria and Egypt, and the work of Thomas Aquinas, a brilliant synthesis of Platonism and Aristotelianism was soon forged. It is important for readers who identify with Western history and culture, and particularly for anyone with a Jewish or Christian historical bias, to understand that it was in the Muslim world, from the tenth to the twelfth centuries, that the spiritual, philosophical, and practical implications of both Platonism and Aristotelianism were developed.

Esotericism in the Renaissance and Modern West

If the account of the esoteric (in relation to the exoteric) in this chapter is accurate, then it would seem to follow that esotericism in the West has evolved along parallel lines, within Christianity, particularly through Platonism and Neoplatonism, and outside, through Pythagoreanism, aspects of Platonism, Gnosticism, and Plotinus. It would also seem to follow that esotericism is of necessity a bit unorthodox, and to the extent that Christianity insisted on dogma and rigid prescriptions, it drove out the esoteric. But by the time of the Renaissance in the West, beginning in the fifteenth century, philosophers and especially artists were ready for a truly profound expression of the Platonic and the Aristotelian.

Just as no one can look at the architecture of Persian and Arab cultures and doubt the ability of these cultures to think through and live out the intimate relationship between timeless ideals, or Platonic Forms, and the Aristotelian concern for the physical, so no one can look at Renaissance churches or sculpture without appreciating the exquisite balance between form and physicality. The Renaissance was a time of elegant and passionate expression of the spirit in intimate creative relation to matter.

It would be interesting as intellectual history, and certainly revealing of esotericism, to trace the interplay of Platonism and Aristotelianism from the Renaissance to the present. All the great thinkers would appear on the stage of Western thought: The brooders and transformers, the celebrators and critics would play their parts in the dramatic play of ideas. But as our task is to focus particularly on the esoteric, this discussion will only summarize the general ways in which the impluse to the esoteric has survived and reasserted itself in the face of the emerging dominance of scientific rationality. Very briefly, the role of the esoteric in this phase of Western thought amounts to a call for an alternative mode of knowing, one that links the inner, or spiritual, of the knower with the inner, the spiritual, of the knowable.

This formulation does not so much distinguish the Platonic from the Aristotelian as it does this way of knowing from the usual way, from the scientific and analytic ways. As a result of the creative celebration of the ideal and the physical in the Renaissance, the Platonic and the Aristotelian could both serve as ways to a more transformative way of knowing. More typically, neither serves the esoteric enterprise: The Platonic perspective often perpetuates the hierarchical dualism between upper and lower, Reality and appearance, Knowledge and opinion, while the Aristotelian often represents commitment to the practical and the sensory at the expense of the Ideal and Transcendent.

The task of the present time, then, would seem to be the creation of a Platonism—an attention to ideal form—that attends to the particularity of the ordinary world, in combination with an Aristotelianism that penetrates the ordinary world so deeply as to discern the ideal form sustaining every particular and enabling it to transcend itself. Happily, there are at least three major thinkers whose thought represents precisely this combination:

- *William James* (1842–1910), American psychologist and philosopher; expert on parapsychological and religious experience. James would be a thoroughgoing Aristotelian except for his artist's eye for the spiritual illumining the ordinary, like the sun shining through the stained-glass windows of a medieval cathedral.
- *Rudolf Steiner* (1861–1925), Austrian esoteric philosopher, scientist, artist, and educator.

• *Carl Gustav Jung* (1875–1961), Swiss psychoanalyst; expert on the transformative power of symbols; contemporary gnostic.

William James

The esoteric in various forms was a deep concern of William James, the most original and influential American philosopher. James did not use the term *esoteric,* and he did not practice an esoteric discipline, but he was deeply involved in the study of mystical, parapsychological, and esoteric experiences.

Born in New York City, James was a member of New England's most prominent family of letters. His father, Henry, Sr., was a religious thinker in his own right as well as a student of the eighteenth-century Christian esoteric teacher Emanuel Swedenborg. William James's brother, Henry, was America's most distinguished novelist and literary critic. His sister, Alice, although overshadowed by her two world-famous brothers, was the author of highly introspective and insightful diaries published only recently, more than seventy years after her death.

After training as a painter, William studied medicine at Harvard University, where he subsequently taught physiology, psychology, and then philosophy. In addition to his writings on pragmatism, which popularized the characteristic perspective of the American philosophical tradition, James authored two masterpieces—one in psychology and one in the study of religion. His monumental *Principles of Psychology* (1890) remains the primary alternative to the psychoanalytic writings of Sigmund Freud. It shows James's gifts for the observation and description of human experience, including perception, habit, and memory, and his chapter on the "Stream of Consciousness" has generated our most powerful aesthetic metaphor. His *Varieties of Religious Experience* (1902) remains the classic study in the field of religious experience, rivaled only by Henri Bergson's *Two Sources of Morality and Religion* (1932).

But James had yet another interest, one that has been largely ignored by students of his psychology, his philosophy, and his study of religious experience: for the last thirty years of his life, James worked tirelessly as a psychical researcher, that is, as an investigator into the claims for telepathy, the ability to move physical objects by thinking, preknowledge of events, and channeling messages from the dead. James's primary purpose in this extremely frustrating research was to hold the middle ground between scientific skepticism and uncritical credulity. James sought to rein in both these extreme and mutually exclusive positions by showing them to be inattentive to the facts of observable experience. James was in search of "one white crow," which could be put on display as a means of showing that although almost all experience is of one kind, there is nevertheless another kind, however rare it may be.

Although psychical research might seem to be quite a different topic from esoteric philosophy, the difference is perhaps not so great and can be attributed to the distinctive requirements of modern Western thought. For Socrates, the meaning of virtue was subject to careful scrutiny, but the oracle of Delphi, his *daimonion,* and the immortality of the soul seemed to him indisputable facts. For Plato, the beliefs of Socrates were still valid, but he felt the need to defend the possibility of another reality and another kind of knowledge. After three hundred years of Western scientific philosophy, James could philosophically assume the truth neither of Socrates' beliefs nor of Plato's case for an exit from the cave.

Although the Pythagorean mystery center and the shrine of the Delphic Oracle were no longer available for James's scrutiny, he wondered whether there might not be individuals whose experiences were comparable to those of the esoteric teachers or their students. James performed a similar service with respect to individuals whose religious experiences pointed to another reality, "a wider self" that is continuous with the "something more" through which saving experiences come.[2] But in addition to studying religious experiences such as conversion, saintliness, and mysticism, James wanted to evaluate, and perhaps make a case for, exceptional experience that could be shown to be noetic, that is, a source of reliable knowledge about realities on the other side of the ordinary.

In the end, James was rather disappointed in the results of his psychical research. Essentially he learned enough to be personally convinced of the possibility of psychic experiences, but not enough to convince anyone who was previously unconvinced. In "Confidences of a Psychical Researcher," written the year before his death, James filed this report:

For twenty-five years I have been in touch with the literature of psychical research, and have had acquaintance with numerous "researchers." I have also spent a good many hours (though far fewer than I ought to have spent) in witnessing (or trying to witness) phenomena. Yet I am theoretically no "further" than I was at the beginning. . . .

The peculiarity of the case is just that there are so many sources of possible deception in most of the observations, that the whole lot of them *may* be worthless, and yet that in comparatively few cases can aught more fatal than this vague general possibility of error be pleaded against the record. Science meanwhile needs something more than bare possibilities to build upon; so your genuinely scientific inquirer—I don't mean your ignoramus "scientist"—has to remain unsatisfied. It is hard to believe, however, that the creator has really put any big array of phenomena into the world merely to defy and mock our scientific tendencies; so my deeper belief is that we psychical researchers have been too precipitate with our hopes, and that we must expect to mark progress not by quarter-centuries but by half-centuries or whole centuries.[3]

Unfortunately, psychical research seems not to have progressed significantly since James described the situation in 1909, but in view of the opposition to the idea of exceptional states of consciousness—and even the concept of consciousness—any case for psychical experience must be counted as positive. In the midst of widespread "new paradigm" thinking, to whom or to which movement or position would one turn for an informed and insightful account of experience not accounted for by standard, thoroughly exoteric, philosophies? I think it must be said that within the orthodox core of Western philosophy, James stands out for his efforts to extend the range of philosophy and to validate the significance of the esoteric and psychic for a philosophical account of experience.

Outside the walls of orthodoxy, that is, outside the topics and methodologies that are ordinarily treated in journals of philosophy, presented at philosophy meetings, and included in textbooks, there are hosts of teachers, movements, practices, claims, and studies that are potentially significant for philosophy. Of these, the most promising would seem to be the esoteric or, specifically, spiritual-scientific philosophy of Rudolf Steiner.

The Spiritual Science, or Anthroposophy, of Rudolf Steiner

In the field of philosophy, as in education, the social sciences, and the arts and sciences, Rudolf Steiner is a bewildering figure. He defies all categories except esoteric: He is a Platonic Aristotelian, a scientist-artist, a Christian exponent of karma and rebirth, and a cosmological visionary who offers detailed suggestions on curriculum and pedagogy appropriate for grades K through 12. He wrote approximately fifty books, and his lectures on many fields within these broad categories were collected in more than two hundred volumes. In addition to writing on science in general, he offered advanced insights into physics, medicine, nutrition, and agriculture, and in art he suggested original and highly influential innovations for painting, sculpture, and architecture, developed a new art form called eurythmics, and presented a series of mystery dramas tracing the inner logic of karma and rebirth over several generations.

All this was possible because Steiner possessed an esoteric capacity—an ability to see/know spiritually or supersensibly. How can we best think of this capability? Metaphorically, or allegorically, we can say that Steiner was one of those who went up out of the cave. Steiner himself, however, would not use this image: Rather, he presents his supersensible capacity in terms closer to Aristotle's conception of active thinking. On studying Steiner's vast and overwhelming spiritual-scientific research, we would do well to follow his lead in thinking of his methodology in Aristotelian terms, but there is nevertheless something entirely Platonic about his way of grasping reality. Perhaps it is accurate to say that his method is Aristotelian, while the result—the astonishing quantity and quality of his works—is more like a Platonic seeing of the Forms, of the inner, ideal qualities that render all experience intelligible.

Yet this division into Aristotelian method and Platonic result is not quite adequate because the reverse seems also to be true: The method is also Platonic because it involves the kind of meditative and transformative discipline characteristic of a mystery center, and the kind of practical result we associate with Aristotle. In fact, Steiner understood himself to be the initiator of a modern mystery school, one that strives for the ideal synthesis of scientific objectivity with spiritual interiority. This combination requires a new way of thinking, one that incorporates feeling and willing.

Jung and the Transformative Power of Symbols

In a letter to Carl Jung in 1911, a year after Jung was elected president of the International Psychoanalytic Association, Sigmund Freud urged Jung not to let his impulse toward the study of the occult take him beyond the bounds of orthodox, or Freudian, psychoanalytic theory and practice:

> I know that your deepest inclinations are impelling you toward a study of the occult, and do not doubt that you will return home with a rich cargo. There is no stopping that, and it is always right for a person to follow the biddings of his own impulses. The reputation you have won with your *Dementia* will stand against the charge of "mystic" for quite a while. Only don't stay too long away from us in those lush tropical colonies; it is necessary to govern at home. . . .[4]

Unfortunately for their relationship, Jung did not take Freud's advice; instead, he stayed in the "lush tropical colonies" of the occult for the next fifty years, until his death in 1961. From Jung's point of view, however, he was both following "the biddings of his own impulses" and governing at home. For Jung, "home" included a vast and complex variety of myths, symbols, and images as revealed through world literature, art, and religion, as well as through the dreams of his patients. By resisting Freud's advice, and Freudian orthodoxy, in favor of these researches into the role of comparative mythology and symbolism in the theory and practice of mythology, Jung was inevitably labeled "mystic" by Freud and others.

What Freud did not realize was the full extent of Jung's impulse toward the so-called occult. Not even Jung's associates and students knew the depth of this impulse until after Jung's death, when his autobiography, revealingly titled *Memories, Dreams and Reflections,* was published. Had Freud had the opportunity to read the following statement, he would have realized that Jung would not be returning to the fold:

What we are to our inward vision, and what man appears to be *sub specie aeternitatis* [from the perspective of eternity], can only be expressed by way of myth. Myth is more individual and expresses life more precisely than does science. Science works with concepts of averages which are far too general to do justice to the subjective variety of an individual life.

Thus it is that I have now undertaken, in my eighty-third year, to tell my personal myth.[5]

This passage represents the final victory in Jung's life of the mythic side over the scientific side. When reflecting on his early years as a student and as a young psychiatrist, he called this mythic side "personality number two," whereas "personality number one" impelled Jung into science, medicine, and psychiatry. At no time in his life was Jung merely a dreamer or visionary. Even in his earliest years, and again in his latest years, when the mythic side was stronger than the scientific side—the reverse of his middle (professional) years—Jung was invariably reflective, practical, and scientific.

But even at his most practical, the influence of his "second side," his lifelong involvement with dreams, visions, symbols, and myths, continues to be felt. As his autobiography begins with a series of childhood dreams and visions, it concludes with the moving confession that his destiny required of him both creativity and loneliness. To a remarkable degree, Jung's life, to use his favorite symbol, came full circle:

As a child I felt myself to be alone, and I am still, because I know things and must hint at things which others apparently know nothing of, and for the most part do not want to know. Loneliness does not come from having no people about one, but from being unable to communicate the things that seem important to oneself, or from holding certain views which others find inadmissible. The loneliness began with the experiences of my early dreams, and reached its climax at the time I was working on the unconscious.[6]

Jung's emphasis on the unconscious, on the universality as well as the particularity of myths and symbols, renders his lifework a model for the present generation of new paradigm thinkers. He is also an example of one who has conducted his own explorations into esoteric experience. Through his voluminous writings (seventeen enormous volumes articulating more than sixty years of intense research), Jung functioned as a model, as an exemplar of the lonely journeyer, but also as a bridge between generally orthodox science, particularly psychiatry, and his own uncharted examination of the myths and symbols of widely disparate peoples.

Jung carefully studied the esoteric traditions, ancient and contemporary, of Europe and, to a lesser extent, of Africa and of the Native Americans, and in all these materials he sought patterns that had proved psychologically beneficial. He did not, however, attempt to sort out his findings with respect to philosophical traditions, or in a way that would advance philosophic understanding.

Why, then, should we consider Jung in this chapter on esoteric philosophy? I think we should admit that there are not many contemporary esoteric philosophers, certainly none of Jung's significance. Further, because the thought of this century seems to me, at least, to have been most radically altered by psychology and anthropology (and not by mathematics or the physical or life sciences, as is ordinarily assumed), a major esoteric philosophy would have to include, and perhaps be based on, these two disciplines. And this is precisely what Jung offers: a view of human nature, illness and disorder individually and culturally considered, with profound, if unarticulated, philosophical implications.

Like James, Jung is a thoroughgoing empiricist who honored a lifelong commitment to observable findings, describable and analyzable psychological phenomena; but unlike James, Jung did not describe his cross-cultural, multilayered research in philosophical terms. Yet Jung's work on the esoteric (or occult) may prove philosophically even more significant than James's work on psychical research because Jung's data are so rich and suggestive for a new view of human nature and culture.

Essentially, Jung's works would commit us to a novel, and perhaps radical, understanding of the self: "The Self is our life's goal, for it is the completest expression of that fateful combination we call individuality."[7] The self attains self-realization by a process Jung calls individuation:

> Individuation means becoming a single, homogeneous being, and insofar as "individuality" embraces our innermost, last and incomparable uniqueness, it also implies becoming one's own self. We could therefore translate individuation as "coming to selfhood" or "self-realization."[8]

Individuation is the complex, lifelong process, culminating in the second half of life, by which the self gradually replaces the ego as the center of the personality. When the ego dominates the self (when the self is not, or not yet, individuated), the unconscious exercises an unhealthy influence. Jung's work would be an essential contribution to contemporary philosophy if only for its brilliant analysis of the ills that at present beset the ego—and consequently the self. Jung shows that both the illnesses of his patients and the obvious illness of our culture—wars, depression, addiction, and so on—issue from an unhealthy image of the ego, of the ordinary conscious "I."

In his effort to find healthy antidotes to the illness he found characteristic of modern Western culture, Jung made a deep and detailed study of other cultures, focusing particularly on their health-giving myths and symbols. Such myths and symbols are derivative of even deeper unconscious creative forces called archetypes. (*Arche* is the Greek word in the first sentence of the Greek translation of the Book of Genesis: "In the beginning," or, just as accurately, "in the original structure, or originating form.") Jung spent the major part of the last decades of his life searching for the myriad manifestations of archetypal images such as the earth mother, the wise old man, death and rebirth, circularity, triangularity, quaternity, the Self.

This anthropological and comparative dimension of Jung's thought constitutes a challenge to the method and dominant assumptions of modern Western (exoteric) philosophy. For a healthy self, and a healthy view of humanity and culture, would seem to require, in addition to the scientific rationality characteristic of philosophy during the past three centuries, a completely different source of insight, one with deep roots in the unconscious and free from the control of the willful, conscious ego.

Unlike Steiner, Jung did not articulate a methodology for the attainment of esoteric knowledge nor create an esoteric mystery school, but he did show by dramatic example his own way to the secrets of the unconscious. In order to experience the interplay of conscious and unconscious in his own life, he spent two years playing the same games he had played as a child. In order to experience the unconscious balancing power of the ancient image of the mandala (a complex form using the triangle, square, and circle), Jung spent two years painting mandalas. He discovered that the mandala offers a picture of the self, or lack of self, in the psyche:

> My mandalas were cryptograms concerning the state of the self which were presented to me new each day. In them I saw the self—that is, my whole being—actively at work. To be sure, at first I could only dimly understand them; but they seemed to me highly significant, and I guarded them like precious pearls. I had the distinct feeling that they were something central, and in time I acquired through them a living conception of the self. The self, I thought, was like the monad which I am, and which is my world. The mandala represents the monad, and corresponds to the microcosmic nature of the psyche.

> I was being compelled to go through this process of the unconscious. I had to let myself be carried along by the current, without a notion of where it would lead me. When I began drawing the mandalas, however, I saw that everything, all the paths I had been following, all the steps I had taken, were leading back to a single point—namely, to the mid-point. It became increasingly plain to me that the mandala is the center. It is the exponent of all paths. It is the path to the center, to individuation.[9]

To the extent that self is dominated by the ego or conscious mind, the unconscious will probably be unable to generate a mandala at all, or if it does it will not generate the interplay of quaternity and circularity characteristic of a self-realized psyche. While the ego dominates, the unconscious will not represent itself as centered. Because this egocentric psyche fails to realize "the almost irresistible compulsion and urge to *become what one is,*" the resulting representation of such a psyche will be a visible distortion of the ideal mandala shape.[10] By contrast, the individuated self will generate a mandala that is centered, harmonious, and depicted by quaternity and circularity, the two shapes that invariably symbolize wholeness.

Jung was convinced that the modern West, including of course exoteric philosophy as a characteristically rational discipline, would not recover its wholeness or health until it gave full and honorable sway to its unconscious life. In order to expose the limitations of Western thought and culture, Jung searched for myths and symbols in virtually every religious and artistic tradition, ancient and contemporary. In this respect, Jung's work is itself a kind of archetype for the last decades of this century and for the next century. While we now know that Jung's understanding of some of the cultures he interpreted was limited by his time and methodology, he nevertheless showed that in the future any attempt to interpret humanity will have to include images and ideas heretofore not dreamed of in modern Western philosophy.

The Present Situation: Global Esotericism

The so-called new paradigm—the emerging new framework, or set of assumptions, for contemporary thought and culture—will almost certainly be characterized by multiculturalism, or globalism. Slowly, but with an undeniable inevitability, we are coming to recognize some of the ways in which modern Western culture is inseparably joined with other cultures, east and west, north and south. The most obvious force for integration is the ecosystem. We breathe the same air, are dependent on the same resources, live by, and off, the same sun, moon, and galaxies.

The second force for integration is the near-global economy. As with the ecosystem, individuals and societies differ in their relation to the world economy (the gap between haves and have-nots, for instance, widens at an alarming rate), but that there is only one system, with no loose ends, is now nearly a fact of life. The third such global bond is technology, particularly communications and transportation. My candidate for the fourth global integrator is music, technologically transmitted—that is, music available by compact disc or cassette. The fifth candidate for global status is the most important, yet least predictable—the impulse toward democratic government and values.

Comparative thought—cross-cultural or multicultural philosophy—has not yet reached the status of these five forces for globalization, but it is proceeding along the same path. If or when a new paradigm does emerge, it seems almost certain that it will be built up out of multicultural and comparative philosophical traditions. If we can judge from current trends, this newly dominant global mode of thinking will be psychologically and anthropologically sophisticated but indifferent to historical specificity.

The new paradigm will almost certainly take as its guru thinkers such people as Jung, for his multicultural psychological insight, and Joseph Campbell, whose thought is derivative of Jung's, for global mythology. Attempts at constructing a new paradigm will continue to build on Jung and Campbell for the extent of their cross-cultural reach and for the extent to which their thought provides a constructive substitute for religion.

Although American culture and values were fashioned out of a profound understanding of history, in recent decades, perhaps owing to the unprecedented mobility and technological speed of daily life, popular culture is now characterized by an appalling indifference to historical context. On its positive side, this ahistorical attitude enables American culture to draw freely from very diverse cultures, ideas and practices that are beneficial; on the negative side, this ability to import and integrate is often cavalier and superficial. Contemporary American culture is in the process of absorbing and Americanizing such "non-Western" teachings and practices as meditation techniques, all forms of Buddhism, teachings on karma and rebirth, Asian art disciplines, and shamanism. Only rarely, however, do individuals and groups who borrow these teachings attend to the philosophical moorings that make them intelligible.

Similarly, the American exports—especially economics, the arts, and democracy—will need to be framed in, or at least accompanied by, the philosophical ideas that support them in the American cultural situation. All this sharing, borrowing, adapting, and comparing will require cultural sympathy born of historical knowledge and philosophical multiculturalism.

Notes

1. Alfred North Whitehead, *Adventures in Ideas* (London: Free Press, 1967), p. 118.
2. William James, *The Varieties of Religious Experience* (New York: Penguin Books, 1982), pp. 508, 515.
3. James, *Essays in Psychical Research* (Cambridge: Harvard University Press, 1986), pp. 361–62.
4. C. G. Jung, *Memories, Dreams, and Reflections*, trans. Richard and Clara Winston (New York: Pantheon Books, 1961), p. 363.
5. Ibid., p. 3.
6. Ibid., p. 356.
7. Jung, *Two Essays on Analytical Psychology*, trans. R. F. C. Hull (New York: Pantheon Books, 1953), p. 238.
8. Ibid., p. 171.
9. Jung, *Memories, Dreams, and Reflections*, pp. 195–96.
10. Jung, *The Archetypes and the Collective Unconscious*, trans. R. F. C. Hull (Princeton: Princeton University Press), 1969), p. 357.

About the Contributors

Roger T. Ames is editor of the international journal *Philosophy East and West*, coauthor of *Thinking Through Confucius*, and translator of Sun-Tzu's *Art of Warfare*. He is professor of philosophy at the University of Hawaii.

J. Baird Callicott has written widely on environmental issues and is coauthor of *Clothed-in-Fur and Other Tales*. He is professor of philosophy at the University of Wisconsin at Stevens Point.

Janet Flesch is completing her doctorate in philosophy at the University of Texas at Austin.

David L. Hall is managing review editor of *Philosophy East and West* and coauthor of *Thinking Through Confucius*. He is professor of philosophy at the University of Texas at El Paso. His most recent books are *Richard Rorty* and a philosophical novel.

Kathleen M. Higgins is author of *Nietzsche's Zarathustra* and *The Music of Our Lives* and of various articles on Nietzsche, aesthetics, and Chinese music. She is also editor of several books, including *The Philosophy of (Erotic) Love*. She is associate professor of philosophy at the University of Texas at Austin.

Robert A. McDermott is author of *The Essential Aurobindo* and *The Essential Steiner* and president of the Institute for Integral Studies in San Francisco.

Eric Ormsby is director of libraries at McGill University in Montreal and a member of the Institute for Arabic Studies. He is the author of *Theodicy* in *Islamic Thought, Handlist of Arabic Manuscripts in the Princeton University Library* and many articles on Arabic thought.

Thomas W. Overholt is coauthor of *Clothed-in-Fur and Other Tales*. He is professor of philosophy at the University of Wisconsin at Stevens Point.

Graham Parkes is editor of *Nietzsche and Asian Thought* and *Heidegger and Asian Thought* and cotranslator of *The Self-Overcoming of Nihilism* by Nishitani Keiji. He is professor of philosophy at the University of Hawaii.

Stephen H. Phillips is author of many articles on Indian philosophy, epistemology, Sanskrit, and the philosophy of religion, and author of *Aurobindo*. He is associate professor of philosophy at the University of Texas at Austin.

Homayoon Sepasi-Tehrani is a graduate student in the Department of Asian and Oriental Languages at the University of Texas at Austin.

Robert C. Solomon is author of many books, including *The Passions*, *From Hegel to Existentialism*, *About Love*, and *The Bully Culture*. He is Quincy Lee Centennial professor of philosophy at the University of Texas at Austin.

Jacqueline Trimier is working on her doctorate in philosophy and African studies at the University of Warwick in Coventry.

Jorge Valadez does research in ontology, social and political philosophy, and pre-Columbian philosophy. He is assistant professor of philosophy at Marquette University.